Reader in Gender Archaeology

This *Reader in Gender Archaeology* presents twenty current, controversial and highly influential articles which confront and illuminate issues of gender in prehistory. The question of gender difference and whether it is natural or culturally constructed is a compelling one. The articles here, which draw on evidence from a wide range of geographic areas, demonstrate how all archaeological investigation can benefit from an awareness of issues of gender. They also show how the long-term nature of archaeological research can inform the gender debate across the disciplines.

The volume:

- Organizes this complex topic into seven sections on key themes in gender archaeology: archaeological method and theory, human origins, division of labor, the social construction of gender, iconography and ideology, power and social hierarchies and new forms of archaeological narrative.
- Includes section introductions which outline the history of research on each topic and present the key points of each article.
- Presents a balance of material which rewrites women into prehistory, and articles which show how the concept of gender informs our understanding and interpretation of the past.

Kelley Hays-Gilpin is Assistant Professor of Anthropology at Northern Arizona University.
David S. Whitley is the US representative of ICOMOS and lectures at UCLA.

ROUTLEDGE READERS IN ARCHAEOLOGY

Series editor: David S. Whitley

Reader in Archaeological Theory
Post-Processual and Cognitive Approaches
Edited by David S. Whitley

Reader in Gender Archaeology

Edited by
Kelley Hays-Gilpin and
David S. Whitley

London and New York

First published 1998
by Routledge
11 New Fetter Lane, London EC4P 4EE

Simultaneously published in the USA
and Canada by Routledge
29 West 35th Street, New York,
NY 10001

Transferred to Digital Printing 2002

Routledge is an imprint of the Taylor & Francis Group

First published in paperback 1998

Typeset in Bell Gothic and Perpetua by
Florencetype Ltd, Stoodleigh, Devon

Printed and bound in Great Britain by
T.J.I. Digital, Padstow, Cornwall

British Library Cataloguing in Publication Data

A catalogue record for this book is available from the
British Library

Library of Congress Cataloguing in Publication Data

Reader in gender archaeology/[edited by]
Kelley Hays-Gilpin and David S. Whitley.

(Routledge readers in archaeology)

Includes bibliographical references and index.

1. Social archaeology. 2. Women, Prehistoric.
3. Sex role–History. I. Hays-Gilpin, Kelley.
II. Whitley, David S. III. Series.

CC72.4.R43 1998

930.1–dc21   97–30383

ISBN 0–415–17359–0 (hbk)
ISBN 0–415–17360–4 (pbk)

CONTENTS

LIST OF CONTRIBUTORS

Bennett, Sharon, State University of New York College, Dept. of Anthropology, Plattsburgh, NY 12901, USA

Cohen, Mark Nathan, State University of New York College, Dept. of Anthropology, Plattsburgh, NY 12901, USA

Conkey, Margaret W., University of California. Dept. of Anthropology, Berkeley, CA 94720–3710, USA

Cyphers Guillén, Ann, Universidad Nacional Autonoma de Mexico, Instituto de Investigaciones Antropologicas, Ciudad Universitaria, Delegacion Coyoacan, 04510, Mexico, DF, Mexico

Davis, Emma Lou, (deceased) Great Basin Anthropological Foundation, San Diego, CA, USA

Dommasnes, Liv Helga, University of Bergen, Historical Museum, Bergen, Norway

Falk, Dean, State University of New York, Dept. of Anthropology, Albany, NY 12222, USA

Galloway, Patricia, Mississippi Dept. of Archives and History, PO Box 571, Jackson, MS 39205, USA

Gibbs, Liv, 76 Millgate, Newark-on-Trent, Notts NG24 4TV, England

Gilchrist, Roberta, University of Reading, Dept. of Archaeology, Whiteknights, Reading, RG6 6AA, England

Kennedy, Mary C., Washington University, Dept. of Anthropology, CB 1114, St. Louis, MO 63130–4899, USA

Knapp, A. Bernard, University of Glasgow, Dept. of Archaeology, Glasgow G12 8QQ Scotland

McCafferty, Geoffrey G., Brown University, Dept. of Anthropology, PO Box 1921, Providence, RI 02912, USA

McCafferty, Sharrisse D., Brown University, Dept. of Anthropology, PO Box 1921, Providence, RI 02912, USA

McKell, Sheila M., James Cook University of North Queensland, Dept. of Anthropology/Archaeology, Townsville, QLD 4811, Australia

Nelson, Sarah M., University of Denver, Dept. of Anthropology, 2130 Race St, Denver, CO, 80208–0174, USA

Russell, Pamela, University of Auckland, Centre for Continuing Education, 28 Ayr Street Parnell, Auckland, 1 New Zealand

Sassaman, Kenneth E., Savannah River Archaeological Research Program, PO Box 371, New Ellenton, SC 29809, USA

Spector, Janet D., University of Minnesota, Dept. of Anthropology, 205 Ford Hall, Minneapolis, MN 55455, USA

Watson, Patty Jo, Washington University, Dept. of Anthropology, CB 1114, St. Louis, MO 63130–4899, USA

Wylie, Alison, University of Western Ontario, Dept. of Philosophy, London, Ontario N6A 3K7, Canada

Zihlman, Adrienne, University of California, Dept. of Anthropology, Santa Cruz, CA 95064, USA

PREFACE

In 1800 John Hays sold his 400 acre farm, located outside of what would become Nashville, Tennessee. It was purchased by Andrew Jackson, who renamed it The Hermitage. In 1829 Jackson became the seventh President of the United States.

In 1997, Kelley Hays-Gilpin, descendant of Andrew Jackson's nephew, and David Whitley, descendant of John Hays (by way of his Great Grandfather x3, Capt. Andrew Jackson Bean) prepared this reader. It is on the archaeology of gender.

We designed it to provide students and other scholars with an introduction to archaeological theory and practice that focusses on understanding sex and gender in prehistory. We selected articles from a variety of journals and edited volumes and excerpted several books to introduce the history and issues behind gender archaeology, provide case studies that address gender issues in a variety of geographic and subject areas, and introduce some of the most important authors in this field.

Gender archaeology is not a unified sub-field of archaeology. These writers do not present a unified front. Not only do their subjects, methods, and theoretical orientations differ, but so do their writing styles. Our brief introductions to each section provide context in plain language that will help make the articles more accessible to interested undergraduates and non-specialists. Further readings on each topic are suggested; these include related work published in English in volumes and journals that should be available at major libraries, or through inter-library loan at smaller ones.

After almost 200 years, we felt it was time for the Jackson and Hays families to get involved in another "project."

ACKNOWLEDGEMENTS

Acknowledgements

We extend our thanks to Margaret Conkey, Carol Kramer and Lyn Wadley for sharing bibliographies and syllabi, and to A. Bernard Knapp for bravely sending unpublished manuscripts to people he has never actually met. Patricia Crown, Louise Lamphere and the other participants of the School of American Research Senior Seminar on sex roles and gender hierarchies in the ancient Southwest US, and the members of the arch-theory internet discussion group, stimulated our thinking and provided a bounty of good ideas and references. Two anonymous reviewers provided invaluable advice on our original proposal. We are grateful to Dean Susanna Maxwell and Vice Provost Henry Hooper at Northern Arizona University for their moral support and allowing us to use university facilities, and to Prof. Joseph Boles of the NAU Women's Studies Program for his encouragement. Of course, this volume would not be a reader at all without the generosity of all the authors who granted permission to reprint their works, sometimes on very short notice. We thank them all very much indeed. Finally, we are indebted to Vicky Peters, Nadia Jacobson, Patricia Stankiewicz and Janet Goss at Routledge for their patient and willing support.

We are indebted to the publishers for permission to reprint the following articles:

Conkey, Margaret W. and Janet Spector (1984) "Archaeology and the Study of Gender," in *Archaeological Method and Theory* 7:1–38, New York: Academic Press.
Gilchrist, Roberta (1991) "Women's Archaeology? Political Feminism, Gender Theory, and Historical Revisionism," *Antiquity* 65:495–501.
Wylie, Alison (1992) "The Interplay of Evidential Constraints and Political Interests: Recent Archaeological Research on Gender," *American Antiquity* 57:15–35.
Zihlman, Adrienne (1989) "Woman the Gatherer: The Role of Women in Early Hominid Evolution," in Sandra Morgen (ed.) *Gender and Anthropology: Critical Reviews for Research and Teaching*, Washington, DC: American Anthropological Association, pp. 21–40.

McKell, Sheila M. (1993) "An Axe to Grind: More Ripping Yarns from Australian Prehistory," in
H. du Cros and L. Smith (eds) *Women and Archaeology: A Feminist Critique*, Occasional
Papers in Prehistory 23, Department of Prehistory, Research School of Pacific Studies,
Canberra: The Australian National University, pp. 115–20.

Falk, Dean (1997) "Brain Evolution in Females: An Answer to Mr. Lovejoy," in L. Hager (ed.)
Women in Human Evolution, London: Routledge, pp. 114–36.

Spector, Janet (1983) "Male/Female Task Differentiation among the Hidatsa: Toward the
Development of an Archaeological Approach to the Study of Gender," in P. Albers and B.
Medicine (eds) *The Hidden Half*, Washington, DC: University Press of America, pp. 77–99.

Sassaman, Kenneth (1992) "Lithic Technology and the Hunter-Gatherer Sexual Division of Labor,"
North American Archaeologist 13:249–62.

Watson, Patty Jo, and Mary C. Kennedy (1991) "The Development of Horticulture in the Eastern
Woodlands of North America: Women's Role," in J. M. Gero and M. W. Conkey (eds)
Engendering Archaeology: Women and Prehistory, Oxford: Basil Blackwell, pp. 255–75.

Galloway, Patricia (1997) "Where Have All the Menstrual Huts Gone? The Invisibility of Menstrual
Seclusion in the Late Prehistoric Southeast," in C. Claassen and R.A. Joyce (eds) *Women
in Prehistory: North America and Mesoamerica*, Philadelphia: University of Pennsylvania
Press, pp. 47–62.

McCafferty, Sharrisse D. and Geoffrey G. McCafferty (1991) "Spinning and Weaving as Female
Gender Identity in Post-Classic Mexico," in M.B. Schevill, J.C. Berlo, and E.B. Dwyer (eds.)
Textile Traditions of Mesoamerica and the Andes: An Anthology, New York: Garland
Publishing, pp. 19–44.

Gibbs, Liv (1987) "Identifying Gender Representation in the Archaeological Record: A Contextual
Study," in I. Hodder (ed.) *The Archaeology of Contextual Meanings*, Cambridge: Cambridge
University Press, pp. 79–89.

Russell, Pamela (1993) "The Paleolithic Mother-Goddess: Fact or Fiction?" in H. du Cros and L.
Smith (eds.) *Women and Archaeology: A Feminist Critique*, Occasional Papers in Prehistory
23, Department of Prehistory, Research School of Pacific Studies, Canberra: The Australian
National University, pp. 93–97.

Cyphers Guillén, Ann (1993) "Women, Rituals, and Social Dynamics at Ancient Chalcatzingo,"
Latin American Antiquity 4(3):209–24.

Cohen, Mark Nathan and Sharon Bennett (1993) "Skeletal Evidence for Sex Roles and Gender
Hierarchies in Prehistory," in B. Miller (ed.) *Sex Roles and Gender Hierarchies*, Cambridge:
Cambridge University Press, pp. 273–96.

Nelson, Sarah M. (1993) "Gender Hierarchy and the Queens of Silla," in B. Miller (ed.) *Sex Roles
and Gender Hierarchies*, Cambridge: Cambridge University Press, pp. 297–73.

Dommasnes, Liv Helga (1991) "Women, Kinship, and the Basis of Power in the Norwegian Viking
Age," in R. Samson (ed.) *Social Approaches to Viking Studies*, Glasgow: Cruithne Press,
pp. 65–73.

Davis, Emma Lou (1978) excerpts from *The Ancient Californians: Rancholabrean Hunters of the
Mojave Lakes Country*. Los Angeles: Natural History Museum of Los Angeles County.

Spector, Janet (1993) excerpts from *What This Awl Means: Feminist Archaeology at a Wahpeton
Dakota Village*. St. Paul, Minnesota: Minnesota Historical Society.

Knapp, A. Bernard (1988) "Boys will Be Boys: Masculinist Approaches to a Gendered Archaeology,"
in xxx (ed.) *Redefining Archaeology: Feminist Perceptives*, Canberra: Australian national
University, Research School of Pacific Studies, pp. xx–xx.

GLOSSARY

gender:	the cultural values inscribed on sex
gender attribution:	the criteria people in a particular society use to assign individuals to gender categories, such as man, woman, transgendered. Criteria may be biological or social, and may not correspond to an individual's own gender identity.
gender identity:	an individual's own feelings about whether s/he is a man or a woman, regardless of biological characteristics.
gender ideology:	meanings and values attributed to gender categories in a given culture, and assignment of gender to non-sexed phenomena or ideas (for example, moon/sun, earth/sky, soft/hard, domestic/public), on the basis of these meanings and values.
gender hierarchy:	inequalities in power relationships between genders, evidenced by physical abuse, differential access to food, sex, wealth, political office, esoteric knowledge, or freedom of movement.
gender role:	what men and women actually do in specific social contexts.
sex:	categories based on observable biological characteristics of females, males, and intersexed individuals. Sex categorization is usually based on the appearance of external genitals, but modern medicine takes into account internal organs, chromosomes, and hormonal differences.
sex roles:	duties and obligations of individuals in a society, based on their sex category. For example, only females may be expected to bear and nurse children, only males may be expected to impregnate females. Other differences are usually gender, rather than sex, based.

(adapted from Spector and Whelan 1989:69 and Jacobs and Roberts 1989:454)

PART I

Sex, gender and archaeology

Chapter 1

INTRODUCTION:
Gendering the Past

Kelley Hays-Gilpin and David S. Whitley

Sex and gender are commonplace. Rightly or wrongly, they are used to define us, our relationships to others, and our place in society. But this personal connection to these two concepts belies many differences in their definition, opinions about their meanings, and their widely varying cultural uses. Most cultures, and most researchers, distinguish the sexes based on observable, biological traits, especially genitalia. But even the specifics of sex categories can differ among cultures (Yates 1993). Gender — cultural values inscribed on sex categories — varies even more. Within our own culture, as in many others, gender categories are contested by political and religious factions. With the emergence of sex change operations, even the biology of sexual division has become a controversy concerning the importance of mind versus body. Just as in our own culture, within archaeology too, sex and gender have often been ignored. Yet archaeology is uniquely situated to reveal aspects of the deep history of sex and gender relations in ways no other discipline can address.

There are many approaches to the cross-cultural study of sex and gender. Anthropologists studying living societies can ask people how they classify babies, children, intersexes (hermaphrodites), homosexuals, reproductively inactive, or aged members of society according to sex and gender. They can observe behavior to find out what these categories mean in terms of differential access to resources and social roles. Historical archaeologists may find clues in written records. But these methods are not available to prehistorians, those archaeologists who attempt to study past, non-literate cultures. Archaeologists and physical anthropologists measure skulls (crania) and pelvic bones to determine the sex of skeletons using known statistical differences in the sizes and shapes of these between males and females in a given population. Archaeologists hope that artifacts such as tools and items of clothing found with sexed skeletons will tell us what activities men and women performed, and whether they dressed differently. Simply assigning adult skeletons to the categories "male" and "female" does not, however, tell us anything about the values and expectations people in the past had of men and women. We do not even know if our own understanding of these two categories matched those of people in the past. Did sex roles, gender identities, and values about gender stay the same or change? Are the sex and gender roles we have today "natural" or are they the product of specific historical and cultural processes? Were the roles and values assigned to men and women different in the past and in other cultures? Could they be different in the future? Because notions about sex and gender differ among living cultures, past ideas most probably were very different from those held today.

Archaeologists have been slow to take on questions like these in spite of a great deal of public interest in our interpretations of what life was like in the past. Popular culture fills its need to justify the present with reconstructions about the past by generating stories based on a few "facts," incomplete contexts, or just plain fiction. Cartoon cave men drag women around by their hair. Fred Flintstone and prehistoric pals cavort with dinosaurs. They shape our children's ideas about their remote ancestors. Buxom Indian maidens on butter cartons and toothsome braves with tomahawks on sports uniforms all project present-day stereotypes or fantasies of Native Americans into the past. In doing so, they create our popular impressions of other cultures. Likewise, the recent construction of a universal Mother Goddess religion from the archaeological investigations of Marija Gimbutas and James Mellaart in Europe says more about today's spiritual needs than about evidence for a pervasive female-centered monotheism from the Paleolithic through the Neolithic (see Russell, chapter 14). Yet proponents of this theory ask important questions that archaeologists have not really explored: What are the origins of male domination in our culture and other cultures? What came before this domination? If males did not dominate, does it follow that females dominated, or were there instead gender-egalitarian, "partnership" societies? Or perhaps societies with multiple status and power hierarchies? What would it have been like to live in such societies?

For archaeologists, this means asking how we can identify evidence for sex and gender *differences*, including equalities and inequalities. It also means examining these in terms of health, nutrition, violence, prestige, productivity, control over labor and surplus, and the way non-sexed phenomena such as kinds of work, art styles, the sun and moon, deities, and landscape features are assigned genders. All this makes archaeology that *investigates* gender — rather than just *assumes* it — relevant.

Archaeologists have long pursued an understanding of social and economic differences, especially the differences between elites and commoners, farmers and foragers, and one ethnic group and its neighbors. But differences between men and women, and between adults and children, have been taken for granted. As in popular culture, archaeologists too have projected stereotypes from the present into the past, resulting in interpretations of archaeological data resting on unsupported assumptions about sex roles and gender identities. Simply assuming that "men hunted and women gathered plants" or that "the warriors were men" is very different from demonstrating with evidence that in a particular time and place most men in a particular age category hunted certain kinds of animals (i.e. large game) more than most women did, or that those individuals who engaged in warfare were all or mostly young to middle-aged adult males. Likewise, if evidence does show that males engaged in hunting large game far more often than females, is saying so a sexist statement? Archaeologist Linda Hurcombe (1995) notes that many of her students want to find evidence that women hunted large game in the past, because *our society* places a high value on hunting. Did early humans place a higher value on hunting or gathering, or were these activities seen as complementary? When did such divisions of labor appear in human prehistory in the first place? These are very difficult questions. Yet they are interesting and important even if they are never answered definitively.

In the 1960s and 1970s, most academic disciplines began to take a look at sex and gender stereotypes, and evaluate the effects of biases and assumptions on their scholarship. This feminist critique opened up new ways of thinking about the world, and challenged researchers to gather new data. For example, primatologists began to systematically record the activities of male and female baboons. Previously, writing down only what the boisterous males did made it easy to assume that baboon societies were organized according to male dominance hierarchies. The source of this assumption is, of course, the fact that American society in the 1950s was in a large part organized around male dominance hierarchies.

By the early 1980s, however, several archaeologists became alarmed that their field was not taking advantage of insights from feminism and gender studies. Margaret Conkey and Janet Spector wrote "Archaeology and the Study of Gender," (chapter 2) to:

1   explain why archaeology must incorporate this topic;
2   provide examples of where simply applying stereotypes and unfounded assumptions resulted in bad science; and
3   suggest some directions for future research.

Spector's 1983 article, "Male/Female Task Differentiation among the Hidatsa: Toward the Development of an Archaeological Approach to the Study of Gender," (chapter 8) provided one of the earliest case studies of the kinds of research they proposed. In spite of Conkey and Spector's promising beginning in one of the most prestigious American publication series on archaeological method and theory, investigations of gender and feminist critiques proceeded much more rapidly and thoroughly in Scandinavia and the United Kingdom than in the United States (see, for example, Dommasnes 1992).

By the late 1980s, few other archaeological studies in the Americas had used gender as an explicit analytical category. Joan Gero and Margaret Conkey organized the Wedge Conference in South Carolina in 1988. They challenged scholars working in different areas and with different kinds of data to incorporate questions about gender into their research. The result, *Engendering Archaeology* (Gero and Conkey eds. 1992, often "jokingly" called *Endangering Archaeology*) stands now as a classic work in this field.

Since the Wedge Conference, many other gender-focused archaeology conferences have convened, notably the 1989 Chacmool Conference (Walde and Willows 1991), the 1991 Boone Conference (Claassen 1992), and the 1991 Women in Archaeology Conference at Charles Stuart University, Albury, Australia (du Cros and Smith 1993). Gender-oriented sessions are regularly held at international, national, and regional archaeology meetings. Archaeologists take part in multidisciplinary gender-focused conferences such as the Gender and Material Culture Conference at the University of Exeter in 1994, where art historians, medievalists, and others shared perspectives on gender (Hurcombe and Donald 1997). Several other excellent compendia of gender archaeology and related papers have appeared in the last decade (Arnold *et al.* 1988; Bacus *et al.* 1993; Claassen and Joyce 1997; Nelson and Kehoe 1990; Scott 1994; Spielmann 1995; Wright 1996). In addition, two textbooks are now available. Margaret Ehrenberg's (1989) *Women in Prehistory* tells the story of how women's lives changed from the European Paleolithic through Iron Age. Janet Spector's (1993) *What this Awl Means: Feminist Archaeology at a Historic Wahpeton Village* (excerpted in chapter 20) explores not only the lives of women and men at the Little Rapids site, but also how archaeology is done. How do we think about what we do in the field? How do we interpret what we have found and present our conclusions to other scholars, the public, the descendants of those whose remains we investigate?

As will become apparent, most researchers working on gender issues are women, but not because women have excluded men from this field (see Knapp, chapter 21). Until very recently, most archaeologists were men (but see Claassen 1994, and discussions of gender equity and career issues in Nelson *et al.*, 1994). Because of the middle-to-upper class European and Euroamerican backgrounds of the majority of archaeologists, gender values of these cultures pervade conventional approaches, whether applied by men or by women. Gender was viewed as a binary classification, and the masculine gender category was taken to be primary. When the past was envisioned as peopled by active individuals, those individuals were envisioned as men. This is not to say that anyone thought there were no women in the past. Instead, they pictured the past as either a mass of genderless beings, or as active men with some passive women in the background doing a limited range of stereotypical and repetitive tasks.

Foregrounding feminine gender identity or feminine tasks required a stretch of imagination. Because it was women, not men, who felt left out of the picture, these stretches of imagination were for the most part undertaken by women. Below,

Roberta Gilchrist's article, "Women's Archaeology? Political Feminism, Gender Theory, and Historical Revisionism," (chapter 3) explains the relationships among feminism and gender studies, and political and scholarly goals, from a British point of view that is equally relevant to the situation in North America. Alison Wylie, leading philosopher of archaeology in general and feminist archaeology in particular, presents her summary of the history and philosophy of gender archaeology in "The Interplay of Evidential Constraints and Political Interests: Recent Archaeological Research on Gender," (chapter 4).

Many of the archaeological studies referenced below could be termed "womanist." They are concerned with "actions, status, or simply presence of women in past societies" (Claassen and Joyce 1997:1). Womanism in archaeology, and gender studies in other fields, have set the stage for exploring many kinds of social difference in prehistory. Currently many studies are moving far beyond the goal of putting women back in the picture. They are moving into the realm of understanding how cultures construct gender differences. The assumption of a simple male/female binary classification is increasingly questioned. The roles of age, reproductive status, occupation, class, and other factors in construction of gender categories are explored. Often more than two gender categories are considered (see for example Whelan 1991). Trying to look at gender in new ways has the happy effect of encouraging one to look at other kinds of difference in new and active ways. In spite of its name, feminist scholarship is by no means limited to the study of women. We are now seeing archaeological studies of children (Lillehammer 1989, Claassen 1992:5; Roveland 1997) and images of masculinity (Bevan 1995; Knapp 1997; Yates 1993). The views of Native peoples are now considered important in archaeological interpretation and practice (Schmidt and Patterson 1995; Spector 1991; Swidler et al. 1997). Historical archaeologists frequently foreground race, ethnicity, class, and gender (Scott 1994). A few archaeologists have begun to consider interests and points of view of homosexuals (Schmidt 1995) and the working class (Paynter 1988, Duke and Saitta 1996). Difference is not just socially constructed, but historically contingent and changing. Feminism, womanism, gender theory, queer theory, and other approaches have much to offer archaeology. What archaeology in turn has to offer women's studies, gender studies, and feminist thinkers in other fields is *time depth*, "a truly historical perspective on the social construction and changing nature and forms of 'difference'" (Conkey 1993:12).

■   ■   ■

Further reading

Barrett, John C. (1988)
Claassen, Cheryl (1992)
—— (1997)
Conkey, Margaret W. (1993)
Conkey, Margaret W. and Joan M. Gero (1991)
Conkey, Margaret W. with Sarah H. Williams (1991)
Dommasnes, Liv Helga (1992)
Engelstad, Ericka (1991)
Fotiadis, Micheal (1994)
Hurcombe, Linda (1995)
Little, Barbara J. (1994)
Nelson (1997)
Paynter, R. (1988)
Wylie, Alison (1991)
—— (1992b)
—— (1994)
—— (1997)

■　■　■

References

Arnold, Karen, Pam Graves, Roberta Gilchrist, and Sarah Taylor (eds) (1988) "Women and Archaeology," *Archaeological Review from Cambridge*, vol. 7, no. 1.

Bacus, Elisabeth A. *et al.* (1993) *A Gendered Past: A Critical Bibliography of Gender in Archaeology*. University of Michigan Museum of Anthropology Report 25, Ann Arbor: University of Michigan.

Barrett, John C. (1988) "Fields of Discourse: Reconstituting a Social Archaeology," *Critique of Anthropology* 7(3): 5–16.

Bevan, Lynne (1995) "Powerful Pudenda: The Penis in Prehistory," *Journal of Theoretical Archaeology* 3/4: 41–58, Glasgow: Cruithne Press.

Claassen, Cheryl (1992) "Questioning Gender: An Introduction," in C. Claassen (ed.), *Exploring Gender Through Archaeology: Selected Papers from the 1991 Boone Conference*, Madison, Wisconsin: Prehistory Press, pp. 1–10.

—— (ed.) (1994) *Women in Archaeology*. Philadelphia: University of Pennsylvania.

—— (1997) "Changing Venue: Women's Lives in Prehistoric North America," in C. Claassen and R. A. Joyce (eds) *Women in Prehistory: North America and Mesoamerica*, Philadelphia: University of Pennsylvania Press, pp. 65–87.

Claassen, Cheryl and Rosemary A. Joyce, (eds.) (1997) *Women in Prehistory: North America and Mesoamerica*. Philadelphia: University of Pennsylvania Press.

Conkey, Margaret (1993) "Making the Connections: Feminist Theory and Archaeologies of Gender," in H. du Cros and L. Smith (eds) *Women and Archaeology: A Feminist Critique*, Occasional Papers in Prehistory 23, Department of Prehistory, Research School of Pacific Studies, Canberra: The Australian National University, pp. 3–15.

Conkey, Margaret W. and Joan M. Gero (1991) "Tensions, Pluralities, and Engendering Archaeology: An Introduction to Women and Prehistory," in J. M. Gero and M. W. Conkey (eds) *Engendering Archaeology: Women and Prehistory*, Basil Blackwell, Oxford, pp. 3–30.

Conkey, Margaret W. and Janet Spector (1984) "Archaeology and the Study of Gender," in *Archaeological Method and Theory* 7: 1–38, New York: Academic Press.

Conkey, Margaret W. with Sarah H. Williams (1991) "Original Narratives: The Political Economy of Gender in Archaeology," in M. DiLeonardo (ed.) *Gender at the Crossroads of Knowledge: Feminist Anthropology in the Postmodern Era*, Berkeley and Los Angeles: University of California Press, pp. 102–39.

Dommasnes, Liv Helga (1992) "Two Decades of Women in Prehistory and in Archaeology in Norway, A Review." *Norwegian Archaeological Review* 25(1): 1–14.

du Cros, H. and L. Smith (eds) *Women and Archaeology: A Feminist Critique*, Occasional Papers in Prehistory 23, Department of Prehistory, Research School of Pacific Studies, Canberra: The Australian National University, pp. 115–20.

Duke, Philip, and Dean Saitta (1996) "An Emancipatory Archaeology for the Working Class," paper prepared for the 1996 Theoretical Archaeology Group Conference, Liverpool, England.

Ehrenberg, Margaret (1989) *Women in Prehistory*. Norman, Oklahoma: University of Oklahoma Press.

Engelstad, Ericka (1991) "Images of Power and Contradiction: Feminist Theory and Post-Processual Archaeology," *Antiquity* 65: 502–14.

Fotiadis, Michael (1994) "What is Archaeology's 'Mitigated Objectivism' Mitigated By: Comments on Wylie." *American Antiquity* 59: 545–55.

Hurcombe, Linda (1995) "Our Own Engendered Species," *Antiquity* 69: 262: 87–100.

Knapp, Bernard (1997) "Boys will be Boys: Masculinist Approaches to a Gendered Archaeology," in J. Hope (ed.) *Women and Archaeology* 3, Sydney: University of Sydney.

Lillehammer, Grete (1989) "A Child Is Born. The Child's World in an Archaeological Perspective." *Norwegian Archaeological Review* 22: 91–105.

Little, Barbara J. (1994) "Consider the Hermaphroditic Mind: Comment on 'The Interplay of Evidential Constraints and Political Interests: Recent Archaeological Research on Gender,'" *American Antiquity* 59: 539–44.

Nelson, Margaret C., Sarah M. Nelson, and Alison Wylie, (eds) (1994) *Equity Issues for Women in Archeology*. Archeological Papers of the American Anthropological Association Number 5, Washington, DC: American Anthropological Association.

Nelson Sarah M. (1997) *Gender in Archaeology: Analyzing Power and Prestige*, Walnut Creek, California: Altamira Press.

Nelson, Sarah M. and Alice B. Kehoe (eds) (1990) *Powers of Observation: Alternative Views in Archaeology*. Archaeological Papers of the American Anthropological Association Number 2, Washington, DC: American Anthropological Association.

Paynter, R. (1988) "Steps to an Archaeology of Capitalism: Material Change and Class Analysis," in M. Leone and P. B. Potter, Jr. (eds) *The Recovery of Meaning: Historical Archaeology in the Eastern United States*, Smithsonian Institution Press, Washington, DC, pp. 407–33.

Roveland, Blythe (1997) "Archaeology of Children," *Anthropology Newsletter* 38(4): 14, Washington, DC: American Anthropological Association.

Schmidt, Peter R. and Thomas C. Patterson (eds) (1995) *Making Alternative Histories: The Practice of Archaeology and History in Non-Western Settings*. Santa Fe, New Mexico: School of American Research Press.

Scott, Elizabeth M. (ed.) (1994) *Those of Little Note: Gender, Race, and Class in Historical Archaeology*. Tucson, Arizona: University of Arizona Press.

Spector, Janet (1993) *What This Awl Means: Feminist Archaeology at a Wahpeton Dakota Village*. St. Paul, Minnesota: Minnesota Historical Society, Chapter 1 and first page of Chapter 2.

Spielmann, Katherine A. (ed.) (1995) "The Archaeology of Gender in the American Southwest," *The Journal of Anthropological Research* 51(2).

Swidler, Nina, Kurt E. Dongoske, Roger Anyon, and Alan S. Downer (eds) (1997) *Native Americans and Archaelogists: Stepping Stones to Common Ground*. Walnut Creek, California: Altamira Press.

Walde, Dale, and Noreen D. Willows (1991) The Archaeology of Gender: Proceedings of the 22nd Annual Chacmool Conference. Calgary: The Archaeological Association of the University of Calgary.

Whelan, Mary K. (1991) "Gender and Historical Archaeology: Eastern Dakota Patterns in the 19th Century," *Historical Archaeology* 25: 17–32.

Wright, Rita P. (ed.) (1996) *Gender and Archaeology*, Philadelphia: University of Pennsylvania Press.

Wylie, Alison (1991) "Gender Theory and the Archeological Record: Why is There No Archaeology of Gender?," in J. M. Gero and M. W. Conkey (eds) *Engendering Archaeology: Women and Prehistory*, Oxford: Basil Blackwell, pp. 31–54.

—— (1992) "Feminist Theories of Social Power: Some Implications for a Processual Archaeology," *Norwegian Archaeological Review* 25(1): 50–68.

—— (1994) "On 'Capturing Facts Alive in the Past' (or Present): Response to Fotiadis and Little," *American Antiquity* 59: 556–60.

—— (1997) "Good Science, Bad Science, or Science as Usual? Feminist Critique of Science," in L. D. Hagar (ed.) *Women in Human Evolution*, Routledge, London, pp. 29–55.

Yates, Tim (1993) "Frameworks for an Archaeology of the Body," in C. Tilley (ed.) *Interpretative Archaeology*, Providence, Rhode Island and Oxford: Berg, pp. 31–72.

Chapter 2

ARCHAEOLOGY AND THE STUDY OF GENDER

Margaret W. Conkey
Janet D. Spector

Introduction

A serious challenge to the function of archaeology in contemporary society has been raised with the assertion that a largely unrecognized rationale for archaeology is the empirical substantiation of national mythology (Leone 1973:129). This use of archaeology reinforces values of which we are not always aware. As archaeologists, we "can properly be accused of being acolytes . . . to our culture," unaware of what we have been doing, and whom we serve (Leone 1973:132). Although Leone has offered a fundamental insight with respect to the relationship of archaeology to a *national* mythology, we show how archaeology similarly provides substantiation for a particular *gender* mythology. That is, the following review of archaeology and the study of gender should make it clear how archaeology has substantiated a set of culture-specific beliefs about the meaning of masculine and feminine, about the capabilities of men and women, about their power relations, and about their appropriate roles in society.

We argue that archaeology, like other traditional disciplines viewed through the lens of feminist criticism, has been neither objective nor inclusive on the subject of gender. Furthermore, because archaeologists lack an explicit framework for conceptualizing and researching gender – and more widely – social roles, we have drawn upon a framework that is implicit and rooted in our own contemporary experience. Thus, we must formulate not only an explicit theory of human social action (see Hodder 1982a, 1982b, 1982c) but also, as part of this, an explicit framework for the archaeological study of gender. This framework must begin with theories and terms that are gender inclusive, not gender specific. As Minnich cogently argues, it is more radical than it appears to develop gender inclusive theories and terms, given that our intellectual tradition is based on a fundamental conceptual error. *Man and mankind* are not general, but exclusive; they are partial, and so is the scholarship about *man and mankind* (Minnich 1982:7).

The role of archaeology in substantiating contemporary gender ideology is complicated. There is virtually no systematic work on the archaeological study of gender. There are no publications in the field with titles like "Methods for Examining Gender through the Archaeological Record"; or "Gender Arrangements and Site Formation Processes"; or "Gender Arrangements and the Emergence of Food Production"; or, more generally, "Gender Structures and Culture Change." We know of no archaeological work in which an author explicitly claims that we can *know* about gender in the past as observed through the archaeological record who then proceeds to demonstrate that knowledge, or to describe *how* we can know.

This does not mean that archaeologists have not said anything about gender structures or gender behavior in past human life. In spite of the absence of serious methodological or theoretical discourse on the subject, the archaeological literature is not silent on the subject of gender. Rather, it is permeated with assumptions, assertions, and statements of "fact" about gender. This is a serious problem.

We have two major purposes in this review of archaeology and the study of gender. First, we critically evaluate and make explicit some of the messages archaeologists convey about gender in their work. These messages exemplify how archaeology functions to provide "empirical" substantiation or justification for contemporary gender ideology. We illustrate that archaeologists, consciously or not, are propagating culturally particular ideas about gender in their interpretations and reconstructions of the past. This aspect of archaeological interpretation not only undermines the plausibility of our reconstructions of the past but also has serious political and educational implications.

Second, we discuss some of the recent literature on gender by feminist scholars inside and outside anthropology. Here we suggest a variety of questions and research problems about gender that might be approached by archaeologists, even by those employing currently accepted methods of analysis. We hope that the feminist critique of archaeology will contribute new ways of thinking about what we do and what we can know about social life in the past. Most important, we hope to bring the subject of gender into the domain of archaeological discourse. In so doing, we hope to call into question the role of archaeology in supporting gender mythology.

A feminist critique of archaeology

Androcentrism in anthropology

The phenomenon of gender bias in scholarship is by no means unique to archaeology or anthropology but rather is a feature of our entire intellectual tradition (see Minnich 1982). To some extent, the male-centered or _androcentric_ bias in archaeology reflects the dependence upon, if not the actual "tyranny" of, the ethnographic record in structuring archaeological work (Wobst 1978). Archaeologists draw heavily on the research of anthropologists and rely upon their ethnographic descriptions as the basis for understanding cultural diversity and regularities. Whether ethnographically derived models are formulated to be tested by archaeological data, or ethnographic interpretations are invoked as analogies or parallels to "explain" archaeological data, all the limitations – the theoretical and methodological biases and problems of the anthropology that generated the ethnographic interpretations and data – are inherited by the archaeologist. Although archaeologists are generally cautious about simplistic ethnographic analogies, this has not been true with regard to the subject of gender. Furthermore, archaeologists cannot be excused for drawing upon gender-biased ethnography and anthropology (Milton 1978) if only because there has been a substantial restructuring of the gender paradigms in ethnography that archaeologists have neither participated in nor drawn upon, either in ignorance or by choice.

In the past decade feminist scholars in sociocultural anthropology have defined and demonstrated pervasive and multifaceted gender bias in anthropological research and studies of cross-cultural life (see Milton 1978; Rogers 1978; Rohrlich-Leavitt _et al._ 1975; Rosaldo and Lamphere 1974a). There is general agreement about the basic dimensions of the problem and the educational and political ramifications of this kind of bias. Just as the scholarly use of racial stereotypes essentially perpetuates racism given the role of academic research in the enculturation process (i.e., the use of our work in the whole educational system), the uncritical use of gender stereotypes in our scholarship perpetuates and supports sexism and gender asymmetry. If our descriptions and interpretations of life in other cultures simply reiterate our own assumptions about gender, we undermine efforts toward explicating cultural diversity or commonalities (one widely accepted goal of anthropology), while at the same time justifying our own gender ideology.

Androcentrism takes several different forms in anthropology. One principal feature is the imposition of ethnocentric assumptions about the nature, roles, and social significance of males and females derived from our own culture on the analysis of other groups. Researchers presume certain "essential" or "natural" gender characteristics. Males are typically portrayed as stronger, more aggressive, dominant, more active, and in general more important than females. Females, in contrast, are presented as weak, passive, and dependent. Given this picture of universal gender dichotomies, it is not surprising to find that many anthropologists directly or indirectly assume biological determinants for gender differences and for the asymmetrical relations between males and females. Biological differences are seen as structuring and, in the case of females, limiting social roles and social position (see Sacks 1979).

A second feature of androcentrism in anthropology is, in part, derived from the first. Many researchers, both male and female, who work with the gender assumptions presented above, place more credence in the views of male informants than in those of females (see E. Ardener 1975). The male perspective is taken to be representative of the culture, whereas the female view is typically portrayed as peripheral to the norm or somehow exceptional or idiosyncratic. In the male-centered view of culture, women are often described primarily in terms of their *lack* of male characteristics. They do not do certain things that men do or they do not hold certain beliefs or participate in certain social networks that men do. Women in many ethnographies are described relative to men or primarily in terms of their relationships to men, for example, as sisters, wives, and mothers.

The emphasis on the native male view of culture is associated with the fact that until recently most ethnographers were men and had greater access to male than to female informants. This contributes to another dimension of androcentrism. Most anthropologists have been western, white, and middle- or upper-class men, and their own position within a race, class, and gender system has shaped their perspective on research, particularly in the selection of research problems. An emphasis on topics like leadership, power, warfare, exchange of women, rights of inheritance, and notions of property – to name a few – can all be cited as issues of special interest to males in particular historic contexts and sociopolitical structures (Sacks 1976; Van Allen 1972). The research problems that have been emphasized are not inherently more important than others nor are they necessarily relevant in many of the cultural contexts examined. They do reflect the perspective of the dominant gender, race, and class of the researchers. The fact that some women have learned this perspective and conduct their research from its vantage point does not deny the sources of the perspective, or that such a perspective has been perpetuated over and above the specific, dynamic contexts of social action among the peoples being studied.

Despite the intensive discussion and dissection of gender bias in sociocultural anthropology and ethnography (e.g., Friedl 1975; Schuck 1974; Slocum 1975), this has barely surfaced as a methodological or theoretical concern in archaeology. It has been said that, in general, a "paradigm lag" characterizes the development of archaeology within the broader discipline of anthropology (Leone 1972). This view is at least partially confirmed by the striking contrast between the rising scholarly interest in gender dynamics in ethnology and the virtual absence of attention to this subject in contemporary anthropological archaeology. The point at hand, however, is that although archaeologists have not participated in the discourse about gender, they have not remained silent on the subject of gender.

Androcentrism in archaeology: some illustrations

All the androcentric problems outlined above are found in archaeological work, but in archaeology the problems are in some ways even more insidious than in sociocultural anthropology. Most archaeologists would agree that "we must resist the temptation to project too much of ourselves into the past" (Isaac 1978a: 104), and that we "cannot assume the same or even similar organization of adaptive behavior" among past societies (Binford 1972: 288). It is precisely because of the intellectual obstacles involved in reconstructing characteristics of social life in the past that so many contemporary archaeologists seek more rigorous methods of analysis.

There has been no rigor in the archaeological analysis of gender. Although archaeologists often make assertions and suggestions about gender arrangements in the past, these are often by-products of the consideration of other archaeological topics or they are so implicit as to be excluded from the attempts of archaeologists to confirm and validate their inferences about past human life. The sources that archaeologists draw upon to derive their implicit notions about past gender arrangements are rarely made explicit. As some case studies discussed here show, it is probable that most derive from androcentric ethnographies or from the researchers' own unexamined, culture-bound assumptions about gender. That is, they do not draw upon nor create a body of theory of social life, or of gender arrangements.

When archaeologists employ a set of stereotypic assumptions about gender, how it is structured, and what it means — what might be called a gender *paradigm* — a temporal continuity of these features is implied. Even when this paradigm is "merely" a cultural backdrop for the discussion of other archaeological subjects (e.g., what an artifact was used for), there is a strongly presentist flavor to archaeological inquiry (Butterfield 1965; Stocking 1965); *presentist* in the sense that the past is viewed with the intent of elucidating features that can be linked with the present. The implicit suggestion of a cultural continuity in gender arrangements from the earliest hominids into the present has two important implications. First, it is part of and contributes to a wider research strategy that emphasizes continuities in many aspects of hominid behavior and evolution (see Pilbeam 1981). Second, the presentist stance forcefully suggests that contemporary gender dynamics are built into the species through unspecified evolutionary processes. Although most American archaeologists research human life after the establishment of modern *Homo sapiens*, these archaeologists inherit a picture of human social life and gender structures that appear to have been established for several million years.

One other important implication of the implicit, presentist gender paradigm is what can be called the *false notion of objectivity*. Archaeologists appear to be objective about what we can know about the past. They are quick to point out that "we have no idea how prehistoric human groups were socially partitioned" (Binford and Binford 1968b: 70). Yet in the very same article, we read about casually made stone tools that indicate presumed occupation by women engaged in plant processing. It has been said that "as long as we do not correct for the imbalance created by the durability of bone as compared with that of plant residues, studies of human evolution will always have a male bias" (Isaac 1978a: 102). Thus female roles and activities are not only distinct from but less visible than those of their male associates, despite the fact that we do not know how adaptive behavior was organized.

We argue that the archaeological "invisibility" of females is more the result of a false notion of objectivity and of the gender paradigms archaeologists employ than of an inherent invisibility of such data. The differential preservation of bones compared to plant remains is *not* the problem, only a diversion. One can claim that female-related data in the archaeological record are invisible only if one makes some clearly questionable assumptions, such as the existence of an exclusive sexual division of labor. It is ironic that a central feature of much contemporary archaeology has been that most of the past is knowable, if only we ask the right questions (Binford 1972: 86). But questions that would elucidate prehistoric gender behavior or organization are rarely asked.

It is important to see how these general notions on androcentrism in archaeology can actually be substantiated in particular archaeological studies. Our review of selected archaeological literature is not meant to be exhaustive. Instead we have chosen to discuss those works that exemplify particular problems of androcentrism, that highlight the kinds of gender imagery conveyed in archaeological studies, and that illustrate some of the ways in which those images are conveyed by authors. Our survey includes literature representing archaeological approaches to the entire temporal span of human existence from the emergence of the earliest hominid populations to ethnoarchaeological research among contemporary gatherer–hunters. Perhaps the most obvious case of androcentricism in archaeology both in conceptualization and mode of presentation occurs in the reconstructions of earliest hominid life. Feminist scholars, drawn to this literature in their search for origins of contemporary sex roles and gender hierarchy, have critically evaluated the Man-the-Hunter model of human evolution and have found it permeated with gender bias (see Dahlberg 1981; Martin and Voorhies 1975; Morgan 1972; Slocum 1975; Tanner 1981; Tanner and Zihlman 1976; Zihlman 1978, 1981).

The Man-the-Hunter model was crystallized by Washburn and Lancaster (1968), elaborated by Laughlin (1968), and was subsequently popularized by numerous writers. This model includes a set of assumptions about males and females – their activities, their capabilities, their relations to one another, their social position and value relative to one another, and their contributions to human evolution – that epitomize the problems of androcentrism. In essence, the gender system presented in the model bears a striking resemblance to contemporary gender stereotypes. In spite of recent revisions of the Man-the-Hunter model as part of the human evolutionary scenario (e.g., Isaac 1978a; Lovejoy 1981), the revised gender arrangements are not substantively different from those first presented by Washburn and Lancaster (see Zihlman 1982 for a review). Thus, among ourselves, to students enrolled in our introductory classes, and to the lay public (e.g., Johanson and Edey 1981), we present a picture of continuity in gender arrangements and ideology from early humans to the present, a continuity that suggests an inevitability, if not the immutability of this sphere of social life.

We consider the Man-the-Hunter model here for several reasons. First, as has been noted above, the gender arrangements assumed to characterize the earliest human populations often serve as a baseline for archaeologists working with fully *sapiens* populations. Second, as a scholarly issue, the deconstruction of the model has been under consideration for a decade. We ought to be able to learn from this in our application of more critical thinking to other reconstructions of prehistory. Third, given that the Man-the-Hunter scenario is one with which most archaeologists are familiar, we can use it not merely as a particular instance of androcentrism but also as an example that, in fact, embodies most of the major issues to be considered in a review of archaeology and the study of gender.

These major issues include:

1   the prevalence of gender-specific models that result in gender-exclusive rather than gender-inclusive reconstructions of past human behavior;
2   the common assumption of a relatively rigid sexual division of labor that results in the sex linking of activities with one sex or the other, which in archaeology is often compounded by assuming sex linkages artifactually (e.g., projectile points as male, ceramics as female); and
3   the differential values placed on the different (and usually sex-linked) activities, such that there is a prevailing overemphasis on those activities or roles presumed to be male associated.

There is also another issue that is not – as are the above three issues – androcentrism or a component of male bias, and this issue is perhaps the most important archaeological issue lurking behind this review. What we find lacking in the Man-the-Hunter model is an explicit theory of human social life and, by implication, the lack of a specific paradigm for the study of gender. Without such theory it is precisely in the attempts to reconstruct prehistoric social life that culturally derived (from our own culture), implicit notions about gender serve as the basis for reconstruction. The study of early hominid social life is one of the more obvious domains of archaeological research in which the lack of archaeological theory for elucidating past human life – including, but not limited to, gender structures – is most glaring.

The gender bias in Man-the-Hunter formulations of hominid evolution is apparent on several levels of analysis. On the surface there is the frequent problem of using *man* and *human* interchangeably when, in fact, the authors are referring to males. Washburn and Lancaster state that "human hunting, if done by males, is based on a division of labor and is a social and technical adaptation quite different from that of other mammals" (Washburn and Lancaster 1968:293). Having established the gender-specific nature of human hunting, they go on to suggest that "the biology, psychology and customs that separate us from the apes – all these we owe to the hunters of time past" (1968:303). The gender-specific character of the model is even further exemplified in the discussion of the relationships between human psychology and hunting in which Washburn and Lancaster report: "the extent to which the biological bases for killing have been incorporated into human psychology may be measured by the ease with which boys can be interested in hunting, fishing, fighting and games of war" (1968:300).

All the statements quoted imply an empirical basis that masks the biases of the model. We are provided little detail on the sources for their reconstructions of early human social life, particularly the strict sexual division of labor. Washburn and Lancaster claim that "in a very real sense our intellect, interests, emotions and basic social life – all are evolutionary products of the success of the hunting adaptation" (1968:293). What accompanies that adaptation is not only a strict division of labor but also a clear asymmetry in the contributions of males and females. There is no explanation as to how the strict sexual division of labor evolved in early hominids (but cf. Lovejoy 1981), nor any supporting data for assuming differential contributions of males and females in the areas of group protection or provisioning. Females are allegedly restricted by their biological characteristics associated with pregnancy, lactation, and childbirth, and circumscribed – almost immobilized – by their presumed roles in childcare. That pregnancy, childbirth, or nursing are disabilities and that childrearing is a full-time, exclusively female activity are not universal ideas. These are culturally specific beliefs and comprise a cultural ideology that has been reflected onto our earliest ancestors.

The fact that Washburn and Lancaster emphasize presumed male activities (e.g., hunting, warfare, sexual competition over females) as critical variables to explain hominid evolution speaks more to the perspective of the researchers than to the reality of prehistoric life. There have been challenges to the argument that hunting by males set the course for human evolution, including brain expansion and sociocultural elaboration, but these have only led to a replacement of that argument by more subtle but still androcentric versions. The "homebase," "central place foraging," and "food-sharing" hypothesis (see Lee 1980a for an early formulation of this hypothesis; Isaac 1978a, 1978b, 1982) that now replaces male hunting as central to the success and biobehavioral divergence of the hominid line remains based not only on the assumption of a strict sexual division of labor, but, to many proponents, on an accompanying set of assumptions including limited female mobility and a differential value of gender-associated activities and foodstuffs. The sexual division of labor is envisioned as the means by which food carrying and the delayed consumption of resources could develop. These behaviors in turn allowed for the food sharing that makes the human career distinctive (Isaac 1978a; Lancaster 1978).

The selective pressures for the primordial hominid sexual division of labor – and hence for the foundation adaptation of human life – are attributed to increasingly encumbered females, monogamous pair-bonding and the nuclear family, and even more rigidly to the provisioning of females and young by increasingly skillful and daring australopithecine hunters (Johanson and Edey 1981; Lovejoy 1981; Pfeiffer 1980).

Although plausible alternative behaviors that also may have led to regular food sharing have been presented by feminist anthropologists (see Tanner 1981; Tanner and Zihlman 1976; Zihlman 1978), the basic features of the Man-the-Hunter model persist in anthropology and the alternatives have been ignored or dismissed (Isaac 1978a). Although the homebase and food-sharing model of early hominid life has come under serious attack recently (Binford 1981), its promoters (e.g., Isaac 1982) continue to direct their methodological energies (e.g., Bunn 1981) toward confirmation of hunting and meat processing as central to early hominid lifeways, rather than toward restructuring the questions asked of the archaeological record (but see Potts 1982 for some modifications).

Feminist critiques of early hominid studies should raise the question of the universality of the sexual division of labor (see Cucchiari 1981). Although the division between the sexes in human life may well be an "elementary structure" (LaFontaine 1978:7–8), the degree to which a division of labor along sex lines exists in any culture is varied, dynamic, and closely interrelated with the social relations of production. A division of labor between males and females should not be assumed but rather be considered a problem or a feature of social structure to be explained (Beechy 1978; Hartman 1975; Hochschild 1973). However, with the "documentation" of a sexual division of labor back in the Plio-Pleistocene, researchers working with archaeologically more recent human groups tend to assume its existence without reflection. In fact, analysis of archaeological work focused on human groups in the more recent past shows that the gender systems presented are suspiciously like those discussed in the context of hominization.

We present here an analysis of five widely cited archaeological studies. These were intentionally selected because there was reason to believe, given their problem orientation, that the subject of gender might be explicitly addressed (see Kennedy 1979). Studies by Winters, Hill, Longacre, and Deetz, published in the Binfords' classic collection, *New Perspectives in Archeology*, (1968a), all attempt to consider aspects of social life as reflected or manifested in the archeological record. Yellen's ethnoarchaeological study of the !Kung San, published almost a decade after the other studies (1977), also was selected for review, in part because the researcher based his report on direct observation of a living population reducing the potential for bias of the "ethnographer-as-middleman." Yellen's work was conducted in a climate of increased interest in gender and heightened awareness of the problems of androcentrism in anthropology. Finally, Yellen's study seemed likely to be more accurate and comprehensive on the subject of gender than other earlier works because of the substantial body of literature about sex roles among the !Kung San that could supplement Yellen's own observations (e.g., Draper 1975; Draper and Cashdan 1974; Howell 1979; Lee 1976, 1980b; Yellen and Harpending 1972). We thought Yellen's work might reveal new perspectives in the archaeological treatment of gender.

All these examples of anthropological archaeology suffer from serious interpretive biases. Though each study has its own particular constellation of problems, there are some general patterns of androcentrism that can be summarized. First, there is a persistent and consistent linkage of certain activities with each sex, combined with a failure on the part of investigators to provide any supporting data to justify such associations. This problem is exacerbated by the presumption of linkages between artifact types and each sex; for example, projectile points are associated with men, pots with women. This kind of reasoning implies a rigid, cross-culturally similar system of sexual division of labor in the past. It also imposes rigidity in interpretations of archaeological assemblages that produces simplistic inferences about social life in prehistoric societies. In short, researchers bring to their work preconceived notions about what each sex ought to do, and these notions serve to structure the way artifacts are interpreted. This circular reasoning surely fails to conform to the rigorous methodological standards advocated by most contemporary archaeologists.

A second general feature revealed in our examination is the differential treatment of males and females in archaeological reporting. The descriptions of male activities are more detailed, and are portrayed more actively and more frequently than female-associated activities. There is asymmetry in the visibility, energy levels, accomplishments, and contributions of the sexes. The very language used to describe or refer to males and females differs to the disadvantage of women. For example, there is a striking absence of the word *activity* used with reference to women, though the phrase *male activity* or some version of that phrase is common. Finally, passive verb forms are typically used for females in contrast to the use of active forms for males. Sex bias then is both reflected and realized by the language of archaeology.

In looking more specifically at these studies, detailed aspects of androcentrism are revealed. Howard Winters's work on mortuary materials illustrates how preconceived notions about gender arrangements can confuse, in fact contort, archaeological interpretations. Winters's approach to mortuary materials, like similar work conducted by others, has been criticized for resting on the simplistic and passive assumption that "status and role differences in life are reflected in treatment at death" (see Pader 1982; Parker-Pearson 1982). But even allowing that assumption, which is basic to Winters's inferences, it has been applied differentially to males and females.

For example, when grinding pestles are found with females in burial contexts, they are interpreted as reflecting the grinding and food-processing activities of women. When such items are found associated with males, however, they suggest to Winters that the men must have manufactured these artifacts (for their women?) or utilized them as hammerstones in pursuing other (less feminine?) tasks. The same kind of reasoning is applied in the interpretation of trade goods. When found with males, Winters infers that this indicates men controlled trading activities. But when found with women, the association suggests only that women possessed such items, not that they participated in trade.

Winters's discussion of the meaning of atlatls when found in association with male and female burials is especially problematic. Atlatl components are found rather commonly with female burials. Winters offers several possible explanations: they may have been purely ceremonial inclusions; they may have been related to the transfer of a corporate estate; the Indian Knoll culture may have included a "platoon of Amazons or a succession of Boadicceas defending the Green River" (Winters 1968: 206); or, finally, the women may have hunted. "But at the moment, all that can be concluded is that the roles of females overlapped those of males in some way, leading to the . . . association with the former of a weapon that one would expect *a priori* to be a symbol of male activities" (Winters 1968: 207). The androcentric problem here is precisely the *a priori* expectations about what males and females did; what materials they manufactured, used, or exchanged; and what the archaeological association of materials with either sex might mean.

The work of Hill, Longacre, and Deetz (all Ph.D. theses presented in summary form in Binford and Binford 1968a) present other, less blatant aspects of andro-centrism in archaeology. None of these studies was explicitly concerned with sex roles, although one could say that the archaeological visibility of women was poten-tially enhanced, given the methodological focus on the role of potters, who were presumed to be female, as a way to document matrilocal residence patterns. The attention to women was in a sense a by-product of archaeologists' efforts to do social anthropology (see Conkey 1977) working with archaeological materials that happened to be linked with a female activity. Unfortunately, these studies do not demonstrate any serious understanding of the complexities of gender arrangements although their concerns with the archaeological expression of social phenomena such as postmarriage residence patterns would seem to demand such knowledge. Although Deetz, Hill, and Longacre depend on ethnographic data to formulate and test hypotheses, they under-utilize these resources as a basis for understanding gender arrangements.

There have been numerous critiques of these "paradigm-setting" studies, but few have considered issues related to gender arrangements. Schiffer has shown some of the methodological weaknesses of these studies in terms of assumptions about site formation processes (1976: 22–25), assumptions that include aspects of gender arrangements and how these social phenomena are expressed archaeologically. All the studies presume prior knowledge about who made and used ceramics, the trans-mission of ceramic design and manufacturing techniques, and about the cultural and spatial contexts of pottery use. None of the studies viewed the ceramics and their makers as active participants in the wider cultural system; rather, the patterning of ceramic variability was seen as reflecting social processes to the archae-ological observer.

The work of Hill, Longacre, and Deetz has the potential to raise important issues about possible female networks, female roles as keepers or transmitters of a symbolic repertoire, or females as socializers. None of these topics is explored. Nor is any consideration given to the role and power of these female potters, given that ceramics might have significance in group boundary-maintenance processes (Washburn 1977) or in extradomestic exchange systems (Plog 1980). Instead, their studies show serious differential treatment of men and women, highlighting the contributions and activities of males while minimizing those of females. Women are portrayed as performing a very limited number of exclusively domestic tasks – they make pots, and cook and process food. Men, in contrast, carry out a broad range of activities in a variety of cultural domains: weave textiles, use clubhouses, make decisions of public concern, and perform ritual, craft, and manufacturing activities (Hill 1968: 117–119).

Some of the criticisms of Longacre, Hill, and Deetz can be attributed to the time at which their work was conducted. Feminist anthropology was not a force in the field and in fact most researchers at the time could be faulted for andro-centric bias. But these are some of the founding treatises of the "new archaeology" and they, like much of the research of the following decade, set the tone for the anthropological archaeology that is, at best, weak on the social theory demanded for the solution of anthropological problems (see Aberle 1968).

The analysis of Yellen's work reveals the persistence of bias well into the 1970s. The differential treatment of men and women in this study is particularly striking because the archaeologist was in the role of observer–reporter and not dependent on limited ethnographic information. Yellen had direct access to information on both male and female activity patterns but his approach parallels that of Winters, Deetz, Longacre, and Hill in peripheralizing women and emphasizing men. This practice in "living" archaeology confirms the suspicions of E. Ardener (1972, 1975) and others who suggest that researchers are more attracted to the models and behaviors of native males regardless of the particular features of the society studied.

Although Yellen acknowledges and reports (1977: 62–63) the importance of female gathering among the !Kung (it constitutes 60–80 per cent of their diet as reported by Lee 1965, 1968), he finds that "in practice it is much easier to talk to the men because each day is in some way unique and stands out in the hunter's mind. Asking women where they went produces much less detailed and reliable information" (1977: 62–63). Yellen does not acknowledge that this may be a problem of the relationship between the male observer and female informant. As Kennedy suggests, "rather than think that the San women wander out of camp, gather food in the Kalahari, and find their way back home again, having no clear recollection of what they did or where they had been, it may be safer to conclude that the San women are reluctant to give detailed accounts of their activities to strange men" (Kennedy 1979: 12). This argument is supported by the amount of detailed and reliable subsistence data collected by female anthropologists from !Kung women (e.g., Draper 1975), including the fact that these women often collect information while out gathering that may be critical in determining the success of male hunters with whom they share this information (Allison Brooks, personal communication, 1977; Heinz 1978).

Even when the contributions and activities of women are observable, as in the case of Yellen's research, the visibility of women is obscured by the mode of reporting. It is interesting to note, for example, that Yellen never identifies women by name in his narrative of events although he frequently does so for men. The women are referred to only in terms of their relationships to men – as someone's spouse or as a member of some specific male's family – or ambiguously and anony-mously as part of the "women." Named male individuals hunt, cooperate, follow, lead, butcher, and carry, whereas unspecified women "set out to gather," "spread out" and "maintain voice contact." Unspecified by name, women appear to be mere adjuncts in group movements, leaving the impression that they have no instrumental role in decisions or actions regarding such movements. As Kennedy states, "If we are constantly presented with a picture of men who move about with nameless, faceless families in tow, we will use that picture when we evaluate the archeological record" (Kennedy 1979: 14–15).

Although our review of archaeological literature is by no means exhaustive, we would argue that it does represent common themes in terms of the treatment of gender as a subject matter. In general, the contributions, activities, perceptions, and perspectives of females are trivialized, stereotyped, or simply ignored. Regardless of the temporal or cultural contexts examined, we are presented with the same imagery of males, of females, and of sexual asymmetry (male dominance and female subordination). Men are portrayed as more active, more important, and more responsible for group maintenance and protection than are women. Women are typically presented as confined to a domestic sphere where their activities and mobility patterns are allegedly restricted by their roles as mothers and wives. Archaeological research, in content and mode of presentation, has been androcentric. Fortunately, a large body of feminist literature and research on gender is now available to undermine this kind of bias and, more important, to serve as a basis for developing explicitly archaeological approaches to the study of gender.

Toward an archaeological approach to the study of gender

The past decade has witnessed the publication of literally hundreds of books and articles in the area of gender studies. Feminist scholars in sociocultural anthropology have played a major role in this discourse (see review articles by Quinn 1977; Lamphere 1977; Rapp 1979; and Atkinson 1982). Although there are no published works attempting to define archaeological approaches to gender, there are publications written by nonarchaeologists within and outside anthropology that explore the origins and evolution of sex roles and gender hierarchy (see Dahlberg 1981; Rorhlich-Leavitt 1977; Slocum 1975; Tanner 1971; Tanner and Zihlman 1976 for examples within anthropology. See Davis 1971; Diner 1973; Morgan 1972; and Reed 1975 for examples in popular literature). Martin and Voorhies's (1975) book is unique in having been authored by archaeologists. Most of the authors contributing to these volumes are unfamiliar with current approaches to archaeological data, inference, or argument, but their work does reflect the enormous interest in evolutionary perspectives on gender as well as the paucity of work by researchers with training in contemporary archaeological methods or theory.

Ethnographic studies now demonstrate complexity and cross-cultural variability in gender arrangements in living societies. These newly formulated examinations focusing on the expression and meaning of gender can serve as the basis for more detailed analysis of the possible material manifestations of various dimensions of gender arrangements, a first and crucial step toward developing methods for interpreting the archaeological record.

Assuming that we will be able to establish some meaningful correlations between the material and nonmaterial aspects of gender systems, we may then be in a methodological position to use the archaeological record to examine long-term evolutionary patterns and processes concerning gender. Ultimately, this line of research could lead to major theoretical contributions explaining the emergence and development of aspects of gender arrangements and the conditions that contribute to diversity and commonalities in those arrangements as observed through time and across space. At the same time, this kind of research will lead to better understandings of the role of gender arrangements and ideology in structuring or affecting other processes of change.

Feminist studies of gender

In the following pages, we provide for archaeologists some background in recent feminist studies of gender and suggest how this research can be used to formulate archaeological approaches to gender. Our intent here is to alert archaeologists to the significance – and the complexity – of the subject and to stimulate discussion among archaeologists about the possible contributions we might make to the study of gender.

The major premise of recent feminist work on gender is expressed in the following statement that introduces a collection of essays on the cultural construction of sexuality and gender:

> The natural features of gender, and natural processes of sex and reproduction, furnish only a suggestive and ambiguous backdrop to the cultural organization of gender and sexuality. What gender is, what men and women are, what sorts of relations do or should obtain between them – all of these notions do not simply reflect or elaborate upon biological "givens," but are largely products of social and cultural processes. The very emphasis on the biological factor *within* different cultural traditions is variable; some cultures claim that male – female differences are almost entirely biologically grounded, whereas others give biological differences, or supposed biological differences, very little emphasis.
>
> (Ortner and Whitehead 1981b:1)

Much feminist research in anthropology today is concerned with gender and sexuality as cultural constructs and with the sources, processes, and consequences of their construction and organization. Although researchers vary in perspective and theoretical orientation, all view gender as a multifaceted and important social phenomenon having several different dimensions, including gender role, gender identity, and gender ideology (for detailed discussion, see Kessler and McKenna 1978; Ortner and Whitehead 1981a).

Gender role refers to the differential participation of men and women in social, economic, political, and religious institutions within a specific cultural setting. Gender roles describe what people do and what activities and behaviors are deemed appropriate for the gender category. *Gender identity* refers to an individual's own feeling of whether she or he is a woman or a man. As we know from the case of transsexuals – a gender category in our culture – this aspect of gender does not necessarily coincide with the gender category others might assign to the individual. *Gender ideology* refers to the meaning, in given social and cultural contexts, of *male, female, sex,* and *reproduction.* The system of meaning includes the prescriptions and proscriptions for males, females, or persons of any other culturally defined gender category (e.g., the *berdache*). Here the emphasis is on gender, sexuality, and reproduction as symbols.

In delineating the components of gender, feminist researchers have shown that these aspects vary from culture to culture and that they vary independently. For example, two cultures may resemble one another in terms of the actual activities performed by men and women but differ dramatically in terms of the meaning attached to the gender assignments or the value of the tasks. It is also important to note that sex roles and gender ideology are not necessarily congruent within a given culture (see LaFontaine 1978; Wallman 1976). Some roles are always and only performed by members of one sex. Others may be assumed by individuals of either sex although, within the group's ideology, there is an explicit conceptual or symbolic association of the role with one or the other sex. The association between actual activity patterns of males and females and symbolic linkages of the activities to males and females may vary and may change over time. This clearly argues against the simplistic and rigid notions of sexual division of labor often presented in archaeological literature.

In summary, feminist scholars conceptualize gender as a complex system of meaning – that is, as a social category that lies at the core of how people in particular cultures identify who they are, what they are capable of doing, what they should do, and how they are to relate to others similar to and different from themselves. Like the social category, *family*, gender is a system of social rather than biological classification that varies cross-culturally and changes over time in response to a constellation of conditions and factors that are as yet poorly understood. It is in this very area of cultural diversity and change through time that archaeology might make a most important contribution to the study of gender, and vice versa.

Approaches in feminist anthropology

Feminist anthropological studies have taken a variety of forms, each useful for archaeologists as we begin to formulate our approaches to gender. For those interested in more systematic examination of the literature now available, there are five types of sources that can be consulted:

1   *major* anthologies of articles (e.g., Caplan and Burja 1979; Dahlberg 1981; MacCormack and Strathern 1980; Matthiason 1974; Ortner and Whitehead 1981a; Reiter 1975; Rohrlich-Leavitt 1975, Rosaldo and Lamphere 1974a; Schlegel 1977);

2   review essays (Atkinson 1982; Lamphere 1977; Quinn 1977; Rapp 1979; Rosaldo 1980);

3   general texts (e.g., Boserup 1970; Friedl 1975; Martin and Voorhies 1975; Sacks 1979; Sanday 1981; Tanner 1981);

4   special issues of journals dealing thematically with women and gender (e.g., *American Ethnologist* 1975: 2(4); *Anthropological Quarterly* 1967: 40(3); *Arethusa* 1973: 6(1); *Ethnology*, 1974: 13(2); *Ethos*, 1973: 1(4); *Western Canadian Journal of Anthropology* 1976: 6(3); and

5   ethnographies emphasizing women and/or gender systems (e.g., Bledsoe 1980; Chiñas 1973; Dwyer 1978; Goodale 1971; Hughes-Jones 1979; Murphy and Murphy 1974; Strathern 1972; Weiner 1976.

Also see review articles above for additional ethnographic sources.

Approaches in feminist anthropology fall into three major categories: feminist critiques of androcentrism in the discipline; studies that can aptly be described as "the anthropology of women"; and work in feminist theory focused either on issues related to sexual asymmetry or on the relationships between gender systems and other facets of social life. In some ways, these categories reflect the chronological development of feminist anthropology from critique to theory building, although the field is still very dynamic, and all three types of studies continue to influence and strengthen the others. Each kind of study is potentially important in working toward archaeological approaches to the subject of gender and is briefly summarized here.

The earliest work in feminist anthropology identified and described male bias in the field. Stimulated by the rising interest in gender arrangements that accompanied the contemporary women's movement, anthropologists reviewed traditional studies in the discipline to learn about the lives of women in other times and places or to consider more generally the treatment of women as subject matter in anthropological work. Previous sections of this chapter discussed the findings of feminist critics in terms of androcentrism in anthropology and these need not be repeated here. The result of the early critiques was to introduce the subject of women as legitimate, interesting, and important in anthropological inquiry. Subsequent and deeper critiques of the field challenge many of the concepts and theories employed by anthropologists, arguing that attention to sex roles and cultural concepts of gender profoundly and essentially alters our analyses and will ultimately transform present understandings of human life (see Atkinson 1982: 249).

In response to the feminist critiques of anthropology, numerous researchers in recent years have initiated new ethnographic studies or reanalyses of previous works in efforts to highlight the roles and contributions of women in specific cultures and to examine female participation and influence in various institutions or domains of social life (e.g., Weiner 1976). Studies in the anthropology of women seek to understand commonalities and diversity in women's lives – interculturally and intraculturally – and to examine women's spheres of power and influence. Studies in the anthropology of women essentially reinvestigate human life with females at the center of analysis (see Murphy and Murphy 1974; Rogers 1975; and Rohrlich-Leavitt 1977).

These studies have been particularly useful in revealing the enormous range of activities undertaken by women when viewed cross culturally, challenging stereo-typic notions common in anthropology that suggest limitations in female roles or task performance. They further call into question basic anthropological under-standings of specific cultures previously examined through the lens of male informants and male observer–analysts (see Rohrlich-Leavitt 1977; Slocum 1975; Weiner 1976; and Zihlman 1981). In all cases these female-centered studies have introduced new and appropriate variables into the analysis of human life.

The third and perhaps the most important area of feminist anthropology focuses on gender theory. Much of the thereotical discourse in the field centers on debates about the universality and expression of sexual asymmetry. The issues were initially presented in what has become a classic in feminist anthropology, *Women, Culture and Society*, edited by Michelle Rosaldo and Louise Lamphere (1974a). The contrib-utors in this volume generally take as given "that all contemporary societies are to some extent male-dominated and although the degree and expression of female subordination vary greatly, sexual asymmetry is presently a universal fact of human social life" (Rosaldo and Lamphere 1974b: 3).

The articles in this collection represent the first serious attempts in contempo-rary anthropology to consider the constellation of factors — economic, social, and ideological — that structure relations between the sexes and, more specifically, deter-mine the social position of females in society. The working assumption of most of the authors in the volume is that there exist distinct gender-linked realms or social spheres: the public–male and the domestic–female. Although many researchers, including those who contributed to *Women, Culture and Society*, have come to abandon this conceptualization, or at least its universality, Rosaldo summarized the perspec-tive as follows:

> Our . . . argument was, in essence, that in all human societies sexual asym-metry might be seen to correspond to a rough institutional division between domestic and public spheres of activity, the one built around reproduction, affective, and familial bonds, and particularly constraining to women; the other, providing for collectivity, jural order, and social cooperation, organized primarily by men. The domestic/public division as it appeared in any given society was not a necessary, but an "intelligible" product of the mutual accom-modation of human history and human biology. . . . From these observations, we argued, one could then trace the roots of a pervasive gender inequality.
> (Rosaldo 1980: 397)

Women, Culture and Society provoked a tremendous response and stimulated serious debates about the presumed universality of sexual asymmetry and the most appro-priate methods and frameworks for studying female status (see Lamphere 1977 for a review of these debates). Many argued that the universality of sexual asymmetry assumed by the authors was more apparent than real and that this idea reflected the continuation of androcentric analyses despite the feminist consciousness of the authors. The critics suggested that the appearance of universal female subordination was rooted in the very categories of analysis used by ethnographers, particularly the public–domestic dichotomy. Many researchers, including Rosaldo (1980), have raised serious questions about the applicability of this dichotomy to small-scale or prestate societies.

The structural opposition inherent in the public–private notion and the gender linkages associated with it may be appropriate in describing western, industrial, suburban societies but it distorts the structure and character of gender relations in many other groups. In fact, all too often the division into public and domestic spheres merely describes presumed male and female domains regardless of the specific spatial or social context of their activities and behaviors. The analytical consequences of a *contrast* between a familial sphere and a political–jural sphere (following Fortes 1969) are not only linked to modern western ideology (Nash and Leacock 1977), but also are "incompatible with the study of [human] relationships" and of their articulation (Rosaldo 1980: 407, citing O'Laughlin 1977; see also Caplan and Burja 1979). There is now systematic critique of research priorities (see Yanagisako 1979) and core concepts in the discipline of anthropology, concepts and vocabularies (see also Schuck 1974) that have been taken as givens and appear on the surface to be "neutral" and "value free:" *social structure, public–domestic, formal–informal*. The point of this criticism is to pull such concepts apart, trace them back to their origins and evaluate their utility in theory building (Spector n.d.). Archaeologists have only to gain from this kind of theory building.

Although debates continue concerning the universality of female subordination and appropriate methods for measuring the status of women cross culturally, most current feminist research in anthropology has moved away from discussion of gender universals and focuses more on variability. Whyte's overview (1978), *The Status of Women in Preindustrialized Societies*, Liebowitz's (1978) examination of the wide range of family structures in human and nonhuman primate societies, and numerous studies examining the complexities of understanding issues of power, status, and influence within one society or cross culturally (see Quinn 1977) mark a departure in feminist anthropology from "our analytical tradition [that] has preserved the 19th century division into inherently gendered spheres" (Rosaldo 1980: 407). Extremely variable contexts and forms of gender-linked organization, status, and behaviors have been demonstrated.

Questions now center on examination of the factors that seem to influence the nature of relations between men and women, the circumstances in which women and men exert power and influence, and the ways that gender arrangements affect or structure group responses to various conditions in their social or natural environments.

Recent work emphasizing the relationships between gender organization and culture change are especially relevant to archaeology and in some respects the approaches taken overlap with the problem-orientation of archaeologists. Several important contributions have been made in the study of colonization and culture contact. These demonstrate the differential impact that these processes have on the roles, activities, and experiences of both men and women (e.g., Bossen 1975; Draper 1975; Etienne and Leacock 1980; Helms 1976; Klein 1976; Leacock 1975; Matthiasson 1976). In certain situations of culture change, gender organization and gender-linked roles are certain not only to be affected but may well structure and set the basis for the new configuration of roles and social organization, from the extractive–productive tasks through the cosmological and ideological realms. Myers (1978) has shown how a period of population decline and demographic anxiety channeled early Israelite women into domestic and reproductive "niches" to meet the crisis, and how this limited role was elaborated and made rigid despite demographic recovery by late biblical times. Silverblatt's study (1978) shows how the very roles and rankings of females in the early Inca state became the means whereby they were later subordinated and excluded first within the Inca Empire and, more extensively, with the Spanish Conquest. Rothenberg (1976) has shown how the "conservatism" of the subsistence strategies of Seneca women after European contact is, in fact, a deliberate and adaptive response to the exigencies of the contact situation.

Other studies of special interest to archaeologists concern the formation of pristine states. These studies generally do not approach the subject through analysis of the archaeological record but are more concerned with processes of state formation as a major reorganization of human social structures, including gender relations. Reiter, for example, criticizes the archaeological systems approach to state formation, arguing that the framework has not brought enough attention to the contexts in which political formations change (Reiter 1978). She suggests that the domain of kinship deserves careful consideration, for it is probably precisely within this domain that dramatic tensions occurred; with the rise of the state, it is kinship-based societies that are being transformed (Reiter 1978:13). The suppression of the kinship base that is so powerful an organizer of social relations in prestate societies undoubtedly triggered important changes in gender status or gender relations (see Sacks 1979).

Reiter argues that "we should expect to find variations within state making (and unmaking) societies over time, and between such societies, rather than one simple pattern" (Reiter 1978:13). The examination of such variability can only be done through the analysis of the contexts of change and the formulation of specific research questions. In this kind of research approach aspects of gender will be illuminated rather than obscured, as is often the case with the broad focus and general scale of analysis typical of archaeological systems studies. Reiter suggests that those approaches that derive models from ethnographic or ethnohistoric accounts have the most-potential for refining the archaeological resolution of state formation questions.

In suggesting new approaches to the study of state formation, Reiter reviews existing literature in archaeology and sociocultural anthropology that she believes can contribute to the "contextualization" of changes, studies including those that emphasize: the politics of kinship (e.g., Adams 1966; Gailey 1976; Ortner 1976; Silverblatt 1978); changing content and roles of cosmologies (e.g., Adams 1966; Eliade 1960; Flannery and Marcus 1976; Nash 1978; Willey 1971); intensification of warfare (e.g., McNamara and Wemple 1973; Muller 1977; Pomeroy 1974; but see also Harris and Divale 1976); and trade (e.g., Adams 1974; Kohl 1975; Mintz 1971; Rohrlich-Leavitt 1977). Within any of these topic areas, questions about gender can and should be formulated to enhance our understanding of state formation. Feminist researchers argue that in studying the rise of the state it is likely that one can learn a great deal about the reorganization of gender behavior (e.g., Muller 1977; Nash 1978). The converse is also true. The examination of gender relations, roles, and ideologies must be included in any comprehensive attempts to explain the rise of the state.

This last point is important in articulating the intersection of interests in feminist anthropology and archaeology. Most of the questions about culture process raised by contemporary archaeologists have a gender component or dimension: site functions; site uses; subsistence systems that are, of course, based on task-differentiation; inter- and intrasite spatial phenomena; settlement systems; the power and role of material culture; mechanisms of integration and cultural solidarity; extradomestic trade and exchange systems; and, above all, the course of culture change.

Archaeology and building critical theory

The task before us in developing archaeological approaches to gender is similar to other theoretical and methodological challenges posed in the field in recent years. Most contemporary archaeologists would agree that our knowledge of the past is not necessarily limited by the fragmentary nature of our data but rather by our epistemologies (Wylie 1981) and by our methods for analyzing the archaeological record. Working from this optimistic perspective, archaeologists in recent years have initiated studies into a wide range of issues and questions to increase our understanding of social life and cultural processes in the past. Examples include renewed interest in the role of the individual (Hill and Gunn 1977); increasing concern with site-formation processes (Binford 1980; Schiffer 1976); household-level or other studies of smaller social units (Flannery and Winter 1976); Wilk and Rathje 1982); emphasis on more structural perspectives (Deetz 1977; Hodder 1982b; Lechtman 1976; Wylie 1982); and more sophisticated and explicit realization of the role and power of symbolic forms, rituals, and cosmologies in past human life (Fritz 1978; Hodder 1982c; Isbell 1976; Leone 1982). Most of these are directly related to the inquiry into prehistoric gender behavior, organization, and ideology, and we advocate the explicit addition of the subject of gender arrangements and ideology to this growing list of concerns of contemporary archaeology. However, the success of any of these new approaches in explaining any aspect of prehistoric life or in accounting for the archaeological record is dependent upon critical theory-building and the development of appropriate epistemologies (Wylie 1981, 1982).

Critical theory-building, simplistically, involves the recognition that one generation's gain is the next generation's problem (Rapp 1982). Although the archaeology of at least the past two decades has advocated the pursuit of culture process and prehistoric social organization (Binford and Sabloff 1982; Flannery 1967; Longacre 1963; Sabloff and Willey 1980), there have been trends associated with this pursuit that have inhibited the archaeological study of gender. This pursuit of culture process is precisely one context within which we might have expected a series of questions into the transformation of cultural forms, including those associated with gender roles and organizations. However, as we have seen, these questions have not been raised. Before we turn to a more positive approach to archaeology and the study of gender it is relevant to consider, albeit briefly, why such gender-related questions have not been raised, why archaeologists have been ignorant of the bulk of feminist research of the 1970s, and why social *action* of most sorts has been absent from archaeological theory and interpretation. Only one major theme of archaeological theory is discussed, but this is clearly this generation's problem despite the significant contributions made by archaeological practitioners of the 1970s and earlier.

Few would disagree that one dominant theme of archaeology has been the systems perspective. Ever since Flannery's classic polarization of archaeology into culture history versus culture process and his advocacy of a systems perspective (Flannery 1967), many researchers have become preoccupied with the analysis of subsystems that interact to compromise the total cultural system to be studied. Binford and Sabloff (1982:139) are still advocating the replacement of the normative paradigm with the preferred systems paradigm.

The systems approach per se does not preclude attention to gender structures or dynamics but the research priorities that have resulted tend to focus on such broad processes and in such functional perspective that the sources of change or the roles of individuals, small groups, or even the role of choice have rarely been considered. Although the systems approach has produced useful analyses of resource-procurement systems, seasonality, scheduling, and other general features of subsystems, the actors who procured resources and made decisions about the allocation of their time and labor have somehow become invisible, if not irrelevant and subservient to the system of which they are a part. This preoccupation with the system(s) behind the Indian and the artifact (after Flannery 1967) is not unique to archaeology, and there are insightful critiques of how this perspective on humans as biotic components in information-processing systems has both dominated research in the social and biological sciences and structured our own concepts of ourselves (Haraway 1979, 1983).

There are a number of other problems with a systems approach in archaeology, particularly for the study of gender. Archaeology has become characterized by fragmented studies of the various subsystems – subsistence, settlement, and so forth – and each has essentially become its own subdiscipline of archaeology with its own vocabulary, cross-cultural analyses, and studies of each across time and space. Instead of doing the culture history of different taxonomic units, many contemporary archaeologists do the culture history of different subsystems.

Another problem with the systems approach as practiced in archaeology is the methodological problem of scale. There is a disjunction between the nature of the archaeological data we have to work with and the very broad processes that are examined within the systems perspective. The archaeological remains that we have on hand are the by-products of so much sociocultural behavior that we have not even begun to find a way to read all or even most of the behavior from the data. Given "the dense load of cultural information that every artifact bears" (Kintigh 1978), we should not be surprised at the relative lack of success we have had in answering broad questions that lack requisite specificity. Furthermore, the scale of analysis of the systems approach that focuses on changes within certain subsystems tends to preclude contextualizing the study of change. Thus, the systems approach promotes an ahistoric archaeology: the *contexts* in which social and political formations change are not brought into focus.

Finally, the systems approach of the past decade has relegated the material culture of past human societies – that which comprises the bulk of the archaeological record – to a passive role in human life. Burial treatment *reflects* status, or the numbers and distributions of ovens or wells *imply* certain household sizes or residential systems.

However, both ethnographically and archaeologically the distributions of such artifacts and features as wells, ovens, or pots can be looked at as layouts or structural features that may have not only promoted or channeled interaction and information exchange among the users, whether male, female, or unknown, but also actually defined social action (Braithwaite 1982). Hodder (1983), for example, has shown how women in western Europe negotiated social positions by the use of decorated pottery during the fourth to fifth millennia BC. Architectural features may also be viewed as potential media through which social action may be defined; there is Carpenter's study (1980) on Islamic house structures of the fifteenth century with room arrangements that are more and less sex-linked in usage, and there is the implication of how rooftop connections in an Iranian village structure patterns of information exchange and female social action (Jacobs 1979).

Just as E. Ardener (1975) has argued that there are other models of society to be obtained, models other than those deriving from the functional approaches to ethnography, there are other models of prehistoric life (e.g., Davis 1978) to be developed than those based on a systemic and functional archaeology. Ardener suggests that these other models for ethnography may best be approached by means of studies of symbolic and ritual behaviors, and certainly these aspects of prehistoric life have been seriously neglected in the past decades. Archaeologists have yet to realize the power of the understanding that the essence of human – and, hence, cultural – life is that it is both material and symbolic simultaneously. We submit that archaeologists must rethink their slavish adoption of the systems perspective and develop a working concept of culture that includes attention to the centrality of symbolic behavior. This is particularly the case if archaeologists want to contribute to the study of gender, and, more broadly, if archaeologists are going to develop an adequate theory of human social and cultural life that must lie behind our research and interpretations. We address some of these broader issues of critical theory-building in the final section of this review, within a discussion of just one possible approach to the archaeology of gender.

An analytical framework for the archaeology of gender

One most promising general approach to the archaeology of gender is an ethnoar-chaeological or ethnohistorical one. The power of the ethnoarchaeological approach in archaeological theory-building has been shown within a variety of theoretical stances (compare Kramer 1979 with Hodder 1982c). Various statements by prac-tioners of ethnoarchaeology (e.g., Binford 1980: 5; Deetz 1972: 115) emphasize that this domain of research has great potential to aid in the construction of models that we need to link the material and nonmaterial world. However, employing ethnoarchaeological approaches in the case of gender is complicated by the perva-siveness and persistence of androcentrism (as shown in the case of Yellen 1977), and, as discussed above, by the theoretical and epistemological preferences that have inhibited attention to gender.

Our first task in undertaking an ethnoarchaeological approach to gender must be the reconceptualization of gender dynamics. This is one reason why we can only gain from a thorough comprehension of contemporary feminist research in anthro-pology. Certainly the foundation must be a theory of social life that explicitly acknowledges the parameters and variations in gender arrangements, the possible material manifestations of those arrangements, and above all the ways in which material culture (and other archaeologically accessible data, such as spatial pattern-ings) actively structure (and restructure) not only gender arrangements but many other sociocultural phenomena.

We illustrate here how a new set of terms for some very basic subjects of archae-ological inquiry can, when based on a reconceptualization of gender dynamics, yield immediate methodological implications for the archaeology of gender. Janet Spector (1981, 1982) has designed an analytical framework that can be used either to orga-nize observations of gender behaviors and materials among living groups or to reanalyze information about gender available in existing primary or secondary written sources. This is called a *task-differentiation* framework, and it is proposed as a new way to think about and research what is usually considered "activities." This task-differentiation framework focuses on the material parameters of gender arrangements, reduces the possibility of androcentric bias, and overall is more sensitive to and allows for variable and changing configurations of human division of labor. We hope that with sufficient cross-cultural application of the framework we can gain more reliable knowledge about variations in gender arrangements, the factors explaining observed variations, and how such variability might be expressed in the archaeological record. Although the task-differentiation framework is still in the formative stages of development and has been applied only in limited cultural contexts utilizing existing written accounts (see Spector 1981, 1982), it is presented here as an illustration of one kind of approach to the archaeology of gender.

The task-differentiation framework highlights dimensions of male and female activity patterns. The assumption underlying this orientation is that what people do – how they are socially, temporally, and materially organized – is achieved by and hence directly related to the types and structure of sites and their "contents" that are the archaeological record. The framework focuses attention on four interrelated aspects of task performance: the social, temporal, spatial, and material dimensions of each task undertaken by any given group.

To use the framework, one first identifies the tasks performed by people in a given cultural setting – tasks associated with resource procurement and processing; those associated with the physical maintenance of the group, including construction and repair of buildings, facilities, and the manufacture of material goods; and tasks associated with social maintenance of the group, that is, those tasks associated with reproduction, ritual life, health, and inter- and intragroup relations. These categories are not meant to be exhaustive, but such a list should imply a far more comprehensive conception of tasks. Too often, studies of activity patterns or division of labor limit attention to tasks directly associated with subsistence or technology.

Once tasks have been identified, one describes the other parameters of task performance. The *social dimension* of task differentiation identifies the sex, age, number, and relationships (age groups, kin groups, non-kin groups) of task performers. At any one time, who performs the task? How are people organized, scheduled, and interacting in the context of the specific task being examined? Do people work in groups? individually? at the same time and place as others performing the same task? Attention to questions of this type on a task-by-task basis begins to suggest the possibilities of intra- and cross-cultural variability. There are clearly many alternative ways to organize people to perform the same task and each alternative has implications in terms of the task system as a whole, and for the social dynamics. The social dimensions of task performance should be described as precisely as possible rather than using generalizing concepts (e.g., *communal, individual, group*) that may mask important details of task organization.

The next aspect of task differentiation to be described is the *temporal dimension*. For each task identified, one inventories the frequency and duration of task performance. It is important to consider when (seasonally, at what time of the month, day, etc.) the task is performed and how long it takes each time it is performed.

These are essentially questions about scheduling and the tempo of people's lives and, again, there is clearly a considerable range of possibilities along this dimension of task differentiation.

The *spatial dimension* of task differentiation identifies where each task is performed within the context of particular site types (depending on the specific subsistence-settlement system being examined). Attention is drawn to tasks that may be spatially discrete in contrast to others that may be performed in various locations. Some tasks always take place within a dwelling or proximate to certain stationary facilities. Other tasks are less restrictive in a spatial sense. Again this dimension of task differentiation has implications in terms of understanding variability in gender systems – for example, differences in the mobility patterns and use of space by men and women within and between cultures – and in terms of understanding possible relationships between gender arrangements and archaeological site formation processes and site structure (see Kent 1980 for a cogent critique of our predetermined notions on these relationships).

Finally, the task-differentiation framework directs attention to the material dimensions of activity patterns. For each task identified, one indicates all the materials associated with task performance. Materials, facilities, and structures are produced, utilized, transformed in the course of use, and left behind as by-products of task performances. One further examines how materials are used by task performers. Are pieces of equipment shared, or individually owned or used? Are some materials that are produced during task performance consistently removed from the location of use? Are there other patternings and structures of materials? It is in this area of investigation that we might begin to learn in a systematic way about similarities and differences between males and females in terms of their use of and knowledge about certain materials, artifact types, and contexts. This is particularly the case if one assumes that the material patternings we observe are brought into existence by cultural classifications and (implicit) cultural knowledge of the makers and users. The picture is clearly more complicated and dynamic than simply identifying one set of tools with males and another with females.

The task-differentiation approach enables those archaeologists interested in gender to consider a number of related questions, some centered on furthering our general understanding of gender as a basic and fundamentally important aspect of human life and other questions more specifically related to the archaeological expression of gender arrangements. In the first case, the approach provides a detailed and quantifiable means of examining and comparing the activity configurations of males and females. Each gender can be separated for analytical purposes to study gender-specific features of the task-differentiation system, including aspects of scheduling, mobility patterns, knowledge of the environment, and resource utilization patterns of men and women. These are all subjects referred to in traditional archaeological studies and treated androcentrically.

Because the framework is cross-culturally applicable, it also allows archaeological researchers to compare groups in different ecological, economic, or social contexts to understand better the expression and sources of variations in gender arrangements. Ultimately, with enough studies of this type, we may begin to approach the archaeological record with sufficient understanding to interpret assemblages in terms of gender. The task framework does begin to illustrate the ways that gender organization and material culture patterning are interactive; these ways are far more complex and variable than previously appreciated.

Finally, the task-differentiation framework allows us to frame research questions that should contribute to the mandatory construction of gender theory. For example, the approach specifies a range of questions to be asked in culture change studies. In cases where we can document the introduction of new elements of technology, we can "model" out the possible differential impact on men and women, given the previously existing task system. Whose labor patterns are likely to be altered? whose mobility patterns affected? whose scheduling patterns?

The task-differentiation framework obviously does not encompass all aspects of gender. Most important, the whole area of the relations between material culture and gender ideology awaits serious investigation (but look for Moore, in press). However, the relevance of such a framework for the archaeology of gender should be clear. At present, the framework involves a methodology of modeling. Certain constraints or attributes (e.g., the spatial dimension of task differentiation) are specified for the construction and testing of paramorphic models (Wylie 1981). These models are built on the basis of better-known contemporary ethnographic or historic contexts, and they are built to represent past cultural contexts, or at least to represent the generative processes that led to the material (and other) output of these contexts. The data of the archaeological record that one is investigating acquire significance as evidence (for gender arrangements or task differentiation) only in relation to the "models of context" that, in this case, the task-differentiation framework can construct (Wylie 1981).

Some conclusions

We are still far from being able to interpret with confidence the archaeological record in terms of gender, and the same can be said for many other features of prehistoric life. Although gender is information that has not regularly and reliably been recovered by archaeologists who lack a theoretical and methodological framework to do so, statements on gender have not been absent in archaeological interpretation. As we have shown, the so-called methodological barriers (the archaeological problem of women; cf. Hayden 1977) have not kept many archaeologists from covert inclusion of assumptions about roles and relationships, nor have these barriers prompted archaeologists to draw upon an increasingly rich literature on human gender. This literature embodies theoretical reconceptualizations, new vocabularies, and a set of research questions immediately relevant to archaeologists.

We are not advocating that archaeologists abandon their currently preferred research objectives and replace them with those that elucidate gender organization, although we do believe that the methodological and theoretical restructuring that this would entail would lead to a much more compelling archaeology. We are not demanding that archaeology try to elucidate whether a male or a female made a certain tool or performed a certain task, nor that archaeologists who have attempted to do so (e.g., Winters 1968) must now empirically support or test their notions.

One thing we *are* saying is that there are certain assumptions about these behaviors that underlie archaeological research and it is these assumptions that must be evaluated and reworked in light of recent feminist research. The organization of gender behavior relates to and is intimately a part of most other aspects of past cultural systems in which archaeologists have always been interested. Archaeologists will have to understand gender dynamics at some level if we are to continue to pursue some research objectives that we have set out for ourselves: site functions and uses; subsistence systems that are, of course, based on task differentiation; inter- and intrasite spatial phenomena; the power and role of material culture; mechanisms of cultural solidarity and integration; extradomestic trade and exchange system; and, above all, the course of culture change.

We hope that our discussion of how archaeologists have perpetuated gender stereotypes stimulates further discussion among archaeologists about appropriate methods for studying gender and about the theoretical implications of including gender in our examination of other archaeological research questions. We hope that this review will stimulate more critical awareness of the role of archaeologists in employing and perpetuating gender stereotypes and androcentric perspectives. We hope also that archaeologists can realize how the roots of the barriers to elucidating past gender arrangements and ideology lie in two related domains. On the one hand, the roots lie more in the sociopolitical contexts of archaeological research than in our inherent abilities to interpret the archaeological record and the past. On the other hand, it will be difficult to do archaeology other than that elicited by contemporary sociopolitical contexts without (1) a critical theory-building that questions aspects of epistemology (e.g., empiricism) and socio-cultural theory (e.g., the primacy of systems), and (2) the development of methods appropriate to the actualization of research goals. In order to begin these latter tasks we must question the rationale and role of archaeology, and this has implications for more than the archaeology of gender.

■ ■ ■

References

Aberle, D. (1968) Comments, in discussion. In *New perspectives in archaeology*, edited by S. R. Binford and L. R. Binford. Chicago: Aldine Press, pp. 353–359.

Adams, R. McC. (1966) *The evolution of urban society*. Chicago: Aldine.

—— (1974) Anthropological perspectives on trade. *Current Anthropology* 15(3): 239–258.

Ardener, E. (1972) Belief and the problem of women. In *The interpretation of ritual: essays in honor of A. I. Richards*, edited by J. S. LaFontaine. London, Tavistock, pp. 135–158.

—— (1975) Belief and the problem of women. The problem revisited. In *Perceiving women*, edited by Shirley Ardener. New York: John Wiley and Sons, pp. 1–28.

Ardener, S. (ed.) (1975) *Perceiving women*. New York: John Wiley and Sons.

Atkinson, J. (1982) Review essay: anthropology, *Signs*, 8(2): 236–258.

Beechy, V. (1978) Women and production: a critical analysis of some sociological theories of women's work. In *Feminism and materialism*, edited by Annette Kohn and Ann-Marie Wolpe. London: Routledge and Kegan Paul, pp. 155–197.

Binford, L. R. (1972) Archaeological Perspectives. In *An archaeological perspective*, New York: Academic Press, pp. 78–104.

—— (1980) Willow smoke and dogs' tails: hunter–gatherer settlement systems and archaeological site formation. *American Antiquity* 45(1): 4–20.

—— (1981) *Bones: ancient men and modern myths*. New York: Academic Press.

Binford, S. R. and L. R. Binford (1968a) *New perspectives in archaeology*. Chicago: Aldine.

—— (1968b) Stone tools and human behavior. *Scientific American* 220: 70–84.

Binford, L. and J. Sabloff (1982) Paradigms, systematics and archaeology. *Journal of Anthropological Research* 38: 137–153.

Bledsoe, C. (1980) *Women and marriage in Kpelle society*. Stanford, California: Stanford University Press.

Boserup, E. (1970) *Women's role in economic development*. New York: St. Martin's Press.

Bossen, L. (1975) Women in modernizing societies. *American Ethnologist* 2: 587–601.

Braithwaite, M. (1982) Decoration as ritual symbol: a theoretical proposal and an ethnographic study in southern Sudan. In *Symbolic and structural archaeology*, edited by I. Hodder. Cambridge: Cambridge University Press. pp. 80–88.

Bunn, H. (1981) Archaeological evidence for meat-eating by Plio-Pleistocene hominids from Koobi Fora and Olduvai Gorge. *Nature* 291: 574–576.

Butterfield, H. (1965) *The Whig interpretation of history*. New York: Norton.

Caplan, P. and J. M. Burja (eds) (1979) *Women united, women divided: comparative studies of ten contemporary cultures*. Bloomington, Indiana: Indiana University Press.

Carpenter, D. (1980) A structural analysis of vernacular architecture. The degree of privatization and its functional implications. BA honors thesis, Department of Anthropology, State University of New York, Binghamton, New York.

Chiñas, B. (1973) *The Isthmus Zapotecs: women's roles in cultural context*. New York: Holt, Rinehart, and Winston.

Conkey, M. W. (1977) By chance: the role of archaeology in contributing to a reinterpretation of human culture. Paper presented at Annual Meetings, American Anthropological Association, Houston, Texas.

Cucchiari, S. (1981) The gender revolution and the transition from bisexual horde to patrilocal band: the origins of gender hierarchy. In *Sexual meanings*, edited by S. Ortner and H. Whitehead. Cambridge, England: Cambridge University Press. pp. 31–79.

Dahlberg, F. (editor) (1981) *Woman the gatherer*. New Haven: Yale University Press.

Davis, E. G. (1971) *The first sex*. New York: Putnam.

Davis, E. (ed.) (1978) *The ancient Californians: Rancholabrean hunters of the Mojave Lakes country*. Los Angeles: Natural History Museum of Los Angeles County, Social Sciences Series 29.

Deetz, James (1968) The inference of residence and descent rules from archaeological data. In *New perspectives in archaeology*, edited by S. R. Binford and L. R. Binford, Chicago: Aldine, pp. 41–48.

—— (1972) Archaeology as a social science. In *Contemporary archaeology*, edited by M. P. Leone. Carbondale, Illinois: Southern Illinois University Press, pp. 108–117.

—— (1977) *In small things forgotten: The archaeology of early American life*. New York: Doubleday Anchor.

Diner, H. (1973) *Mothers and amazons: The first feminine history of culture*. New York: Doubleday Anchor.

Draper, P. (1975) !Kung women: contrasts in sexual egalitarianism in foraging and sedentary contexts. In *Toward an anthropology of women*, edited by R. R. Reiter. New York: Monthly Review Press. pp. 77–109.

Draper, P. and E. Cashdan (1974) The impact of sedentism on !Kung socialization. Paper presented at Annual Meetings of the American Anthropological Association, Mexico City.

Dwyer, D. (1978) *Images and self-images: male and female in Morocco*. New York: Columbia University Press.

Eliade, M. (1960) Structures and changes in the history of religions. In *City invincible*, edited by K. Kraeling and R. Adams. Chicago: University of Chicago Press, pp. 361–366.

Etienne, M. and E. Leacock (1980) *Women and colonization: anthropological perspectives*. New York: Praeger.

Flannery, K. V. (1967) Culture-history vs. culture-process. Review of *An introduction to American archaeology: North and Middle America* (vol. 1) by Gordon R. Willey. *Scientific American* 3: 399–426.

Flannery, K. V. and J. Marcus (1976) Formative Oaxaca and the Zapotec cosmos. *American Scientist* 64: 374–383.

Flannery, K. V. and M. C. Winter (1976) Analyzing household activities. In *The early Mesoamerican village*, edited by K. Flannery, New York: Academic Press, pp. 34–44.

Fortes, M. (1969) *Kinship and the social order*. Chicago: Aldine.

Friedl, E. (1975) *Women and men*. New York: Holt, Rinehart and Winston.

Fritz, J. M. (1978) Paleopsychology today: ideational systems and human adaptation in prehistory. In *Social archaeology: beyond subsistence and dating*, edited by C. Redman *et al*. New York: Academic Press, pp. 37–57.

Gailey, C. (1976) The origin of the state in Tonga. Gender hierarchy and class formation. Paper presented at American Anthropological Association meetings, Washington, DC.

Goodale, J. (1971) *Tiwi wives: a study of the women of Melville Island, North Australia*. Seattle, Washington: University of Washington Press.

Haraway, D. (1979) Sex, mind, and profit: from human engineering to sociobiology. *Radical History Review* 20: 206–237.

—— (1982) Signs of dominance. *Studies in History of Biology* 6: 129–219.

Harris, M. and W. T. Divale (1976) Population, warfare, and the male supremacist complex. *American Anthropologist* 78: 521–538.

Hartman, H. (1975) Capitalism, partriarchy, and job segregation by sex. *Signs: Journal of Women in Culture and Society* 1 (3, Part 2): 137–169.

Hayden, B. (1977) Stone tool functions in the Western Desert. In *Stone tools as cultural markers: change, evolution and complexity*, edited by R. V. S. Wright. New Jersey: Humanities Press, Inc, pp. 178–188.

Heinz, H. J. (1978) *Namkwa: life among the Bushmen*. London: Cape Publishers.

Helms, M. W. (1976) Domestic organization in Eastern Central America: The San Blas Cuna, Miskito, and Black Carib compared. *Western Canadian Journal of Anthropology* VI (3): 133–163. Special issue: *Cross-sex relations: native peoples*, edited by P. A. McCormack.

Hill, J. N. (1968) Broken K Pueblo: patterns of form and function. In *New perspectives in archaeology*, edited by S. R. Binford and L. R. Binford. Chicago: Aldine. pp. 103–142.

Hill, J. and J. Gunn (1977) *The individual in prehistory*. New York: Academic Press.

Hochschild, A. (1973) A review of sex role research. *American Journal of Sociology* 78(4): 1011–1025.

Hodder, I. (1982a) Theoretical archaeology: a reactionary view. In *Symbolic and structural archaeology*, edited by I. Hodder. Cambridge, England: Cambridge University Press, pp. 1–16.

—— (1982b) (ed.) *Symbolic and structural archaeology*. Cambridge, England: Cambridge University Press.

—— (1982c) *Symbols in action: Ethnoarchaeological studies of material culture*. Cambridge, England: Cambridge University Press.

—— (1983) Burials, houses, women and men in the European Neolithic. In *Ideology and social change*, edited by D. Miller and C. Tilley. Cambridge, England: Cambridge University Press.

Howell, N. (1979) *Demography of the Dobe !Kung*. New York: Academic Press.

Hughes-Jones, C. (1979) *From the Milk River: spatial and temporal processes in Northwest Amazonia*. Cambridge, England: Cambridge University Press.

Isaac, G. L. (1978a) The food-sharing behavior of protohuman hominids. *Scientific American* 238(4): 90–108.

—— (1978b) Food sharing and human evolution: archaeological evidence from the Plio-Pleistocene of South Africa. *Journal of Anthropological Research* 34: 311–325.

—— (1982) Bones in contention: competing explanations for the juxtaposition of Early Pleistocene artifacts and faunal remains. Paper presented at 4th International Archaeozoology Congress, London.

Isbell, W. (1976) Cosmological order expressed in prehistoric ceremonial centers. *Actes du XLII Congres International des Americanistes* IV: 269–297.

Jacobs, L. (1979) Tell-i-Nun: archaeological implications of a village in transition. In *Ethnoarchaeology*, edited by C. Kramer. New York: Columbia University Press, pp. 176–191.

Johnson, D. and M. Edey (1981) *Lucy: the beginnings of humankind*. New York: Simon and Schuster.

Kennedy, M. C. (1979) Status, role, and gender: Preconceptions in archaeology. Manuscript, Department of Anthropology, University of Minnesota, Minneapolis.

Kent, S. (1980) Search and what shall ye find: a holistic model of activity area use. Paper presented at annual meetings, Society for American Archaeology. Philadelphia, Pennsylvania.

Kessler, S. and W. MacKenna (1978) *Gender: an ethnomethodological approach*. New York: John Wiley and Sons.

Kintigh, K. (1978) A study in the archaeological inference of aspects of social interaction from stylistic artifact variation. Preliminary paper. Department of Anthropology, Ann Arbor: University of Michigan.

Kohl, P. (1975) The archaeology of trade. *Dialectical Anthropology* 1: 43–50.

Klein, L. (1976) "She's one of us, you know" – the public life of Tlingit women: traditional, historical, and contemporary perspectives. In *Western Canadian Journal of Anthropology*, VI, (3): 164–183. Special issue: *Cross-sex relations: Native Peoples*, edited by P. A. McCormack.

Kramer, C. (1979) Introduction. In *Ethnoarchaeology. Implications of ethnography for archaeology*, edited by C. Kramer. New York: Columbia University Press, pp. 1–20.

LaFontaine, J. S. (1978) Introduction. In *Sex and age as principles of social differentiation*. ASA Monograph 17, New York: Academic Press, pp. 3–20.

Lamphere, L. (1977) Review essay: anthropology. *Signs, Journal of Women in Culture and Society* 2(3): 612–627.

Lancaster, J. B. (1978) Caring and sharing in human evolution. *Human Behavior* 1(2): 82–89.

Laughlin, W. S. (1968) Hunting: An integrating biobehavior system and its evolutionary importance. In *Man the hunter*, edited by R. Lee and I. Devore. Chicago: Aldine, pp. 304–320.

Leacock, E. B. (1973) Introduction. In *The origin of the family, private property and the state*, by F. Engels, New York: International Publishers.

—— (1975) Class, commodity, and the status of women. In *Women cross-culturally: change and challenge*, edited by R. Rohrlich-Leavitt. The Hague: Mouton, pp. 601–616.

—— (1977) Women in egalitarian societies. In *Becoming visible. Women in European History*, edited by R. Bridenthal and C. Koonz. Boston: Houghton-Mifflin, pp. 11–35.

—— (1978) Women's status and egalitarian society: implications for social evolution. *Current Anthropology* 19 (2): 247–254.

Lee, R. B. (1965) Subsistence ecology of !Kung bushmen. Unpublished Ph.D. dissertation, Department of Anthropology, University of California, Berkeley.

—— (1968) What hunters do for a living, or how to make out on scarce resources. In *Man the hunter*, edited by R. B. Lee and I. DeVore. Chicago: Aldine, pp. 30–48.

—— (1976) !Kung spatial organization: an ecological and historical perspective. In *Kalahari hunter–gatherers*, edited by R. B. Lee and I. DeVore. Cambridge, Massachusetts: Harvard University Press, pp. 74–97.

—— (1980a) The hand-to-mouth existence: a note on the origin of human economy. Appendix in *The !Kung San*. Cambridge: Cambridge University Press (originally 1968), pp. 489–494.

—— (1980b) *The !Kung San. Men, women, and work in a foraging society*. Cambridge: Cambridge University Press.

Lechtman, H. (1976) Style in technology – some early thoughts. In *Material culture. Style, organization, and dynamics of technology*, edited by H. Lechtman and R. Merrill. Proceedings of American Ethnological Society, 1975. St. Paul: West Publishing, pp. 3–20.

Leone, M. P. (1972) Issues in anthropological archaeology. In *Contemporary archeology*, edited by M. Leone. Carbondale, Illinois: Southern Illinois University Press, pp. 14–27.

—— (1973) Archaeology as the science of technology: Mormon town plans and fences. In *Research and theory in current archaeology*, edited by C. L. Redman. New York: John Wiley and Sons, pp. 125–150.

—— (1982) Some opinions about recovering mind. *American Antiquity* 47(4): 742–760.

Liebowtiz, L. (1978) *Males, females, families*. North Scituate, Mass: Duxbury Press.

Longacre, W. A. (1963) Archaeology as anthropology: a case study. Ph. D. dissertation, Department of Anthropology, University of Chicago.

—— (1968) Some aspects of prehistoric society in east-central Arizona. In *New perspectives in archeology*, edited by S. R. Binford and L. R. Binford. Chicago: Aldine, pp. 89–102.

Lovejoy, C. O. (1981) The origin of man. *Science* 211, (4480): 341–350.

MacCormack, C. and M. Strathern (eds) (1980) *Nature, culture and gender*. Cambridge: Cambridge University Press.

Martin, M. K. and B. Voorhies (1975) *Female of the species*. New York: Columbia University Press.

Matthiasson, C. (ed.) (1974) *Many sisters: women in cross-cultural perspective*. New York: Free Press.

Matthiasson, J. (1976) Northern Baffin Island women in three cultural periods. In *Western Canadian Journal of Anthropology* VI, (3): 201–212. Special Issue: *Cross-sex relations: native peoples*, edited by P. A. McCormack.

McNamara, J. and S. Wemple (1973) The power of women through the family in medieval Europe: 500–1100. *Feminist Studies* I(3–4): 126–141.

Milton, K. (1978) Male bias in anthropology. *Man* (n. s.) 14: 40–54.

Minnich, E. (1982) A devastating conceptual error: how can we *not* be feminist scholars? *Change Magazine* 14(3): 7–9.

Mintz, S. (1971) Men, women and trade. *Comparative Studies in Society and History* 13(3): 247–269.

Moore, H. (ed.) in press *Women, archaeology and material culture*. Cambridge: Cambridge University Press.

Morgan, E. (1972) *The Descent of Woman*. New York: Stein and Day.

Muller, V. (1977) The formation of the state and the oppression of women: A case study in England and Wales. *Radical Review of Political Economy* 9: 7–21.

Murphy, Y. and R. Murphy (1974) *Women of the forest*. New York: Columbia University Press.

Myers, C. (1978) The roots of restriction: women in early Israel. *Biblical Archeologist* 41(3): 91–103.

Nash, J. (1978) The Aztecs and the ideology of male dominance. *Signs: Journal of Women in Culture and Society* 4(2): 349–362.

Nash, J. and E. Leacock (1977) Ideologies of sex: archetypes and stereotypes. *Annals of the New York Academy of Science* 285: 618–645.

Ortner, S. B. (1976) The virgin and the state. *Michigan papers in anthropology* 2.

Ortner, S. B. and H. Whitehead (1981a) *Sexual meanings: the cultural construction of gender and sexuality*. Cambridge: Cambridge University Press.

—— (1981b) Introduction: accounting for sexual meanings. In *Sexual meanings*. Cambridge: Cambridge University Press.

Pader, E. (1982) Symbolism, social relations and the interpretation of mortuary remains. *British Archeological Reports*, International Series, 130.

Parker-Pearson, M. (1982) Mortuary practices, society and ideology: an ethnoarcheological study. In *Symbolic and structural archaeology*, edited by I. Hodder. Cambridge: Cambridge University Press, pp. 99–114.

Pfeiffer, J. (1980) Current research casts new light on human origins. *Smithsonian* 11(3): 91–103.

Pilbeam, D. (1981) Major trends in human evolution, in *Current arguments on early man*, edited by L.-K. Königsson. New York and Oxford: Pergamon Press.

Plog, S. (1980) *Stylistic variation of prehistoric ceramics: design analysis in the American southwest*. New York: Cambridge University Press.

Pomeroy, S. (1974) *Goddesses, whores, wives and slaves: women in classical antiquity*. New York: Schocken.

Potts, R. (1982) Caches, campsites and other ideas about earliest archaeological sites. Paper presented at Symposium, Origins of Culture: Johns Hopkins University Medical School, Baltimore, Maryland.

Quinn, N. (1977) Anthropological studies on women's status. *Annual Review of Anthropology* 6: 181–225. Palo Alto: Annual Reviews, Inc.

Rapp, R. (1979) Review essay: anthropology. *Signs: Journal of Women in Culture and Society* 4(3): 497–513.

—— (1982) Introduction to Worlds in Collision: the impact of feminist scholarship in anthropology. A Symposium presented at the 1982 annual meetings, American Anthropological Association, Washington, D.C.

Reed, E. (1975) *Women's evolution: From matriarchal clan to patriarchal family*. New York: Pathfinder Press.

Reiter, R. R. (1975) *Toward an anthropology of women*. New York: Monthly Review Press.

—— (1978) The search for origins: unraveling the threads of gender hierarchy. *Critique of Anthropology* 3(9–10): 5–24.

Rogers, S. C. (1975) Female forms of power and the myth of male dominance: a model of female/male interaction in peasant society. *American Ethnologist* 2(4): 727–755.

—— (1978) Women's place: a critical review of anthropological theory, *Comparative Studies in Society and History* 20(1): 123–162.

Rohrlich-Leavitt, R. (ed.) (1975) *Women cross-culturally: change and challenge*. The Hague: Mouton.

Rohrlich-Leavitt, R. (1977) Women in transition: Crete and Sumer. In *Becoming visible: Women in European History*, edited by R. Bridenthal and C. Koonz. Boston: Houghton-Mifflin Co, pp. 36–59.

Rohrlich-Leavitt, R., B. Sykes, and E. Weatherford (1975) Aboriginal women: male and female anthropological perspectives. In *Toward an anthropology of women*, edited by R. R. Reiter. New York: Monthly Review Press, pp. 110–126.

Rosaldo, M. Z. (1980) The use and abuse of anthropology: reflections on feminism and cross-cultural understanding. *Signs: Journal of Women in Culture and Society* 5(3): 389–417.

Rosaldo, M. Z. and L. Lamphere (eds) (1974a) *Woman, culture, and society*. Stanford, California: Stanford University Press.

—— (1974b) Introduction to *Woman, culture and society*. Stanford, California: Stanford University Press. pp. 1–16.

Rothenberg, D. (1976) Erosion of power – an economic basis for the selective conservatism of Seneca women in the 19th century. *Western Canadian Journal of Anthropology* VI, (3). Special issue: *Cross-sex relations: native peoples*, edited by P. McCormack: 106–122.

Sabloff, J. and G. Willey (1980) *A history of American archaeology* (2d ed.) San Francisco: W. H. Freeman and Co.

Sacks, K. (1976) State bias and women's status. *American Anthropologist*, 78(3): 565–569.

—— (1979) *Sisters and wives: the past and future of sexual equality*. Westport, Connecticut: Greenwood Press.

Sanday, P. R. (1981) *Female power and male dominance: On the origins of sexual inequality*. Cambridge: Cambridge University Press.

Schiffer, M. B. (1976) *Behavioral archeology*. New York: Academic Press.

Schlegel, A. (ed.) (1977) *Sexual stratification: a cross-cultural view*. New York: Columbia Press.

Schuck, V. (1974) A symposium: masculine blinders in the social sciences. *Social Science Quarterly* 55(3): 563–585.

Silverblatt, I. (1978) Andean women in the Inca empire. *Feminist Studies* 4: 37–61.

Slocum, S. (1975) Woman the gatherer: male bias in anthropology. In *Toward an anthropology of women*, edited by R. R. Reiter. New York: Monthly Review Press, pp. 36–50.

Spector, J. D. n.d. On building a feminist base in anthropology. Manuscript on file, Department of Anthropology, University of Minnesota, Minneapolis, Minnesota.

—— (1981) Male/female task differentiation: A framework for integrating historical and archeological materials in the study of gender and colonization. Paper presented at the 5th Berkshire Conference on the History of Women, Vassar College, Poughkeepsie, New York.

—— (1982) Male/female task differentiation among the Hidatsa: toward the development of an archeological approach to the study of gender. In *The hidden half: studies of native plains women*, edited by P. Albers and B. Medicine. Washington, DC: University Press of America.

Stocking, G. (1965) On the limits of "presentism" and "historicism" in the historiography of the behavioral sciences. *Journal of the History of the Behavioral Sciences* I: 211–218.

Strathern, M. (1972) *Women in between: female roles in a male world: Mount Hagen, New Guinea*. London: Seminar Press.

Tanner, N. (1981) *On becoming human*. Cambridge: Cambridge University Press.

Tanner, N. and A. Zihlman (1976) Women in evolution. Part I. Innovation and selection in human origins. In *Signs: Journal of Women in Culture and Society* 1(3): 104–119.

Van Allen, J. (1972) Sitting on a man: colonialism and the lost political institutions of Igbo women. *Canadian Journal of African Studies* 6: 165–181.

Wallman, S. (1976) Difference, differentiation, discrimination. *New Community: Journal of the Community Relations Commission* V (1–2).

Washburn, D. K. (1977) *A symmetry analysis of upper Gila area ceramic design*. Peabody Museum Papers, 68. Cambridge, Massachusetts: Harvard University Press.

Washburn, S. and C. S. Lancaster (1968) The evolution of hunting. In *Man the hunter*, edited by R. Lee and I. DeVore. Chicago: Aldine, pp. 293–303.

Weiner, A. (1976) *Women of value, men of renown*. Austin: University of Texas Press.

Whyte, M. K. (1978) *The status of women in preindustrialized societies*. Princeton, N.J.: Princeton University Press.

Wilk, R. and W. Rathje (eds) (1982) *Archaeology of the household: building a prehistory of domestic life*. A Special issue of *American Behavioral Scientist* 25(6): 611–724.

Willey, G. (1971) Commentary on: "The emergence of civilization in the Maya Lowlands". In *Observations on the emergence of civilization in Mesoamerica*, edited by R. Heizer. Contributions of the University of California Archaeological Research Facility (Berkeley), No. 11: 97–109.

Winters, H. (1968) Value systems and trade cycles of the late archaic in the Midwest. In *New perspectives in archeology*, edited by S. R. Binford and L. R. Binford. Chicago: Aldine, pp. 175–222.

Wobst, H. M. (1978) The archaeo-ethnology of hunter-gatherers, or the tyranny of the ethnographic record in archaeology. *American Antiquity* 43: 303–309.

Wylie, M. A. (1981) Positivism and the new archeology. Unpublished PhD dissertation, Department of Philosophy, State University of New York, Binghamton.

—— (1982) Epistemological issues raised by a structural archaeology. In *Symbolic and structural archaeology*, edited by I. Hodder. Cambridge: Cambridge University Press, pp. 39–56.

Yanagisako, S. (1979) Family and household: the analysis of domestic groups. *Annual Review of Anthropology*, 8: 161–205.

Yellen, J. (1977) *Archaeological approaches to the present*. New York: Academic Press.

Yellen, J. and H. Harpending (1972) Hunter-gatherer populations and archaeological inference. *World Archaeology* 4(2): 244–253.

Zihlman, A. (1978) Women in evolution, part II: subsistence and social organization in early hominids. *Signs: Journal of Women in Culture and Society* 4(1): 4–20.

—— (1981) Women as shapers of the human adaptation. In *Woman the gatherer*, edited by F. Dahlberg. New Haven, Connecticut: Yale University Press, pp. 72–102.

—— (1982) Whatever happened to woman-the-gatherer? Paper presented at annual meetings, American Anthropological Association, Washington, DC.

Chapter 3

WOMEN'S ARCHAEOLOGY?
Political Feminism, Gender Theory and
Historical Revision

Roberta Gilchrist

Women's issues are deservedly a growing concern in archaeology, with concerns that run from the power (im)balance
between the sexes in the present practice of archaeology to
the technical question of how gender-relations are, or are
not, recoverable from archaeological context. The several
aspects that lie within the phrase "women's archaeology" are
explored.

Introduction

Archaeology has not been eager to address the issues, or indeed
the existence, of women's archaeology. An avoidance assisted by
cultivated misconceptions as to what "women's archaeology" might
constitute, whether women's support groups rallying in excavation
trenches or the nice irony of women-only fora on sexual discrimination. By such means do those who mistrust, or misunderstand,
political feminism, dismiss the value of this (so-called) "women's
archaeology".

But what is women's archaeology? Indeed, does it, or should it,
exist? Archaeology was slow to respond to the two decades of
lobbying and research which mark the emergence of women's
studies. Moreover, now that this debate has finally been engaged,
its effectiveness has been compromised by a confusion of issues,
particularly those surrounding the place of equity issues in archaeological theory and practice. The last decade has seen the kindling
of archaeological debate surrounding women, feminism and gender.
Progress – and publication – has been hindered by the conflation

of, and frequent confusion between, issues which are actually separate. And since much of the discussion has taken place at unpublished conferences, the recognition of a clear agenda has been prevented by an inability to disaggregate practical, political and theoretical motivations. It is the purpose of this paper to disentangle the positions and issues which have run together to form an impression of "women's archaeology":

1   political feminism, including equal opportunities within the profession;
2   gender theory; and
3   historical revision surrounding women in the past.

At first, archaeology reacted in a fashion akin to that seen in more traditional disciplines, such as art history; it is said feminist interpretation was marginalized within publication and conferences (Pollock 1987: 3). While anthropologists published seminal works of feminist theory (e.g. Rosaldo 1980; Ortner and Whitehead 1981), archaeologists remained silent. The first explicit archaeological expositions on gender considered the subject as one which might be tackled through archaeological methodology (Conkey and Spector 1984). More recently, gender has been regarded primarily as a conceptual issue, of central importance in considering the structure of past societies (e.g. Sørensen 1988; Barrett 1988). The women's movement has heightened our awareness of the place of women, both in archaeological employment and in the past which we study, while feminist theory has contributed to the topics and approaches of academic archaeology.

Political feminism

Feminist approaches are varied and cannot be characterized as a single school of thought (e.g. see the diversity of approaches in Hirsch and Keller 1990). More radical, "standpoint" feminists question the structures within which knowledge is constructed, sometimes suggesting a greater validity for explicitly feminist research. Other "empiricist" feminists negotiate within existing structures of knowledge, methodologies and notions of science (see discussion in Harding 1986). Feminist archaeology is defined by its political motivation, to recognize and work to change the patriarchal nature of society, archaeology and our perceptions of the past. Within this broad definition may be considered issues of archaeological employment, education and contributions to archaeological theory-building.

Practical conditions of employment for men and women in archaeology are often considered under the auspices of "feminism", or as is argued below, incorrectly, of "gender archaeology" (e.g. Theoretical Archaeology Group Conferences 1982–90; Chacmool 1988 "Archaeology and Gender"). Problems raised include equality for men and women in opportunities, employment and recognition within professional and academic archaeology, although to a great extent mirroring the pattern of other professions and society at large. Even where long-term career structures exist, these are designed to suit men, whose security may be gained at the expense of those outside this structure, often women. In Britain, the sexual balance of archaeological employment, for instance, may come under threat with the increasing tendency for short contracts of employment and the disintegration of the long-fought-for, if precarious, professional structure. Competition for employment will favour those men and women who are free from personal responsibilities, such as child care.

Discussion has highlighted the absence of women in top positions of archaeological management, fieldwork, teaching and research, and the tendency for women to specialize in categories of finds work, which Gero has likened to "archaeological housework" (1985: 344). Many of these observations have been anecdotal (e.g. Damm 1986), although statistically valid surveys are now being conducted for figures of women in research and employment in British, American, German, Australian and Norwegian archaeology (e.g. respectively, Lomas 1988; Kramer and Stark 1988; Mertens and Kästner 1990; *Women's Congress* 2 1990; Commasnes and Kleppe 1988, and *Kvinner i arkeologi i Norge* from 1984 onwards). Equity issues have been placed firmly on the agenda of international archaeology, featuring, for example, as the major themes of the January 1991 editions of the magazines of both the Society for American Archaeology (*Bulletin* 9.1) and the (British) Institute of Field Archaeologists (*The Field Archaeologist* 14).

These exploratory surveys offer interesting contrasts on the cultural construction of gender rôles in the profession of archaeology. For example, in Britain and Germany, the paucity of women in management and university teaching appears to be the most problematic issue; in Australia, in contrast, women have been pressured into filling positions of Cultural Resource Management, representing about 80 per cent of the professionals in this sector (Smith 1990). The definition of "archaeological housework" varies internationally, depending upon the relative status of tasks such as finds work and CRM. The Institute of Field Archaeologists has convened an Equal Opportunities Working Party to investigate personal attitudes, conditions of work and provisions made by employers within British archaeology. The preliminary results have been checked across data sets collected from individuals, employers, societies, universities and the professional institutes. While women can be seen to be better represented in archaeology (*c.* 35 per cent) than in equivalent professions, they are discriminated against in a number of ways. Despite women holding equal (or apparently better) academic qualifications than their male counterparts, they are less likely to hold management positions or to achieve professional qualifications; they are concentrated in the lower salary bands and levels of responsibility; and they specialize in particular areas of archaeological competence, especially finds, environmental archaeology, excavation, post-excavation and research, rather than survey, buildings study, teaching and administration (IFA 1991).

Archaeologists have begun to consider the negative implications of sexual stereotyping in children's archaeology books (Burtt 1987), which convey a uniform past peopled by dominant men and passive women. Teachers have shown concern to offer a more challenging archaeological programme, less coloured by the preconceptions of our own time. Initiatives include the Joint Matriculation Board Archaeology Syllabus for English "A" level (secondary education), and personal projects in American universities, for example Spector and Whelan's "Incorporating gender into archaeology classes". Perhaps reaching the largest audiences are those museum projects which use interpretation and display to promote consciousness-raising (Jones and Pay 1990). This approach confronts traditional interpretation and entrenched social attitudes by presenting women in the past as having led varied, prominent and, above all, valued lives.

Early feminist contributions to archaeological theory considered the importance of language in the discipline's structural sexism, for example in the use of terms such as "mankind" (Braithwaite 1982a). Feminist theoretical archaeology has been largely concerned with critique. The feminist review of androcentrism (male bias) in archaeological interpretation (e.g. Gero 1985; Conkey and Spector 1984), has been credited with assisting archaeology to mature into a more self-critical discipline (Hodder 1986: 159). Among new topics feminist archaeologists have introduced to archaeology are the nature of personal agency, sexuality and the social control of the human body and reproduction (e.g. Gilchrist 1988).

It has been noted that the feminist contribution to a value-committed, post-processual archaeology is surprisingly under-developed (Shanks and Tilley 1987: 191), although these same commentators have used feminist archaeology to illustrate the validity of subjectivity as an intellectual premise (Shanks 1989; Tilley 1989). Indeed some "standpoint" feminists would agree that studies of women in the past can only be sensitively conducted by female archaeologists in response to their own subjectivity (e.g. Damm 1986). Many others argue to the contrary, insisting that strong theorizing cannot be built out of an inner, intuitive sense of female reasoning (Dobres 1988). While acknowledging itself to be politically motivated, feminist archaeology does not necessarily advocate relativism. Recently, feminists have identified a contradiction within their general aims: the encouragement of multiple perspectives is at odds with the need for a developed science which will categorically refute androcentrism (e.g. Hawkesworth 1989). Indeed, the historical specificity of the construction of gender must be appreciated in order to develop an analysis of power relations which is not androcentric. At another level, it may be argued that post-processual theories of the individual are anti-feminist. These approaches continue to subsume the female agent under a gender neutral individual which is implicitly male, thus blocking the political impetus of feminism by negating the feminist collective in favour of the individual.

Feminism cannot be condensed into a single set of beliefs of goals, post-processualist or otherwise. Feminist archaeology is consistent only in its political aims. Although feminist subjectivity has inspired the critique which has helped to spur disciplinary development, few feminists would support a body of theory based on the subjectivity of being a woman, regardless of time, space, age or ethnicity.

Gender theory

The academic study of gender is not restricted to the feminist arena, nor is it a topic studied exclusively by women. Gender is distinct from the biological static of sex; its study is equally concerned with men and women. Gender centres on the social construction of masculinity and femininity: the social values invested in the sexual differences between men and women. In this respect gender archaeology is part of the study of social structure, as significant as rank in the social stratification and the evolution of past societies.

Processualist studies first approached the issue of gender by attempting to recognize artefact patterns characteristic of male and female, so as to define activity areas and zones of spatial control (e.g. the Glastonbury Lake Village, Clarke 1972, and the Mesoamerican Village, Flannery and Winter 1976). These studies involved implicit assumptions concerning male and female rôles and the sexual division of labour. The problem remains as to whether artefacts should be linked to male and female on the basis of ethnographic parallel − a form of analogy currently out of favour − or only where sexed skeletons are associated with grave goods. The approach behind artefact correlates often assumes an exclusive means of male and female signification, or an exclusive sexual division of labour. The emphasis is on making gender, or more specifically women, visible in the archaeological record. This premise relies on recognizing women's behaviour as deviant to a standard which is male. Artefact correlates remain problematic, particularly now that many archaeologists recognize the androcentrism of their social interpretations. Each of the theoretical frameworks must continually, and critically, re-assess their assumptions regarding gender.

A feminist approach put forward an explicit theory of gender, to combat interpretations which accepted modern-day gender stereotypes as timeless, objective and "natural" (Conkey and Spector 1984). Within archaeological literature gender came to be defined as a social, rather than biological, classification of rôles, relationships and cultural imagery. Emphasis was first placed on study of the sexual division of labour in past societies, Conkey and Spector suggesting methodologies, in particular the "task-differentiation framework", which would quantify the artefact-related activities of men and women.

Archaeologists influenced by structuralism focused greater attention on the signification of material culture and spatial patterning, often defining gender as sets of male and female binary oppositions. Braithwaite, for example, considered decoration as a means of encouraging encounters between opposed social and symbolic categories, such as male and female (1982b: 81). Likewise, Sørensen asserted that bronze object typologies were based in selected oppositional structures, including male and female, which could reveal the basic decisions, choices and values exercised by a past society (1987:94). Although these particular binary oppositions are viewed as socially constructed, they suggest a universal contradiction between male and female cultural categories. This pairing of male and female structural oppositions negates alternative gender constructions, such as trans-sexualism and, in certain societies, the existence of eunuchs as a third gender. Is male–female the only standard structure to be expected in the gender relations of past societies?

Gender archaeologists have struggled against essentialism, in terms of universal male and female oppositions, and the cross-cultural subjectivity attributed to being a man or woman in each and every society. To this end, recent work has explored the potential meanings derived from archaeological context. Gibbs, for example, set out to examine the visibility of females in a variety of data sets from Bronze Age Denmark, including hoards, burials, settlements, art and figurines, in order to assess changing "gender tensions" over time (1987). Male and female rôles and spaces within settlements were examined for Iron Age Noord-Holland by Therkorn (1987), who determined gender domains according to deposits associated with household hearths and communal halls. Such gender studies often rely on the sexing of skeletons and the assignment of male or female categories to associated artefacts.

Studies which emphasize the quantification of data and its context have been criticized for placing undue stress and confidence in methodology (Sørensen 1988: 14). Contextualist and processualist approaches to gender have often concentrated on the recognition of male and female cultural definitions in the archaeological record. Such exercises seek to demonstrate the visibility of women and pay little heed to the development of conceptual frameworks for understanding gender in past societies. To date archaeological studies of gender have been concerned with structuralist, symbolic definitions of material culture. For some post-processualists gender is not a material correlate to be excavated, nor is it simply a form of cultural signification. Gender can be used as a starting point for exam-ining social structure, community relationships and change. Barrett, in particular, has centred on gender in the process of structuration, in order to examine the relationship between the individual and social structure, and the rhythms of daily life (1988). Archaeological approaches have concentrated on gender as a form of categorization, with analysis limited to the naming of sexual difference. An overtly feminist gender archaeology might study gender as power relations. Here the ulti-mate aim would be to move beyond the naming of sexual difference, to its analysis and disruption.

Gender is no longer considered a problem of methodology, but rather one of social theory. As such, gender archaeology can be conducted within any political framework (including non-feminist), and with reference to existing methodologies and programmes of research. Indeed the future of gender archaeology may lie in its integration within mainstream social interpretations, as, for example, in Bender's recent study of Palaeolithic communities (1989). Our goals will be partly realized when gender is considered not as an optional issue, but as another structuring prin-ciple fundamental to interpreting past societies.

Historical revision

While feminism has encouraged archaeology to consider the issue of male bias within interpretation, the advent of women's studies has promoted new topics for analysis and new histories of the discipline. A critical historiography of archaeology, in which the contributions of men and women are evaluated according to their social context, has yet to emerge. Recently, however, balance has been sought by acknowledging women in histories of archaeology. Attention has been drawn to 19th-century women travellers and antiquaries, such as Gertrude Bell, and to women who were unusual in achieving professional and academic prominence, like Kathleen Kenyon and Dorothy Garrod. No sociological analysis of women in our historiography has yet been written, nor do these studies assess the significance of individual women's contributions. Instead the aim in this work is to write biographies of women as rôle-models who will inspire future generations of women archaeologists (e.g. Williams 1981).

While archaeology now acknowledges "women" as forming a topic for analysis, many observers remain intolerant: they caricature such endeavours as part of the lunatic fringe. Few practitioners are pledged to discover mother goddesses, and where the female figurine is the centre of analysis, studies aim to examine patterns in society and belief (e.g. Gimbutas 1989). Most are dedicated to redressing the balance of content and coverage within archaeological textbooks. Can a "missionary purpose" yield balanced interpretations (Hawkes 1990)? Or do alternative archaeologies consist of nothing more than an uncritical revision of history to suit contemporary politics? The rapidly increasing number of publications on women in the past can be justified on the basis of three arguments.

First, this is an aspect of archaeology which hitherto has been ignored; scholarship on women is required if we are to write comprehensive histories. Second, if our discipline does not address the issue of women in the past, then others will. Alternative narrative histories for women already exist, which are less critical and more strategically political than anything which we would wish to write as archaeologists (e.g. French 1985). Third, studies of women in the past can meet some of the objectives of feminist archaeology; they possess shock value, and are catalysts for the consciousness-raising which leads to a re-evaluation of social attitudes.

While the principles behind studies of women in the past are unassailable, each analysis must earn its own academic merit. Ultimately, revisionist histories for women are no more unprovable than the male-dominated narratives which they replace. But these studies must be of equal academic weight; they must be accurate and convincing in addition to being thought-provoking. Only in this way can the study of women assist feminism and contribute to gender studies. Far from "perpetuating the split between practical and academic archaeology" (Sørensen 1988: 15), this dialogue may actually increase the accessibility of theoretical archaeology. Reviewing Ehrenberg's *Women in prehistory*, Jacquetta Hawkes was critical of the volume's factual content, but concluded "I hope it may even encourage diggers and thinkers to exert themselves more to distinguish the lives and handiwork of prehistoric women" (Hawkes 1990).

Conclusion: integration versus isolation

Clearly, the practical, political and theoretical issues which shelter under "Women's archaeology" or "Women and archaeology" interest the discipline at large, not only women. Feminist archaeology, promoting greater social responsibility within the profession, has developed a critique which has assisted theory-building. Fresh topics on the academic agenda have elevated gender to an issue of social structure. These approaches welcome a more accessible theoretical archaeology, in which the daily lives of men and women are considered. Studies of women in the past and in our own historiography promise a greater balance for future understanding. To date, feminism, gender and the study of women have been marginal to mainstream archaeology. In some cases this is partly a product of choice, since women-only groups are thought more supportive, and because integration within the establishment might be thought to compromise feminist aims and theory. But surely we must challenge existing attitudes at their source? The significance of feminism, gender and women in archaeology will be acknowledged only when our future is built through integration with the wider discipline.

■ ■ ■

References

Barrett, J. C. (1988). Fields of discourse: reconstituting a social archaeology, *Critique of Anthropology* 7(3): 5–16.

Bender, B. (1989). The roots of inequality, in D. Miller, M. Rowlands and C. Tilley (eds), *Domination and resistance*: 83–95. London: Unwin Hyman.

Braithwaite, M. (1982a). *Archaeologia chauvinistica*: bare-faced but not naked ape, *Archaeological Review from Cambridge* 1(2): 62–3.

—— (1982b). Decoration as ritual symbol: a theoretical proposal and an ethnographic study in southern Sudan, in I. Hodder (ed.), *Symbolic and structural archaeology*: 80–88. Cambridge: Cambridge University Press.

Burtt, F. (1987). "Man the hunter": bias in children's archaeology books, *Archaeological Review from Cambridge* 6(2): 157–74.

Clarke, D. (1972). A provisional model of an Iron Age society and its settlement system, in D. Clarke (ed.), *Models in archaeology*: 801–69. London: Methuen.

Conkey, M. W. and J. Spector. (1984). Archaeology and the study of gender, *Advances in archaeological method and theory* 7: 1–29.

Damm, C. (1986). An appeal for women in archaeology, *Archaeological Review from Cambridge* 5(2): 215–18.

Dobres, M. (1988). Feminist archaeology and inquiries into gender relations: some thoughts on universals, Origins stories and alternating paradigms, *Archaeological Review from Cambridge* 7(1): 30–44.

Dommasnes, L. and E. Johansen Kleppe. (1988). Women in archaeology in Norway, *Archaeological Review from Cambridge* 7(2): 230–34.

Ehrenberg, M. (1989). *Women in prehistory*. London: British Museum Publications.

Flannery, K. V. and M. C. Winter. (1976). Analysing household activities, in K. V. Flannery (ed.), *The early Mesoamerican village*: 34–47. New York: Academic Press.

French, M. (1985). *Beyond power: on women, men and morals*. London: Jonathan Cape.

Gero, J. M. (1985). Socio-politics and the woman at home ideology, *American Antiquity* 50(2): 342–50.

Gibbs, L. (1987). Identifying gender representations in the archaeological record: a contextual study, in Hodder (1987): 79–87.

Gilchrist, R. (1988). The spatial archaeology of gender domains: a case study of medieval English nunneries, *Archaeological Review from Cambridge* 7(1): 21–8.

Gimbutas, M. (1989). *The language of the goddess*. London: Thames & Hudson.

Harding, S. (1986). *The science question in feminism*. Ithaca (NY): Cornell University Press.

Hawkes, J. (1990). Review of M. Ehrenberg *Women in prehistory*, *Antiquity* 64: 424–5.

Hawkesworth, M. E. (1989). Knowers, knowing, known: feminist theory and claims of truth, *Signs* 14(3): 533–57.

Hirsch, M. and E. F. Keller (eds). (1990). *Conflicts in feminism*. London: Routledge.

Hodder, I. (1986). *Reading the past*. Cambridge: Cambridge University Press.

—— (ed.). (1987). *The archaeology of contextual meanings*. Cambridge: Cambridge University Press.

IFA [Institute of Field Archaeologists]. (1991). *Women in archaeology: IFA Equal Opportunities in Archaeology Working Party Report*.

Joint Matriculation Board "A" and "AS" Level Archaeology Group. (1989). Draft syllabus. Unpublished.

Jones, S. and S. Pay. (1990). The legacy of Eve, in P. Gathercole and D. Lowenthal (eds), *The politics of the past*: 160–71. London: Unwin Hyman.

Kramer, C. and M. Stark. (1988). The status of women in archaeology, *Anthropology Newsletter* 29(9): 1, 11–12.

Lomas, H. (1988). Power structures in contemporary archaeology from a feminist perspective. Paper presented to the Theoretical Archaeology Group Conference.

Mertens, E. and S. Kästner. (1990). Women in German archaeology. Paper presented to the Theoretical Archaeology Group Conference.

Ortner, S. and H. Whitehead. (1981). *Sexual meanings: the cultural construction of gender and sexuality*. Cambridge: Cambridge University Press.

Pollock, G. 1987. Women, art and ideology: questions for feminist art historians, *Women's Studies Quarterly* 15(1/2): 2–9.

Rosaldo, M. Z. 1980. The use and abuse of anthropology: reflections on feminism and cross-cultural understanding, *Signs* 5(3): 389–417.

Shanks, M. 1989. Identity, the past and an archaeological poetics. Paper presented to the Theoretical Archaeology Group Conference.

Shanks, M. and C. Tilley. 1987. *Social theory and archaeology*. Cambridge: Polity.

Smith, L. 1990. Feminist issues in cultural resource management. Paper presented to the Theoretical Archaeology Group Conference.

Sorensen, M. L. S. 1987. Material order and cultural classification: the role of bronze objects in the transition from Bronze Age to Iron Age Scandinavia, in Hodder (1987): 90–101.

—— 1988. Is there a feminist contribution to archaeology?, *Archaeological Review from Cambridge* 7(1): 9–20.

Spector, J. D. and M. K. Whelan. 1987. Incorporating gender into archaeology classes. Paper presented to the 86th annual meeting of the American Anthropological Association.

Therkorn, L. 1987. The inter-relationships of materials and meanings: some suggestions on housing concerns within Iron Age Noord-Holland, in Hodder (1987): 102–10.

Tilley, C. 1989. Science, subjectivity and archaeological discourse. Paper presented to the Theoretical Archaeology Group Conference.

Williams, B. 1981. *Breakthrough: women in archaeology*. New York (NY): Walker.

Chapter 4

THE INTERPLAY OF EVIDENTIAL CONSTRAINTS AND POLITICAL INTERESTS:
Recent Archaeological Research on Gender

Alison Wylie

In the last few years, conference programs and publications have begun to appear that reflect a growing interest, among North American archaeologists, in research initiatives that focus on women and gender as subjects of investigation. One of the central questions raised by these developments has to do with their "objectivity" and that of archaeology as a whole. To the extent that they are inspired by or aligned with explicitly political (feminist) commitments, the question arises of whether they do not themselves represent an inherently partial and interest-specific standpoint, and whether their acceptance does not undermine the commitment to value neutrality and empirical rigor associated with scientific approaches to archaeology. I will argue that, in fact, a feminist perspective, among other critical, explicitly political perspectives, may well enhance the conceptual integrity and empirical adequacy of archaeological knowledge claims, where this is centrally a matter of deploying evidential constraints.

It is a striking feature of North American archaeology that there is very little in print advocating or exemplifying a feminist approach to archaeology; certainly there is nothing comparable to the thriving traditions of feminist research on women and gender that have emerged, in the last twenty years, in such closely aligned fields as sociocultural anthropology, history, various areas in the life sciences (including evolutionary theory), classics, and art history. The first paper to explore systematically the relevance of feminist insights and approaches for archaeology was published in 1984 by Conkey and Spector, and the first collection of essays dedicated to reporting original work in the area has just appeared (Gero and Conkey, *Engendering Archaeology: Women and Prehistory*, 1991). This collection is the outcome of a small working conference convened in South Carolina in April 1988 specifically for the purpose of mobilizing interest in the questions about women and gender that had been raised by Conkey and Spector in 1984. Its organizers, Gero and Conkey, were concerned that, in the four years since the appearance of this paper, very little work had appeared, or seemed imminent, that took up the challenges it posed (see Gero and Conkey 1991:xi–xiii). They approached colleagues who represented a wide range of research interests in prehistoric archaeology and asked if they would be willing to explore the implications of taking gender seriously as a focus for analysis in their fields; most had never considered such an approach and had no special interest in feminist initiatives, but agreed to see what they could do. In effect, Gero and Conkey commissioned a series of pilot projects on gender that they hoped might demonstrate the potential of research along the lines proposed by Conkey and Spector in 1984.

Between the time of this initial conference and the appearance of *Engendering Archaeology*, many of the papers prepared for discussion in South Carolina were presented in a session on gender and archaeology at the annual meeting of the Society for American Archaeology in April 1989; they drew a substantial and enthusiastic audience, to the surprise of many of the participants. But most significant, one much more public conference, the 1989 Chacmool conference held the following November at the University of Calgary, took "The Archaeology of Gender" as its focal theme. It drew *over 100* contributions on a very wide range of topics, all but four of which (the invited keynote addresses) were submitted, directly or indirectly, in response to an open call for papers (most will appear in Walde and Willows [1991]). So despite the fact that little more than Conkey and Spector's 1984 paper was in print at the time the Chacmool conference was being organized and the SAA session presented, an awareness of the issues they raised and an enthusiasm about the prospects for archaeological work on gender seemed to have taken hold across the length and breadth of the field.

This precipitous emergence of broadly feminist initiatives raises a number of questions. First are questions about the development itself: why has there been no sustained interest before now in women and gender as subjects of archaeological inquiry and/or in scrutinizing the interpretive assumptions routinely made about women and gender in extant practice; and, why is such an interest emerging at this juncture? These are questions I have addressed elsewhere (Wylie 1991a, 1991b), but which bear brief discussion here as a basis for considering a second set of issues to do with the implications of embracing, or tolerating, feminist approaches. For many I believe the real question raised by these developments is not why research on gender is emerging (only) now, but why it should ever emerge. The genre of question posed in this connection is, "why do we need it?"; "what does it have to offer?" or, more defensively, "why should we take any of this seriously?" (after Wylie

1991b). Often the most dismissive responses reflect, not just uneasiness about feminist initiatives, but a general wariness about intellectual fads and fashions. Given the rapid emergence of the scientific new archaeology, displacing so-called "traditional" modes of practice, and now the equally dramatic reaction against the new archaeology and the emergence of a plethora of warring anti- or postprocessualist and critical alternatives, many are deeply weary of debate. Renfrew's review of "isms" of our time (Renfrew 1982:8) and the challenge Watson (in Watson and Fotiadis 1990) issues to the advocates of some of these "isms" to deliver the goods, as it were, convey a sense of alarm at the instability of this succession of research programs. Viewed in this light, the call to study women and gender may seem especially tenuous, even self-destructive.

I want to argue that a feminist perspective, which questions entrenched assumptions about women and gender and directs attention to them as subjects of inquiry, promises to enhance substantially the conceptual and empirical integrity – the "objectivity," properly construed – of archaeological inquiry. To this end, I consider how feminist initiatives have arisen and how the debate over "isms" has unfolded such that they might be viewed with particular scepticism. I offer general arguments against this scepticism, questioning the terms of abstract debate from which it derives, and then turn, in the final section, to an analysis of several examples of the new research on gender, drawn from *Engendering Archaeology* (Gero and Conkey 1991), which illustrates how evidential considerations can challenge and constrain political and theoretical presuppositions, even where these constitute the encompassing framework of inquiry.

Why now? Why ever?

Why is the Archaeology of Gender emerging only now?

Where the preliminary questions – "why not before now?" and, "why now?" – are concerned, my thesis is that a number of factors have been relevant both in forestalling and in precipitating these developments in archaeology, similar to the situation described by Longino (1987) and by Longino and Doell (1983) for the life sciences. The conceptual and methodological commitments of scientific, processual archaeology have tended to direct attention away from what Binford (1983, 1986a, 1989: 3–23, 27–39) has vilified, in his most uncompromising defenses of processual approaches, as "ethnographic," internal variables; gender dynamics, which would be included among such variables in most analyses, are just one example of the sort of factor he considers explanatorily irrelevant and scientifically inaccessible (for a more detailed analysis, see Wylie [1991a:35–38]). While anti- and postprocessual challenges to this general orientation have certainly been crucial in opening a space for the development of an interest in gender, among other symbolic, ideational, social, and broadly "ethnographic" dimensions of the cultural past, it is striking that none of the chief exponents of postprocessualism have done a great deal to develop a feminist analysis of archaeological method or theory. Indeed, as Ericka Engelstad (1991) argues, they have largely avoided any sustained reflexive critique of their own proposals and practice, with the result that these remain resolutely androcentric. Moreover, postprocessualists had established the need for work on variables like gender fully a decade ago, and yet there was no sustained archaeological work on gender, *per se*, and no serious consideration of the implications for archaeology of feminist research in other fields, until the last few years. Given this, I suggest that social and political (i.e., "external," non-cognitive) factors must play a central role in the emergence of an interest in gender at this juncture.

To be more specific, it would seem implausible, given the experience reported in other disciplinary contexts, if the preparedness to consider questions about gender, and in some cases, the willingness to champion research that addresses them, did not have to do with the influence of explicitly political, feminist thinking on practitioners in the field (Wylie 1991b). In most cases I expect this influence will be only indirect; whether many practitioners identify as feminists or are in any sense sympathetic to feminism, a great many will have been affected by a growing if still liminal appreciation of women's issues, starting with equity issues, that grows out of second-wave feminist activism and has become evident, in recent years, in the discourse and practice of archaeologists. No doubt this is closely tied to the demands for equity they face as members of academic institutions, consulting businesses, and government agencies, and to resulting changes in the representation, roles, and status of women in these larger institutional contexts. But however they arise, and however welcome or unwelcome they may be, as these changes enforce some level of awareness of gender politics in contemporary contexts they also produce (in some) a growing awareness that gender is not a "natural," immutable given, an insight which is seen by many as the pivotal discovery of feminist theory (Flax 1987; Harding 1983). And (in some) this has influenced, in turn, scholarly thinking about the subjects of archaeological study. Whatever their political commitments, they may begin to question entrenched assumptions about sexual divisions of labor and the status of women in prehistory, and to consider previously unexplored questions about the diversity of gender structures in prehistoric contexts, about the significance of gender dynamics in shaping past cultural systems, and about the origins and emergence of contemporary and/or ethnohistorically documented sex/gender systems.

In some cases the influence of feminist thinking has been direct. For example, both organizers of the South Carolina conference have long been active on issues to do with the status of women in archaeology. Gero has published a number of groundbreaking articles on these issues and been actively involved in promoting research on the political dynamics, including the gender dynamics, of the discipline (Gero 1983, 1985, 1988). And Conkey was a member of the American Anthropological Association (AAA) Committee on the Status of Women from 1974 (chair in 1975–1976) in which capacity she was drawn into the organization of a panel for the 1977 AAA meetings on gender research in the various subfields of anthropology. Charged with presenting a section on archaeological research on gender, Conkey confronted the dearth of literature in the area; for the most part she found that "women [and gender] were considered by chance rather than by design," if they were considered at all (M. Conkey, personal communication 1991). In these connections both organizers were drawn into contact with feminists working in other fields, especially sociocultural anthropology, and were aware of the insights, both critical and constructive, that had resulted from the systematic investigation of questions about the status, experience, and roles of women in their various research fields. It was quite explicitly this exposure to, and engagement in, feminist discourse outside archaeology that led them to question the assumptions about gender underlying archaeological theorizing and to see both the need and the potential for a focused program of feminist research in archaeology. As they came to question the assumptions about gender that underpin *contemporary* sex roles, they came to see that these same assumptions infuse the theories about other people's lives they were engaged in constructing as archaeologists. In organizing events and publications that they hoped would generate wider interest among archaeologists in questions about gender they, and, specifically, the feminist commitments that had come to inform their own work, have been instrumental in mobilizing the latent grass-roots interest in these questions that now seems widespread, even among archaeologists who would never identify as feminists and have had no contact with feminist research in other contexts. On this account it is, most simply, the experience of women and, more important, the emerging feminist analysis of this experience, which figures as a key catalyst (both directly and indirectly) for skepticism about entrenched conceptions of women and gender and for research in this area as it is now emerging in archaeology.

Relativist implications

But if this is the case – if the new research on gender is motivated and shaped, at least in part, by explicitly feminist commitments – does it not follow that it is to be identified and, for many, dismissed, with the extreme anti-objectivist positions defended by postprocessualists? Does it not exemplify precisely the sort of partisan approach to inquiry that they endorse, and that Binford (1989:32), for example, has condemned as conceptual "posturing"? To be more specific, if political interests are allowed to set the agenda of archaeology, do they not irrevocably compromise the commitments to objectivity and value neutrality – most broadly, the commitment to settle empirical questions by appeal to the "world of experience" (Binford 1989:27; see also Binford 1982:136), rather than to prejudgments or sociopolitical interests – that stand as a hallmark of science? And in this case, what credibility can such inquiry claim on its own behalf; are its results not as limited and biased as those they are meant to displace? Perhaps more disturbing, if an explicitly partisan feminist standpoint reveals the partiality (the unacknowledged standpoint specificity) of our best existing accounts of the past and brings into view a different past, or new ways of understanding the past, does it not follow that any number of other standpoints might do the same? And in this case, what is to stop the proliferation of conflicting views of prehistory and, with this, a slide into extreme standpoint relativism according to which the credibility of each of these "versions" is strictly context or perspective and interest specific?

Such conclusions only follow, I argue, if you accept the sharply polarized terms in which much current debate about the aims and status of archaeology has been cast, and assume that any critique of objectivist ideals, any break with the scientific canons of processual archaeology (originally construed in rigidly positivist terms), leads irrevocably to what Trigger (1989:777) calls "hyperrelativism." This oppositional response to questions about the standards and goals of inquiry is not unique to archaeology; on Trigger's account the social sciences as a whole are marked by:

> an increasingly vociferous confrontation . . . between, on the one hand, an old-fashioned positivist certainty that, given enough data and an adherence to "scientific" canons of interpretation, something approximating an objective understanding of human behavior can be achieved . . ., and on the other hand, a growing relativist skepticism that the understanding of human behavior can ever be disentangled from the interests, prejudices, and stereotypes of the research.
>
> (Trigger 1989:777; see also Bernstein 1983; Wylie 1989b)

On the former view, the aim of producing "objective" knowledge – knowledge which is credible, "true" transhistorically and cross-contextually, not just given a particular standpoint (Bernstein 1983:8–25) – can only be realized if researchers scrupulously exclude all "external," potentially biasing (idiosyncratic or contextually specific) factors from the practice of science, so that judgments about the adequacy of particular knowledge claims are made solely on the basis of "internal" considerations of evidence, and of coherence and consistency. Positivist/empiricist theories of science, including those that influenced North American archaeology in the 1960s and 1970s and are still evident in archaeological thinking, made much of a distinction between the context of discovery, in which such "external" factors might be given free reign, and the context of verification or confirmation in which the fruits of creative speculation, however inspired or shaped, would be subjected to rigorously impartial testing against (independent) evidence; the body of empirical "facts" deployed as evidence was presumed to be the stable foundation of all (legitimate, nonanalytic) knowledge, and was, in this capacity, the final arbiter of epistemic adequacy.

It is by now commonly held that this view of knowledge production (specifically scientific-knowledge production) is deeply problematic. The sharp distinction between the contexts of discovery and verification, and "foundationalist" faith in facts as the source and ground of legitimate knowledge, has broken down in face of a number of challenges. Even the proponents of a robust (empiricist/positivist) objectivism had, themselves, long acknowledged that all available evidence (sometimes even all imaginable evidence) routinely "underdetermines" interesting knowledge claims about the world, that is, evidence rarely entails or supports a unique explanatory or interpretive conclusion and eliminates all potential rivals (for a summary, see Laudan and Leplin [1991]; Newton-Smith [1981]; Suppe [1977]). Furthermore, the analyses of "contextualist" theorists (e.g., Hanson 1958; Kuhn 1970) suggest that the facts, data, or evidence against which theoretical constructs are to be tested are all too intimately connected with these constructs to stand as a secure and autonomous "foundation" of knowledge; data are, famously, "theory laden." This opens up considerable space for the insinuation of "external" interests and values into the processes of both formulating and evaluating empirical knowledge claims. Indeed, sociologists of science have argued, on the basis of innumerable detailed studies of the practice (rather than just the products) of science, that "facts" are as much made as found and that judgments about their evidential significance are radically open. The most thoroughgoing "social constructivists" among them maintain that facts, and the theoretical claims they are used to support, are equally a product of the local, irreducibly social and political, interests that inform the actions and interactions of scientific practitioners in particular contexts; in their most radical moments, they seem to suggest that scientists quite literally create the world they purport to know (see Woolgar's [1983:244] discussion of the range of positions at issue here). It seems a short step from the original contextualist and constructivist arguments against native objectivism and foundationalism to the conclusion that cognitive anarchy is unavoidable; "anything goes" in the sense (not intended by Feyerabend [1988:vii, 1–3]) that virtually any knowledge claim one can imagine could, in principle, find some perspective or context in which it is compelling, and that there are no overarching grounds for assessing or challenging these context-specific judgments.

In an archaeological context, the outlines of this reaction emerge in some anti- or postprocessual literature. The point of departure is typically a "contextualist" argument to the effect that, where archaeological data must be theory laden to stand as evidence, it is unavoidable that archaeologists have always, of necessity, actively *constructed* (not reconstructed, recaptured, or represented) the past, no matter how deeply committed they may have been to objectivist ideals. In some of his early critical discussions, Hodder insists, in this connection, that any use of archaeological data as test evidence is mediated by "an edifice of auxiliary theories and assumptions which *archaeologists have simply agreed not to question*" (Hodder 1984a:27, emphasis added); evidential claims thus have nothing but conventional credibility. In short, archaeologists literally "create 'facts'" (Hodder 1984a:27). From this it follows that archaeologists are "without any ability to test their reconstructions of the past" (Hodder 1984a:26); as Shanks and Tilley put the point four years later, "there is literally nothing independent of theory or propositions to test against . . . any test could only result in tautology" (Shanks and Tilley

1987b:44, 111). As a consequence, archaeological data, test evidence, and interpretive claims about the past must be regarded as all *equally* constructs: "knowledge consists of little more than the description of what has already been theoretically constituted" (Shanks and Tilley 1987a:43; see also 1987a:66). "Truth is," they declare, "a [mobile] army of metaphors" (Shanks and Tilley 1987b:22). More specifically, Shanks and Tilley argue that what counts as true or plausible, indeed, what counts as a "fact" in any relevant sense, is determined by contextually specific interests: individual, micropolitical interests, as well as class interests, broadly construed. It is thus unavoidable that archaeology is a thoroughly and irredeemably political enterprise, one which is engaged in creating a past thought expedient for, or dictated by, present interests (Shanks and Tilley 1987b:209–212, but see also 192–193). And where there are no independent factual resources with which to counter the influence of "external" factors – where pretensions to objectivity can only be, on their account, a masking of the effects of these influences – Shanks and Tilley advocate self-consciously political reconstruction of the past(s) thought necessary for "active intervention in the present" (Shanks and Tilley 1987b:103). In this vein, Hodder (1983:7) once enjoined archaeologists to avoid "writ[ing] the past" for others, or for societies in which they are not themselves prepared to live.

The process of polarization described by Trigger (1989:777) is complete when objectivists, reacting against what they consider the manifestly untenable implications of "hyperrelativism," insist that there *must* be "objective foundations for philosophy, knowledge, [and] language" (Bernstein 1983:12); they reject out of hand the critical insights that arose, originally, from the failure of objectivist programs cast in a positivist/empiricist mold, and renew the quest for some new Archimedean point, some "stable rock upon which we can secure our lives," and our knowledge, against the insupportable threat of "madness and chaos where nothing is fixed" (Bernstein 1983:4; see also Wylie 1989b:2–4). Just such a turn is evident, in the context of archaeological debate, in the exceedingly hostile counterreaction of (some) loyal processualists: in the caricatures in terms of which the positions of anti- and postprocessualists are assessed and rejected (e.g., in Binford's [1989:3–11] "field guide" and discussion of "yippie" archaeology; and in R. Watson's [1990] treatment of Shanks and Tilley); in uncompromising restatements of the central doctrines of processualism (e.g., by Binford [1983:137, 222–223; and by Renfrew 1989:39; for fuller analysis of Binford's position, see Wylie [1989a:103–105]); and in the frequent accusations, on both sides, that the opposition has simply missed the point, that they indulge in "wafting . . . [red herrings] in front of our noses" (Shanks and Tilley 1989:43; Binford 1989:35; see discussion in Wylie 1992).

It is clear where feminist research initiatives will be placed in the context of debates such as these. In the past two decades, feminist-inspired research across the social and life sciences has provided strong substantive grounds for questioning the "self-cleansing" capacity for scientific method; feminists have identified myriad instances of gender bias that have persisted, not just in instances of "bad science," but in "good" science, "science as usual," and frequently they have done this by bringing to bear the distinctive "angle of vision" afforded by various feminist and, more generally, women's perspectives (for a summary see Wylie [1991a:38–44]). In this, feminist researchers have made clear (sometimes unintentionally) the theory- and interest-laden, contextual, and constructed nature of scientific knowledge. Where debate is polarized in the manner described by Trigger (1989), some argue that the move to embrace a radically deconstructive, postmodern standpoint is irresistible; it is the logical outcome of their critiques (see Harding 1986).

But are the polarized options defined in the context of these debates the only ones open to archaeologists or other social scientists who have been grappling with an acute awareness "of how fragile is the basis on which we can claim to know anything definite about the past or about human behavior" (Trigger 1989:777)? More specifically, is the radically anti-objectivist stance endorsed, most strongly, by Shanks and Tilley the only alternative to uncompromising faith in the foundational nature of "facts" and the capacity of the "world of experience" to adjudicate all "responsible" claims to knowledge? In fact, as has been noted by virtually every commentator on their work, both sympathetic and critical (e.g., see comments published with Shanks and Tilley [1989]; Wylie 1992), Shanks and Tilley are not consistent, themselves, in maintaining a radically deconstructive position. Indeed, this ambivalence is a consistent feature of anti- or postprocessual literature. As early as 1986, Hodder had substantially qualified his earlier position (1983), insisting that, although "facts" are all constructs, they derive from a "real world," which "does constrain what we can say about it" (Hodder 1986:16). He has recently urged what seems a rapprochement with processualism, and endorsed a "guarded commitment to objectivity" (Hodder 1991:10). Although Shanks and Tilley (1987a:192) indicate distaste for this attempt to "neutralize and depoliticize" archaeological inquiry, they themselves hasten to add, in the same context, that they "do not mean to suggest that all pasts are equal" (Shanks and Tilley 1987a:245); there is a "real" past (Shanks and Tilley 1987a:110), moreover, archaeological constructs are to be differentiated from purely fictional accounts of the past by the fact that they are constrained by evidential considerations ("data represents a network of resistances") that can "challenge what we say as being inadequate in one manner or another" (Shanks and Tilley 1987a:104). The turn away from an uncompromising constructivism seems to come, in every case, at the point where anti- or postprocessualists confront the problem that radical constructivism (or, its "hyperrelativist" implications) threatens to undermine their own political and intellectual agendas as much as it does those they repudiate.

It is striking, in this connection, that many *feminists* working in the developed traditions of feminist research outside archaeology are likewise deeply "ambivalent" about the relativist implications that are sometimes seen to follow from their own wide-ranging critiques of objectivism (see Lather 1986, 1990; Fraser and Nicholson 1988). For example, despite endorsing postmodern approaches, the feminist philosopher of science, Sandra Harding, argues that we cannot afford to give up either the strategic advantages that accrue to more conventional modes of scientific practice – in effect, feminist uses of the tools of science – or the emancipatory vision embodied in postmodern transgressions of these "successor science" projects (Harding 1986:195; see Wylie 1987). Others (like biologist Fausto-Sterling [1985]) quite clearly want to preserve the option of defending feminist insights as *better* science in quite conventional terms, and a great many social scientists routinely privilege "facts" of some description – often as the grounds for conclusions about the gender-biased nature of the theories they criticize – even when they insist that facts cannot be treated as a stable, given "foundation" of knowledge (for a more detailed account, see Wylie [1991c]). One commentator from political science, Mary Hawkesworth (1989:538), takes the even stronger position that "the feminist postmodernists' plea for tolerance of multiple perspectives is altogether at odds with feminists' desire to develop a successor science that can refute once and for all the distortions of androcentrism" (Hawkesworth 1989:538). She clearly hopes that feminism has not reached "such an impasse that its best hope with respect to epistemological issues is to embrace incompatible positions and embed a contradiction at the heart of its theory of knowledge" (Hawkesworth 1989:538).

I myself find inescapable the suspicion that strong constructivist and relativist positions embody what seems patently an ideology of the powerful. Only the most powerful, the most successful in achieving control over their world, could imagine that the world can be constructed as they choose either as participants or as observers. Any who lack such power, or who lack an investment in believing they have such power, are painfully aware that they negotiate an intransigent reality that impinges on their lives at every turn. Certainly, any serious attempt to change inequitable conditions of life requires a sound understanding of the forces we oppose; self-delusion is rarely an effective basis for political action. It is, then, precisely their political commitment to the emancipatory potential of feminism – their commitment to learn about how gender structures operate so that they can act effectively against the inequities that these structures perpetuate – that enforces, for many feminist practitioners and theorists, as much scepticism about extreme relativisms as about the (untenable) objectivism that has so long masked androcentric bias in the social and life sciences (this point is acknowledged in Hodder 1991). They are persistently forced back from either of the extremes that emerge in abstract debate by a clear appreciation of how intransigent are the practical, empirical constraints binding on both inquiry and activism. A similar turn is evident in postpositivist philosophy of science; the critical insights of "contextualists" and "constructivists" are by now incontrovertible, where directed against "received view" positivism and empiricism (Suppe 1977), but the positions that have carried these critiques to an extreme have proven as untenable as those they displace. Consequently, there has been considerable interest in making sense of how, exactly, data come to be "laden" with theory, such that it acquires evidential significance through rich interpretive construction, and yet still has a capacity to surprise, to challenge settled expectations (see, e.g., Shapere [1985] on the constitution of "observations" in physics, and Kosso [1989] on observation in science generally;

see also the recent work on experimental practice, e.g., Galison [1987]; Hacking [1983, 1988]; for further discussion of how this bears on archaeology, see Wylie ([1990]).

Where feminist initiatives in *archaeology* are concerned, the encompassing philosophical problem at issue is precisely that which has attracted attention in recent postpositivist history and philosophy of science, and from feminist theorists in many contexts, viz., that of how we can conceptualize scientific inquiry so that we recognize, without contradiction, *both* that knowledge is constructed and bears the marks of its makers, *and* that it is constrained, to a greater or lesser degree, by conditions that we confront as external "realities" not of our own making. I want to argue that just this sort of mediating position is emerging in and through the new archaeological work on gender. It is political and should be aligned with antiprocessualist approaches insofar as it repudiates narrow objectivism of a positivist/scientistic cast. But it is not altogether assimilable to, indeed, it embodies a serious, politically and epistemically principled critique of, the more extreme claims associated with post-processualism. That is to say, social and political factors are crucial in directing attention to questions about gender but, at least in the case of the South Carolina conference, which I will take as the focus of my analysis here, these do not account for the successes of the research they inspire or inform. It is the substantive results of this research that make it a serious challenge to extant practice, and these results are to a large degree autonomous of the political motivations and other circumstances responsible for the research that produced them.

"Engendered" archaeology

The results of the preliminary investigations presented at the South Carolina conference are remarkable in a number of respects. Most of the contributors reported that they began with serious reservations about the efficacy of the approach urged on them by Gero and Conkey; they did not see how questions about gender could bear on research in their fields or subfields, given that they had never arisen before. But even the most sceptical conceded that attention to such questions did result in quite striking "discoveries" of gender bias in existing theory and in clear evidence of gender-related variability in familiar data bases that had been completely overlooked.

One especially compelling critical analysis, due to Watson and Kennedy (1991), exposes pervasive androcentrism in explanations of the emergence of agriculture in the eastern United States. Whatever the specific mechanisms or processes postulated, the main contenders – Smith (1987) and the proponents of coevolutionary models that postulate a local, independent domestication, and Prentice (1986), among those who support a diffusionist model – all read women out of any active, innovative role in developing cultigens, even though it is commonly assumed that women are primarily responsible for gathering plants (as well as small game) under earlier foraging adaptations, and for the cultivation of domesticates once a horticultural way of life was established. Prentice does attribute some degree of initiative to members of Archaic period societies in adopting imported cultigens, but he identifies this firmly with the authority and magical/religious knowledge of shamans, who are consistently referred to as male (Prentice 1986, as cited in Watson and Kennedy 1991:263). It was their role as "high-status" (commerce-oriented) culture brokers that would have ensured the success of an agricultural innovation, once introduced, and it was they, Prentice maintains, who "would have had the greatest knowledge of plants" (Prentice 1986, as cited in Watson and Kennedy 1991:263), and the motivation to cultivate and domesticate them. To be more specific, it was the knowledge they would have developed plants for ritual purposes, and their interest in securing a source of rattles and exotic medicine, that led to the introduction of tropical gourds (*cucurbita*) and, subsequently, to the development of indigenous cultigens in the Eastern Woodlands. In effect, women passively "followed plants around" when foraging, and then passively tended them when introduced as cultigens by men.

The dominant alternative, as articulated by Smith (1987), postulates a process whereby horticultural practices emerged as an adaptive response to a transformation of the plant resources that occurred without the benefit of any deliberate human intervention. At most, human patterns of refuse disposal in "domestilocalities," and the associated disturbance of the environment around base camps and resource-exploitation camps, would have unintentionally introduced artificial selection pressures that generated the varieties of indigenous plants that became domesticates. On this account "the plants virtually domesticate themselves" (Watson and Kennedy 1991:262), and women are, once again, assumed to have passively adapted to imposed change.

Watson and Kennedy make much of the artificiality of both models. Why assume that dabbling for ritual purposes would be more likely to produce the knowledge and transformations of the resource base necessary for horticulture than the systematic exploitation of these resources (through foraging) as a primary means of subsistence (Watson and Kennedy 1991:268)? And why deny human agency altogether when it seems that the most plausible ascription of agency (if any is to be made) must be to women (Watson and Kennedy 1991:262–264)? Watson and Kennedy make a strong case against the presumption, central to the coevolution model, that cultural change as extensive as adopting or developing domesticates could plausibly have been an "automatic process" (Watson and Kennedy 1991:266–267), and observe that they are "leary of explanations that remove women from the one realm that is traditionally granted them, as soon as innovation or invention enters the picture" (Watson and Kennedy 1991:264). Their assessment is that both theories share a set of underlying assumptions, uncritically appropriated from popular culture and traditional anthropology, to the effect that women could not have been responsible for any major culture transforming exercise of human agency (Watson and Kennedy 1991:263–264).

In a constructive vein, a second contributor who works on Prehispanic sites in the central Andes, Hastorf, drew on several lines of evidence to establish that gendered divisions of labor and participation in the public, political life of Prehispanic Sausa communities were profoundly altered through the period when the Inka extended their control in the region; that is, the household structure and gender roles encountered in historic periods cannot be treated as a stable, "traditional" feature of Andean life that predates state formation (Hastorf 1991:139). In a comparison of the density and distribution of plant remains recovered from household compounds dating to the periods before and after the advent of Inka control, Hastorf found evidence of both an intensification of maize production and processing, and of an increase in the degree to which female-associated processing activities were restricted to specific locations within the sites over time. In addition, she reports the results of stable-isotope analysis of skeletal remains recovered from these sites, comparing male and female patterns of consumption of meats, and various plant groups (mainly tubers and quinoa, and maize). Although the lifetime dietary profiles of males and females are undifferentiated through the period preceding the advent of Inka control in the valley, she finds evidence, consistent with the results of the paleobotanical analysis, that the consumption of maize increased much more dramatically for (some) men than for any of the women, at the point when evidence of Inka presence appears in the valley (Hastorf 1991:150). Given ethnohistoric records that document Inka practices of treating men as the heads of households and communities, drawing them into ritualized negotiations based on the consumption of maize beer (*chicha*) and requiring them to serve out a labor tax that was compensated with maize and *chicha*, she concludes that, through this transitional period, the newly imposed political structures of the Inka empire had forced a realignment of gender roles. Women "became the focus of [internal, social and economic] tensions as they produced more beer [and other maize foodstuffs] while at the same time they were more restricted in their participation in the society" (Hastorf 1991:152); indeed, their increased production was an essential basis for the political order imposed by the Inka, an order that drew male labor and political functions out of the household.

Similar results are reported by Brumfiel (1991) in an analysis of changes in household production patterns in the Valley of Mexico through the period when the Aztec state was establishing a tribute system in the region. She argues, through analysis of the frequencies of spindle whorls, that fabric production, largely the responsibility of women (on ethnohistoric and documentary evidence), increased dramatically in outlying areas but, surprisingly enough, decreased in the vicinity of the urban centers as the practice of extracting tribute payments in cloth developed. On further analysis, she found evidence of an inverse pattern of distribution and density in artifacts associated with the production of labor-intensive and transportable (cooked) food based on the use of tortillas; the changing proportion of griddles to pots suggests that the preparation of griddle-cooked foods increased near the urban centers and decreased in outlying areas, where less-demanding (and preferred) pot-cooked foods continued to predominate. She postulates, on this basis, that cloth may have been exacted directly as tribute in the hinterland, while populations living closer to the city center intensified their production of transportable food so that they could take advantage of "extra-domestic institutions" in the Valley of Mexico (Brumfiel 1991:243) – markets and forms of production that "drew labor away from the household context" (Brumfiel 1991:241) – that required a mobile labor force. In either case, Brumfiel points out, the primary burden of (directly or indirectly) meeting the tribute demands for cotton and maguey cloth imposed by Aztec rule was shouldered by women and was met by strategic realignments of their household labor. Where the Aztec state depended on such tribute to maintain its political and economic hegemony, its emergence, like the spread of the Inka state, as studied by Hastorf, must be understood to have transformed, and to have been dependent on a transformation of, the way predominantly female domestic labor was organized and deployed.

Finally, several contributors considered assemblages of "artistic" material, some of them rich in images of women, and explored the implications of broadening the range of conceptions of gender relations that inform their interpretation. Handsman undertook a critical rethinking of the ideology of gender difference, specifically, the "male gaze" (Handsman 1991:360), that infused a British exhibition of "The Art of Lepenski Vir" (Southampton, 1986), a Mesolithic site along the Danube River dating to the sixth millennium BC. Where this "art" is represented as the product of men who "were not ordinary hunter-gatherers" (Handsman 1991:332), while the women of Lepenski Vir are treated exclusively as their subjects (Handsman 1991:335), Handsman objects to the ways in which this exhibit, and archaeological discourse generally, is "productive and protective of [hierarchical relations between men and women] inside and outside the discipline" (Handsman 1991:334), especially where it represents these hierarchies as timeless and natural, as "a priori, as a constant and universal fact of life" (Handsman 1991:338). In short, he challenges the notion that gender (or "art") can be treated in essentialist terms in this or in any context. In countering the uncritical standpoint of the exhibit, Handsman explores several interpretive strategies by which "relational histories of inequality, power, ideology and control, and resistance and counter-discourse" might be explored, where gender dynamics are concerned (Handsman 1991:338–339). And in the process, he points to a wide range of evidence – features of the "artistic" images themselves, differences between them and other lines of evidence, and associations with architectural and artifactual material that (could) provide them context – that constitute "clear signs" (Handsman 1991:340) of complexities, contradictions, "plurality and conflict" (Handsman 1991:343), which undermine the simple story of natural opposition and complementarity told by the exhibit.

In a similar vein, Conkey has developed an analysis of interpretations of paleolithic "art," especially the images of females or purported female body parts, in which she shows how "the presentist gender paradigm" (Conkey with Williams 1991:13) – the contemporary ideology of gender difference that represents current definitions and relations of men and women as "a matter of bipolar, essential, exclusive categories" (Handsman 1991:335), locked in stable and predetermined relations of inequality – has infused most reconstructions of Upper Paleolithic 'artistic' life," yielding accounts in which "sexist 20th century notions of gender and sexuality are read into the cultural traces of 'our ancestors'" with remarkable disingenuity (Conkey with Williams 1991:13). She concludes that whatever the importance of these images and objects, it is most unlikely that they were instances of either commodified pornography or "high art," as produced in contemporary contexts, which is indeed how many treatises on such images consider them (see also Mack 1990). Moreover she, like Handsman, urges that we scrutinize the ideological agenda that lies behind the quest for closure in such cases, viz., the compulsion to naturalize those features of contemporary life most crucial to our identity as human and cultural beings, by tracing them back to our "origins" (as human and cultural).

None of these researchers, not even Handsman who moves furthest in the direction of a deconstructive (postprocessual) stance, considers their results merely *optional*, standpoint-specific alternatives to the androcentric models and paradigms they challenge. They purport to *expose* error, to demonstrate that formerly plausible interpretive options are simply false (empirically) or untenable (conceptually), and to improve on previous accounts. Watson and Kennedy (1991:267–268) draw attention to a straightforward contradiction implicit in much current theorizing about the emergence of horticulture in the Eastern Woodlands: women are persistently identified as the tenders of plants, whether wild or under cultivation, and yet are systematically denied any role in the transition from foraging to horticulture, whatever the cost in terms of theoretical elegance, plausibility, or explanatory power. Hastorf, and Brumfiel, bring into view new facts about the structure of well-understood data bases that call into question, not just the conceptual integrity but also the empirical adequacy of otherwise credible models of the political and economic infrastructure of states in Mesoamerica and the Andes. Brumfiel advances, on this basis, an alternative model that effectively fills (some of) the gaps and solves (some of) the puzzles she exposes as problematic for extant theories. And Handsman, and Conkey, argue that, although the artistic traditions they deal with are enormously rich and enigmatic, some interpretive options, including many that accord with the assumptions about gender taken for granted in our own contemporary societies, are simply unsustainable. Although the quest for closure, for one right answer, may be misguided when dealing with this sort of material, it does not follow that "anything goes."

Evidential constraints

In all of these cases, the results – both critical and constructive – turn on the appraisal of constraints imposed by, or elicited from, various kinds of relevant evidence. This is significant inasmuch as it suggests that however thoroughly mediated, or "laden," by theory archaeological evidence may be, it routinely turns out differently than expected; it generates puzzles, poses challenges, forces revisions, and canalizes theoretical thinking in ways that lend a certain credibility to the insights that sustain objectivist convictions. Consequently, while we cannot treat archaeological data or evidence as a given – a stable foundation – it is by no means infinitely plastic. It does, or can, function as a highly recalcitrant, closely constraining, "network of resistances," to use the terms of Shanks and Tilley's (1987a:104) discussion. What we need now is a nuanced account of *how* data are interpretively laden such that, to varying degrees, they can stand as evidence for or against a given knowledge claim. Such an account has not been developed by Shanks and Tilley, or by Hodder, even though they are themselves manifestly ambivalent about their strongest constructivist claims. Their response has been to juxtapose with claims about the radical instability of all evidence and the vicious circularity of all empirical testing, counterclaims to the effect that archaeological data can (and sometimes do) decisively resist theoretical appropriation. But, with the exception of Hodder's (1991) most recent discussion, they do not then reassess their original constructivist assertions. The result is incoherence.

The point of departure for an account that could make sense of these contradictory insights must be the now-familiar thesis that the empirical evaluation of knowledge claims, including claims about the past, is never a "lonely encounter of hypothesis with evidence" (Miller 1987:173). Evidential relevance is constructed as a three-place relation (Glymour 1980); archaeologists inevitably constitute data as evidence or, ascribe it "meaning" (Binford 1983) as evidence of specific events or conditions in the past, by means of linking hypotheses and interpretive principles. The key to understanding how evidence (as an interpretive construct) can constrain is to recognize, first, that the content and use of these linking principles is, itself, subject to empirical constraint and, second, that a great diversity of such principles figure in any given evidential argument. The credibility of these principles is by no means necessarily a matter of convention, but can often be established empirically and quite independently of any of the theories or assumptions that inform archaeological theorizing (i.e., the theories that might be tested against interpretively constituted evidence). Their independence from one another further ensures that error in any one line of interpretation may be exposed by incongruity with others that bear on the same (past) subject. Archaeologists thus exploit a great variety of evidence when they evaluate knowledge claims about the past; not just different kinds of archaeological evidence, but evidence from a wide range of sources, which enters interpretation at different points, and which can be mutually constraining when it converges, or fails to converge, on a test hypothesis.

In the cases considered here and, indeed, in most archaeological interpretation, claims about the past are invariably shaped by an encompassing theory, or at least by some set of precepts about the nature of the cultural subject, which can also inform the interpretation of archaeological data as evidence for or against these claims. When the theoretical framework is closely specified, a structurally circular interdependence between test evidence and test hypotheses can emerge, i.e., where the test hypothesis in question derives from a theory about cultural dynamics that also supplies the linking principles used to interpret the data as evidence for or against this hypothesis. It is presumably circularity of this sort that led post-processualists to declare that archaeologists quite simply "create facts" (Hodder 1984a:27), and that testing is inevitably futile, being viciously circular.

When practice is examined more closely, however, I suggest that any examples of full-fledged circularity that antiprocessualists might cite fall at one end of a continuum of types of interpretive inference, most of which do not sustain radically pessimistic judgments about the indeterminacy of archaeological inference and hypothesis evaluation. Even when the threat of self-validating circularity is realized, which is, in part, what Watson and Kennedy (1991) object to in explanations for the emergence of horticulture in the eastern United States, it is often possible, as they demonstrate, to establish evidential grounds for questioning the assumptions that frame both the favored hypothesis and the constitution of data as supporting evidence. Sometimes even data used to support the hypothesis can play this role. A traditional model of gender relations, underpinned by sexist assumptions about the nature and capabilities of women, infuses the interpretations of archaeological data that Watson and Kennedy consider, ensuring that, inevitably, these data will be seen as evidence of a "natural" division of labor in which women are consistently passive and associated with plants. Nevertheless, this does not (also) ensure that the record will obligingly provide evidence that activities identified as male in the terms of this model mediated the transition from a foraging to a horticultural way of life, however strong the expectation (on this model) that they must have. Where Smith's coevolution hypothesis is concerned, Watson and Kennedy point out that a very large proportion of the activities around "domestilocalities," which he cites as causes of the disturbances that would have transformed the weedy plant species into indigenous domesticates, were the activities of women, given (for the sake of argument) the traditional model they find presupposed by his account (Watson and Kennedy 1991:262).

But even if the interpretation of archaeological data as evidence is so "overdetermined" by orienting presuppositions that tensions and contradictions such as these never arise, critiques of these presuppositions – including critiques of the linking principles used to establish the evidential significance of specific data, as well as of the central tenets of the encompassing conceptual framework – may be based on independent evidence, that is, evidence generated outside the (archaeological) context to which these presuppositions are applied, evidence established in the "source" contexts from which interpretive linking principles are drawn. Watson and Kennedy make effective use, in this connection, of background (botanical) knowledge about the range and environmental requirements of the relevant varieties of maize to argue that many of the contexts in which they appear prehistorically are far from optimal (indeed, "inhospitable," "adverse"; Watson and Kennedy [1991:266]). Hence, it is not altogether plausible that they could have arisen under conditions of neglect; it is "more plausible" that humans knowledgeable about these plants (e.g., women foragers) must have taken a role in their cultivation and development. When Watson and Kennedy call into question the proposal that male shamans must have played this role (due to Prentice [1986]), they indicate some appreciation that the traditional model of sexual divisions of labor, which they find implicit in all the hypotheses they consider and accept for the sake of argument, is itself profoundly problematic given ethnographic evidence of foraging practices and the (gendered) distribution of botanical information among members of foraging societies (Watson and Kennedy 1991:256–257, 268). Over the past three decades, feminist anthropologists have documented enormous variability in the roles played by women, in the degrees to which they are active rather than passive, mobile rather than bound to a "home base," and powerful rather than stereotypically dispossessed and victimized. All of this decisively challenges any presupposition that women are inherently less capable of self-determination and strategic manipulation of resources than their male counterparts. Where independent botanical and ecological information provides a basis for calling into question specific interpretive principles (i.e., concerning the import of data bearing on the spatiotemporal distribution of early maize varieties in the eastern United States), these ethnographic data challenge the credibility of the interpretive framework itself, rendering suspect any interpretation that depends on such an assumption, quite independently of archaeological results.

Straightforward circularity is generally not the central problem in archaeological interpretation, however. Given the state of knowledge in the relevant fields, explanatory hypotheses about particular past contexts, and the linking principles deployed to interpret the record of these contexts, are rarely integrated into a single, unified, encompassing culture theory; indeed, given the complexity of most archaeological subjects, it is almost unimaginable that a single unified theory (e.g., of cultural systems) would have the resources to provide both the necessary explanatory hypotheses and the grounds for testing them (i.e., the relevant linking principles) in a given archaeological context. Despite disclaimers, analogical inference is generally the basis for ascribing evidential significance to archaeological data, and here the worry is usually underdetermination, not overdetermination. Nevertheless, as in the case just described, analogical inference is subject to two sets of evidential constraints that can significantly limit the range of evidentially viable options: those determining what can be claimed about the analog based on knowledge of source contexts and those deriving from the archaeological record that determine its applicability to a specific subject context (Wylie 1985). In linking women with the use of spindle whorls in weaving, and with the use of pots and griddles in food preparation, Brumfiel (1991) relies on a direct historic analogy that postulates that the same sorts of food and cloth production were involved in archaeological as in ethnohistoric contexts (given a judicious reading of codices dating to the sixteenth century; Brumfiel [1991:224–230, 237–239, 243–245]); this is, in turn, the basis for postulating further limited similarities in the relations of production where gender is concerned. Similarly, archaeologists dealing with evidence of horticultural lifeways routinely postulate a division of labor in which women are primarily responsible for agricultural activities, but they base this not on an appeal to the completeness of mapping between source and subject, which Brumfiel's case illustrates, but on the persistence of this association across histori- cally and ethnographically documented contexts, however different they may be in other respects (see, for example, Ehrenberg's discussion of the ethnographic bases for assuming these correlates; Ehrenberg 1989:50–54, 63–66, 81–83, 90–105).

In these cases, evidence of extensive similarity (the completeness of mapping) between source and subject contexts, and of reliable correlation between clusters of attributes in source contexts, suggests that the linkage postulated between archae- ologically observed material and its inferred functional, social, ideational, or other significance is not entirely arbitrary. To be specific, this kind of source-derived information constitutes evidence that the general association of women with the foraging of plant resources and with horticulture, and their local association with cooking and weaving in Aztec contexts, is to some (specifiable) degree non- accidental; it is at least preliminary evidence that an underlying "determining struc- ture" links the artifactual material in question to specific functions, gender associa- tions, or activity structures securely enough to support an ascription of the latter attributes to the archaeological subject (for the details of this analysis, see Wylie [1985, 1988]). A change in background knowledge about the sources, as much as in what archaeologists find in the record, can decisively challenge these interpretive claims. Where the feminist research on foraging societies (mentioned above) calls into question all aspects of the assumption that women passively "followed plants around" (as Watson and Kennedy characterize the traditional model), indeed, where it provides evidence that the "gathering" activities of women often include the hunting of small game, it becomes necessary to reconsider simplistic interpretive assumptions to the effect that "hunting" artifacts are indicative of the presence or activities of men. But most important, when the linking principles used to "ascribe meaning" to archaeological data as evidence are uncontested – when their credibil- ity is well established and independent of any of the hypotheses that archaeologists might want to evaluate – archaeological evidence can very effectively stabilize the assessment of comprehensively different claims about the cultural past. The power of the challenge posed by Brumfiel to extant models of the economic base of the Aztec empire depends on precisely this. Her identification of spindle whorls, and pots and griddles, with cloth and food production by women is unproblematic for any she might engage in debate and wholly independent of both the hypotheses she challenges and those she promotes. Hence, when she shows that variability inheres in these data that cannot be accounted for on standard models *when interpreted in these shared terms*, she establishes a challenge that is by no means an artifact of the feminist standpoint that led (directly or indirectly) to her analysis, or that is compelling only for those who share a feminist understanding of gender relations.

Insofar as analogical inferences often allow considerable scope for (independent) empirical assessment, they fall into the middle ranges of a continuum of types of inference, where degrees of insecurity and the potential to be systematically insulated from critique (as in the case of vicious circularity) are concerned. The limiting case on this continuum of theory-ladening inferences – the ideal of security in the ascription of evidential significance to data – are instances where archaeologists can draw on completely independent, nonethnographic sources for biconditional linking principles (laws or law-like principles) that specify unique causal antecedents for specific components of the surviving record. Among the cases considered here, Hastorf's use of the analysis of bone composition comes closest to the ideal. If the background knowledge deployed in stable-isotope analysis is reliable (and this is always open to critical reassessment) it can establish, in chemical terms, what dietary intake would have been necessary to produce the reported composition of the bone marrow recovered from archaeological contexts. And where this can be linked, through paleobotanical analysis, to the consumption of specific plant and animal resources, it can underwrite the inference of dietary profiles that is very substantially independent of, and can seriously challenge (can provide a genuine test of), any interpretive or explanatory presuppositions about subsistence patterns and/or social practices affecting the distribution of food that archaeologists might be interested in testing. The independence and security of linking arguments based on background knowledge of this physical, chemical, bioecological sort is exploited in many other areas: in morphological analyses of skeletal remains that provide evidence of pathologies and physical stress; in radiocarbon, archeomagnetic, and related methods of dating; and in some reconstructions of prehistoric technology and paleo-ecology, to name a few such examples. As the degree of independence between linking principles and test hypotheses or framework assumptions evident in these cases is approximated, archaeologists secure a body of evidence that establishes provisionally stable parameters for all other interpretation and a stable basis for piecemeal comparison between contending claims about the cultural past (a further analysis of independence is developed in Wylie [1990]). Something along the lines of these limiting cases constitute the ideal on which Binford bases his arguments for middle-range theory (e.g., Binford 1983:135, 1986b:472).

It is important to note, however, that the import of evidence of this sort (i.e., evidence that is constituted on the basis of extremely reliable, deterministic, and independent linking principles) is often very limited, taken on its own. As indicated, Hastorf must rely on a number of collateral lines of evidence to establish that the anomalous shift in diet evident in male skeletons was likely due to increased consumption of maize beer, to link this to the advent of Inka-imposed systems of political control in the valley, and to draw out the implication that this political transformation depended on a profound restructuring of gender relations at the level of the household. Indeed, this reliance on multiple lines of evidence is an important and general feature of archaeological reasoning; archaeologists rarely ascribe evidential significance to items taken in isolation. But this is not necessarily cause for despair. In such cases the security of archaeological evidence depends not just on the credibility of particular linking principles, taken in isolation, or on their independence from the test claims they are used to support or refute, but also, and crucially, on the independence *from one another* of the various linking principles used to establish diverse lines of evidence bearing on these claims. That is to say, where the constraints inherent in the relation between evidence and hypothesis operate on *a number of different vertical axes* (i.e., running from different elements of the data base, via a range of linking hypotheses, to the claims in question), a network of "horizontal" constraints comes into play between the lines of inference by which various kinds of data, bearing on a particular past context, are interpreted as evidence of this context. If diverse evidential strands all converge on a given hypothesis – if you can use different means to triangulate on the same postulated set of conditions or events – then you may be able to provide it decisive, if never irreversible, support simply because it is so implausible that the convergence should be the result of compensatory error in all the inferences establishing its evidential support (for philosophical discussion of these considerations, see Kosso [1988:456]; Hacking [1983:183–185]).

Like Hastorf, Brumfiel operates under this sort of constraint when she shows that independently constituted lines of evidence concerning both cloth and food production converge on the counter-hypothesis that change in the organization of domestic labor was a key component in establishing the economic basis for the Aztec empire. This convergence is a strong argument for her account precisely because it cannot be counted on. Even when, taken separately, each line of evidence relevant to a particular model of past events or conditions of life enjoys strong collateral support (i.e., from the sources that secure the linking principles on which they depend), undetected error or weakness may become evident when one line of evidence persistently runs counter to the others, when dissonance emerges among lines of interpretation; the failure to converge on a coherent account makes it clear that error lies somewhere in the system of auxiliary assumptions and linking principles, however well entrenched they may be. In the extreme, which might be represented by the sorts of cases Handsman and Conkey consider (i.e., interpretations of "artistic" images and traditions), persistent dissonance may call into question the efficacy of *any* interpretive constitution of the data as evidence. Ultimately, there may be no determinate fact of the matter where the symbolic import of gender imagery is concerned or, as Conkey suggests, we may have to conclude that we simply are not (and may never be) in a position to determine what the fact of the matter is in such cases. It is, paradoxically, the fragmentary nature of the archaeological record that is its strength in setting up evidential constraints of these sorts, even in establishing the limits of inquiry.

The key point to be taken from reflection on these examples of gender research in archaeology is that although archaeological data stand as evidence only under (rich) interpretation, the process of interpretation – of ladening data with theory so that it has evidential import – is by no means radically open ended. The linking principles and background knowledge that mediate the constitution of data as evidence are by no means necessarily or inherently arbitrary conventions, as Hodder

(1984a:27) once suggested. Values and interests of various kinds do play a crucial role not just in setting the agenda of archaeological inquiry – determining what questions will be asked – but in determining what range of interpretive and explanatory options will be considered fruitful or plausible; in this they shape not just the direction, but also the content and outcome of archaeological research. But this does not mean that such "external" influences determine the shape of inquiry seamlessly, or irrevocably; they can be very effectively challenged on conceptual and empirical grounds, as has been demonstrated repeatedly by feminist social scientists over the past two decades, and by the critical analyses described here. It is significant, however, that the impetus for reassessing a discipline's "taken-for-granteds," at all levels (i.e., at the level of specific interpretations and linking principles, as well as at that of broad framework assumptions), very often comes from those who bring to bear a standpoint, a socially and politically defined "angle of vision," that differs from that typical of the established status quo in a field (whatever form this takes). It is precisely a shift in the values and interests informing the work of these critics that directs their attention to new questions, which throws into relief gaps and incongruities in established theories, and which leads to a questioning of settled judgements of plausibility that have otherwise never been challenged (see Longino 1990). And while the insights that result from such a turn, for example, from the work of those who bring to bear a feminist perspective, are always themselves open to further critique – as feminist discussions of class and ethnic, cultural, and racial difference have made clear, they have their own limitations – it is not the case that they are on the same footing, in this respect, as the (partial) perspectives they critique and sometimes displace. Once our understanding is expanded (indeed, many argue, transformed) so that it takes women and gender fully into account, there is no return to the traditional androcentric models described by Watson and Kennedy; the process of inquiry is, in this sense, open-ended, but it is not anarchic.

Conclusion

Although it can no longer be assumed that there is one set of standards or reference points to which all models, hypotheses, and claims can be referred – there is no "transcendental grid" (Bernstein 1983; Wylie 1989b) – at any given time, there will be a number of stable, shared evidential reference points that can be exploited piecemeal in the comparison and evaluation of contending claims, and these can sometimes yield "rationally decisive" (Bernstein 1983), if never final, conclusions. This means that, at least sometimes, it is plausible to say that we have quite literally "discovered" a fact about the world, or that we have shown a formerly plausible claim to be "just false." Such claims are established by a good deal of politically motivated, explicitly feminist research, including that which has begun to emerge in archaeology; the critical analysis by Watson and Kennedy, and the constructive proposals of Hastorf, and of Brumfiel, are cases in point. In other cases the outcome of inquiry is more equivocal. As Handsman, and Conkey, illustrate, sustained investigation may lead us to question basic assumptions about the existence and the accessibility of certain "facts" about a given subject domain. In short, there is a whole continuum of inferences, ranging from the viciously circular, through analogical and other forms of ampliative inference, to the nearly deductive naturalistic inferences favored by Binford, that manifest enormously different degrees of security and open-endedness; none of these parts should be read for the whole.

I suggest, then, that the question of what epistemic stance is appropriate – whether we must be relativists or objectivists, processualists, or postprocessualists – should be settled locally, in light of what we have come to know about the nature of specific subject matters and about the resources we have for their investigation. We should resist the pressure to adopt a general epistemic stance appropriate to all knowledge claims. The ambivalence expressed by Harding (1986) and inherent in the contradictory impulses evident in postprocessualism is well founded, but need not lead us to build inconsistencies into the core of our epistemology and practice.

If these general points are accepted, it follows that feminist research, including feminist research in archaeology, is not "political" in any especially distinctive or worrisome sense (Wylie 1991b). Sociopolitical factors are key in explaining how and why it has arisen at this point, but the results of inquiry are not the "overdetermined" products of (viciously) circular inference that takes, as both point of departure and conclusion, the political convictions from which it draws inspiration. In fact, if any general lesson is to be drawn from reflection on feminist practice, it is that politically engaged science is often much more rigorous, self-critical, and responsive to the facts than allegedly neutral science, for which nothing much is at stake.

■ ■ ■

References

Arnold, K., R. Gilchrist, P. Graves, and S. Taylor (editors) (1988) Women in Archaeology. *Archaeological Reviews from Cambridge* 7(1):2–8.

Barstow, A. (1978) The Uses of Archeology for Women's History: James Mellaart's Work on The Neolithic Goddess at Çatal Hüyük. *Feminist Studies* 4(3):7–17.

Bernstein, R. J. (1983) *Beyond Objectivism and Relativism: Science, Hermeneutics, and Praxis.* University of Pennsylvania Press, Philadelphia.

Bertelsen, R., A. Lillehammer, and J. Naess (eds) (1987) *Were They All Men?: An Examination of Sex Roles in Prehistoric Society.* Arkeologist museum i Stavanger, Stavanger, Norway.

Binford, L. R. (1982) Objectivity – Explanation – Archaeology 1981. In *Theory and Explanation in Archaeology*, edited by C. Renfrew, M. J. Rowlands, and B. A. Segraves, pp. 125–138. Academic Press, New York.

—— (1983) *Working at Archaeology*. Academic Press, New York.

—— (1986a) Data, Relativism, and Archaeological Science. *Man* 22:391–404.

—— (1986b) In Pursuit of the Future. In *American Archaeology Past and Future*, edited by D. J. Meltzer, D. D. Fowler, and J. A. Sabloff, pp. 459–479. Smithsonian Institution Press, Washington, DC.

—— (1989) *Debating Archaeology*. Academic Press, New York.

Braithwaite, M. (1984) Ritual and Prestige in the Prehistory of Wessex *c.* 2200–1400 BC: A New Dimension to the Archaeological Evidence. In *Ideology, Power, and Prehistory*, edited by D. Miller and C. Tilley, pp. 93–110. Cambridge University Press, Cambridge.

Brumfiel, E. M. (1991) Weaving and Cooking: Women's Production in Aztec Mexico. In *Engendering Archaeology: Women and Prehistory*, edited by J. M. Gero and M. W. Conkey, pp. 224–251. Basil Blackwell, Oxford.

Conkey, M. W., and J. D. Spector (1984) Archaeology and the Study of Gender. In *Advances in Archaeological Method and Theory*, vol. 7, edited by M. B. Schiffer, pp. 1–38. Academic Press, New York.

Conkey, M. W. with S. H. Williams (1991) Original Narratives: The Political Economy of Gender in Archaeology. In *Gender at the Cross-roads of Knowledge: Feminist Anthropology in the Post-Modern Era*, edited by M. di Leonardo. University of California Press, Berkeley.

Ehrenberg, M. (1989) *Women in Prehistory*. University of Oklahoma Press, Norman.

Engelstad, E. (1991) Images of Power and Contradiction: Feminist Theory and Post-Processual Archaeology. *Antiquity* 65: 502–514.

Fausto-Sterling, A. (1985) *Myths of Gender: Biological Theories About Men and Women*. Basic Books, New York.

Feyerabend, P. (1988) *Against Method*. 2nd ed. Verso, London.

Flax, J. (1987) Postmodernism and Gender: Relativism in Feminist Theory. *Signs* 12: 621–643.

Fraser, N., and L. J. Nicholson (1988) Social Criticism without Philosophy: An Encounter Between Feminism and Postmodernism. *Communications* 10: 345–366.

Galison, P. (1987) *How Experiments End*. University of Chicago Press, Chicago.

Gathercole, P., and D. Lowenthal (1989) *The Politics of the Past*. Unwin Hyman, London.

Gero, J. M. (1983) Gender Bias in Archaeology: A Cross-Cultural Perspective. In *The Socio-Politics of Archaeology*, edited by J. M. Gero, D. M. Lacy, and M. L. Blakey, pp. 51–58. Research Report No. 23. Department of Anthropology, University of Massachusetts, Amherst.

—— (1985) Socio-Politics and the Woman-at-Home Ideology. *American Antiquity* 50: 342–350.

—— (1988) Gender Bias in Archaeology: Here, Then and Now. In *Feminism Within the Science and Health Care Professions: Overcoming Resistance*, edited by S. V. Rosser, pp. 33–43. Pergamon Press, New York.

Gero, J. M., and M. W. Conkey (eds) (1991) *Engendering Archaeology: Women and Prehistory*. Basil Blackwell, Oxford.

Gibbon, G. (1989) *Explanation in Archaeology*. Basil Blackwell, New York.

Glymour, C. (1980) *Theory and Evidence*. Princeton University Press, Princeton, New Jersey.

Hacking, I. (1983) *Representing and Intervening*. Cambridge University Press, Cambridge.

—— (1988) Philosophers of Experiment. *PSA 1988*, vol. 2, edited by A. Fine and J. Leplin, pp. 147–156. Philosophy of Science Association, East Lansing, Michigan.

Handsman, R. (1991) Whose Art Was Found at Lepenski Vir?: Gender Relations and Power in Archaeology. In *Engendering Archaeology: Women and Prehistory*, edited by J. M. Gero and M. W. Conkey, pp. 329–365. Basil Blackwell, Oxford.

Hanson, N. R. (1958) *Patterns of Discovery*. Cambridge University Press, Cambridge.

Harding, S. (1983) Why Has the Sex/Gender System Become Visible Only Now? In *Discovering Reality: Feminist Perspectives on Epistemology, Metaphysics, Methodology and Philosophy of Science*, edited by S. Harding and M. B. Hintikka, pp. 311–325. D. Reidel, Dordrecht, Holland.

—— (1986) *The Science Question in Feminism*. Cornell University Press, Ithaca.

Hastorf, C. A. (1991) Gender, Space, and Food in Prehistory. In *Engendering Archaeology: Women and Prehistory*, edited by J. M. Gero and M. W. Conkey, pp. 132–159. Basil Blackwell, Oxford.

Hawkesworth, M. E. (1989) Knowers, Knowing, Known: Feminist Theory and Claims of Truth. *Signs* 14: 533–557.

Hodder, I. (1982) *Symbols in Action*. Cambridge University Press, Cambridge.

—— (1983) Archaeology, Ideology and Contemporary Society. *Royal Anthropological Institute News* 56:6–7.

—— (1984a) Archaeology in 1984. *Antiquity* 58:25–32.

—— (1984b) Burials, Houses, Women and Men in the European Neolithic. In *Ideology, Power, and Prehistory*, edited by D. Miller and C. Tilley, pp. 51–68. Cambridge University Press, Cambridge.

—— (1985) Post-processual Archaeology. In *Advances in Archaeological Method and Theory*, vol. 8, edited by M. B. Schiffer, pp. 1–25. Academic Press, New York.

—— (1986) *Reading The Past: Current Approaches to Interpretation in Archaeology*. Cambridge University Press, Cambridge.

—— (1991) Interpretive Archaeology and Its Role. *American Antiquity* 56:7–18.

Kehoe, A. (1983) The Shackles of Tradition. In *The Hidden Half: Studies of Plains Indian Women*, edited by P. Albers and B. Medicine, pp. 53–73. University Press of America, Washington, D.C.

Kelley, J. and M. Hanen, (1992) Gender and Archaeological Knowledge. In *Metaarchaeology*, edited by L. Embree. Boston Studies in Philosophy of Science. Reidel, Holland.

Knorr, K. and M. Mulkay (ed) (1983) *Science Observed: Perspectives on the Social Study of Science*. Sage Publications, London.

Kosso, P. (1988) Dimensions of Observability. *British Journal of Philosophy of Science* 39:449–467.

—— (1989) Science and Objectivity. *Journal of Philosophy* 86:245–257.

Kramer, C. and M. Stark 1988 The Status of Women in Archaeology. *American Anthropological Association Newsletter* 29(9):1, 11–12.

Kuhn, T. S. (1970) *The Structure of Scientific Revolutions*. 2nd ed. University of Chicago Press, Chicago.

Lather, P. (1986) Issues of Validity in Openly Ideological Research: Between a Rock and a Soft Place. *Interchange* 17(4): 63–84.

—— (1990) Postmodernism and the Human Sciences. *The Humanist Psychologist* 18: 64–83.

Latour, B. (1987) *Science in Action*. Harvard University Press, Cambridge.

Latour, B. and S. Woolgar (1986) *Laboratory Life: The Construction of Scientific Facts*. Princeton University Press, Princeton, New Jersey.

Laudan, L. and J. Leplin (1991) Empirical Equivalence and Underdetermination. *Journal of Philosophy* 88:449–472.

Longino, H. E. (1987) Can There Be a Feminist Science? *Hypatia* 2:51–65.

—— (1990) *Science as Social Knowledge*. Princeton University Press, Princeton, New Jersey.

Longino, H. E. and R. Doell (1983) Body, Bias, and Behavior: A Comparative Analysis of Reasoning in Two Areas of Biological Science. *Signs* 9:206–227.

Mack, R. (1990) Reading the Archaeology of the Female Body. *Qui Parle* 4:79–97.

Miller, D. and C. Tilley (eds) (1984) *Ideology, Power, and Prehistory*. Cambridge University Press, Cambridge.

Miller, R. (1987) *Fact and Method: Explanation, Confirmation and Reality in the Natural and Social Sciences*, Princeton University Press, Princeton, New Jersey.

Moore, H. L. (1988) *Feminism and Anthropology*. Polity Press, Cambridge.

Mukhopadhyay, C. C. and P. J. Higgins (1988) Anthropological Studies of Women's Status Revisited: 1977–1987. *Annual Review of Anthropology* 17:461–495.

Newton-Smith, W. H. (1981) *The Rationality of Science*. Cambridge University Press, Cambridge.

Pickering, A. (1984) *Constructing Quarks: A Sociological History of Particle Physics*. Edinburgh University Press, Edinburgh.

—— (1987) Essay Review: Forms of Life: Science, Contingency and Harry Collins. *British Journal for the History of Science* 20:213–221.

—— (1989) Living in the Material World: On Realism and Experimental Practice. In *The Uses of Experiment: Studies in the Natural Sciences*, edited by D. Gooding, T. Pinch, and S. Schaffer, pp. 275–297. Cambridge University Press, Cambridge.

Prentice, G. (1986) Origins of Plant Domestication in the Eastern United States: Promoting the Individual in Archaeological Theory. *Southeastern Archaeology* 5: 103–119.

Renfrew, C. (1982) Explanation Revisited. In *Theory and Explanation in Archaeology*, edited by C. Renfrew, M. J. Rowlands, and B. A. Segraves, pp. 5–23. Academic Press, New York.

—— (1989) Comments on Archaeology Into the 1990s. *Norwegian Archaeological Review* 22(1): 33–41.

Rosaldo, M. Z., and L. Lamphere (ed) (1974) *Women, Culture, and Society*. Stanford University Press, Stanford.

Rudner, R. (1966) *Philosophy of the Social Sciences*. Prentice Hall, Englewood Cliffs, New Jersey.

Shanks, M., and C. Tilley (1987a) *Re-constructing Archaeology*. Cambridge University Press, Cambridge.

—— (1987b) *Social Theory and Archaeology*. Polity Press, Cambridge.

—— (1989) Archaeology Into the 1990s; Questions Rather Than Answers. Reply to Comments on Archaeology Into the 1990s. *Norwegian Archaeological Review* 22(1): 1–14, 42–54. (With comments, pp. 15–41.)

Shapere, D. (1985) The Concept of Observation in Science and Philosophy. *Philosophy of Science* 49: 485–525.

Smith, B. D. (1987) The Independent Domestication of the Indigenous Seed-Bearing Plants in Eastern North America. In *Emergent Horticultural Economies of the Eastern Woodlands*, edited by W. Keegan, pp. 3–47. Occasional Paper No. 7. Center for Archaeological Investigations, Southern Illinois University, Carbondale.

Spector, J. D. (1983) Male/Female Task Differentiation Among the Hidatsa: Toward the Development of an Archeological Approach to the Study of Gender. In *The Hidden Half: Studies of Plains Indian Women*, edited by P. Albers and B. Medicine, pp. 77–99. University Press of America, Washington, DC.

Suppe, F. (1997) *The Structure of Scientific Theories*. 2nd ed. University of Illinois Press, Urbana.

Trigger, B. G. (1989) Hyperrelativism, Responsibility, and the Social Sciences. *Canadian Review of Sociology and Anthropology* 26: 776–797.

Tringham, R. E. (1991) Households with Faces: The Challenge of Gender in Prehistoric Architectural Remains. In *Engendering Archaeology: Women and Prehistory*, edited by J. M. Gero and M. W. Conkey, pp. 93–131. Basil Blackwell, Oxford.

Walde, D. and N. Willows (eds) (1991) *The Archaeology of Gender*, Proceedings of the 22nd Annual Chacmool Conference. The Archaeological Association of the University of Calgary, Calgary.

Watson, P. J. and M. Fotiadis (1990) The Razor's Edge: Symbolic-Structuralist Archaeology and the Expansion of Archeological Inference. *American Anthropologist* 92: 613–629.

Watson P. J. and M. C. Kennedy (1991) The Development of Horticulture in the Eastern Woodlands of North America: Women's Role. In *Engendering Archaeology: Women and Prehistory*, edited by J. M. Gero and M. W. Conkey, pp. 255–275. Basil Blackwell, Oxford.

Watson, R. A. (1990) Ozymandias, King of Kings: Postprocessual Radical Archaeology as Critique. *American Antiquity* 55: 673–689.

Weitzenfeld, J. S. (1984) Valid Reasoning by Analogy. *Philosophy of Science* 51: 137–149.

Wildeson, L. E. (1980) The Status of Women in Archaeology: Results of a Preliminary Survey. *American Anthropological Association Newsletter* 21(5): 5–8.

Woolgar, S. (1983) Irony in the Social Study of Science. In *Science Observed: Perspectives on the Social Study of Science*, pp. 239–266. Sage Publications, London.

Wylie, A. (1985) The Reaction Against Analogy. In *Advances in Archaeological Method and Theory*, vol. 8, edited by M. B. Schiffer, pp. 63–111. Academic Press, New York.

—— (1987) The Philosophy of Ambivalence: Sandra Harding on *The Science Question in Feminism*. *Canadian Journal of Philosophy* (supplementary volume) 13: 59–73.

—— (1988) "Simple" Analogy and the Role of Relevance Assumptions: Implications of Archaeological Practice. *International Studies in the Philosophy of Science* 2(2): 134–150.

—— (1989a) Matters of Fact and Matters of Interest. In *Archaeological Approaches to Cultural Identity*, edited by S. Shennan, pp. 94–109. Unwin Hyman, London.

—— (1989b) Archaeological Cables and Tacking: The Implications of Practice for Bernstein's "Options Beyond Objectivism and Relativism." *Philosophy of the Social Sciences* 19: 1–18.

—— (1990) The Philosophy of Archaeology: Varieties of Evidence. Paper presented at the Annual Meeting of the American Philosophical Association Meetings, Eastern Division, Boston.

—— (1991a) Gender Theory and the Archaeological Record: Why Is There No Archaeology of Gender?. In *Engendering Archaeology: Women and Prehistory*, edited by J. M. Gero and M. W. Conkey, pp. 31–54. Basil Blackwell, Oxford.

—— (1991b) Beyond Objectivism and Relativism: Feminist Critiques and Archaeological Challenges. In *The Archaeology of Gender*, Proceedings of the 22nd Annual Chacmool Conference, edited by D. Walde and N. Willows. The Archaeological Association of the University of Calgary, Calgary.

—— (1991c) Reasoning About Ourselves: Feminist Methodology in the Social Sciences. In *Women and Reason*, edited by E. Harvey and K. Okruhlik. University of Michigan Press, Ann Arbor, Michigan.

—— (1992) On "Heavily Decomposing Red Herrings": Scientific Method in Archaeology and the Ladening of Evidence with Theory. In *Metaarchaeology*, edited by L. Embree. Boston Studies in the Philosophy of Science. Reidel, Holland.

PART II

Human origins

INTRODUCTION

Most archaeologists work with the remains of *Homo sapiens sapiens*, who have only roamed the earth for about 200,000 years, but human origins are interesting to all of us. One question we would like to answer is, of the many kinds of differences between men and women, which differences are biologically determined, and which are culturally constructed? When in the course of human evolution does "culture" emerge? Physical anthropologists, paleontologists, and some archaeologists work together to investigate fossils and tools of our hominid ancestors, such as *Australopithecus*, and *Homo erectus*. Primatologists contribute to an understanding of our early ancestors by comparing the physical characteristics and behaviors of monkeys and apes to try to understand what behaviors they have in common, and what evolutionary and environmental factors might account for their differences.

Most non-human primates obtain their own food. Mothers share food with their own offspring until they can forage for themselves. Chimpanzees, our closest non-human relatives, share food with other relatives, and occasionally with non-relatives. For example, males share meat with each other and with sexually receptive females. But no non-human primate societies have what we would call a division of labor beyond the fact that females take care of their offspring. In contrast, most human societies divide labor along gender lines that usually coincide with male and female sexes. This division of labor is most frequently characterized as "males hunt animals" while "females gather plants." Scientists do not agree about when and why this sexual division of labor emerged, or even if it accurately characterizes any human society.

Until the 1970s, scientists thought that hunting was the key to human evolution. Because men hunt large animals in most living societies, and women do not, they assumed that "physically superior" male human ancestors hunted in the remote past and shared meat with passive females, who stayed home in base camps caring for dependent infants and children. Sherwood Washburn, C.S. Lancaster, and William Laughlin elaborated this theme in papers given at a 1965 conference titled, "Man the Hunter" (Lee and Devore 1968). At the same conference, studies of living hunter-gatherer societies, particularly the !Kung of southern Africa, showed that women's plant-gathering activities actually provided most of the food consumed by these small, highly mobile groups of families. Men's hunting provided variety in the diet, and personal prestige, but was far less reliable than plant gathering as a food source. A few years later, Sally (Slocum) Linton wrote "Woman the Gatherer," summarizing and critiquing the traditional male-oriented picture of human evolution, and presenting a newer, more gender-balanced version. Still, many saw this model as simply "turning the tables" to place higher value on women's activities. Subsequent research has broken down the hunting/gathering dichotomy to some degree, noting that women sometimes hunt large game, and often hunt small game. The very definition of "hunting," then, becomes problematic, because we have preconceived ideas about what it means.

The importance of a more gender-balanced view has been supported by subsequent research. Adrienne Zihlman, for example, has continued to pursue many lines of evidence for the development of sex and gender differences in early human evolution. She wrote the article (chapter 5), entitled "Woman the Gatherer," to help anthropology professors incorporate new data and new ideas about early humans into introductory courses.

In her article, "An Axe to Grind" (chapter 6) Sheila McKell discusses the use of stone tools by traditional Australian Aboriginal men and women, to demonstrate that hunter-gatherers in recent history had flexible and varied approaches to tool-making and tool use. If recent hunter-gatherers lacked a rigid division of labor, why assume our ancient hunting and gathering ancestors included only hunting men and gathering women, or as Lovejoy (1981) has argued, hunting *and* gathering males provisioning child-tethered females?

In chapter 7 Dean Falk (1997) takes on the Lovejoy hypothesis with an altogether different approach in "Brain Evolution in Females." Data on the evolution of the human brain show small but interesting differences indicating that most male and female humans perceive the world and act in slightly different ways. Falk directly addresses the question of the biological differences between modern men and women, and what this implies about human evolution by getting at the "heart" of the matter, the human brain. She is careful to map out how studies were undertaken, and to present quantitative results showing that the differences she discerns do not necessarily apply to any individual man or woman, but to "averages" or statistical norms in large populations. She summarizes increasing evidence that subtle, yet significant, differences exist between male and female brain structure. These can be used to refute the passive "stay-at-home" role for women in human evolution, such as the Lovejoy hypothesis. Falk's primary goal is not to point out how men and women today act or should act, but to understand what brain differences observed today might tell us about the behavior of our remote ancestors.

Further reading

Balme, Jane and Wendy Beck (1993)
Fedigan, Linda Marie (1982)
—— (1986)
Hager, Lori D. (1997)
McGrew, W. C. (1981)
Morbeck, Mary Ellen, *et al.* (1997)
Slocum Sally (Linton), (1975)

Sperling, Susan (1991)
Taylor, Timothy (1996)
Zihlman, Adrienne L. (1981)
—— (1993)
—— (1997)

■ ■ ■

Bibliography

Balme, Jane, and Wendy Beck (1993) "Archaeology and Feminism: Views on the Origins of the Division of Labour," in H. du Cros and L. Smith (eds) *Women and Archaeology: A Feminist Critique*, Occasional Papers in Prehistory 23, Department of Prehistory, Research School of Pacific Studies, Canberra: The Australian National University, pp. 61–74.

Fedigan, Linda Marie (1982) *Primate Paradigms: Sex Roles and Social Bonds*, Montreal: Eden Press.

—— (1986) "The Changing Role of Women in Models of Human Evolution," *Annual Review of Anthropology* 15: 22–66.

Hager, Lori D. (1997) "Sex and Gender in Paleoanthropology," in L. Hager (ed.) *Women in Human Evolution*, London: Routledge, pp. 1–28.

Lee, R. B. and I. DeVore (eds) (1968) *Man the Hunter*, Chicago: Aldine.

Lovejoy, C. O. (1981) The Origin of Man, *Science* 211: 341–350.

McGrew, W. C. (1981) "The Female Chimpanzee as a Human Evolutionary Prototype," in F. Dahlberg (ed.) *Woman the Gatherer*, New Haven: Yale University Press, pp. 35–74.

Morbeck, Mary Ellen, Alison Galloway and Adrienne L. Zihlman (eds) (1997) *Evolving Female: A Life-History Perspective*, Princeton, New Jersey: Princeton University Press.

Slocum Sally (Linton), (1975) "Woman the Gatherer: Male Bias in Anthropology," in R. R. Reiter (ed.) *Toward an Anthropology of Women*, New York: Monthly Review Press, pp. 36–50.

Sperling, Susan (1991) "Baboons with Briefcases vs. Langurs in Lipstick: Feminism and Functionalism in Primate Studies," in M. DiLeonardo (ed.) *Gender at the Crossroads of Knowledge: Feminist Anthropology in the Postmodern Era*, Berkeley and Los Angeles: University of California Press, pp. 204–234.

Taylor, Timothy (1996) *The Prehistory of Sex: Four Million Years of Human Sexual Culture*, Bantam Books: New York.

Zihlman, Adrienne L. (1981) "Women as Shapers of the Human Adaptation," in F. Dahlberg (ed.) *Woman the Gatherer*, New Haven: Yale University Press, pp. 75–120.

—— (1993) "Sex Differences and Gender Hierarchies Among Primates: An Evolutionary Perspective," in B. Miller (ed.) *Sex and Gender Hierarchies*, Cambridge: Cambridge University Press, pp. 32–56.

—— (1997) "The Paleolithic Glass Ceiling: Women in Human Evolution," in L. D. Hager (ed.) *Women in Human Evolution*, London: Routledge, pp. 91–113

Chapter 5

WOMAN THE GATHERER:
The Role of Women in Early Hominid Evolution

Adrienne L. Zihlman

Orientation

The purpose of this chapter is to provide guidance for incorporating women and their activities into discussions of hominid evolution and early hominid life. "Woman the gatherer" developed as a countertheme to "man the hunter" in order to generate an image of women as active and autonomous participants in the evolutionary process and in early hominid society. It is a view consistent with evolutionary principles and takes into account a wide range of information. Complementary information can be found by Fedigan and Fedigan (1989), Lancaster (1989), and Spector and Whelan (1989).

An approach to studying the past

This chapter focuses on the early stage of human evolution some 2–4 million years ago. For this period of time there is minimal direct information to assist us. Consequently, reconstructions of the human past often rely on assumptions based upon cultural values and stereotypes or individual experience. However, there is available "indirect" information about the evolutionary process, about our close relatives, and about contemporary people who live a nomadic way of life.

Because this chapter presents an evolutionary perspective, several kinds of information are relevant: time, fossil record, living species and the evolutionary process.

1. *Time* establishes when events happened in the past and makes it possible to determine their sequence and duration (for example, when human physical characters appear during pre-history). But

other events also are of interest: Did food sharing come before or after gathering? Did a sexual division of labor appear in the earlier stages of human evolution or perhaps much later, when more permanent settlements emerged? The time chart (Table 1) provides a general sequence of events for orientation and discussion.

2 *Fossil record*. The direct evidence for events some 2–4 million years ago consists of fossil bones and teeth and, later, stone artifacts, uncovered in eastern and southern Africa. From teeth and bones we identify the fossils as hominid (in the human family) and can measure brain and tooth size, limb length, and proportions. Within general parameters, this evidence offers possibilities for inferring diet and development from the teeth, locomotion from the pelvic and foot bones, brain size from the skull, and body size from joints and limb bones. The early fossils record that a human form of bipedal locomotion emerged much earlier in time than did a large brain.

3 *Living species*. Fossils cannot speak with a distinct voice. Therefore the past (direct) evidence must be integrated with present (indirect) evidence of living species in order to explain human prehistory. For example, genetically chimpanzees are the closest living relatives to humans. Thus, it is not surprising that early hominids resemble chimpanzees in many features of brain size, dental development, and joint and bone structure. Chimpanzee behavior cannot be identical to that of early hominids; nonetheless, it provides a basis for speculating about some aspects of early hominid behavior, such as object manipulation, communication, and social bonds. Modern gathering-hunting societies illustrate the interrelationships of several aspects of behavior – for example, how food is obtained and processed, by whom and with what kinds of tools; and how subsistence intersects with other activities such as food sharing, care of children and women's work. An approach to the past that combines the fossil and archeological record with the behavior of living chimpanzees and foraging peoples offers ways to look at women's activities and to place hunting and male activities into perspective.

4 *Evolutionary process*. Evolution by natural selection means three things: individuals in a population survive to adulthood, they mate and produce offspring, and they rear their offspring to reproductive age. Given mammalian, and specifically primate, reproduction, females are central in producing and rearing offspring and are a limiting resource in population expansion. Therefore an evolutionary perspective of past human societies must consider the female life cycle and reproductive effort.

To ensure that women are included in the human species, I avoid the use of the generic *man* and adopt the term *humans*. Language shapes our perspective and can structure our thinking. Phrases like "the evolution of man," "the social life of early man," or "mysteries of mankind" are cases in point.

The evolution of social life: contrasting hypotheses

Behavior does not fossilize, yet it is behavior rather than bones and teeth alone that interests us about human evolution. Reconstructions of human behavior that

Table 1   Time chart: Major events in human evolution

Time scale (Years before present)	Events	Possible interpretation of way of life
10,000	Domestication of plants and animals in the Old World	Major changes in family and gender relationships? Food sources concentrated; Permanent settlements
100,000	Spread of *Homo sapiens* throughout Old World	Gathering-hunting well developed
200,000	Origin of *Homo sapiens* in Africa Humans throughout Old World	Expanding resource base Beginning of single hunting in temperate regions?
1,500,000	Human populations into Asia and Europe	Gathering successful in habitats outside Africa
2,500,000	Bone tools, evidence of digging Stone tools; some in association with animal bones; some bones with cutmarks	Effective procurement of plant foods (digging) Occasional butchering of large animals for meat Predation continues Expanding home range size
3,000,000	Hominid fossils in North Central, East, South Africa – 2 or more species	Collecting and sharing wide range of plant foods; predation on small animals
4,000,000	Hominid fossils in East Africa; hominid jaws and teeth *Australopithecus anamensis*	Early hominids adapting to savanna collecting dispersed foods bipedally with organic tools
5,000,000	Divergence of humans and chimpanzees (molecular evidence)	
6–8,000,000	Savanna mosaic habitat becomes widespread in Africa	

developed during the 1960s (and are still very much in evidence) can be summarized as "man the hunter." This view of human evolution is known for its emphasis on meat eating and hunting and on the activities of males. According to this view, distinguishing features of the human way of life encompass a diet in which meat is a main item, in contrast to the presumed vegetarian apes; hunting by males as a means to obtain it, and consequently an early division of labor by sex; pair bonding so males would share meat with their mates and offspring and ensure social stability within the group; and the loss of estrus and acquisition of continual sexual receptivity of females to attract males.

The gathering hypothesis or "woman the gatherer" was developed as a corrective to the omission of women and women's activities in traditional reconstructions; this perspective is useful for keeping gender in human evolution. When first proposed, this view emphasized both the importance of plant foods in the diet and gathering as a method for obtaining plants and small animals for food and as an impetus in the development of the human way of life (Linton 1971; Tanner and Zihlman 1976; Zihlman and Tanner 1978).

In the hunting hypothesis, early hominid behavior is interpreted as a result of men's hunting activities: bipedal locomotion, tool using and making, food sharing, formation of pair bonds, and the sexual division of labor. In contrast, the gathering hypothesis stresses that obtaining plant foods with tools, especially by women, was the basis for the human way of life, and that plants were major food items, a focus for technological innovation and for changes in social behavior. Behaviors once thought to be exclusive to a hunting way of life are equally if not more important to a gathering one: upright posture, bipedal locomotion, and the ability to walk long distances and carry; sharing food, making and using tools; having knowledge and communicating about the environment. Women as well as men were developing these skills.

The gathering hypothesis has been seen in opposition to hunting and as exclusively about women. But a more central issue is timing: when did hunting emerge in human evolution and what preceded it? It is likely that innovations around plant foods developed in the earliest stages of human evolution and that hunting came later in time. There is a great deal of information from the fossil record, studies of the behavior of chimpanzees, and the role of women in contemporary gathering-hunting societies to support the gathering hypothesis. Evidence for utilizing meat from large animals by early hominids appears in the archeological record almost 2 million years after the first appearance of hominids. Unequivocal evidence for hunting is much later in time.

The fossil record and its interpretation

Direct evidence from the australopithecine fossils dated from between 2 and 3 million years ago provide information on diet and development from dentition, locomotion from pelvic and foot bones, hand function from hand bones and body proportions from skeletal remains.

Dentition

All early hominids have large, well worn, thickly enameled molar and premolar teeth. Relative to estimated body size, these teeth are larger than they are in any contemporary ape or human. The corresponding muscles of mastication − the temporalis and masseter − have left well-developed markings on the skull and jaws. These features are associated with a dental mechanism effective for grinding foods that are tough or foods from the ground that are gritty and wear down the teeth (Wallace 1975). The dental mechanism of early hominids is convergent with that of bears and pigs. Thickly enameled posterior teeth are also found among primates, such as orangutans and cebid monkeys, which dentally process fruits with tough outer coverings.

The dental evidence is consistent with an omnivorous diet that probably included various kinds of fruits, seeds and nuts, fibrous vegetation, as well as roots and tubers from underground. Early hominids were very likely eating some animal protein, and their dentition does not rule this out. But features of the chewing apparatus point to a diet that contained many items that required dental preparation. At this early stage in evolution, tool use for extensive preparation of food, such as pounding or cooking, was probably not well developed.

Recent studies on rate of tooth formation and eruption have changed our ideas about the developmental pattern and chronological age of individual fossil hominids (Beynon and Dean 1988). Previously it was supposed that australopithecine maturation was prolonged, as in modern humans, and was a departure from the faster developmental rate in apes (Mann 1975). These new studies now indicate that dental formation is similar to that of chimpanzees, and that growth and development were on a faster rather than a slower track.

Canine teeth in early hominids are small, about the size of the incisors, and show little variation. In contrast, canine teeth of male monkeys and apes are usually notably larger than those of females and are associated with male–male competition or defense against predators. The small canine teeth in hominids indicate little difference in function between females and males but suggest changes in social interaction, especially between males, and in antipredator strategies.

Locomotor anatomy

Bipedal locomotion is a defining characteristic of the human family, the *Hominidae*, and its hallmark is endurance rather than speed (Zihlman and Brunker 1979). There is evidence for this form of locomotion by 3.5 mya based on hominid footprints from Laetoli, Tanzania, although the fossil hominid pelvis, lower limbs and foot bones retain a number of chimpanzee-like features (Leakey and Hay 1979; Stern and Susman 1983). A new first metatarsal almost 2 million years old resembles that of humans more than apes, but its joint surface suggests that the characteristic toe-off mechanism of human gait was absent (Susman and Brain 1988).

Brain and body proportions

More recently discovered fossils indicate that the cranial capacity of hominids between 2 and 3 million years ago is well within the range of chimpanzees (Falk 1987). Brain reorganization as deduced from preserved surfaces of fossil brains may have been minimal and more similar to an ape than to a human pattern. A partial skeleton almost 3 million years old (AL 288, called "Lucy") preserves arm and thigh bones and suggests the body proportions were intermediate between chimpanzee and humans. Compared to chimpanzees, early hominids probably had a lower center of gravity, which would have increased stability in an upright position. Because the fossils are rarely complete or even nearly so (the famous Lucy has 40 per cent of the entire skeleton), it is difficult to establish body size and its range in the population. Some of the fossils, like Lucy, are very small; other individual bones, such as the thigh or foot bones, are quite large. At this time it is not clear how many species of hominids these bones represent and what size range might have existed within each species. This information is important for establishing how much bigger in body size males might have been than females.

Hand bones

Modern human hands have short straight finger bones, well-developed thumb bones and associated muscles, and a mobile palm. In contrast, ape hands have long, curved robust fingers, relatively small thumb bones and associated muscles, and limited mobility in the palm. Fossil hand bones of 3 million years ago are still quite curved and bear resemblance to those of African apes (Susman et al. 1984). However, the palm region indicates greater mobility than that of apes and the potential to grip objects and strongly manipulate them (Marzke 1983). At these hominid sites (Hadar, Ethiopia) no objects are preserved that can be interpreted as hominid tools.

But at a fossil site about 2 million years of age (Swartkrans) newly discovered hominid hand bones and tools are preserved together. The thumb bone suggests well-developed muscles and an ability to grasp tools firmly (Susman 1988). The associated stone and bone artifacts show signs of having been used for digging.

Animals bones and stone tools

For many years the animal bones that had accumulated in South African caves along with the hominids were thought to be the result of hominid activities. Subsequent research on these and other sites demonstrates that bones may accumulate and be modified by natural processes, such as weathering, sorting and transporting by water, trampling by animals, and collecting, breaking, and destruction by carnivore predators and scavengers.

Some of this early research involved comparing the bone collecting behavior and consumption patterns of several species of carnivore, including hyena, cheetah, leopard, porcupine, and owl, with human food remains from Middle and Late Stone Age archeological sites (Brain 1981). This analysis provides a compelling argument that the bone accumulations in the caves were the result of hunting behavior of carnivores (primarily leopards) and that the early hominid bones at the same sites were remains of the hunted and not the hunters. *no man the hunter - yet*

Stones (and a few bones) with unmistakable signs of wear or workmanship show up in the archeological record between 2 and 2.5 million years ago. These implements consist of flakes, choppers, and unmodified pieces that show wear or are of foreign materials transported from another area. The function of stone tools is not always obvious. But now microscopic study of wear patterns on some stone implements suggest that they were used for cutting soft plant materials, for scraping and sawing wood and for cutting animal tissue (Keeley 1977; Keeley and Toth 1981). Flake tools and choppers could have been used to clean, cut up, and pound plant foods, for preparing effective wooden implements or for bashing open marrow cavities of long bones for marrow. New bone tools from Swartkrans found with hand bones and mentioned above show a polish similar to that produced experimentally on bones used for digging in hard ground.

The association of animal bones, stone tools, and hominid remains from East African sites led to the conclusion that the bones were the debris accumulated by hominids at home bases (Isaac 1978). More recent studies indicate that bone breakage and concentration may be due primarily to carnivore activities and make it unlikely that these areas are campsites or home bases as once thought (Potts 1984, 1988).

At a few sites between 1 and 2 million years ago, cutmarks on animal bones may have been made by stone tools and suggest that the hominids were butchering large animals (Bunn 1981; Potts and Shipman 1981). But there is no evidence that the animals butchered were killed by human actions, and it is difficult to establish with any certainty how early people obtained meat prior to 130,000 years ago (Klein 1987). Animal bone and stone tool associations may reflect a mixture of hominid and carnivore activities (Potts 1988). *(or as assumed b/c of assumed male hunting)*

Supporting information from chimpanzees and foraging peoples

The fossil and archeological record of 2–3 million years ago give insight about diet, development, locomotion, and manipulative skills of early hominids. Animal bone accumulations, stone and bone implements and associations with bones help sort out hominid from carnivore activity. Information about chimpanzee behavior offers suggestions about the kinds of behavior that might have been present in the ancestral ape population, and contemporary gathering-hunting societies illuminate the nature of women's roles in a nomadic way of life.

Molecular data

During the 1960s new techniques to study the genetic material of living species revealed that chimpanzees and gorillas were the closest living relatives to humans and the two groups may have separated some 5 million years ago, rather than 20 or 30 mya, as previously thought (Sarich and Wilson 1967). Recent techniques comparing DNA indicate that chimpanzees and humans are more closely related to each other than either is to the gorilla (Sibley and Ahlquist 1984; Williams and Goodman 1989). This close genetic relationship between chimpanzees and humans suggests that the common ancestor to both groups may have resembled chimpanzees more than any other primates. Behaviors observed in chimpanzees may have been present in the common ancestor and early hominids.

Chimpanzee behavior

Chimpanzees in their natural habitat are more similar to humans in a number of behaviors than previously recognized or appreciated. For example, chimpanzees, like humans and most other primates, are best described as omnivorous because they eat a variety of both plant and animal foods; they are not strictly vegeterian (Harding and Teleki 1981). Their diverse diet includes a preponderance of fruits, supplemented by insects and small animals. It is likely that the early hominids, even if relying primarily on plant foods, also preyed upon small animals for food.

Chimpanzees also prepare and use tools, occasionally walk bipedally and communicate social and environmental information (Goodall 1986). Both females and males modify and use materials in a variety of ways – leaves as sponges, twigs as probes to obtain termites, rocks and sticks as hammers to crack open nuts and as missiles. Female chimps spend more time than males fishing for termites and in cracking open nuts more efficiently (Boesch and Boesch 1984; Goodall 1986). The most significant variable related to the sex difference in frequency and efficiency in nut cracking may be social. Adult males prefer to maintain visual contact with other group members and often stop the activity in order to engage in social interactions. Adult females in contrast, continue cracking nuts even if there is a conflict or if the group moves on.

Sharing food among chimpanzees was first reported in the context of predation and eating meat, with adult males sharing more frequently (Goodall 1968; Teleki 1973). As more data were collected, it became apparent that plants are widely shared, and over half the instances occur between mother and offspring pairs. Most of the food shared is plant material and most sharing (in 86 per cent of instances) is between related individuals (McGrew 1975; Silk 1978).

Among pygmy chimpanzees (*Pan paniscus*) food sharing seems to occur more frequently than is the case for *Pan troglodytes* (Kano 1982; Kuroda 1984). Juvenile animals are the most frequent recipients, and adult females are donors four times more often than are adult males.

Long-term studies on several species of free-ranging primates demonstrate that chimpanzees, like other primates, form relationships between mothers and offspring and among siblings that endure throughout life. These small family groups form the social core in most primate species. Primatologists discovered that rank and status in the group passes from mothers to their offspring, a contrast to previous assumptions that dominance rank is something earned simply by the fighting abilities of big and strong males (Sade 1972; see Fedigan and Fedigan 1989).

Chimpanzee social organization is flexible (fission–fusion type) and suited to ranging over many square miles in search of food. Groups change in size and composition and are not headed by a leader male. Friendships and kin ties influence the day to day associations of animals. An extensive communicative repertoire of postures, gestures, vocalizations and facial expressions permits varied and complex responses to different social situations.

Like group composition, sexual activity is variable with several patterns: opportunistic or noncompetitive mating where a female in estrus may mate with several different males during a single cycle; or a short-term exclusive relationship where a male prevents other males from mating with his temporary mate; or a consortship where a male and female leave the group for a week or more and remain away from other chimpanzees (Tutin 1979). No single mating pattern accurately describes this highly social species.

Female chimpanzees spend most of their adult life pregnant and lactating and invest more time and energy in rearing offspring than do males. Adult males in chimpanzee groups are generally protective of all infants and young; and through patrolling territorial boundaries maintain the home range of the chimpanzee community from neighboring males.

In their omnivorous diet, object manipulation, social development, flexibility in sexual activity, and fission–fusion social organization, chimpanzees may resemble the early hominids and illustrate the active role females play in this range of activities. There is a tendency to emphasize the differences between chimpanzees and ourselves. But for this early period of human evolution it is instructive to emphasize our similarities with chimpanzees and the continuity between the ape ancestor and the earliest hominids.

Gathering-hunting peoples

A nomadic, gathering-hunting way of life persisted in some form from the time of human origins 5 million years or so ago. Only after about 10,000 years ago did human populations begin to settle down in some parts of the world, to cultivate plants and domesticate animals. Therefore, modern-day nomadic peoples provide a more realistic model for helping to conceptualize early hominid societies than do Western industrialized ones.

The significance of gathering first became apparent at the same conference on "hunting-gathering" peoples, where Washburn and Lancaster and Laughlin presented their ideas on hunting (Lee and DeVore 1968). Several studies reported that the majority of tropical hunter-gatherer groups in Africa, Asia, Australia, and North America subsists mainly on plant foods gathered by women, or on fish, and much less by hunting *per se*. In actuality most such groups are "gatherer-hunters," which led Lee and DeVore (1968) to conclude that vegetable foods were probably always available and that early hominid women likely played an active role in subsistence – collecting food, making and using tools, as well as caring for infants.

The savanna mosaic environment illustrated by the bushveldt and woodlands of the Kalahari in southern Africa contains many species of plants that are used for food, medicine, and materials for making many kinds of tools. One population, for example, utilizes 80 plant species as food, 11 of which are staple items in the diet. These include various types of melon, beans, roots, tubers, leaves and gum; they are tasty, nutritious, abundant, predictable and accessible. These people also hunt or gather some 50 kinds of animals, though their role in overall diet varies seasonally (Tanaka 1980). The heavy reliance on plant foods of tropical savanna gatherer-hunters contrasts with earlier assumptions that the main food items in a savanna environment would necessarily be meat.

The task of gathering food falls primarily to women. They go out collecting, often with other women, carrying their nursing infants, their digging implements and sharpening stone; the kaross, a garment made of animal skin, serves as a baby sling, as well as a container for gathered food (Lee 1968, 1969). The work effort of women is considerable, and they frequently walk long distances and carry heavy loads. It is not unusual for a woman to return home after a journey of several miles, carrying the equivalent of 75 per cent of her body weight in food, firewood and baby (Lee 1979; Peacock 1985). Among the Kalahari San, women carry their babies continually for the first two years, an estimated 2400 km, which decreases to 1800 km in the third year and 1200 by age four (Lee 1979). Children of this age weigh from about 6 to 15 kg, which is added to the food and goods a woman might carry. After children are weaned they remain in camp with other adults and children while the mother again goes out gathering. Women are responsible for about 90 per cent of child care (Lee 1979).

Women also contribute protein to the diet. Killing birds and small mammals with a club or collecting tortoises and insects can be considered a form of gathering. Women may report back to camp on the animals and tracks observed while gathering, and this information may be used later by men during hunting. Men also gather food, but this may consist of picking and eating plants while hunting, though occasionally men return from hunting with plants, birds' eggs, or firewood. Women among the Kalahari San do not hunt by bow and arrow, but in some cultures they do (Estioko-Griffin and Griffin 1981).

Overall, the picture of women we now have from gathering-hunting societies is one of active, mobile individuals, who walk long distances, carry heavy loads, and contribute a major source of food to their families. They prepare food, use tools, and at the same time become pregnant, lactate, and care for children.

Early hominid behavior from a woman's perspective

Locomotion and travel

Bipedal locomotion is a terrestrial, savanna adaptation for covering long distances while carrying food and water, digging sticks, objects for defense, and offspring. A large home range is necessary for obtaining the widely dispersed resources on the savanna, especially of plant foods. The evidence suggests that both women and men engaged in these activities.

For women there are social aspects of bipedal locomotion. A hominid mother probably carried and nursed her baby almost continually for three years, as do chimpanzees and women in foraging societies. Without a grasping foot like that of chimpanzees to cling to their mother's hair, hominid babies could not hold on to their mothers as well. Consequently the mother had to take a more active role in carrying the infant. A sling for support might have been an early hominid "tool" that would have freed the mother's arms and hands for other activities.

Tool making and using

Stone tools persist better through time than food plants or implements made from organic materials, but both were probably important in early hominid subsistence (Lee 1968). Given the importance of organic tools among gatherer-hunters and the facility of chimpanzees with grass stems and twigs and wooden hammers, many implements used by early hominids were probably made of organic material and used for digging. This type of implement may represent a straightforward transition from chimpanzee termiting sticks to the simple, multi-purpose digging tools of modern gatherer-hunters (see Spector and Whelan, 1989). Similarly, the stones used by chimpanzees for cracking open nutshells would not be readily recognized as tools in the archeological record.

Development and learning

If the hominid way of life depended upon bipedal locomotion and making and using tools, then from a child's point of view, the gathering way of life required extended time to acquire motor and cognitive skills. In turn, it required a long dependence on adults (Zihlman 1983). An early hominid child could not be physically independent until it was weaned and could walk long distances. For chimpanzees this occurs about age 5, but a contemporary child does not develop the stamina to walk long distances until about age 8.

A young chimpanzee does not master the art of termiting with tools until about age 5, and skills for cracking open nuts with stone and wooden hammers are not developed until adolescence. Presumably it would have taken an early hominid child at least 5 years to learn motor and cognitive skills for using tools effectively. Learning these, as well as social skills, would have taken place within the protective social environment of the mother and group, and so equipped the young to survive, reproduce and rear offspring.

Mating patterns and sexuality

Although early hominid mating patterns are usually presented as monogamous or pair bonded, these suggestions can only be speculative. Nonetheless, I would conjecture that mating patterns were variable, as they are among chimpanzees, and stress flexibility and female choice. The dependency of young after weaning would have been facilitated if males, as well as females, shared food and cared for the young. The males need not have been the biological fathers. They might have developed friendships that have been described for female and male baboons and chimpanzees. Females might view males with these traits as more sexually attractive and so choose them as mates. The small canine teeth in early hominids suggest that social changes occurred among early hominids, perhaps a reduction in aggression among males, and between females and males, compared to chimpanzees.

Sexual division of labor

The nature of a sexual division of labor and when it developed during human evolution have been major issues for theories of human evolution. In human societies it is reciprocal and expected. Among chimpanzees there are differences in frequency of tasks by sex and by age, but there is no formalized sharing or exchange. Early hominids were probably more similar to this pattern than to that of gatherer-hunters. My own view is that the sexual division of labor as we know it today probably developed quite recently in human evolution, perhaps in the Later Pleistocene when hunting begins to be effective, or even later when people began to live in settlements and give up a nomadic way of life.

Summary

Information derived from the fossil record, primate behavior, and gatherer-hunters gives a firm basis for delineating women's reproductive, economic, and social activities and contributions to human evolution. We can conclude that women made and used tools to obtain food for themselves, as well as to sustain their young after weaning; walked long distances; and carried food and infants bipedally on the African savannas (Tanner 1981; Tanner and Zihlman 1976). It is also reasonable to conclude that hunting did not emerge at the earliest stage in human evolution. Rather, hunting probably developed much later in human history and derived from the technological and social base in gathering (Zihlman 1978, 1981).

There are limitations to what the record of human prehistory can reveal about the behavior of women and men. Details of social behavior can never be known with any certainty and will always be a focus for conjecture and debate. But a balanced understanding of human evolution should incorporate women as well as men, children as well as adults into the picture and include the range of activities throughout the life cycle on which natural selection acts, rather than a narrower focus on one or two of them. It is as much through the willingness to incorporate the available information as it is through the information itself that we can gain a more complete view of our ancient human ancestors.

■ ■ ■

References

Beynon, A. D. and M. C. Dean (1988) Distinct Dental Development Patterns in Early Fossil Hominids. *Nature* 335: 509–514.

Boesch, C., and Helwig Boesch (1984) Possible Causes of Sex Differences in the Use of Natural Hammers by Wild Chimpanzees. *Journal of Human Evolution* 10: 585–593.

Brain, C. K. (1981) *The Hunters or the Hunted? An Introduction to African Cave Taphonomy*. Chicago: University of Chicago Press.

Bunn, H. T. (1981) Archaeological Evidence for Meat-Eating by Plio-Pleistocene Hominids from Koobi Fora and Olduvai Gorge. *Nature* 291: 574–577.

Estioko-Griffin, Agnes and P. Bion Griffin (1981) "Woman the Hunter: The Agta". In *Woman the Gatherer*. F. Dahlberg (ed.) pp. 121–151. New Haven: Yale University Press.

Falk, Dean (1987) Hominid Paleoneurology. *Annual Review of Anthropology* 16: 13–30.

Fedigan, L. M. and L. Fedigan (1989) Gender and the Study of the Primates. In *Gender and Anthropology*: Critical Reviews for Research and Teaching. S. Morgen (ed.) pp. 41–64. Washington, DC. American Anthropological Association.

Goodall, Jane (1968) The Behaviour of Free-living Chimpanzees in the Gombe Stream Reserve. *Animal Behavior Monographs* 1: 165–311.

—— (1986) *The Chimpanzees of Gombe*. Cambridge: Harvard University Press.

Harding, R. S. O. and G. Teleki (eds) (1981) *Omnivorous Primates: Gathering and Hunting in Human Evolution*. New York: Columbia University Press.

Isaac, G. L. (1978) The Foodsharing Behavior of Protohuman Hominids. *Scientific American* 238(4):90–108.

Kano, T. (1982) The Social Group of Pygmy Chimpanzees (*Pan paniscus*) of Wamba. *Primates* 23:171–188.

Keeley, L. H. (1977) The Functions of Paleolithic Flint Tools. *Scientific American* 237(5):108–126.

Keeley, L. H. and N. Toth (1981) Microwear Polishes on Early Stone Tools from Koobi Fora, Kenya. *Nature* 293:464–465.

Klein, R. G. (1987) Reconstructing How Early People Exploited Animals: Problems and Prospects. In *The Evolution of Human Hunting*. M. Nitecki and D. Nitecki (eds), pp. 11–45. New York: Plenum.

Kuroda, S. (1984) Interaction over Food among Pygmy Chimpanzees. In *The Pygmy Chimpanzee: Evolutionary Biology and Behavior*. R. L. Susman (ed.) pp. 301–324. New York: Plenum.

Lancaster, J. B. (1989) Women in Biosocial Perspective. In *Gender and Anthropology: Critical Reviews for Research and Teaching*. S. Morgen (ed.) pp. 95–115. Washington, DC: American Anthropological Association.

Leakey, Mary D. and R. L. Hay (1979) Pliocene Footprints in the Laetolil Beds at Laetoli, Northern Tanzania. *Nature* 278:317–323.

Lee, R. B. (1968) What Hunters Do for a Living or How to Make Out on Scarce Resources. In *Man the Hunter*. R. B. Lee and I. De Vore (eds) pp. 30–48. Chicago: Aldine.

—— (1969) !Kung Bushman Subsistence: An Input-Output Analysis. In *Ecological Studies in Cultural Anthropology*. P. Vayda (ed.), pp. 47–79. Garden City, NY: Natural History Press.

—— (1979) *The !Kung San: Men, Women and Work in a Foraging Society*, Cambridge: Cambridge University Press.

Lee, R. B. and I. DeVore (1968) *Man the Hunter*. Chicago: Aldine.

Linton, Sally (1971) "Woman the Gatherer: Male Bias in Anthropology". In *Women in Cross-Cultural Perspective*. Sue-Ellen Jacob (ed.) Champaign: University of Illinois Press. Reprinted under Sally Slocum in *Toward an Anthropology of Women*, 1975 R. Rapp Reiter (ed.) pp. 36–50. New York: Monthly Review Press.

Mann, Alan (1975) Paleodemographic Aspects of the South African *Australopithecines*. *Anthropology Publications* No. 1. Philadelphia: University of Pennsylvania Press.

Marzke, M. (1983) Joint Functions and Grips of the *Australopithecus afarensis* Hand, with Special Reference to the Region of the Capitate. *Journal of Human Evolution* 12:197–211.

McGrew, W. C. (1975) Patterns of Plant Food Sharing by Wild Chimpanzees. Proceedings of the 5th Congress, International Primatology Society (Nagoya, Japan), pp. 304–309.

Peacock, Nadine (1985) Time Allocation, Work and Fertility among Efe Pygmy Women of Northeast Zaire. PhD dissertation, Harvard University.

Potts, R. (1984) Home Bases and Early Hominids. *American Scientist* 72:338–347.

—— (1988) *Early Hominid Activities at Olduvai*. Hawthorne, NY: Aldine de Gruyter.

Potts, R. and Pat Shipman (1981) Cutmarks Made by Stone Tools on Bones from Olduvai Gorge, Tanzania. *Nature* 291:577–580.

Sade, D. S. (1972) A Longitudinal Study of Social Behavior of Rhesus Monkeys. In *Functional and Evolutionary Biology of Primates*. R. H. Tuttle (ed.) pp. 378–398. Chicago: Aldine.

Sarich, V. M., and A. C. Wilson (1967) Immunological Time Scale for Hominid Evolution. *Science* 158:1200–1203.

Sibley, C. B. and J. Ahlquist (1984) The Phylogeny of the Hominoid Primates as Indicated by DNA–DNA hybridization. *Journal of Molecular Evolution* 20:2–15.

Silk, J. B. (1978) Patterns of Food Sharing among Mother and Infant Chimpanzees at Gombe National Park, Tanzania. *Folia Primatologica* 29:129–141.

Spector, J. D. and M. K. Whelan (1989) Incorporating gender into archaeology classes, in Sandra Morgan (ed.) *Gender and Anthropology: Critical Reviews for Research and Teaching*, Washington, DC: American Anthropological Association, pp. 65–94.

Stern, J. and R. L. Susman (1983) The Locomotor Anatomy of *Australopithecus afarensis*. *American Journal of Physical Anthropology* 60:279–318.

Susman, R. L. (1988) Hand of *Paranthropus robustus* from Member 1, Swartkrans: Fossil Evidence for Tool Behavior. *Science* 240:781–783.

Susman, R. L. and T. M. Brain (1988) New First Metatarsal (SKX 5017) from Swartkrans and the Gait of *Paranthropus robustus*. *American Journal of Physical Anthropology* 77:7–15.

Susman, R. L., J. T. Stern and W. L. Jungers (1984) Arboreality and Bipedality in the Hadar Hominids. *Folia primatologica* 43:113–156.

Tanaka, J. (1980) *The San Hunter-Gatherers of the Kalahari*. Tokyo: Tokyo University Press.

Tanner, Nancy (1981) *On Becoming Human*. New York: Cambridge University Press.

Tanner, Nancy and Adrienne Zihlman (1976) Women in Evolution: Innovation and Selection in Human Origins. *Signs* 1(3 pt. 1):585–608.

Teleki, G. (1973) The Omnivorous Chimpanzee. *Scientific American* 228 (I):33–42.

Tutin, Caroline E. G. (1979) Mating Patterns and Reproductive Strategies in a Community of Wild Chimpanzees *(Pan troglodytes schweinfurthii). Behavioral Ecology and Sociobiology* 6:29–38.

Wallace, J. A. (1975) Dietary Adaptations of *Australopithecus* and *Early Homo*. In *Paleoanthropology, Morphology and Paleoecology*. R. H. Tuttle (ed.) pp. 203–223. The Hague: Mouton.

Williams, S. A., and M. Goodman (1989) A Statistical Test That Supports a Human/Chimpanzee Clade Based on Noncoding DNA Sequence Data. *Molecular Biology and Evolution* 6:325–330.

Zihlman, A. L. (1978) Women in Evolution, Part II. Subsistence and Social Organization Among Early Hominids. *Signs* 4(1):4–20.

—— (1981) Women as Shapers of the Human Adaptation. In *Woman the Gatherer*. Frances Dahlberg (ed.) pp. 75–120. New Haven: Yale University Press.

—— (1983) A Behavioral Reconstruction of *Australopithecus*. In *Hominid Origins: Inquiries Past and Present*, K. J. Reichs (ed.) pp. 207–238. Washington, DC: University Press of America.

Zihlman, A. L., and Lynda Brunker (1979) Hominid Bipedalism: Then and Now. *Yearbook of Physical Anthropology* 22:132–162.

Zihlman, A. L. and N. Tanner (1978) Gathering and the Hominid Adaptation. In *Female Hierarchies*. L. Tiger and H. Fowler (eds) pp. 163–194. Chicago: Beresford Book Service.

Chapter 6

AN AXE TO GRIND: MORE RIPPING YARNS
FROM AUSTRALIAN PREHISTORY

Sheila M. McKell

Despite the fact that much of a positive nature has been said over
the past decade or so within the discipline of social anthropology
with respect to sex roles and gender in foraging societies (for
example, Draper 1975; Leacock 1978; Bell 1983; Tiffany 1984;
Moore 1988), this discussion has had little or no impact on archaeological theory. Therefore this chapter will attempt to illuminate
the masculinist nature of the greater amount of archaeology practised within Australia at the present time. It will briefly review
some of the current models of human evolution and how women
are portrayed within them, question the appropriateness of the
gatherer/hunter distinction as a means of categorising foraging societies, and introduce the concept of gender and gender systems as
a tool to allow us a better understanding of prehistoric lifeways.
Finally it will examine the potential that ethnoarchaeological
research within Australia has or could have in providing some
possible answers to the issues that I will render problematical.

In a previous discussion of the following issues (McKell 1989)
I critiqued some of the current models of human evolution and
was especially interested in how women are portrayed in them.
Most of the literature on which these models are based have a
white European male bias which either completely ignored women's
activities or trivialised them as being secondary to male activities
(Ardrey 1961; Morris 1967; Tiger 1969; Wilson 1975). One classic
example of this bias can be seen in the "man the hunter" myth
which has led to the popular notion that male hunting was the
pivotal adaptation that separated hominids from the primates. Males
using tools and cooperating, behaviours which they see as essential for hunting large animals, were also bringing meat back to the

home base to share with the dependent females and their young, that is their family, the *homo erectus* family so similar to our own. The proponents of this model appeal to the archaeological record to validate these highly speculative scenarios but there is no archaeological evidence to back the man myths because the so called "tools" men and women used would have been essentially organic and therefore not preserved in the archaeological record (Washburn and Lancaster 1968).

With an eventual increase in awareness that there was no archaeological evidence to back the ideas proposed in the "man the hunter" myth and in the face of much negative evidence, man the hunter became "man the provisioner" who, instead of hunting, now provisions the dependent female and her young with gathered food. Here we are still confronted with the same basic ideas with respect to the primitive nuclear family where males are still viewed as pivotal in the selection process and women still dependent (Lovejoy 1981).

In reaction to the explicitly sexist scenarios outlined above, feminist anthropologists outlined a theory in which it is argued that the distribution and sharing of gathered, rather than hunted, food, by women rather than men, initiated the complex exchange behaviours that gradually evolved into social roles and reciprocal obligations. This issue of food sharing is particularly important with respect to mother/child interactions. As the period of infancy lengthened, mothers probably continued to share food with their young after weaning. This could lead to sharing among matrilines and then between child and parent, the effects of which would be that adults would live longer and the children could benefit from the acquired knowledge. The end result of the sharing discussed above would be that women needed to provide more food for their increasingly dependent young, therefore a digging stick and some sort of receptacle, which would ultimately become a baby-carrier, was needed. The implications of this is that the selection pressure would be on females rather than on males. While this proposal has to some extent brought women into the prehistoric picture, we are still limited by the restrictive categories of men hunting and women gathering (Slocum 1975; Zihlman 1978; Zihlman and Tanner 1978; McGrew 1981).

Conkey and Spector (1984) suggest that there are three major problems associated with the man myths, especially when archaeologists make use of them in their studies of more recent societies. They tend to be gender exclusive and they mostly assume a division of labour by sex. This is often carried over into the linking of artefacts by sex and the prevalence of value-laden male activities, that is, women's activities are not given equal coverage. They argue that the discipline of archaeology is not as free from cultural values as its practitioners would have us believe. Archaeology has substantiated through its theories, the projection of these cultural sex stereotypes into not only the recent past but into the far distant past as well. This is a situation which impacts more on the probable roles of women than on men.

The hunting model, which stresses the critical importance of a sexual division of labour and that meat procured by male hunting was the major source of nutrient, has persisted even when confronted by evidence to the contrary. In 1968 Lee and

DeVore suggested that it was now necessary to review models such as these with a view to changing them in the face of much ethnographic evidence which suggests that societies which depend primarily on hunting for their subsistence are few in number and most utilise resources such as plant food, fish and shellfish. Since then we have also been made aware of the importance, both throughout human evolution and in contemporary foraging societies, of the very substantial amount of food gathered by women.

In defence of the gatherer/hunter distinction the suggestion has been made on a number of occasions, especially by the proponents of the man myth, that women are biologically incapable of hunting. In a brief review of the ethnographic literature we find a number of societies in which women hunt and use stone tools. Among these are the Ainu of Japan who, although the women cannot touch men's hunting equipment, stress that it is for religious reasons rather than some psychological or physiological deficiency on the part of women (Watanabe 1968). The Agta women of the Philippines hunt in treacherous rainforest with babies on their backs (Estioko-Griffin 1984). Amongst the Batek De' of Malaysia each person respects the capabilities of the other. There is no sexual division of labour therefore if a woman wants to hunt she is free to do so. Conversely, if a man wishes to gather tubers he has that same freedom of choice. Neither sexes' contribution is considered less than the other and each has equal access when food is shared (Endicott 1981). Again, amongst the Mbuti of Zaire, women hunt using bow and arrows and spears and play a large part in net hunting which is a team activity. Once more we find that amongst the Mbuti women their physiological functions are in no way viewed as a hindrance (Estioko-Griffin and Griffin 1981).

I would emphasise at this point that the behaviours outlined above have some very real implications for the theory, methodology and interpretations of the archaeological record. Conkey and Spector (1984) suggest that when archaeologists argue that women are invisible archaeologically because of the differential preservation of stone, bone and plant material, this should be viewed as a diversionary tactic. The real problem lies in the imposition of the strict sexual division of labour, which also has all the characteristics of sex roles in our own society, and blinds archaeologists to women in the archaeological record. The end result of the imposition of this inflexible sexual division of labour and the material remains associated with it, which has its origins in and is best exemplified by the man the hunter model, is that subsistence activities such as gathering and hunting are assigned exclusively to one sex or the other. This situation is further exacerbated as the artefacts are also assigned according to these sex roles. That is, men use stone tools and women do not (Conkey and Spector 1984).

Yet again, a search through the Australian literature is revealing with these ideas in mind, in that as early as 1847 the explorer Leichhardt noted some women on the Isaac River in the Herbert/Burdekin area using hafted stone axes to extract a bee's nest from a tree (Leichhardt 1847). On Bathurst Island the Tiwi woman's axe was of vital importance to her when out hunting. Today their axes are made of steel but in the past they used edge ground stone axes. The Tiwi women considered the ground edge axe to be superior to the flaked tools which they suggest were made in a hurry. The women also made and hafted their own stone axes. As one old woman said "In old days, I can't make proper axe so my aunti [sic] make me good one. She makes lots of good axe" (Goodale 1971:155). When the Tiwi women went bush hunting they used their axe as a primary tool and to make their own digging sticks (Goodale 1971). Hamilton (1987) notes that women in the Western Desert used stone axes, choppers and adzes. A horsehoof core was used to chop mulga wood for their digging sticks and when shaping a coolamon they used a sharp edged stone, flaking it as it blunted, and then an adze to finish it off. If these stone axes were to be excavated in Australia today the archaeologist would almost always assume that they were used by men as primary tools and again by men to make secondary tools for women.

One particularly good example of the visibility of women archaeologically is in a site in northwest Arnhem Land on one of the Nourlangie Rock outliers. The site is Anbangbang 1 and it is unusual in that it has a high concentration of organic remains, especially remains of women's activities, unusually well preserved in the upper level. Whilst recognising the many pitfalls associated with trying to identify the differences between male and female activities in the material remains, several authors (Jones 1985; Jones and Johnson 1985; Clarke 1988, 1989) have suggested that some of the material remains are indicative of women's activities. This unusual preservation of organic material allows us an insight into an Aboriginal community's daily routine that has never been possible previously. A large proportion of the plant food deposited in the site would also have been obtained by women, as would the turtles, terrapins, crocodile eggs, goannas and freshwater mussels (Jones and Johnson 1985). There were 35 pieces of two, three and four ply string made from wood, hair and fur and a piece of woven dilly bag all known ethnographically to be made by women. Also recovered from the site but not necessarily deposited there by women were adze/chisels, slugs, scrapers, a grinding slab, bone tools, ochre, gum resin, 38 wooden tools, barbed points, bamboo goose spears, firesticks, wood shavings and animal fur (Jones 1985: 60–5). Jones and Johnson (1985) suggest that the large number of quartzite leilira blades contained in the site are also indicative of women's activities. Elsewhere in the literature these blades are also referred to as being women's knives in the Central Desert (Mulvaney 1989). Again as with the Tiwi women's axes the suggestion is made that the women at Anbangbang 1 were using them not only as primary tools but to make their own wooden secondary tools. The preservation in this site is highly unusual and it therefore presents a unique opportunity to examine those aspects of Aboriginal subsistence activities usually absent from the archaeological record in the tropics, that is, women's activities.

Language is a major obstacle to change in archaeology as it does not have the ability to represent difference without hierarchy. Basically what has happened in response to the recent feminist criticism in archaeology overseas is that some attempts have been made to remove sexist language in the literature. While this is to be applauded, what we now have is a genderless pre-history and, people being what they are, if you do not specify the sex of an individual they will presume it to be male. Spector and Whelan (1989) report that the "man the hunter" myth still appears in the literature, albeit in muted form. While some authors have questioned the validity of the theory, but not the imposition of the division of labour, most preferred to find fault with the model on other grounds and none referred to the debate between feminists and others. As was mentioned earlier, women have merely been superimposed onto the same old sexist myths, that is, woman the gatherer on to the man the hunter myths and in doing so many prehistorians believe that the "women problem" has gone away. Within Australia these problems are best exemplified in a recent publication by Thorne and Raymond (1989). While women are indeed given credit for collecting most of the food, we are still given the impression of a sexual division of labour in which men hunt and women gather. An even more insidious bias in the chapter on gatherer/hunters is that there is only one illumination of a Tasmanian Aboriginal woman and that is a sketch drawn by Nicholas Petit in 1802 (Thorne and Raymond 1989: 68). The woman is breast feeding her baby and, whilst acknowledging that the woman is fulfilling a biological function necessary to the survival of the species, she is not shown carrying out any of the many economic activities that women in foraging societies engage in, whereas the other half dozen pictures of men show them fishing, hunting, collecting turtle eggs and mangrove worms. So while the intention of the author might have been to give an even-handed coverage of the tasks that both men and women engage in, visually, the overall impression one is left with is that male subsistence activities are more important than female activities. What is missing in archaeology at the present time is a theory that encompasses human behaviour in its totality, both male and female, and which is free from western sex stereotypes and assumptions with respect to the supposed capabilities of the sexes in other societies.

Some recent ethnoarchaeological studies have shown the adaptability, or flexibility, of the sex roles in contemporary gatherer/hunter subsistence behaviour (Estioko-Griffin and Griffin 1981; Meehan 1982; Cane 1984; Estioko-Griffin 1984). They have also made us aware that many of our anthropological models to date are inadequate and allowed us to envision alternate scenarios. There is a need to move away from the restrictive categories of "hunting" and "gathering" and to become more aware of the potential variability of what people do in other cultures today and in the past. What is needed now are many more ethnoarchaeological studies along the lines suggested by Davidson (1988) which will allow us to learn more about the actual, rather than the assumed, dimensions of sex and gender roles in contemporary foraging societies (Conkey and Spector 1984).

Ethnoarchaeology has the potential to illuminate gender roles but anthropologists have to first transform the perspectives that they have of gender in non-Western societies. This can be achieved through familiarising oneself with certain aspects of feminist anthropological research. It is in this way that anthropologists who have an interest in gender will be able to formulate a theory of human behaviour that can recognise and encompass the differences in gender roles cross-culturally and how these might be expressed materially (Conkey and Spector 1984).

For whatever reason, an awareness of these various arguments has not, to any great extent, filtered through to the discipline of archaeology within Australia and neither has there been any systematic study of the concept of gender in archaeology. Again what is needed in the discipline is a feminist critique to expose the inherent biases and the adoption of new concepts and methods for the archaeological study of gender. By placing gender at the centre of our studies we can generate new unimagined scenarios. There has been a tremendous amount of new research in social anthropology which has shown how variable gender is cross-culturally, that is, some activities will be valued differently from others. One would hope that the recognition of this variability would argue against rash generalisations, but unfortunately archaeologists within Australia still persist in promoting their ethnocentric ideas with respect to the supposed capabilities of the sexes (Spector and Whelan 1989).

Spector argues that, when assessing the variability in male/female activity patterns, we must move beyond the gatherer/hunter distinction as each of these two categories has a number of smaller tasks within it that can be organised in an infinite number of ways cross-culturally. We must recognise that each task contains information about group composition, the environment, location, season, frequency, duration, all artefacts and any other objects associated with the task, traces of which should be identifiable in the material and spatial organisation of sites. Once we have developed an awareness of the cross-cultural variability of gender, with this method we will then be in a position to appreciate the variety of possible responses to changes in the physical and social environment throughout pre-history (Spector and Whelan 1989).

A basic tenet of archaeology is that the past is knowable, that is, that there is a relationship between people's activities, the types of sites and the contents which make up the archaeological record (Schiffer 1976). Information with respect to gender is no different, it is often visible, but archaeologists need to revise their concepts and methods in order to understand how it might be expressed. Binford (1962) suggests that all cultural behaviour is visible, that is, has a material correlation. Therefore if, as has been suggested by Conkey and Spector (1984), gender is a cultural phenomenon, its material manifestations should be as visible archaeologically as any other culturally determined behaviour.

Some final solutions would be to stress the need to problematise the idea of gender and where possible in our writings present a balanced treatment of male and female activities. Most importantly, we have to recognise difference rather than universals and to assume we don't know what gender configurations were throughout prehistory instead of the wholesale transfer of an assumed sexual division of labour onto the past.

■ ■ ■

References

Ardrey, R. (1961) *African Genesis: A Personal Investigation into the Animal Origins and Nature of Man*. New York: Atheneum.

Bell, D. (1983) *Daughters of the Dreaming*. Melbourne: McPhee Gribble Publishers.

Binford, L. (1962) Archaeology as anthropology. *American Antiquity* 28(2): 217–25.

Cane, S. (1984) Desert Camps: A case study of some artefacts and Aboriginal behaviour in the Western Desert. Unpublished Ph.D thesis, The Australian National University, Canberra.

Clarke, A. (1988) Archaeological and ethnobotanical interpretations of plant remains from Kakadu National Park. In B. Meehan and R. Jones (eds) *Archaeology with Ethnography: An Australian Perspective*, pp. 123–36. Canberra: Department of Prehistory, Research School of Pacific Studies, The Australian National University. *Occasional Papers in Prehistory*, No. 15.

—— (1989) Macroscopic plant remains. In W. Beck, A. Clarke and L. Head (eds) *Plants in Australian Archaeology*. St. Lucia, Brisbane: University of Queensland. *Tempus* 1:54–84.

Conkey, M. and J. Spector (1984) Archaeology and the study of gender. In M. B. Schiffer (ed.) *Advances in Archaeological Method and Theory* 7:1–29. New York: Academic Press.

Davidson, I. (1988) The naming of parts: Ethnography and the interpretation of Australian prehistory. In B. Meehan and R. Jones (eds) *Archaeology with Ethnography: An Australian Perspective*, pp. 17–33. Canberra: Department of Prehistory, Research School of Pacific Studies, The Australian National University. *Occasional Papers in Prehistory*, No. 15.

Draper, P. (1975) !Kung women: Contrasts in sexual egalitarianism in foraging and sedentary contexts. In R. R. Reiter (ed.) *Toward an Anthropology of Women*, pp. 77–110. New York: Monthly Review Press.

Endicott, K. L. (1981) The conditions of egalitarian male-female relationships in foraging societies. *Canberra Anthropology* 4(2):1–10.

Estioko-Griffin, A. and P. B. Griffin (1981) Woman the hunter: The Agta. In F. Dahlberg (ed.) *Woman the Gatherer*, pp. 121–51. New Haven: Yale University Press.

Estioko-Griffin, A. (1984) The ethnography of south-eastern Cagayan Agta hunting. Unpublished MA thesis, Department of Anthropology, University of the Philippines, Diliman, Quezon City.

Goodale, J. C. (1971) *Tiwi Wives: A Study of the Women of Melville Island, North Australia*. Seattle: University of Washington Press.

Hamilton, A. (1987) Dual social system: Technology, labour and women's secret rites in the eastern Western Desert of Australia. In W. H. Edwards (ed.) *Traditional Aboriginal Society: A Reader*, pp. 34–53. Melbourne: The Macmillan Company of Australia Pty Ltd.

Jones, R. (1985) Archaeological conclusions. In R. Jones (ed.) *Archaeological Research in Kakadu National Park*, pp. 291–8. Canberra: Department of Prehistory, Research School of Pacific Studies, The Australian National University. *Special Publication* No. 1.

Jones, R. and I. Johnson (1985) Rockshelter excavations: Nourlangie and Mt Brockman massifs. In R. Jones (ed.) *Archaeological Research in Kakadu National Park*, pp. 39–71. Canberra: Department of Prehistory, Research School of Prehistory, The Australian National University. *Special Publication*, No. 1.

Leacock, E. (1978) Women's status in egalitarian society: Implications for social evolution. *Current Anthropology* 19(2):247–75.

Leichhardt, L. (1847) *Journal of an Overland Expedition in Australia from Moreton Bay to Port Essington, a Distance of Upwards of 3,000 Miles, During the Years 1844–1845.* Adelaide: Australiana Facsimile Editions 16 (1964).

Lovejoy, C. O. (1981) The Origin of Man. *Science* 211(4480):341–50.

McGrew, W. C. (1981) The female chimpanzee as a human evolutionary prototype. In F. Dahlberg (ed.) *Woman the Gatherer*, pp. 35–73. New Haven: Yale University Press.

McKell, S. M. (1989) "Women never hunt" and other ripping yarns from prehistory. Unpublished B. A. (Hons) thesis, James Cook University of North Queensland, Townsville.

Meehan, B. (1982) *Shell Bed to Shell Midden.* Canberra: Australian Institute of Aboriginal Studies.

Moore, H. L. (1988) *Feminism and Anthropology.* Cambridge: Polity Press.

Morris, D. (1967) *The Naked Ape.* New York: McGraw-Hill.

Mulvaney, D. J. (1969) *The Prehistory of Australia.* London: Thames and Hudson.

Reiter, R. R. (1977) The search for origins: Unravelling the threads of gender hierarchy. *Critique of Anthropology* 3:5–24.

Schiffer, M. (1976) *Behavioral Archaeology.* New York: Academic Press.

Slocum, S. (1975) Woman the gatherer: Male bias in anthropology. In R. R. Reiter (ed.) *Toward an Anthropology of Women*, pp. 36–51. New York: Monthly Review Press.

Spector, J. and M. K. Whelan (1989) Incorporating gender into archaeology courses. In S. Morgen (ed.) *Gender and Anthropology: Critical Reviews for Research and Teaching.* pp. 65–94. Washington, DC: American Anthropological Association.

Incorporating gender into archaeology courses. (Unpublished typescript).

Thorne, A. and R. Raymond (1989) *Man on the Rim: The Peopling of the Pacific.* North Ryde: Angus and Robertson Publishers.

Tiffany, S. W. (1984) Introduction: Feminist perceptions in anthropology. In D. O'Brien and S. W. Tiffany (eds) *Rethinking Women's Roles: Perspectives from the Pacific*, pp. 1–13. Los Angeles: University of California Press.

Tiger, L. (1969) *Men in Groups.* New York: Vintage Books.

Washburn, S. L. and C. S. Lancaster (1968) The evolution of hunting. In R. B. Lee and I. DeVore (eds) *Man the Hunter*, pp. 293–303. Chicago: Aldine Publishing Company.

Watanabe, H. (1968) Subsistence and ecology of northern food gatherers with special reference to the Ainu. In R. B. Lee and I. DeVore (eds) *Man the Hunter*, pp. 69–77. Chicago: Aldine Publishing Company.

Wilson, E. O. (1975) *Sociobiology: The New Synthesis.* Cambridge: Harvard University Press.

Zihlman, A. L. (1978) Women in evolution, Part 2: Subsistence and social organization among early hominids. *Signs* 4:4–20.

Zihlman, A. L. and N. Tanner (1978) Gathering and hominid adaptation. In L. Tiger and H. Fowler (eds) *Female Hierarchies*, pp. 163–94. Chicago: Beresford Book Service.

Chapter 7

BRAIN EVOLUTION IN FEMALES
An answer to Mr Lovejoy

Dean Falk

A little more than a decade ago, the field of paleoanthropology was visited with a new hypothesis about the role of women in human origins in an article in *Science* entitled "The Origin of Man" (Lovejoy 1981). The reasoning underlying this new hypothesis went something like this: since the origin of hominids may have coincided with that of bipedalism (but not with the beginnings of tool production or brain expansion which occurred later), if one can explain the origin of bipedalism then one will understand the "*sine qua non* of human origin" (*ibid.*: 341). Lovejoy theorized that bipedalism was selected for in males who travelled over increased daily ranges and gathered food to be hand-carried back to female – offspring groups who remained in core areas. Differential selection for bipedalism in males was presumed to be under strong positive selection that resulted in (a) lowered mobility for females and therefore a reduced accident rate in females and their offspring; (b) reduced exposure to predators, and (c) an intensification of parenting behavior. The net result was more and better hominids. According to this view, early hominid females were left not only four-footed, pregnant, hungry, and in fear of too much exercise in a central core area, they were also left "waiting for their man." In other words, western idealized monogamy and the nuclear family were the order of the prehistoric day. Why? According to Lovejoy, this enabled males to travel away from core areas without fretting about the possibility that the calories they retrieved might actually be nurturing someone else's offspring rather than their own. With faithful mates, males could rest assured of their paternity.

All of this scenario building was couched in demographic, comparative ethological, and sociobiological theory. However, one

[handwritten marginal note: rationale doesn't even make sense]

needn't get that technical to realize how weak this particular "just so" story really is. Think of it – a sexually dimorphic terrestrial primate (but one that curiously lacks dimorphism in canines) in whom the females are so fragile that mobility is a threat to mother/offspring survivorship. The females can't walk. They don't have big canines with which to defend themselves. They live in "novel and varied habitats, especially mosaics" (ibid.: 347). Although it is well known that severe predator pressure is associated with such habitats, it is never explained how an absence of males from core areas results in reduced exposure to predators in helpless females rather than increasing it. Thus, even at a superficial level, the Lovejoy scenario appears questionable.

exactly

The Lovejoy hypothesis may also be viewed at an entirely different level, i.e., as being preoccupied with questions/anxieties about male sexuality. At its most basic level, the hypothesis focuses on the evolution of how men got/get sex. The focal point is on males because it is already known how human females got/get sex. To wit, they "are continually sexually receptive" (Lovejoy 1981: 346) and, ever since those first days when male bipedalism ushered in humanity, females have waited faithfully for their men to return to exercise "copulatory vigilance" (ibid.). Male early hominids, on the other hand, were beset with sexual anxieties as is clear from the worries implied in Lovejoy's article: Will I ever have children? (Yes, if you provide proper nutrition for the mother.) Will my children be healthy? (Sure, if you don't compete with them for food.) Will they be safe? (Yes, as long as they and their mothers don't have to move around too much.) Will I have enough children? (Yes, if you exercise copulatory vigilance and get that interbirth spacing reduced.) How will I know I'm the father? (Because she's pair-bonded with you.) How can I be sure of her love? (Not to worry, she's hooked on your unique epigamic characters.) But I worry that she might like someone else? (She won't – she's monogamous.) Are you sure I won't have to compete with other males for the mother's affections? (No, polygyny is out. You get your own female, they get theirs.) Amazingly, this preoccupation with successful male sexuality was even expressed in a friendly affirmation of the sexual prowess of one of the author's friends. I refer, of course, to documentation of the assertion that "human females are continually sexually receptive" with footnote no. 79 that read "D. C. Johanson, personal communication" (Lovejoy 1981: 346).

But all of this is yesterday's news, right? After all, it's 1997 and nobody believes this stuff anymore. Wrong. Despite a number of reasonable hypotheses about the origins of bipedalism that have been suggested over the past decade and a half, Lovejoy's scenario is still widely invoked. Furthermore, concern with male sexuality continues to be confused with "scientific" endeavors. For example (and to continue a thread), D. C. Johanson of footnote no. 79 writes:

so ridiculous

> In a joke that eluded the editors, Owen attributed the assertion in his *Science* article that "human females are continually sexually receptive" to "D. C. Johanson, personal communication," as though I was the *scientific source* for

all assumptions prejudice

this bit of information; maybe that's why I was nicknamed "the Don Juan of paleoanthropology" by one of my colleagues in a recent book [emphasis mine].

(Johanson, Johanson and Edgar 1994: 80)

The saddest thing about continued promotion of Lovejoy's hypothesis is that the research and substantiated ideas of a number of serious paleoanthropologists and physiologists with alternative hypotheses have not been given the full consideration they deserve. But perhaps I can now offer an alternative model that will be more to the liking of those who accept Lovejoy's basic assumptions?

The origin of humans

Despite the above observations, a number of Lovejoy's basic assumptions derive from standard paleoanthropological and biological theory and these will be incorporated into my own model. For example, my hypothesis will include comparative data for mammals and will also "directly address the few primary differences separating humans from apes" (Lovejoy 1981: 341). My model, like Lovejoy's, will include inferences about causes of humanity that predate the appearance of tools and enlarged brains. Additionally, I will accept that sex differences are more than merely superficial (in fact, I will document it), and even that selection might have occurred differentially on one or both sexes. Because it was so important to the Lovejoy scenario, I have decided to incorporate discussion about how males acquired sexual partners during human evolution. Lovejoy states that "man's most unique character is without question his enormous intelligence" (1981: 347), and I fully agree (and also believe this is true for women). I concur with Lovejoy's statement that intense social behavior was important for the development of human intelligence. In fact, I agree so strongly with these last two points that I must disagree with another point. Although Lovejoy believes that human origins could be sufficiently elucidated by explaining the causes of bipedalism, I do not. After all, all early hominid species were bipedal, but not all of them evolved into humans. The present chapter will therefore focus on brain evolution because it is our brains (or our minds) that make us truly human. If one focuses on brains instead of feet, the evolutionary picture that emerges is quite different from that envisioned by Mr Lovejoy. Indeed, a good deal of evidence suggests that selection may have acted differentially on the brains (intelligence) of males and females. And if this is so, one can easily spin a scenario that favors the latter.

Sex differences in the brain

The gross anatomy of the brain differs between men and women. Adult men have on average larger brains than adult women. Across the globe, female brains average

91 per cent (ranging between 88–94 per cent for different populations) of the mean male brain size (calculated from Table 1 of Pakkenberg and Voigt 1964: 298). The average brain size of many series of adult human males is 1,345 grams (*ibid.*), 91 per cent of that mean is 1,222 grams as an estimated average adult female brain size. However, several caveats should to be noted about brain size estimates. Brain weights vary with cause of death and frequently become heavier with postmortem absorption of fluids (*ibid.*). (For example, people of both sexes who hang themselves have relatively heavy brains.) Brain size also varies with age, peaking at approximately 20 years of age in males, in whom roughly 100 grams are lost between the ages of 25 and 70. Brain size may peak at a younger age in human females as is the case for female as compared to male rhesus monkeys (Masters, Falk and Gage 1991) although there are not yet enough data for humans to be conclusive on this point (Pakkenberg and Voigt 1964: 301). Finally, using regression analysis, Pakkenberg and Voigt have determined that "brain weight depends significantly on height, but not on body weight" (1964: 303). Holloway (1980) analyzed the same data set used by Pakkenberg and Voigt but showed that the relationship between brain size and height is significant only for males. On the other hand, Holloway finds the relationship between brain size and body weight to be significant for males but only reaches significance for females between 56 and 65 years of age:

> It is clear that for males, there are relationships between brain and body size that appear very much stronger than they do in female samples. It is tempting to try to offer a uniform explanation, such as more lean body mass in males, or concomitantly, more body fat in females which is not directly innervated.
>
> (Holloway 1980: 117)

In other words, because of extra body fat in females, brain size is not as tightly correlated with body size as is the case for males. Furthermore, since females have extra fat, presumably their ratios of brain size/body size are somewhat decreased compared to those of leaner males.

Despite the above, the bottom line that is usually presented is that men have bigger brains than women. This fact is frequently (sometimes gleefully) quoted. But what does the extra 123 grams in "average" male brains mean? Recently, a PhD student in the author's department (Froese 1997), analyzed and reconciled contradictory results of Ankney (1992), Ho *et al.* (1980), Holloway (1980), and Pakkenberg and Voigt (1964) regarding brain size in adult men and women. Froese found that, for any given body size (be it weight or height), relative brain size (brain weight divided by weight or stature) is indeed larger in males than in females. However, brains scale allometrically, i.e., they are relatively larger in smaller than in bigger people (as is the case with other animals), and the average woman is neither as heavy nor as tall as the average man. As it turns out, the average brain size/body weight ratio is slightly but significantly greater in women than in men (Ho *et al.* 1980; Holloway 1980). (Since females have "extra fat" compared to males, one can't help but wonder how much larger their brains would be relatively speaking if all that "body fat . . . which is not directly innervated" [Holloway 1980: 117] were left out of the equation.) Another way to control for body size is to calculate an index of encephalization (EQ) that expresses actual brain size divided by that expected for a given body size. Holloway found EQ to be slightly higher for 165 women (7.154) than for 165 men (7.145), but not significantly so.

Froese's (1997) results show that the relatively large brains of average females is due to scaling factors associated with smaller bodies, whereas the extra 110–150 grams in male brains may not be attributed to allometry because males have larger brains than females of the same body size. How, then, to explain the larger brains of males? As detailed below, it is likely that certain cognitive specialization evolved differentially (but not exclusively) in men and women, and that these parallel sex differences occur in some other animals. A classic example is visuospatial processing which is generally more developed in males than females of certain species, including *H. sapiens*. Although such abilities are not reflected in higher EQs for human males, they may require more neurological hardware.

How else do brains differ between adult men and women? The neuronal densities of brains of females are significantly higher than the densities of males' brains (Haug 1987). Put another way, although the female brain is about 100–150 cubic centimeters smaller than the male brain, females and males have the same total number of neurons. (When it comes to brain tissue, cubic centimeters of volume are essentially interchangeable with grams of weight.) Interestingly, the density of glial ("helper") cells does not appear to depend on brain size since a difference does not exist between male and female brains (*ibid.*). (Thus, male brains have more glial cells simply because they are larger.) Since the same number of neurons occupy a smaller space (braincase) in females than in males, one wonders what besides glial cells takes up the extra space in males. One possibility that must apparently be ruled out is relatively enlarged ventricles in males since the ventricles appear to be the same size in both sexes (Willerman *et al.* 1991).

In addition to the differences in brain size and density of neurons, there are also a number of sexual dimorphisms in the average sizes of certain anatomical structures of the brain. One dimorphic region of the human brain is an area of the hypothalamus which contains specific centers (nuclei) that are involved in sexual behavior. Two "interstitial" nuclei located in the front part of the hypothalamus that is the principal region for male-typical sexual behavior (i.e., the medial preoptic area) have been shown to be larger on average in men than in women (Allen *et al.* 1989). (The ventromedial nucleus that is important for female-typical sexual behavior is approximately the same size in both sexes.)

Other sexually dimorphic regions of the brain are not so obviously related to sexual behavior. For example, various reports have suggested that the large pathway connecting neurons that course between the right and left sides of the brain, known as the corpus callosum, is larger in women than in men. However, these findings have been controversial (see Witelson and Kigar 1987; Hines 1990 for reviews) and it now appears that the corpus callosum is about the same absolute size in the two sexes. If so, the corpus callosum is relatively larger in women because of their smaller brains (LeVay 1993: 102). Since women and men have approximately the same absolute number of neurons (see above), it makes sense that the pathway connecting similarly positioned neurons in the two hemispheres would also be approximately the same absolute size. The anterior commissure is another smaller, phylogenetically "older" connection between the two hemispheres that is absolutely larger in women than in men (Allen and Gorski 1986). Still another band of fibers that connects the thalami of the two sides (across the third ventricle), the massa intermedia, is present more often in females than in males (Rabl 1958). Interestingly, there is some evidence that males with a massa intermedia may have lower nonverbal IQs than males who lack this structure (Lansdell and Davie 1972).

Still another sexual dimorphism, but one that does not directly involve pathways connecting the two sides of the brain, has been reported for planimetric measurements of the superior surface of the temporal lobe (known as the planum temporale). In most human adults, the left planum is larger than the right (Geschwind and Levitsky 1968). However, of the minority in whom the temporal planes are "reversed" so that the right side is larger than the left, significantly more are women than men (Wada et al. 1975). This dimorphism in brain shape goes along with another one: in general, right-handed people tend to have right frontal lobes that project farther than the left frontal lobes (known as a "right frontal petalia") and left occipital lobes that extend farther than their right counterparts ("left occipital petalia") (LeMay 1976). This pattern causes the brain and overlying skull to appear somewhat lopsided. As it turns out, reversals of the typical petalia patterns are more common in women than in men (Bear et al. 1986).

The known significant anatomical differences between the "average" brains of adult men and women can easily be summarized: men have brains that are approximately 10 per cent larger than those of women, but women average significantly larger brains relative to body weight because of allometric scaling. Brains of women have a higher density of neurons. Two nuclei of the hypothalamus that are involved in male-typical sexual behavior are larger in men. Three structures that connect the right and left hemispheres of the brain are larger or more frequently present in females. Finally, the normal lopsided shape of the brain is more often reversed in females, as is the typical asymmetry in the relative sizes of the top surfaces of the temporal lobes. What all this boils down to is that, on average, the brains of men and women are "wired" differently. And that relates to cognition.

Sex differences in cognition

As discussed above, converging evidence suggests that, on average, the brains of men and women are wired or "configured" differently. The anatomical differences that have been summarized are relatively dramatic and probably represent superficial

we don't really understand how the brain works

correlations of more subtle neurochemical dimorphisms (see below). Since "the mind is just the brain doing its job" (LeVay 1993: 31), it is reasonable to ask whether sexually dimorphic brains manifest dimorphisms in what they "do," i.e., in cognitive abilities. Just as the above discussion of anatomical dimorphisms began with the general (brain size, density of neurons) and moved towards the specific (certain brain regions), the present discussion of cognition will also move from the general (performance on IQ tests) to the specific (dimorphisms in particular abilities).

Recent advances in medical imaging technology have allowed noninvasive determination of the size of the brain and/or its components. When analyzed in conjunction with the imaged volunteers' performances on IQ tests, this new technology provides a powerful tool for examining the relationship between brain size and intelligence (i.e., as defined by conventional tests). For example, in a recent magnetic resonance imaging (MRI) study of 20 high IQ (i.e., > 130 on the Wechsler Adult Intelligence Scale-Revised [WAIS-R]) and 20 relatively low IQ individuals (i.e., score < 103) in which each group was equally divided between men and women, results showed that the high IQ group had greater brain size (corrected for body size) for both sexes (Willerman et al. 1991). (Interestingly, average IQ men were significantly taller than high IQ men.) With sexes pooled, the IQ-adjusted brain-size correlation was r=0.51, a significant correlation that is somewhat higher than previous reports because of the use of extreme IQ groups (ibid.).

not equal numbers

This general finding was confirmed in another MRI study of 37 adult males and 30 adult females (Andreasen et al. 1993) whose WAIS-R IQs were within the normal range (the mean full-scale IQ was 116 [SD=14]; the mean performance IQ was 114 [SD=13], and the mean verbal IQ was 114 [SD=15]). IQs did not differ significantly between the sexes. This latter study imaged specific parts of the brain as well as intracranial volume and examined the interaction of their sizes with the three types of IQ scores noted above. Once body size was corrected for, larger brains were again found to be correlated with higher IQs in both sexes. However, among the specific components that were measured, only those constituted of gray matter showed a significant positive correlation with intelligence. This was postulated to reflect a greater number of nerve cells and their dendritic branches.

Gender differences were shown in the pattern and number of correlations between sizes of brain regions and performances on different types of IQ tests (ibid.). Specifically, females had significant correlations between verbal IQ and intracranial, cerebellar, cerebral, temporal lobe and hippocampal volumes. (The Wechsler verbal scale traditionally includes tests of information, vocabulary, digit span, comprehension, similarities, and arithmetic.) Men, on the other hand, showed stronger correlations between sizes of brain regions and *performance IQ* and had generally fewer significant correlations overall (ibid.). (The Wechsler performance scale includes items such as block design, picture completion, picture arrangement, object assembly, and digit symbol tests.)

Men's and women's brains were shown to age differently in another MRI study of 69 healthy adults ranging in age from 18–80 years (Gur et al. 1991). In elderly men, the greatest amount of atrophy was in the left hemisphere whereas in women age effects were symmetric. The authors concluded that men are particularly susceptible to aging effects on left hemispheric functions (described below), whereas women are less vulnerable to age-related changes in mental abilities.

The above findings based on MRI research confirm numerous previous studies which demonstrate that, as populations, men and women test differently for certain abilities that are neurologically lateralized, i.e., subserved more by one hemisphere of the brain than the other (see below and Falk 1992a for review). Some workers have questioned the utility of studying such differences because there is usually massive overlap in the distributions of these traits for the two sexes. In such cases, numerous individuals of the weaker sex (sometimes males, sometimes females depending on the task) outperform many of the stronger sex. However, despite the fact that sex differences are frequently small, they are often statistically significant.

Figure 1 shows the traits that are lateralized in most human brains. This diagram represents generalizations that are based upon many thousands of clinical, experimental, and anatomical studies (it should be remembered, however, that there are many individual exceptions). The right hemisphere is associated with global, holistic pursuits. Its visuospatial and mental imaging skills are superb, and it is also associated with musical abilities. It has a noticeably greater role than the left hemisphere in expressing emotions in general as well as in reading them in other people. (The right hemisphere has a special role in processing negative emotions.) It also provides tone of voice and has an edge over the left hemisphere in recognizing faces, in the ability to understand metaphor, and in certain aspects of humor. The left hemisphere, on the other hand, is associated with language functions, skilled movements (e.g., of the right hand), and analytical, time-sequencing processes. This hemisphere is also involved in processing positive emotions.

Given that sexual dimorphism exists in three different pathways that connect the right and left sides of the brain (described above) and that the hemispheres of women may on average be more interconnected, it is not particularly surprising that men and women differ in their "average" performances for certain abilities that are lateralized to one hemisphere more than the other (see Bradshaw and Rogers 1993; Falk 1992a; McGlone 1980 for reviews). Men tend to outperform women on perception and manipulation of spatial relationships, such as mental rotation of figures, map-reading, rod-and-frame test, and remembering positions of numbers. They are also better at left-right discriminations, disembedding figures, and localizing points. Males outperform females in certain areas of mathematics, particularly on calculus and geometry problems. There is also some indication that males excel at musical composition. Women, on the other hand, outperform males on tests of verbal abilities, including reading comprehension, anagrams, essay-writing, and measures of spoken language. Compared with males, females are also subtly biased for certain emotional skills such as understanding non-verbal body language.

The reader will recall that women more often have "reversals" of certain typical brain shape asymmetries than men (above). This added anatomical evidence that

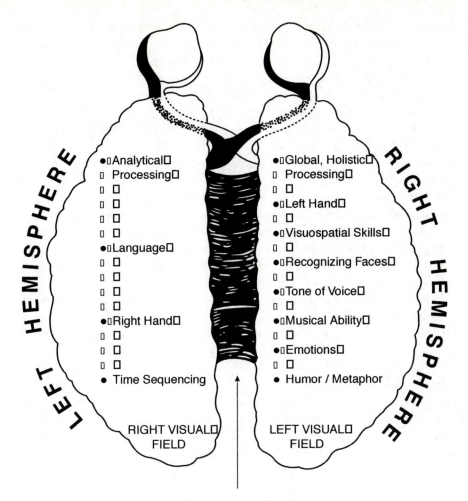

Figure 1 Right and left hemispheres of the brain

"connectedness" across the hemispheres is sexually dimorphic goes along with a survey which found that females seem to process certain kinds of information with both hemispheres, whereas males tend to rely more on one hemisphere or the other (McGlone 1980). For example, the incidence of aphasia (an inability to understand or use words) after left-hemisphere lesions is at least three times higher in men than in women. This suggests that females may process language more with both hemispheres. Despite this generalization, however, females appear to be more left-hemisphere biased for general motor expression than males, as shown by their greater rightward skill for fine motor tasks such as cursive writing and finger-tapping tasks.

The above findings are based on many hundreds of studies across a diverse spectrum of human activities that entail visuospatial, auditory, musical, motor, emotional, and linguistic skills. Despite the confusion, complexity, and related political issues that abound in the literature, this body of information converges on a clear bottom line: finely shaded but significant sex differences characterize human behaviors. As discussed above, MRI research has shown that the "performance" skills that males excel at are significantly correlated with the sizes of various brain structures (corrected for body size) in males, whereas verbal IQs of females are significantly correlated with corrected sizes of specific parts of their brains (Andreasen *et al.*, 1993). Because of the converging evidence that brains of men and women are on average wired differently, one cannot attribute these dimorphisms exclusively to environmental factors. Although environmental factors are of course crucial for "programing" organisms, one should not discount the importance of the biological machinery itself. Like it or not, what the brain "does" is significantly dependent on how the brain "is." Of all the differences between men and women, the largest is the one in which males are favored for a variety of visuospatial skills (Linn and Petersen, 1985). I believe the fact that males (in an average or statistical sense) are particularly good at reading maps, tracing mazes, and mentally manipulating spatial arrangements, whereas females excel at language skills and decoding social interactions, partially represents the end product of a remarkable evolution in our species.

Numerous studies suggest that differential exposure to sex hormones during prenatal development is responsible for sex differences in cerebral lateralization (Geschwind and Galaburda 1987) and in cognition (Hines 1990). For example, male visuospatial abilities are probably the result of organization during perinatal development by gonadal steroids such as testosterone (Williams and Meck 1991; Bachevalier and Hagger 1991). Hines summarizes other evidence (see Falk 1992a for more) and notes that exposure to low levels of hormones during development is always associated with reduction in male-typical cognitive traits, whereas exposure to high levels of hormones increases these traits:

> First, adolescent girls and young women exposed to excess testosterone and other androgens prenatally, because they have a genetic defect called congenital adrenal hyperplasia (CAH), have been reported to show enhanced performance on measures of visuospatial abilities. Second, men exposed to lower than normal levels of androgen from early life, because they have idiopathic hypogonadotrophic hypogonadism, have been found to show reduced visuospatial abilities. Third, women exposed to higher than normal levels of estrogen prenatally, because their mothers were prescribed the synthetic estrogen, diethylstilbestrol (DES), during pregnancy, have been found to show increased language lateralization. Finally, girls and women exposed to lower than normal levels of hormones, because of prenatal ovarian regression associated with the genetic disorder of Turner syndrome, have reduced visuospatial abilities and reduced language lateralization.

This pattern of results may provide convergent evidence for hormonal influences on the development of sex differences in cognition.

(Hines 1990: 54–55)

Even as adults, certain sexually dimorphic lateralized cognitive skills of men and women are influenced by cyclical (menstrual for women, seasonal for men) alterations in levels of hormones (Hampson and Kimura 1988; Chiarello *et al.* 1989). Men apparently perform better at visuospatial tasks in the spring, when presumably their testosterone levels are optimal for such tasks (Gouchie and Kimura 1991), than in the autumn. Women, on the other hand, perform better at some visuospatial tasks such as line orientation judgements during the follicular phases of their menstrual cycles when estrogen levels are rising (Chiarello *et al.* 1989, but see Hampson and Kimura 1988). Apparently, there is a hormonal basis in adults for gender differences in at least some visuospatial skills. As noted above, of all the sexually dimorphic cognitive differences that have been reported, the largest differences exist in visuospatial skills such as mental rotation of geometrical figures (Linn and Petersen 1985). It is also noteworthy that these differences can be detected across the lifespan (*ibid.*).

The evolution of brain lateralization

Because of the way genes from parents mix and match in their offspring, traits that are selected for in one sex are automatically selected for in the other sex ("sex-linked" traits located on the twenty-third pair of chromosomes are an exception). This would account in large part for the huge overlap in the distributions of sexually dimorphic abilities in men and women. Nevertheless, as outlined above, men "on average" excel at visuospatial tasks whereas women tend to outperform men on verbal tests and decoding social cues. In general, these skills depend upon a highly evolved lateralized primate brain. One way to investigate the evolutionary history behind human visuospatial and verbal (or other) skills is to examine them (and their relationship to sex if known) in other animals and to compare their anatomical substrates across species. A large number of investigations utilizing this "comparative method" on rodents, birds, nonprimate mammals, and primates show that brain lateralization has had a long evolutionary history (Bradshaw and Rogers 1993), and that humans are extremely lateralized compared to other animals, including nonhuman primates (Falk 1992a).

As detailed elsewhere (Falk 1992a), studies of rodents suggest that brain lateralization for visuospatial activities may have originally started in conjunction with preferential circling in one direction or the other. Male and female rats have a slight but significant tendency to circle in opposite directions. Such sex differences in locomotor asymmetries are the rule for a variety of rodent species rather than the exception (Robinson *et al.* 1985). Furthermore, the direction of preferred circling correlates with an asymmetrically high concentration of dopamine deep within the opposite side of the brain in rats (Zimmerberg *et al.* 1974). Although most people are unaware of it, they also have a tendency to circle. People are sexually dimorphic in their preferred directions of circling and there is some evidence that the underlying asymmetry in the dopaminergic systems of humans is even more pronounced than is the case for rats (Bracha *et al.* 1987).

But why circle in one direction if you are a rat or, for that matter, a person? Simply put, if one wanders away, one wanders back to the safety of the nest, if one is a rodent, or full circle back to the starting point, if one is a human who is lost in the woods. At least for the rodent, finding the way back to the nest would be an adaptive trait favored by natural selection. That is, such rodents would live longer and leave more offspring than their conspecifics who lack a "sense of direction." Also, rats who don't have to waste time deciding which way to turn might have an edge over getting away from attackers (Stanley Glick, personal communication).

Voles provide a clue about the possible selective value of enhanced visuospatial skills in males. These small burrowing rodents come in two kinds. Prairie voles from the Midwest United States are monogamous, whereas meadow voles from Pennsylvania are polygynous. Studies based on trapped voles fitted with radio transmitters and then released have shown that male meadow voles travelled far afield during the breeding season in order to mate with as many females as possible (Gaulin and FitzGerald 1988; 1989). However, female meadow voles and monogamous prairie voles of both sexes did not expand their ranging patterns during the mating season. When the voles were subsequently retrapped and tested for visuospatial ability in mazes, only polygynous meadow voles showed consistent male superiority on spatial tasks. This suggests that visuospatial skills evolved in male meadow voles in conjunction with their far-ranging search for mates. That is, voles with good internal compasses travelled further, encountered more mates, and left more offspring. Put simply, research on voles suggests that selection for enhanced visuospatial skills in males of various polygynous species may be related to an earlier evolution (selection) for increased mating opportunities.

Nonhuman primates appear to be lateralized for visuospatial skills. As with humans, the right hemisphere of monkeys has an advantage when discriminating between photographs of faces (Hamilton and Vermeire 1985) and there may be a sexual dimorphism in certain aspects of this ability (Hamilton and Vermeire 1983, 1985). Monkeys also appear to be lateralized for discriminating line orientations (Hamilton and Vermeire 1985) as well as other visuospatial patterns (Jason *et al.* 1984) but, curiously, in a direction that is *opposite* to that of humans (i.e., these tasks are left-hemisphere dominant in monkeys). This is particularly interesting in light of a recent demonstration of mental rotation for visual imagery in baboons, which is the first indication that such capabilities exist in a nonhuman species (Vauclair *et al.* 1993). Again, as was the case for certain visuospatial tasks in monkeys, mental rotation in baboons is lateralized to the left hemisphere rather than the right hemisphere. Monkeys and humans differ in this respect.

As outlined above, the comparative mammalian evidence indicates a very deep time-scale for asymmetries related to visuospatial skills (see Bradshaw and Rogers 1993 for review). Furthermore, there is some evidence which suggests that enhanced visuospatial skills may initially have been selected for in polygynous males in conjunction with finding mates. But what about the evolutionary underpinnings of the verbal abilities that are left- rather than right-hemisphere dominant and relatively enhanced in women? Is there any comparative evidence that social vocalization of one sort or another has had a long evolutionary history or that related skills may have been favored in females? As it turns out, a number of studies show that, like humans, macaque monkeys are left-hemisphere dominant for processing socially meaningful (as opposed to socially neutral) vocalizations (Petersen *et al*. 1978, 1984; Heffner and Heffner 1984, 1986).

Ehret (1987), in a study on the house mouse, suggests that lateralization for processing social vocalizations to left hemispheres may have evolved early in mammals. This study also offers an important clue about the possible selective advantage of this trait in females since the ultrasonic calls emitted by young mice were recognized only by the left hemisphere and evoked maternal caring behavior in mothers. On the other hand, no advantage was detected for either hemisphere in virgin females who were trained to respond to the same ultrasonic calls by conditioning (*ibid*.). Since a calling pup who is displaced from the litter is retrieved to the nest by its mother, lateralization for processing socially meaningful vocalizations in females may have functioned throughout evolution to increase differential survivorship.

To summarize, humans have highly lateralized brains that are the end product of millions of years of evolution. Statistically speaking, each sex excels in certain lateralized skills and there is some evidence that these skills may have contributed to the fitness of our ancestors. That is, enhanced visuospatial skills may have increased breeding opportunities in males, whereas processing social vocalizations may have increased the survivorship of females' offspring. Although evidence is limited, these are reasonable hypotheses in light of the known comparative data.

Of all animals tested, human males (and some females) are relatively adept circlers. Not only do they circle their bodies in preferred directions as they go about their daily business (Bracha *et al*. 1987), but their lateralized brains are proficient at rotating perceived objects in their imaginations (mental rotation tasks)! Furthermore, the fact that baboons and people are lateralized in different hemispheres for mental rotation suggests that brain lateralization continued to evolve with respect to visuospatial tasks during anthropoid (and possibly hominid) evolution. It is also clear that lateralization for processing social vocalizations continued to evolve during hominid evolution since only humans have language as we know it.

A fairly large literature (reviewed above) indicates that "on average" the brains of men and women are connected differently across the hemispheres and that the sexes manifest different patterns of functional lateralization. It is possible that the ongoing development of visuospatial and vocal/communication skills during the evolution of *Australopithecus/Homo* was dramatic and involved reorganization of brain lateralization itself (e.g., with left-hemisphere language functions "displacing" certain visual tasks to the right hemisphere). But what could have driven such evolution?

Early hominid evolution

Somewhere around 5.0 million years ago (myr) in Africa, the first hominids diverged from the ancestors of chimpanzees. No one knows for sure why this happened, but it may have been related to the opening of new niches in mosaic habitats. Although the earliest hominids probably continued to sleep in trees, it is likely that they were terrestrial during much of the day. It is generally believed that at the time of divergence hominids had already begun the long evolutionary process of refining bipedalism. (Hopefully, additional discoveries of the oldest known australopithecines [White, Suwa and Asfaw 1994] will eventually shed light on this matter.) Scientists agree that by 2.5 myr at least two kinds of australopithecines (gracile and robust) had evolved. However, they do not agree about *when* australopithecines first speciated into more than one contemporaneous species. Until recently, proponents of "Lucy" (*A. afarensis*) as the mother of us all believed that only one species of hominid lived before 3.0 myr. Although the recent discovery of 4.4-myr-old *A. ramidus* dispels this notion, there is presently no consensus about whether more than one evolving *lineage* of australopithecine is represented before 3.0 myr. I continue to believe that more than one species of australopithecine coexisted long before "Lucy" and that she was not the mother of us all (Falk 1990; Falk *et al.* 1995). At any rate, most paleoanthropologists concur that gracile rather than robust australopithecines gave rise to the genus *Homo*. Some also think that the two types of australopithecines lived in distinctly different niches and that the ancestors of *Homo* spent a good deal of time moving about the sunny open grasslands.

So much for generalizations. A key part of Lovejoy's scenario rests on the assumption that early hominids formed monogamous pair bonds. This assumption weakens, however, in face of comparative primate evidence. Not one species of terrestrial nonhuman primate is monogamous, nor are any of the three great apes. The terrestrialism and sexual dimorphism manifested in fossils of early hominids are usually correlated with polygyny in living primates. Furthermore, 80 per cent of contemporary human societies are not monogamous. (See Hrdy 1981 for review.) Recent research on female sexuality and "female choice" in a number of terrestrial primates suggests that "females embarking upon the human enterprise were possessed of an aggressive readiness to engage in both reproductive and nonreproductive liaisons with multiple, but selected, males" (*ibid*. 176). Indeed, much of the world appears to fear that this might still be the case, as indicated by the universal close observation and control of sexual conduct in women in human communities (*ibid*. 186), not to mention all those male insecurities simmering beneath the surface of Lovejoy's hypothesis. Given these observations, the most reasonable assumption to make about early hominid mating patterns is that they were polygynous.

but really don't know

If early hominids were not monogamous, bipedalism could not have been differentially selected for in males in order to provision their helpless "other halves" as hypothesized by Lovejoy. This raises the question of why bipedalism *did* occur in hominids. Although many interesting ideas have been offered to account for bipedalism (reviewed in Falk 1992a), one of the most synthetic is a physiological theory put forward by Pete Wheeler (1988). According to this theory, protohominids of both sexes had to travel through open country to find patches of food scattered within the mosaic environment. In so doing, they encountered intense solar radiation. Like pygmy chimpanzees, these protohominids were probably capable of a certain amount of bipedalism, i.e. they were preadapted for the eventual development of habitual bipedalism. The earliest hominids were therefore able to minimize the amount of body surface that was directly exposed to damaging solar radiation by walking bipedally so that only the shoulders and top of the head took a direct beating from the rays of the sun when it was overhead. With this shift to bipedalism, a naked skin and associated sweat glands evolved to facilitate increased evaporation. According to Wheeler, these features led to "whole-body cooling" that regulated temperature of blood circulating to (among other regions) the brain, helped prevent heatstroke, and thereby released a physiological constraint on brain size in *Homo*.

Since Wheeler formulated this provocative theory, my own research on the evolution of cranial blood flow has resulted in the "radiator" theory of brain evolution, which supports and complements Wheeler's ideas (Falk 1990; 1992a and b). Although a detailed discussion of this theory is beyond the scope of the present chapter, it should be noted here that fossil and comparative evidence shows that a special network of veins that selectively cool the brain under conditions of hyperthermia evolved in our direct early hominid ancestors. This "radiator" evolved as a correlate of two factors, bipedalism and living in a hot savanna environment, and it released a thermal constraint that previously kept brain size from increasing. Thus, both Wheeler and I view the increase in brain size in *Homo* as a consequence of bipedalism occurring in an environment that selected for certain vascular mechanisms that could regulate brain temperature. These physiological theories are mechanistic. That is, they suggest that the human brain was only able to enlarge after a thermal constraint had been released, but do not identify the behaviors/abilities that were subsequently selected for. That topic is, of course, at the heart of what makes us human.

Whatever its cause, brain size "took off" somewhere around 2.0 million years ago in the genus *Homo*, so much so that by 100,000 years ago (i.e., by the time of Neandertals) brain size had doubled from approximately $700cm^3$ to over $1,400cm^3$ (Falk 1992b). Since the time of Darwin, there have been many speculations about a possible single cause ("prime mover") of the dramatic increase in brain size (reviewed in Falk 1980). Prime-mover candidates that have been suggested over the years include warfare, work, language, tool production, throwing, hunting, and social intelligence. As one might surmise from this list, more credit for brain evolution has traditionally been given to activities that are typically (but not exclusively) pursued by males (*ibid*. Falk 1992a and b). Although Lovejoy (1981) focused on bipedalism rather than brain evolution as the *sine qua non* of human evolution, he carried on this biased tradition with his hypothesis by stating that bipedalism was selected for exclusively in males.

However, it wasn't bipedalism that made us human (bipedal robust australopithecines never got there), it was our brains. But what does it mean to have a human brain? Put another way, what can a human brain do that a chimpanzee brain cannot? Looking above at the list of potential prime movers, a number of activities that were previously ascribed exclusively to humans are now known to occur in both chimpanzees and humans. Both make war, make tools (e.g., fishing poles), and hunt (Goodall 1986). Like humans, chimpanzees can concentrate on and carry out a task (work). For example, in addition to solving problems under experimental conditions (summarized *ibid*.), chimpanzees can learn how to knap stone tools from human teachers (Toth *et al*. 1993). They can also throw (*ibid*.). That leaves just two candidates, language and social intelligence.

Chimpanzees, like most anthropoid primates, are intensely social. For this reason, I have been reluctant to entertain social (or "Machiavellian") intelligence as realistic prime mover of human brain evolution (Falk 1992b). Dunbar (1993), on the other hand, argues that the enlarged human neocortex evolved primarily to keep track of multiple social relationships in increasingly enlarged social groups. My colleague Bruce Dudek and I recently analyzed the same sets of data on brain and group size that Dunbar studied and confirmed that larger primates tend to have larger brains and neocortices, and more often live in larger groups (Falks and Dudek 1993). However, which is cause, which is effect, and which relationships are spurious are not questions that can be unambiguously answered from this data set (*ibid*.). Interestingly, Dunbar notes that:

> in human conversations about 60 per cent of time is spent gossiping about relationships and personal experiences. Language may accordingly have evolved to allow individuals to learn about the behavioral characteristics of other group members more rapidly than was feasible by direct observation alone.
>
> Dunbar 1993: 618

Dudek and I agree with Dunbar's assessment that language is a social phenomenon, and that humans use language to "groom" each other. However, language is used to impart and absorb all kinds of information in addition to that which is social. Thus social intelligence *per se* probably was not the prime mover of human brain evolution. Language was. This is true because, despite the considerable abilities of signing, computer-using, plastic symbol-manipulating, tool-knapping apes, no amount of training has ever resulted in a chimpanzee who could read, write or talk anything like a human does (Falk 1992a). Unlike the brains of other primates, human brains *do* language.

The evolution of women: an answer to Lovejoy

The comparative neuroanatomical evidence summarized in this chapter allows one to speculate about the brains of the very first hominids. Certainly they were lateralized (Falk 1987). As is the case for at least some rodents and primates, processing of meaningful vocal communications was probably dependent upon left hemispheres. Like Old World rhesus monkeys and baboons, certain visuospatial skills such as the ability to discriminate line orientations or other spatial relationships were probably also left-hemisphere dominant, while others, like recognition of faces, were right-hemisphere dominant. During the course of hominid evolution two things probably happened with respect to brain lateralization: the left hemisphere expanded its role in processing vocal communications to include language functions (speech, understanding of spoken language, and eventually reading and writing). The right hemisphere, on the other hand, incorporated certain visuospatial tasks that were previously the domain of the left hemisphere (e.g., mental rotation, discriminating the orientation of lines and other shapes). In other words, during hominid evolution, skills at which females excel today (statistically speaking) displaced those at which males excel from the left to the right hemisphere.

If selection acted differentially on the behaviors of male and female hominids, as Lovejoy asserts, then the neuroanatomical and cognitive sexual dimorphisms that exist today in humans, along with the comparative mammalian evidence, suggest that processing of vocal communications was selected for differentially in females at the same time that visuospatial skills were continuing to evolve in males. And why shouldn't the prime mover of human brain evolution be the result of differential selection on females? If a mother mouse recognizes the distress calls of her young with her left hemisphere and is prompted to return that young to the nest, it is not surprising that Old World monkey mothers also recognize distress calls of their young or that they (and the males of their species) process socially meaningful vocalizations of conspecifics with their left hemispheres. The fundamental social unit for even relatively solitary higher primates like orangutans is the mother/offspring pair. It is primarily the *female*'s reading of and responding to social and environmental cues that escort the genes of her offspring into the future. Therefore it is reasonable to speculate that female hominids evolved better abilities than males for reading social cues and communicating with conspecifics, be they one offspring or a whole troop.

In sexually dimorphic primates like baboons, large male body size is viewed as the anatomical reflection of aggression for male–male competition over mates and for defense of the social group (Lancaster 1984). Smaller female body size, on the other hand, is believed to reflect the energy demands for pregnancy and lactation (*ibid.*). In other words, males are built for breeding/defending and females for mothering. Robust australopithecines were clearly sexually dimorphic, and it is generally assumed that gracile australopithecines were too. (Indeed, there is so much variation in so-called *A. afarensis* that it could easily represent more than one dimorphic species.)

If our gracile australopithecine ancestors were sexually dimorphic as is true for terrestrial primates today, then it is not surprising that the underlying nervous system of humans is sexually dimorphic in ways that reflect cognitive correlates related to breeding/mothering (i.e., testosterone-mediated visuospatial skills/verbal abilities). As discussed elsewhere (Falk 1980; 1992b), of the various candidates that have been put forward as possible prime movers of brain evolution, language seems to be the most reasonable. If so, then a hypothesis that entails differential selection on females may not be as outlandish as some might suppose, especially if one views language as an outgrowth of selection for "social intelligence" (Dunbar 1993). This is not to say that the slight but significant edge that women have over men in verbal tasks indicates that most men are without wonderful language skills (or that a majority of women lack impressive visuospatial abilities). As already noted, there is huge overlap in the distributions of verbal performance on a variety of tests for the two sexes. However, one cannot discount the possibility that men evolved their loquaciousness "clinging to the apron strings of the women," as suggested by some versions of the "Woman the Gatherer" model (Fedigan 1986: 35).

One thing is for sure. I do not see early hominid males as bipedally bringing home the veggies to helpless, quadrupedally locomoting females and their (his) young. Contrary to Lovejoy (1981), the relatively large bodies of males suggest they were polygynous, competed for mates, and aggressively defended their social groups. It may even be that early hominid males patrolled their borders like modern-day chimpanzees from Gombe (Goodall 1986), i.e., that they sought aggressive encounters with strangers. From this point of view, it is interesting that testosterone is viewed as a major organizer of the developing human brain in males (Geschwind and Galaburda 1987) and that it is correlated with both visuospatial skills and aggression in adults.

At least in my culture, more men than women seem to have an inordinate fascination with warfare, and with sports that involve propelling missiles (often balls) at targets (points, holes or spaces). In autumn, when testosterone levels are increasing in men (Dabbs 1990), the visuospatial love of putting balls in specified places merges with aggression during the football season in the US. The lack of sexual dimorphism in early hominid canine size may even indicate that females sexually selected less aggressive males with smaller teeth (Zihlman 1978), and that males were already on their way to sublimating their aggression through male-bonded sports activities. In other words, while she was out gathering food for dinner (kids in tow and no doubt muttering to herself) (Zihlman 1985), he and his buddies were out on the savanna inventing golf.

To summarize, my hypothesis is based on an extensive number of scientific studies that span psychology, zoology, the neurosciences, and recent advances in medical imaging: although brains of males are somewhat larger than those of females of the same body size, the average brain size/body weight ratio of males is significantly smaller because of scaling factors associated with larger bodies (Froese 1997). Brains of males are also characterized by a lower density of neurons. Three structures that connect the right and left hemispheres are, on average, larger or more frequently present in females. As discussed above, a variety of research converges on the conclusion that men's and women's brains are "wired" differently and suggests that these differences form at least part of the substrate for superior average performance on verbal tasks (and assessing social cues) in women versus enhanced scores on visuospatial tests in men. Furthermore, magnetic resonance imaging studies show that, for each sex, the typical cognitive strengths (at least as demonstrated with standardized tests) are significantly correlated with the size of related brain structures. Along other lines, comparative studies on a variety of mammals suggest that the cognitive specialties of men and women are likely to have evolved for reasons to do with classical "reproductive fitness" – i.e., superior visuospatial skills may have first developed in polygynous male ancestors of hominids for finding mates (and the way home) whereas enhanced abilities to interpret vocalizations may have been selected in female ancestors in conjunction with mothering.

The reader may rightfully question whether or not my hypothesis of selective brain evolution is as biased in favor of females as Lovejoy's scenario regarding the origins of bipedalism is towards males. I have written this chapter in order to emphasize that sexual dimorphism in the human brain can no longer be ignored by evolutionary biologists. Indeed, medical imaging technology in combination with cognitive psychological investigations is in the process of revolutionizing our understanding of how brains look and think, and I predict that an increasing amount of evidence will further document the fact that brains of men and women differ, on average, in their wiring. In any event, if one assumes that it is the brain rather than bipedalism that made us human, then my scenario is already supported by a good deal of evidence and is at least plausible.

But I want to add a final caveat. The problem with my interpretation, as with Lovejoy's, is with the assertion that certain skills that may (or may not) have been differentially selected for in one sex were somehow more valuable for the evolution of our species than other advanced abilities (Lovejoy's "*sine qua non* of human origin"). Indeed, it is this line of reasoning that has led some workers (including myself) to choose language as the most likely prime mover of human brain evolution. However, to suggest that certain skills may have been the focus of brain evolution is one thing; to suggest that they alone account for what makes us human is another. Granted, reading and writing are unique human accomplishments. But so are building airplane engines, composing symphonies, and playing football. The reality that men and women, on average, engage in these activities at different levels and frequencies at least partially reflects the fact that lateralized brains of men and women are wired somewhat differently (Falk 1987). In the final analysis, if one believes that our species has benefited from a wide array of enhanced cognitive abilities, then it is best to abandon the assertion that one sex or the other is more "intelligent" or that one sex should take more credit for the unique evolutionary history that made us "human." Agreed, Mr Lovejoy?

■ ■ ■

References

Allen, L. S. and Gorski, R. A. (1986) "Sexual Dimorphism of the Human Anterior Commissure," *Anat. Rec.* 214: 3A.

Allen, L. S., Hines, M., Shryne, J. E. and Gorski, R. A. (1989) "Two Sexually Dimorphic Cell Groups in the Human Brain," *J. Neurosci.* 9: 497–506.

Andreasen, N. C., Flaum, M., Swayze, V., O'Leary, D. S., Alliger, R., Cohen, G., Ehrhardt, J. and Yuh, W. T. C. (1993) "Intelligence and Brain Structure in Normal Individuals," *Amer. J. Psychiatry* 150: 130–34.

Ankney, C. D. (1992) "Sex Differences in Relative Brain Size: The Mismeasure of Women Too?" *Intelligence* 16: 329–336.

Bachevalier, J. and Hagger, C. (1991) "Sex Differences in the Development of Learning Abilities in Primates," *Psychoneuroendocrinology* 16: 177–88.

Bear, D., Schiff, D., Saver, J., Greenberg, M. and Freeman, R. (1986) "Quantitative Analysis of Cerebral Asymmetries," *Arch. Neurol.* 43: 598–603.

Bracha, H. S., Seitz, D. J., Otemaa, J. and Glick, S. D. (1987) "Rotational Movement (Circling) in Normal Humans: Sex Difference and Relationship to Hand, Foot and Eye Preference," *Brain Res.* 411: 231–35.

Bradshaw, J. L. and Rogers, L. J. (1993) *The Evolution of Lateral Asymmetries, Language, Tool Use, and Intellect*, San Diego: Academic Press.

Chiarello, C., McMahon, M. A. and Schaefer, K. (1989) "Visual Cerebral Lateralization Over Phases of the Menstrual Cycle: A Preliminary Investigation," *Brain and Cognition* 11: 18–36.

Dabbs, J. M., Jr. (1990) "Age and Seasonal Variation in Serum Testosterone Concentration Among Men," *Chronobiology Int.* 7: 245–49.

Dunbar, R. I. M. (1993) "Co-evolution of Neocortical Size, Group Size and Language in Humans," *Behav. Brain Sci.* 16: 681–735.

Ehret, G. (1987) "Left Hemisphere Advantage in the Mouse Brain for Recognizing Ultrasonic Communication Calls," *Nature* 325: 249–51.

Falk, D. (1980) "Hominid Brain Evolution: The Approach from Paleoneurology," *Yrbk. Phys. Anthropol.* 23: 93–107.

—— (1987) "Brain Lateralization in Primates and its Evolution in Hominids," *Yrbk. Phys. Anthropol.* 30: 107–125.

—— (1990) "Brain Evolution in *Homo*: The 'Radiator' Theory," *Behav. Brain Sci.* 13: 333–81.

—— (1992a) *Braindance*, New York: Henry Holt.

—— (1992b) "Evolution of the Brain and Cognition in Hominids," the 62nd James Arthur Lecture, New York: The American Museum of Natural History.

—— and Dudek, B. (1993) "Mosaic Evolution of the Neocortex," *Behav. Brain Sci.* 16: 701–2.

——, Gage, T. B., Dudek, B. and Olsen, T. R. (1995) "Did More Than One Species of Hominid Coexist Before 3.0 Ma?: Evidence From Blood and Teeth," *J. Hum. Evol.* 29: 591–600.

Fedigan, L. M. (1986) "The Changing Role of Women in Models of Human Evolution," *Ann. Rev. Anthrop.* 15: 25–66.

Froese, N. (1997) "Relative Brain Size in Men and Women: Who Has More Upstairs and Does It Matter?" under review.

Gaulin, S. J. C. and FitzGerald, R. W. (1988) "Home-range Size as a Predictor of Mating Systems in *Microtus*," *J. Mammal.* 69: 311–19.

—— (1989) "Sexual Selection for Spatial-learning Ability," *Animal Behav.* 37: 322–31.

Geschwind, N. and Galaburda, A. M. (1987) *Cerebral Lateralization: Biological Mechanisms, Associations, and Pathology*, Cambridge: MIT Press.

Geschwind, N. and Levitsky, W. (1968) "Left/right Asymmetries in Temporal Speech Region," *Science* 161: 186–87.

Goodall, J. (1986) *The Chimpanzees of Gombe*, Cambridge: Belknap Press.

Gouchie, C. and Kimura, D. (1991) "The Relationship Between Testosterone Levels and Cognitive Ability Patterns," *Psychoneuroendocrinology* 16: 323–34.

Gur, R. C., Mozley, P. D., Resnick, S. M., Gottlieb, G. L., Kohn, M., Zimmerman, R., Herman, G., Atlas, S., Grossman, R., Berretta, D., Erwin, R. and Gur, R. E. (1991) "Gender Differences in Age Effect on Brain Atrophy Measured by Magnetic Resonance Imaging," *Proc. Natl. Acad. Sci.* 88: 2845–9.

Hamilton, C. R. and Vermeire, B. A. (1983) "Discrimination of Monkey Faces by Split-brain Monkeys," *Behav. Brain Res.* 9: 263–75.

—— (1985) "Complementary Hemispheric Superiorities in Monkeys," *Soc. Neurosci. Abs.* 11: 869.

Hampson, E. and Kimura, D. (1988) "Reciprocal Effects of Hormonal Fluctuations on Human Motor and Perceptual-spatial Skills," *Behav. Neurosci.* 102: 456–59.

Haug, H. (1987) "Brain Sizes, Surfaces, and Neuronal Sizes of the Cortex Cerebri: A Stereological Investigation of Man and His Variability and a Comparison with Some Mammals (Primates, Whales, Marsupials, Insectivores, and One Elephant)," *Amer. J. Anat.* 180: 126–42.

Heffner, H. E. and Heffner, R. S. (1984) "Temporal Lobe Lesions and Perception of Species-specific Vocalizations by Macaques," *Science* 226: 75–6.

—— (1986) "Effect of Unilateral and Bilateral Auditory Cortex Lesions on the Discrimination of Vocalizations by Japanese Macaques," *J. Neurophysiol.* 56: 683–701.

Hines, M. (1990) "Gonadal Hormones and Human Cognitive Development," in J. Balthazart (ed.). *Hormones, Brain and Behaviour in Vertebrates. 1. Sexual Differentiation, Neuroanatomical Aspects, Neurotransmitters and Neuropeptides*, Basle: Karger. *Comp. Physiol.* 8: 51–63.

Ho, K., Roessmann, U., Straumfjord, J. V., and Monroe, G. (1980) "Analysis of Brain Weight: Adult Brain Weight in Relation to Body Height, Weight, and Surface Area," *Arch. Pathol. Lab. Med.* 104: 640–5.

Holloway, R. L. (1980) "Within-species Brain–Body Weight Variability: A Re-examination of the Danish Data and Other Primate Species," *Amer. J. Phys. Anthropol.* 53: 109–21.

Hrdy, S. B. (1981) *The Woman That Never Evolved*, Cambridge, MT: Harvard University Press.

Jason, G. W., Cowey, A. and Weiskrantz, L. (1984) "Hemispheric Asymmetry for a Visuo-spatial Task in Monkeys," *Neuropsychologia* 22: 777–84.

Johanson, D., Johanson, L., and Edgar, B. (1994) *Ancestors: In Search of Human Origins*, New York: Villard Books.

Lancaster, J. B. (1984) "Introduction," in M. F. Small (ed.) *Female Primates: Studies by Women Primatologists*, New York: Alan Liss.

Lansdell, H. and Davie, J. C. (1972) "Massa Intermedia: Possible Relation to Intelligence," *Neuropsychologia* 10: 207–10.

LeMay, M. (1976) "Morphological Cerebral Asymmetries of Modern Man, Fossil Man, and Nonhuman Primates," *Ann. N. Y. Acad. Sci.* 280: 349–60.

LeVay, S. (1993) *The Sexual Brain*, Cambridge: MIT Press.

Linn, M. C. and Petersen, A. C. (1985) "Emergence and Characterization of Sex Differences in Spatial Ability: A Meta-analysis," *Child Development* 56: 1479–98.

Lovejoy, C. O. (1981) "The Origin of Man," *Science* 211: 341–50.

McGlone, J. (1980) "Sex Differences in Human Brain Asymmetry: A Critical Survey," *Behav. and Brain Sci.* 3: 215–63.

Masters, A. V., Falk, D. and Gage, T. B. (1991) "Effects of Age and Gender on the Location and Orientation of the Foramen Magnum in Rhesus Macaques (*Macaca mulatta*)," *Amer. J. Phys. Anthropol.* 86: 75–80.

Pakkenberg, H. and Voigt, J. (1964) "Brain Weights of the Dane," *Acta Anat.* 56: 297–307.

Petersen, M., Beecher, M., Zoloth, S., Moody, D., and Stebbins, W. (1978) "Neural Lateralization of Species-specific Vocalizations by Japanese Macaques (*Macaca fuscata*)," *Science* 202: 324–27.

Petersen, M. R., Beecher, M. D., Zoloth, S. R., Green, S., Marler, P. R., Moody, D. B. and Stebbins, W. C. (1984) "Neural Lateralization of Vocalizations by Japanese Macaques: Communicative Significance is More Important Than Acoustic Structure," *Behav. Neurosci* 98: 779–90.

Rabl, R. (1958) "Strukturstudien an der Massa Intermedia des Thalamus Opticus," *J. Hirnforsch.* 4: 78–112.

Robinson, T. E., Becker, J. B., Camp, D. M. and Mansour, A. (1985) "Variation in the Pattern of Behavioral and Brain Asymmetries due to Sex Differences," in. S. Glick (ed.) *Cerebral Lateralization in Nonhuman Species*, New York: Academic Press.

Toth, N., Schick, K. D., Savage-Rumbaugh, S. S., Sevcik, R. A. and Rumbaugh, D. M. (1993) "Pan the Tool-maker: Investigations into the Stone Tool-making and Tool-using Capabilities of a Bonobo (*Pan paniscus*)," *J. Archaeol. Sci.* 20: 81–91.

Vauclair, J., Fagot, J. and Hopkins, W. D. (1993) "Rotation of Mental Images in Baboons when the Visual Input is Directed to the Left Cerebral Hemisphere,' *Psych. Sci.* 4: 99–103.

Wada, J. A., Clarek, R. and Hamm, A. (1975) "Cerebral Hemispheric Asymmetry in Humans," *Arch. Neurol.* 32: 239–46.

Wheeler, P. E. (1988) "Stand Tall and Stay Cool," *New Scientist*, 12 May: 62–5.

White, T. D., Suwa, G. and Asfaw, B. (1994) "*Australopithecus ramidus*, a New Species of Early Hominid from Aramis, Ethiopia," *Nature* 371: 306–312.

Willerman, L., Schultz, R., Rutledge, J. N. and Bigler, E. D. (1991) "*In vivo* Brain Size and Intelligence," *Intelligence*," 15: 223–28.

Williams, C. L. and Meck, W. H. (1991) "The Organizational Effects of Gonadal Steroids on Sexually Dimorphic Spatial Ability," *Psychoneuroendocrinology* 16: 155–76.

Witelson, S. F. and Kigar, D. L. (1987) "Neuroanatomical Aspects of Hemisphere Specialization in Humans," in. D. Ottoson (ed.) *Duality and Unity of the Brain, Proceedings of an International Symposium at the Wenner-Gren Center*, Stockholm, May 29–31, 1986, New York: Macmillan, pp. 446–95.

Zihlman, A. L. (1978) "Women in Evolution, Part II: Subsistence and Social Organization among Early Hominids," *Signs* 4(1): 4–20.

——(1985) "Gathering Stories for Hunting Human Nature," *Fem. Studies* 11: 364–77.

Zimmerberg, B., Glick, S. D. and Jerussi, T. P. (1974) "Neurochemical Correlate of a Spatial Preference in Rats," *Science* 185: 623–25.

PART III

Identifying "sexual" divisions of labor

INTRODUCTION

Most anthropologists see the division of labor between men and women as the most basic division in human societies (Durkheim 1964; Murdock and Provost 1973). All societies assign some kinds of work to men and other kinds to women. The specifics vary – for example, pottery-making is men's work in India, women's work in the Hopi Pueblos. Degree of flexibility varies. In many cultures, each individual simply does what needs to be done in spite of cultural norms. In others, strong cultural taboos are enforced against men or women. For example, many cultures prohibit women from touching weapons (Brightman 1996). Anthropologists disagree, however, about when a sexual division of labor emerged in human prehistory (Bender 1989, Cucchiari 1981), about the degree to which the division of labor is biologically or culturally determined (Peacock 1991), and whether differences in work roles always lead to differences in status and prestige. For archaeologists, a first task was to find out whether sexual divisions of labor leave material traces. This approach takes for granted the notion that past societies had categories for "men" and "women" that mirror our contemporary notions that conflate sex and gender, i.e. all female-sexed skeletons represent the remains of individuals with similar feminine social identities.

Most archaeologists assume that artifacts and their spatial distribution can tell us about the activities undertaken in houses and other activity areas. In one early attempt to differentiate gendered activities, Kent Flannery and Marcus Winter (1976:34–47) demonstrated how to develop hypotheses about men's and women's activities, and find their spatial correlations. They began with artifacts on house floors, then used archaeological and ethnographic information to interpret their uses. They examined burial data to find out what kinds of "tool kits" appeared with male and female skeletons, then examined the spatial distribution of tools and other artifacts on the house floors as well in groupings that represent larger social units. They identified women's tools, such as grinding stones, pots used for soaking corn in lime, deer bone cornhuskers, and spindle whorls, and men's tools, such as antler tine pressure flakers, projectile points, and many hide-working tools. In some Oaxaca house sites dating to the Formative period, "women's" tools seemed to occur on one side of the house, with "men's" tools clustered on the other side.

Janet Spector's "Male/Female Task Differentiation among the Hidatsa: Toward the Development of an Archaeological Approach to the Study of Gender," (chapter 8) begins with ethnographic data and ends with a discussion of the implications for archaeology. This article was an important early effort to develop methods to help archaeologists consider questions about past divisions of labor. Other studies followed, using a variety of methods.

Sex differences and their archaeological implications have also been investigated by physical anthropologists. Walker and Erlandson (1986) examined evidence for diet in two California Channel Island cemeteries to examine possible changes in men's and women's food procurement activities. Although it appears that women collected and ate more plant foods, while men fished more and ate more protein, this pattern *changed*. In later times, both men and women probably had equal access to fish and women reduced their use of plant foods. This shows that one must not simply *assume* an association between women and plant gathering any more than one can assume that men hunt, and that one cannot generalize from one population or time period to another. Walker and Erlandson's use of dental caries as evidence for dietary differences is an example of using physical remains to compare the diets, health, and nutrition of adult males and females (children's skeletons cannot be sexed).

Evidence for occupational stresses can also be useful. For example, in the Puebloan culture area of the United States Southwest, female skeletons often have robust muscle attachment points in their necks and shoulders, together with arthritic knees, suggesting that they carried heavy loads and spent many hours daily grinding maize. Men's skeletons often have pelvic marks indicating they spent many hours sitting down, perhaps weaving (Wesson and Martin 1995). Patricia Bridges (1989) finds that traces of muscle attachments on arm bones document a change in males' weaponry from spears to the bow and arrows in the Eastern United States. Female skeletons showed no comparable asymmetries, suggesting they did not wield bows.

Kenneth Sassaman moves beyond simply identifying who did what tasks in the past in "Lithic Technology and the Hunter-Gatherer Sexual Division of Labor" (chapter 9). He examines the possible effects of a sexual division of labor on the archaeological interpretation of settlement patterns in the Eastern Woodlands of North America. He assumes that men hunted game, using a stone tool technology, namely hafted bifaces, that was distinct from that used by women for other activities. In the absence of ceramics, archaeologists identify sites and place them in chronological order based on biface types, thus emphasizing kill sites, and butchering sites, probable masculine activities and localities. Ceramics appear long after hafted bifaces. Ceramic period sites are recognized and dated based on pottery types. Presuming that women made, used, and discarded most pottery, archaeologists interpret later sites by emphasizing feminine activities. The full range of women's activities then becomes more visible, including stone tools they probably made and used for a wide variety of tasks. Sassaman argues that the apparent shift from bifaces to smaller, more expedient, and more varied tools might be partly due to a shift in archaeologists' gaze from men's hunting localities to habitation sites where both men and women used stone tools.

Patty Jo Watson, one of the most prominent woman archaeologists working in North America, and her former student, Mary C. Kennedy, show how to engender the past without reference to artifacts and their spatial patterning in "The Development of Horticulture in the Eastern Woodlands of North America: Women's Role" (chapter 10) They investigate:

1   botanical remains to show when and where domesticated plants emerged in the eastern United States;

2   the ethnohistoric record on Native American plant use in the Eastern Woodlands in historic times;

3   comparative ethnographic studies about the division of labor in living cultures;

4   they evaluate several previous hypotheses about the origins of agriculture in the Eastern Woodlands and evaluate them in terms of this evidence.

Watson and Kennedy conclude that Woodland women are likely to have domesticated wild plants by about 2500 BC. Then, after the introduction of maize from Mesoamerica, women actively developed new maize varieties that were better suited to their northern climate.

Many authors, too numerous to include here, have investigated the gendering of certain kinds of labor and craft products and have concluded that the sexual division of labor is really more about gender than sex, and that more than two categories of workers must almost always be considered. Just as women were once thought to be irrelevant or invisible in the archaeological record, the activities and identities of children, elders, and possible third (or more) gender categories are rarely considered, but should be. Still, asking whether the activities of men and women are visible at all in material residues of past activities, and trying to develop some methods for studying gendered activities, were important steps in the history of archaeology. Karen Olsen Bruhns (1991), for example, took on the "ignoble history" of interpreting gender-linked task identification in archaeology, broke down some common assumptions into their constituent parts, and used Mesoamerican ethnographic data on the production of different kinds of textiles and the many uses of grinding stones to illustrate how complicated the gendered division of labor really is – and probably always has been, even in "traditional" societies. Prudence Rice (1991), one of the most important analysts of archaeological ceramics, asked whether any physical differences between the sexes affect the gendering of pottery making as women's work in many cultures, and the gendering of the potter's wheel as male in others. Instead, she proposes that gender *symbolism* and non-biologically-based economic structures play a larger role in the division of labor than sex.

■   ■   ■

Further reading

Benfer, Robert A. Jr. (1990)
Bridges, Patricia S. (1989)
Bruhns, Karen Olsen (1991)
Crown, Patricia L. and W.H. Wills (1995)
Gero, Joan M. (1991)
Hastorf, Christine (1991)
Hollimon, Sandra E. (1992)
Larsen, Clark Spencer (1984)
Peacock, Nadine (1991)
Pohl, Mary and Lawrence H. Feldman (1982)
Rice, Prudence (1991)
Sassaman, Kenneth E. (1992)
Smith, Maria O. (1996)
Walker, Philip L. and Jon M. Erlandson (1986)
Wright, Rita P. (1991)

■ ■ ■

References

Bender, Barbara (1989) "The Roots of Inequality," in D. Miller, M. Rowlands and C. Tilley (eds) *Domination and Resistance*, London: Unwin Hyman, pp. 83–95.

Benfer, Robert A. Jr. (1990) "The Preceramic Site of Paloma, Peru: Bioindications of Improving Adaptation to Sedentism," *Latin American Antiquity* 1:4:284–318.

Bridges, Patricia S. (1989) "Changes in Activities with the Shift to Agriculture in the Southeastern United States," *Current Anthropology* 30:385–394.

Brightman, Robert (1996) "The Sexual Division of Foraging Labor: Biology, Taboo, and Gender Politics." *Comparative Studies in Society and History* 38(4):687–729.

Bruhns, Karen Olsen (1991) "Sexual Activities: Some Thoughts on the Sexual Division of Labor and Archaeological Interpretation" in D. Walde and N. D. Willows (eds.) *The Archaeology of Gender: Proceedings of the 22nd Annual Chacmool Conference*, Calgary: The Archaeological Association of the University of Calgary, pp. 420–429.

Crown, Patricia L., and W. H. Wills (1995) "The Origins of Southwestern Ceramic Containers: Women's Time Allocation and Economic Intensification," *Journal of Anthropological Research* 51(2):173–186.

Cucchiari, Salvatore (1981) "The Gender Revolution and the Transition from Bisexual Horde to Patrilocal Band: The Origins of Gender Hierarchy," in S. B. Ortner and H. Whitehead (eds), *Sexual Meanings: The Cultural Construction of Gender and Sexuality*, Cambridge: Cambridge University Press, pp. 21–79.

Durkheim, Emile (1964) *The Division of Labor in Society*. New York: Free Press.

Gero, Joan M. (1991) "Genderlithics," in J. M. Gero and M. W. Conkey (eds.) *Engendering Archaeology: Women and Prehistory*, Oxford: Basil Blackwell, pp. 163–193.

Hastorf, Christine (1991) "Gender, Space, and Food in Prehistory," in J. M. Gero and M. W. Conkey (eds.) *Engendering Archaeology: Women and Prehistory*, Oxford: Basil Blackwell, pp. 132–159.

Hollimon, Sandra E. (1992) "Health Consequences of Sexual Division of Labor Among Native Americans: The Chumash of California and the Arikara of the Northern Plains," in C. Claassen (ed.) *Exploring Gender Through Archaeology: Selected Papers of the 1991 Boone Conference*, Madison: Prehistory Press, pp. 81–88.

Larsen, Clark Spencer (1984) "Health and Disease in Prehistoric Georgia: The Transition to Agriculture," in M. Cohen and G. Armelagos (eds.) *Paleopathology at the Origins of Agriculture*, Orlando, Florida: Academic Press, pp. 367–392.

Murdock, George Peter and C. Provost (1973) "Factors in the Division of Labor by Sex: A Cross-cultural Analysis," *Ethnology* 12:202–25.

Peacock, Nadine (1991) "Rethinking the Sexual Division of Labor: Reproduction and Women's Work among the Efe," in M. DiLeonardo (ed.) *Gender at the Crossroads of Knowledge: Feminist Anthropology in the Postmodern Era*, Berkeley and Los Angeles: University of California Press, pp. 339–360.

Pohl, Mary, and Lawrence H. Feldman (1982) "The Traditional Role of Women and Animals in Lowland Maya Economy," in K. V. Flannery (ed.) *Maya Subsistence: Essays in Memory of Dennis E. Puleston*, New York: Academic Press, pp. 295–311.

Rice, Prudence (1991) "Women and Prehistoric Pottery Production," in D. Walde and N. Willows (eds.) *The Archaeology of Gender: Proceedings of the 22nd Annual Chacmool Conference*, Calgary: The Archaeological Association of the University of Calgary, pp. 436–443.

Sassaman, Kenneth E. (1992) "Gender and Technology at the Archaic-Woodland 'Transition,'" in C. Claassen (ed.) *Exploring Gender Through Archaeology: Selected Papers of the 1991 Boone Conference*, Madison, Wisconsin: Prehistory Press, pp. 71–79.

Smith, Maria O. (1996) "Bioarchaeological Inquiry into Archaic Period Populations of the Southeast: Trauma and Occupational Stress," in K. Sassaman and D. Anderson (eds.) *Archaeology of the Mid-Holocene Southeast*, Gainesville: University of Florida Press, pp. 137–157.

Walker, Philip L. and Jon M. Erlandson (1986) "Dental Evidence for Prehistoric Dietary Change on the Northern Channel Islands, California," *American Antiquity* 51: 375–383.

Wesson, A. L. and Debra L. Martin (1995) "Women Carried Heavy Loads while Men Were Weaving: Precontact Sexual Division of Labor at Black Mesa, Arizona," paper presented at the 64th Annual American Association of Physical Anthropologists meeting, Oakland, California.

Wright, Rita P. (1991) "Women's Labor and Pottery Production in Prehistory," in J. M. Gero and M. W. Conkey (eds.) *Engendering Archaeology: Women and Prehistory*, Oxford: Basil Blackwell, pp. 194–223.

Chapter 8

MALE/FEMALE TASK DIFFERENTIATION
AMONG THE HIDATSA:
Toward the Development of an Archeological
Approach to the Study of Gender

Janet D. Spector

The rise of feminist anthropology raises a series of challenging questions for archeologists. The significance of gender in social life has been well documented in numerous recent publications (see Rosaldo and Lamphere 1974; Reiter 1975 for collections of articles on the anthropological study of gender), but to date, the study of gender behavior has not been the focus of archeological research. The present investigation was stimulated by two essentially archeological questions about gender and society. First, how might our views of patterns of adaptation, change and stability in prehistory or early historic periods be altered by the consideration of gender? In other words, what role did gender behavior play in shaping the responses of populations to changes in their social or natural environments? This kind of question immediately raises the issue of archeological methods, a second concern stimulating this study: to what extent is it possible to retrieve information about gender from archeological sites and assemblages? The desire to bring together perspectives of contemporary archeology and feminist anthropology has stimulated the development of a new analytical framework, male/female task differentiation, introduced and illustrated in this paper using data on the historically known Hidatsa Indians of the Great Plains.

Introduction

The approach taken in this study is similar to the work of a number of other "ethnoarcheologists" interested in social organizational or behavioral questions (see David 1971; Binford 1975; Schiffer

1976:5–6; Yellen 1977 for examples of ethnoarcheology). In this kind of approach the archeologist initially examines the relationships between material and non-material dimensions of specified behavior in contemporary or ethnographically known cultural settings so that ". . . understandings of the relationships between material and non-material derived from maximum information well controlled can then be fed back into the traditional archeological contexts for more precise inference" (Deetz 1972:115). Lewis Binford, for example, studied the butchering practices of contemporary Eskimo hunters and the animal remains left behind at their butchering sites, to better understand the distributional patterns of various animal bones at archeological sites (Binford 1975:11–30). Similarly, William Longacre is examining the transmission of knowledge about ceramic manufacturing techniques in a group which still produces pottery for domestic use to more reliably interpret the spatial distribution and variability of ceramic remains in archeological contexts (Longacre, personal communication). The long range goal of these and other ethnoarcheological investigations is to enhance our ability to describe and explain cultural processes operant in the past by increasing our capacity to interpret archeological assemblages.

The attempt to design and employ an ethnoarcheological research approach to the study of gender began with the development of an analytical framework suitable for the reanalysis of selected ethnographic data – that is, a framework which highlights information of particular interest to the archeologist. At the core of the proposed framework is the analysis of activities, an orientation similar to that suggested by Michael Schiffer (1976:49–53, 1977:3). More specifically, the task differentiation framework focuses on the organization of males and females in the execution of tasks and the spatial, temporal and material dimensions of those tasks. This focus on activities reflects the primary concerns of the research: first, to explore the feasibility of studying gender in archeological contexts and second, to better understand the relationships between gender and patterns of adaptation, change and stability.

In the first case, it seems logical to assume that the structure of archeological sites – the frequency, variability and distribution of material remains and the spatial arrangements and physical characteristics of structures and facilities – is related to the kinds of activities engaged in by a given population within a particular environmental setting. In discussing the structure of archeological sites, archeologists have often focussed on the cultural and natural factors operating after site abandonment and the way factors like erosion, decay or conditions of abandonment alter or distort the archeological record (Schiffer 1976:27–43). In the present study, the approach taken first examines the possible relationships between the activity patterns of males and females and their activity settings in ethnographically known contexts. When relationships between gender and activity settings can be demonstrated in on-going cultural systems, we can then consider the factors which might act to distort these relationships in archeological sites, hopefully setting the stage for the eventual examination of gender utilizing the archeological record.

The activity orientation of the task differentiation framework is also relevant to the study of gender behavior and adaptation, change and stability through time. It seems reasonable to suggest that men and women in a given population might respond differentially to changes in their social or natural environments depending on the kinds of tasks they engage in; the geographical spaces they utilize in the performance of tasks; the scheduling of their tasks; and the materials (artifacts, structures, facilities) they use and/or produce as a part of their task assignments. The framework proposed here illuminates similarities and differences in the activity patterns of males and females by permitting the analytical separation of the sexes prior to generalization about the group as a whole. As important, the framework reduces the likelihood of androcentrism (male centered biases) which has too often characterized anthropological research and discourse (see Reiter 1975; Rosaldo and Lamphere 1974; Noble 1978; Leacock 1978 for discussion of androcentric bias in anthropology).

This paper presents the results of preliminary research on the task differentiation approach. Much work remains to be done before the framework might be adapted for the study of gender in archeological contexts. The purpose of this paper is to introduce the framework and to illustrate some of the implications of the framework through the case of the 19th-century Hidatsa Indians. In an effort to refine and test the utility of the approach, data presented on the Hidatsa by Bowers (1965) and Wilson (1917, 1934, 1971) were re-analyzed. Not unexpectedly, the analysis was handicapped by certain problems in the ethnographic accounts. Both Bowers and Wilson studied the Hidatsa during the early decades of the 20th century, working with elderly informants to reconstruct traditional Hidatsa culture. In many cases their descriptions lack chronological control, making it difficult to get a sense of the group at any one point in time. Second, these ethnographers, like many of their contemporary counterparts, were not interested in specific details of material culture, so important to archeologists. Finally, neither Wilson nor Bowers was particularly concerned with the sexual division of labor. The Bowers account of Hidatsa social and ceremonial organization suffers from a pervasive androcentrism, peripheralizing the roles and experiences of Hidatsa females by emphasizing the lives of men and boys. Wilson, in contrast, focused his attention almost exclusively on women, but his work is limited to a narrow range of activities. In spite of these limitations, combining information provided by Bowers and Wilson within the task differentiation framework, did permit the refinement of the approach and suggested implications of the framework for future research on gender.

General background on the 19th-century Hidatsa

The Hidatsa are commonly described as one of the earth lodge village groups of the Great Plains. These groups were basically sedentary hoe agriculturalists whose subsistence depended primarily on horticultural products and secondarily on bison and other animal resources prior to the disruptions and cultural changes triggered by events of the contact period (Spencer and Jennings 1965:339). Linguistically, the Siouan speaking Hidatsa were closely related to the Crow, but their cultural patterns during the 19th century resembled those of their neighbors, the Mandan.

During the early years of the 19th century, the Hidatsa reportedly consisted of three, independent village groups, distinct both culturally and historically, living in close proximity along the Knife River in North Dakota. By 1837, following smallpox epidemics which greatly reduced their numbers, these three groups coalesced and along with members of the Mandan tribe, they moved to a new village on the Knife, known as "Like-a-Fishhook." By 1862, they were joined at that village by the Caddoan speaking Arikara. These three groups continued to live together on the Knife River, until 1885 when they were forced to move to the Fort Berthold Reservation (Bowers 1965:10–35).

In describing the Hidatsa during the mid-19th century, both Bowers and Wilson relied on the recollections of elderly informants interviewed in the early decades of the 20th century. According to Bowers, traditionally the basic economic unit of the Hidatsa was the household, or "extended matrilinear family," based on matrilocal residence (Bowers 1965:159). Typically, he reports, a household consisted of older parents, daughters with their husband or husbands, unmarried daughters and sons, and usually a few orphans belonging to the clan of the females (Bowers 1965). According to Wilson's major informant, Buffalo Bird Woman, there were about 70 earth lodges housing these family units in Like-a-Fishhook village during the 1840s (Wilson 1971:44). Though this village was the permanent home base of the Hidatsa, groups of households often left the village at different times of the year to hunt buffalo and other animals, setting up temporary camps along the route to the animals. The people also moved to temporary winter camps, close to fuel (wood) supplies, but for the most part Hidatsa household units lived together in the permanent village, with each extended family residing in their own earth lodge.

Hidatsa task differentiation

The attempt to reanalyze the ethnographic data on the Hidatsa presented by Bowers and Wilson in terms of gender behavior, started with the identification of tasks performed by males and females. Operationally, a task has been defined here as a segment of activity which has discrete parameters in terms of the social unit of task performance, that is, the segment of the population engaged in the task; the season, frequency and duration of the task; the location of task performance; and the material – artifacts, structures and facilities – associated with the execution of the task. The following table illustrates how information was organized within the framework for the analysis of activities involved in the procurement and processing of horticultural products (cultigens).

Unfortunately, given the limitations of the Bowers and Wilson reports, it was not possible to establish a complete task inventory for the mid-19th century Hidatsa.

Some activities – the procurement and processing of cultigens, lodge construction, buffalo procurement and processing – are described in considerable detail. Other activities, including small game hunting, warfare, ceremonies, childrearing, trading, to name but a few, are activities alluded to in the ethnographies but poorly described for purposes of this research. Even when particular tasks involved in activities could be defined, details on task organization, timing, locations and materials were not specific enough to permit full employment of the task differentiation framework. Nonetheless the focus on male and female activity patterns did offer new perspectives on the Hidatsa obscured in the reports of Bowers and Wilson.

The most striking feature of Hidatsa task differentiation is the contrast between the activity patterns of the men and women. With the exception of actually killing animals, Hidatsa women procured and processed all food resources. From what can be abstracted from the ethnographic accounts, the women also collected and processed other natural resources utilized by the group – wood, water, wild plants, herbs, bark and reeds. Female work groups similarly performed the tasks associated with processing buffalo and other animal skins, and constructing and maintaining structures (e.g. earth lodges, temporary dwellings, specialized activity structures) facilities (e.g. drying racks, storage racks, cache pits) and household furnishings. The only male participation reported for resource procurement and processing or in the construction and maintenance of structures and facilities was some occasional assistance in the gardens of elderly men; some male assistance in transporting harvested crops from gardens to the village; the killing and butchering of meat; the procurement and processing of tobacco; and the erection of the four main poles in earth lodges. The men appear to have been engaged for the most part preparing for hunts and raids, preparations which involved long hours of discussion, days of fasting, vision quests and self-torture.

In addition to distinctions in the kinds of tasks performed consideration of parameters of task differentiation highlights other differences between the sexes. Women of individual households – sisters, mothers and daughters – constituted the major unit of female labor, with most tasks performed by one to three women of an earth lodge. Male activities, in contrast, do not appear to have followed this household pattern. Male task groups tended to be larger than female groups and involved members of several households with labor commonly divided by age. On summer buffalo hunts, for example, younger men performed tasks concerned with scouting for buffalo and tending horses. Older men participated in planning and ritual acts associated with the hunt. The men of other age groups engaged in activities like policing the hunting camps or actually killing and butchering the animals.

Task settings, like task organization, were significantly different for Hidatsa men and women. Women's activities took place primarily in gardens, located within a mile of the permanent village, lodge interiors and the areas immediately adjacent to their lodges. Though men spent some time inside the lodges visiting with other men or planning hunts and raids, many more of their activities took them outside the boundaries of the villages or temporary camps. This pattern can again

Table 1 Tasks associated with the procurement and processing of cultigens

Task	Social unit	Task setting	Task time	Task materials
Garden clearing	Women of lodge; occasionally assisted by elderly men	Gardens (¾ mile from summer village)	Spring–Fall	hoes, rakes, digging sticks
Planting	Women of lodge; assistance from related women from other lodges	Gardens (¾ mile from summer village)	mornings; Spring –early summer	hoes, rakes, wooden bowls
Weeding	Women of lodge; occasionally assisted by elderly men	Gardens (¾ mile from summer village)	Early summer	hoes, rakes
Crop protection	Young girls of lodge, usually two	Gardens (¾ mile from summer village)	daily/all day; late summer – harvest in fall	scarecrows, watching stage, ladder, associated cook hut and cooking equipment
Corn harvesting	Women of lodge; young men assist in transport of crop to village	Gardens (¾ mile from summer village	August–September	Baskets, horses and gear for transportation
Corn husking	2–3 women of lodge with assistance of young men	Gardens (¾ mile from summer village)	September	?
Corn shelling	Women of lodge	Threshing booth – lodge exterior	September	Threshing booth, flail stick, mussel shells
Corn cob burning	1 or 2 women of the lodge	Periphery of village	daily; after day's threshing; September	baskets; skin wrappers
Corn storage	Women of lodge; often mother daughter	lodge interior/lodge exterior	September–November	cache pit, skins
Corn grinding	1–2 women of the lodge	lodge interior	daily; year round	corn mortar

Table 1 continued

Task	Social unit	Task setting	Task time	Task materials
Corn cooking	1–2 women of the lodge	lodge interior	daily; year round	clay pot, wooden stirring spoons, paddles, wooden bowls, horn spoons, sticks, corn mortar, hearth
Bean harvesting		NO INFORMATION		
Bean threshing	1–2 women of the lodge	garden	Fall	tent cover (skin), stick, basket or wooden bowl
Bean storage	1–2 women of the lodge	lodge exterior	Fall	cache pit, skin bag
Bean cooking	1–2 women of the lodge	lodge interior	daily; year round	central hearth and cooking equipment (see corn cooking)
Squash harvesting	1–2 women of the lodge	garden	Fall	baskets
Squash drying (includes picking, slicing, stringing, drying)	Women of lodge and "hired" old women of village assisted by young males	lodge interior/lodge exterior	one month; fall	baskets, squash knife, spits, skin robes, wooden needle, drying stage (lodge exterior), squash rack (lodge exterior), drying stage (lodge interior)
Squash storage	1–2 women of the lodge	lodge interior/lodge exterior	Fall	Old tent cover or skin; cache pits (with corn)
Squash cooking	1–2 women of the lodge	lodge interior	daily; year round	clay pots, wooden paddles, wooden bowl, hearth
Sunflower harvesting	Probably women of the lodge	garden	?Fall	?

Table 1 continued

Task	Social unit	Task setting	Task time	Task materials
Sunflower threshing	1–2 women of the lodge	lodge roof/lodge exterior	late fall	baskets, knife, skins, stick
Sunflower parching	1–2 women of the lodge	lodge interior	late fall	clay pot, stick, horn spoon, wooden bowl
Sunflower storage	1–2 women of the lodge	lodge interior	late fall	skin bags
Sunflower grinding	1 woman of the lodge	lodge interior	late fall	corn mortar
Sunflower cooking	1–2 women of the lodge	lodge interior	daily; year round	clay pot, wooden paddle, wooden bowl, central hearth
Processing gourds		NO INFORMATION		
Clearing tobacco gardens	older males	tobacco garden	early spring	hoe, rake and/or buffalo rib
Tobacco planting	1–2 men	tobacco garden	spring	buffalo rib
Weeding tobacco garden	1–2 men	tobacco garden	May–June	buffalo rib
Harvesting tobacco	1–2 men; girls of lodge might assist old men	tobacco garden	June–August: blossoms; Sept.-Nov.: plants	bark and scrotum (buffalo) baskets
Tobacco drying	1 man	blossoms: lodge interior (near lodge shrine); plants: lodge interior near cache pits	June-August: blossoms; Sept.-Nov.: plants	hides, plank, spit
Tobacco storage	1 man	lodge interior	September–November	cache pit or skin package

be illustrated in the example of the summer hunt. Both males and females of various households travelled great distances from the permanent village in search of buffalo herds. Once they located the animals the men generally stayed outside of the camps killing and butchering buffalo, while the women remained at the camps processing meat and hides inside or near the lodges or tipis.

The temporal dimensions of men's and women's lives also differed. Though the details of timing in terms of task frequency and duration are poorly documented in the ethnographies, it appears that men had few activities scheduled on a daily basis. Groups of men are reported to have spent days at a time away from the villages on raiding expeditions, stopping along the way to hunt and perform rituals with few indications of time constraints. In contrast, Hidatsa women had a number of tasks at any time of the year scheduled on a daily basis. Garden work, resource processing like cooking or manufacturing implements, all seem to have been rather tightly scheduled each day. Women's activities also appear to have been more closely tied to seasonality than men's, in part a function of the time defining characteristics of horticultural work.

The material dimension of Hidatsa task differentiation, like temporal features, was difficult to abstract from the accounts of Bowers and Wilson. Wood and animal skins were the primary raw materials used in the manufacture of structures, facilities, clothing and artifacts. Responsibility for collecting wood and processing hides was with the women. Given the greater number and variety of tasks performed by the women, it seems likely that they utilized more materials and a wider range of materials than the men did. They do appear to have been engaged in the production of more material goods than men.

Implications of the task differentiation approach

There is certainly much more to know about Hidatsa task differentiation than was possible working with the published reports of Wilson and Bowers. The value of the reanalysis of their data in terms of the framework was that it permitted a clearer understanding of the implications of the approach for future research on gender.

The potential of the approach is perhaps best illustrated by describing how the framework might be used to structure research in the field where a group could be observed directly. A primary value of reanalyzing the Hidatsa data was that it helped to specify the kinds of information crucial to the full employment of the framework. The initial step in such a study would be to determine the full range of tasks engaged in by the population and the organizational, spatial, temporal and material characteristics of each task. Once these basic descriptive data are collected, the analysis could move to a higher level of abstraction emphasizing the sets of relationships between tasks and the dimensions of task differentiation. This step of the research can be envisioned as the construction of a series of activity maps wherein the investigator would essentially map out or graphically represent the types of tasks taking place at any given time.

One series of activity maps should focus on task organization, highlighting the spatial and temporal relationships between task actors. We know that among the Hidatsa, small groups of women from each household performed a series of horticultural tasks on a daily basis. In mapping these tasks it would be important to determine how each work unit was related to other work units. One picture might be that each female task unit worked in their gardens at the same time as other household units, implying some kind of temporal coordination of women through scheduling. If the gardens were located in close proximity, the actors would also be connected in a spatial sense. If the task actors are spatially and temporally linked in this way, they have the potential of interactions precluded in a system where the task units are separated either spatially or temporally. For any one task identified for a community, there are various time and space relationships possible between the work units. The units may be working independent of other units performing the same task; they may be linked through scheduling but separated spatially; or they may be performing their tasks at the same time and in locations close enough to permit social interaction. Each variant of the time/space organization of task actors suggests different kinds of relationships between members of the community.

A second kind of activity mapping should highlight the temporal dimension of task organization. By plotting out the range of tasks engaged in by a population at any given time period (time of the day, week, season etc.) we would have another means of studying the relationships between particular tasks and task actors. When Hidatsa women were in their gardens, for example, it would be important to see what tasks were being performed by other women and men near the gardens or in settings distant from the gardens. A series of time-specific maps would illustrate the scheduling system for the group as a whole; the distribution of the population geographically at various times; and indicate some of the equipment demands of the task system. If many tasks are scheduled concurrently and take place in settings separated by considerable distances, a higher demand for equipment would exist for the group as a whole than would be the case if tasks were scheduled sequentially or if they were performed in close proximity permitting the sharing of equipment and facilities.

A third type of activity mapping could focus directly on the spatial dimensions of task differentiation. In addition to identifying the locations of each task performed, it would be useful to distinguish those spaces used for many tasks, i.e. multi-purpose settings, from those locations which are more task specialized. The interiors of earth lodges among the Hidatsa were dense with activity as many different female tasks took place in that setting. We might expect that lodge size and the arrangement of artifacts and facilities in the lodges would be different if they were used for a smaller number or another set of activities. The spatial maps would also allow the graphic representation of proximic relations between men and women performing different tasks at the same time, permitting the detection of regularities in such relationships. Finally the focus on the spatial dimension of task differentiation might draw attention to possible distinguishing characteristics of spaces used primarily by women compared to spaces used primarily by men. Among the Hidatsa, the only hint of such gender distinctions is the fact that the settings utilized primarily by females tend to be characterized by a greater number of stationary facilities – drying racks, storage racks and pits, wooden mortars and so on – than the spaces used primarily by men.

A final set of activity maps constructed to define relationships between task differentiation parameters could focus on the material dimensions of tasks. In the study of the Hidatsa it was sometimes possible to define the material unit of different tasks – those artifacts, facilities and structures associated with the tasks – but the material linkages between task actors could not be determined. In graphically representing these relationships the emphasis would be on the way materials were used during task performance, that is, whether actors shared the materials necessary for executing the task or if each actor was essentially materially autonomous, possessing their own set of necessary equipment. The sharing of equipment suggests very different kinds of spatial and temporal relationships between actors than the kind of time and space flexibility permitted if each individual has his or her own set of equipment.

The notion of activity mapping has been used to illustrate some of the possible relationships between task parameters of particular interest to the ethnoarcheologist interested in the study of gender. The manner in which actors use materials, combined with the organizational, scheduling and locational aspects of task performance all presumably structure the material demands and characteristics of the task system. These equipment demands in turn affect the frequency and duration of resource procurement tasks necessary to supply raw materials for the manufacture of that equipment. It is doubtful that the specific regularities in these kinds of relationships can be systematically examined through analysis of existing ethnographic information. It may well be necessary to conduct ethnographic field studies, like Binford, Longacre and other ethnoarcheologists, before the task differentiation framework can be adapted for application to archeological assemblages. We still need to know much more about the specific relationships between gender behavior as seen through task differentiation patterns and activity settings.

Though the archeological application of the framework must await further research, the reanalysis of Hidatsa data did demonstrate the potential of the approach for purposes of studying possible relationships between gender and culture change. In spite of limitations of the ethnographies, it can be established that the lives of Hidatsa men and women during the mid-19th century were impressively separate and distinct. The males and females participated in different, often unrelated tasks; they utilized different geographical spaces; the tempo of their lives was different; and the volume and kinds of materials produced and used by each sex was different. This kind of sexual segregation or gender autonomy was not indicated by either Bowers or Wilson, yet it seems a crucially important aspect of Hidatsa life.

First, the distinctiveness of male and female activity patterns among the Hidatsa (and other sexually segregated groups) suggests that generalizations about the "culture" of the group must be made with great caution. The importance of households, clans, age grades or other conventionally used ethnographic constructs may differ significantly in reference to men and women in groups with this type of task differentiation system. Among the Hidatsa the household does seem to be an important social unit if the analysis centers on the lives and activities of women. It seems less appropriate for describing men's activities which are typically organized in a manner cross-cutting household units. Even generalizations about seasonal patterns or life cycle in a system like the Hidatsa must be made separately for the men and women prior to generalizations about the group as a whole.

The task differentiation framework also exposed some of the dangers involved in the assessment of relative status between men and women, a subject of considerable interest in recent years to a number of anthropologists (see Rosaldo and Lamphere 1974). Many researchers have pointed out the problems of androcentrism in studying status differences where the assumption is made that what men do is of greater importance than what women do. Bowers is certainly guilty of this kind of bias. In describing the social organization of the Hidatsa, for example, Bowers emphasizes the importance of councils and leadership, cultural domains dominated by the men. It appears that the women did not participate in planning hunts or in raiding, activities centrally important to the men and routinely discussed in council meetings of older, prominent men. It was in the context of hunts and warfare that male leadership among the Hidatsa is most conspicuously important. However, in working with Wilson's data it becomes equally apparent that the men were excluded from participation in female activities, particularly resource procurement and processing, or the construction of structures, facilities, and material goods all centrally important to the lives of the women and to the survival of the group.

In a sexually segregated task system like the Hidatsa, both males and females have access to information, knowledge and materials unavailable to the opposite sex. Though the data are not altogether clear, it appears that decision-making was also sexually segregated among the Hidatsa with women in control of their spheres of activity and men involved in decision-making about male activities. It becomes problematic to determine the relative status of men and women in this type of system without arbitrarily attaching more importance to the experience and activities of males, as Bowers did, or females. A more fruitful and interesting focus of analysis may well be the examination of the specific bonds between males and females when they seem most systematically linked to members of their own sex.

In addition to demonstrating the dangers of generalizing about groups as a whole and illustrating the potential of a framework which permits the analytical separation of the sexes for a better understanding of gender behavior, the task differentiation approach also offers new perspectives on the subjects of adaptation, change and stability patterns through time – one of the central concerns inspiring the research. In reanalyzing the ethnographic data in terms of this framework it became clear that the introduction of new items of technology, contact with new groups, population fluctuations and other changes in the social or natural environment are all factors which would have differentially affected Hidatsa men and women. Though it was not possible to fully employ the framework, with more precise information about a group, it should be possible to trace the specific impacts of any single change factor throughout the task differentiation system and eventually to compare the impact of the same kind of change factor on groups with different task systems. One might suggest that changes which draw off male or female labor in a sexually segregated task system like the Hidatsa would affect the group quite differently than in a system where men and women work together in performing tasks. Similarly, changes which affect task scheduling, materials or settings will all have varying effects on a group and on the male and female actors within the group depending on the task system operating.

Conclusions

This study was stimulated by the desire to bring together the concerns and perspectives of feminist anthropology and contemporary archeology, potentially adding an important time dimension to the study of gender and society. Research began by examining some of the possible relationships between the material and non-material aspects of gender behavior in an ethnographically documented cultural setting, a basic step toward enhancing our abilities to interpret archeological assemblages more reliably. For purposes of reanalyzing selected ethnographic data on the Hidatsa Indians a new framework, male/female task differentiation, was developed. This framework highlights distinctive features of male and female activity patterns, focusing particularly on tasks and their organizational, temporal, spatial, and material dimensions, all aspects of behavior theoretically observable in the archeological record.

The research on task differentiation is still in its preliminary stages. The analysis of the Hidatsa, handicapped in some ways by limitations of the ethnograpic reports, did permit refinement of the approach and illustrated the potential of the framework for archeology and ethnography. For the Hidatsa specifically, implementation of the framework exposed a number of important contrasts in the lives of men and women. Though a complete description of Hidatsa task differentiation was not possible, the analysis demonstrates that generalizations about Hidatsa culture must be made with great caution, clearly distinguishing the lives and experiences of men and women. The analysis further suggests that Hidatsa men and women undoubtedly responded differently to conditions of change brought about by contact with Euro-Americans during the latter part of the 19th century.

The next steps toward testing the utility and promise of the approach are to increase the sample of groups analyzed, particularly through implementation of the framework in a field setting where collection of data can be carefully controlled.

Through expansion of the ethnographic sample we can begin to define regularities and variability in task differentiation patterns. Equipped with better understanding of this aspect of gender behavior, we can eventually transform the framework for archeological purposes, adding new dimensions to the study of fundamental cultural processes of adaptation, change and stability.

References

Binford, Lewis (1975) Historical Archeology: Is it Historical or Archeological? *Popular Archaeology* 4 (3–4): 11–30.

Bowers, Alfred (1965) Hidatsa Social and Ceremonial Organization. Smithsonian Institution. *Bureau of American Ethnology Bulletin*, 194.

David, Nicholas (1971) The Fulani Compound and the Archaeologist. *World Archaeology* 3: 111–131.

Deetz, James (1972) Archaeology as a Social Science. In: *Contemporary Archeology: A Guide to Theory and Contributions*, Mark P. Leone (ed.), pp. 108–117.

Leacock, Eleanor (1978) Women's Status in Egalitarian Society: Implications for Social Evolution. *Current Anthropology*, 19(2): 247–275.

Longacre, William (1977) Personal communication.

Noble, Barbara (1978) *Sexual Politics and Theorizing: An Example from Anthropology.* Mimeographed, Department of Anthropology, University of Minnesota.

Reiter, Rayna (ed.) (1975) *Toward an Anthropology of Women.* Monthly Review Press.

Rosaldo, Michelle, and Louise Lamphere (eds) (1974) *Woman, Culture and Society.* Stanford University Press.

Schiffer, Michael (1976) *Behavioral Archeology.* Academic Press.

—— (1977) A Preliminary Consideration of Behavioral Change. To appear in: *Transformations: Mathematical Approaches to Culture Change*, Colin Renfrew and Kenneth Cooke (eds.) Academic Press.

Spencer, Robert F., and Jesse D. Jennings (1965) *The Native Americans: Prehistory and Ethnology of the North American Indians.* New York: Harper and Row.

Wilson, Gilbert (1917) Agriculture of the Hidatsa Indians: An Indian Interpretation. *Studies in the Social Sciences*, No. 9. University of Minnesota.

—— (1934) The Hidatsa Earthlodge. *Anthropological Papers*, Vol. XXXIII, Part V. The Museum of Natural History.

—— (1971) Waheenee: An Indian Girl's Story Told by Herself to Gilbert L. Wilson. Reprinted in: *North Dakota History* 38(1, 12).

Yellen, John (1977) *Archaeological Approaches to the Present.* Academic Press.

Chapter 9

LITHIC TECHNOLOGY AND THE HUNTER-GATHERER SEXUAL DIVISION OF LABOR

Kenneth E. Sassaman

A technological change from formal to expedient core reduction marks the "transition" from mobile to sedentary prehistoric societies in many parts of the world. The phenomenon has often been attributed to changes in the organization of men's activities, particularly hunting. Considering, however, that the change coincides with the adoption of pottery, technology usually attributed to women, an alternative explanation must be considered. From the standpoint of archaeological systematics, the addition of pottery turns our focus away from places where hafted bifaces were discarded toward places where pottery was discarded. The latter are largely domestic contexts: locations at which women, as well as men, employed expedient core technology for a variety of tasks. Thus, the perceived change in core technology reflects the increased visibility of women's activities in the archaeological record. This recognition provides a basis for incorporating gender variables into our interpretations of prehistoric technology and labor organization.

Within American archaeology, studies of lithic technology are burgeoning in new and productive directions. Moving away from the traditional pursuits of chronology and function, lithic analysts are developing method and theory for relating stone tool technology to issues of broad anthropological relevance. These efforts have been particularly important in the study of hunter-gatherers, societies whose traces are often limited to stone tools and the by-products of their manufacture and use. Interpretations of hunter-gatherer settlement-subsistence organization (Amick, 1987; Jefferies, 1982; Raab et al., 1979), mobility (Kelly, 1988; Lurie, 1989; Parry and Kelly, 1987; Shott, 1986), time management (Torrence, 1983), and risk avoidance (Bleed, 1986; Myers, 1989; Torrence, 1989) have all been derived from studies of lithic technology (see Nelson, 1991 for recent review).

A common denominator in this work is that technological variation is referable to environmental variation – the geological occurrence of rock, the seasonality and spatial distribution of food resources, and so forth. Lithic studies that focus on social dimensions of technology are lagging behind the ecological or techno-environmental efforts. With few exceptions (e.g., Cross, 1990), studies addressing social issues – the organization of labor, inequality, control, and the like – concern relatively complex societies (e.g., Clark, 1987; Gero, 1989). The lack of similar approaches to hunter-gatherer technology might be traced to stereotypes about simple societies – that by being egalitarian, all members of the group have access to technology, including the materials and information needed to make and use tools, as well as the products of labor. We simply do not expect much social differentiation in the manufacture, distribution, and consumption of hunter-gatherer stone tools.

While this assumption is itself a subject of debate, there is one dimension of social variation that we accept in hunter-gatherers ethnographically, but do not explicitly incorporate into our models of hunter-gatherers archaeologically. That dimension is the division of labor by sex.

Nearly all recent attempts at modeling hunter-gatherer lithic technology have treated groups as if they were composed of undifferentiated members. The issue I want to address in this article is simply whether or not we can continue to develop models of lithic technology while ignoring the sexual division of labor. It seems apparent that most lithic analysts have implicitly assumed that only men made and used flaked stone tools. However, recent reviews of ethnographic literature render this position untenable (Bird, 1988; Gero, 1991). Moreover, even if women did not make and use stone tools in some prehistoric societies, it is unrealistic to assume that the economic activities of women were not factored into decisions about the production, use, and discard of men's technology.

I want to add to the growing recognition of women's roles in stone tool production and use by pointing out how attention to gender variables can enhance extant interpretations of technological variation and change. My basic argument is quite simple: if we allow that women and men alike used stone tools, we should anticipate that any differences in the productive activities of men and women involving stone tools would contribute to technological variation in the material records of those activities. Such differences might include spatial patterns of work, work schedules, scale of production, access to raw materials, and discard behavior, to name but a few potential axes of variation. Needless to say, these sorts of variables are central to our perceptions and interpretations of prehistoric society.

I employ as a case study the purported change from formal to expedient core technology that is thought to mark the transition from mobile to sedentary prehistoric societies in many parts of the world. This shift has been recently attributed to changes in the organization of male hunting activities (Torrence, 1989) and to changes in patterns of residential mobility (Parry and Kelly, 1987). I will show how a consideration of gender provides alternative readings of the data.

Archaeological time–space systematics

To begin, I propose that the perceived transition from formal to expedient core technology is in part shaped by the categories used to order archaeological time. As a foundation for this proposition, let us assume that there was a basic division of labor whereby men hunted game, and women collected plants and small animal resources. Let us also assume that hunting technology was distinct from other lithic technology, and that the technological requirements of hunting game contributed to regularities in tool design that are now useful in dividing archaeological time into meaningful phases or periods. It follows that time–space systematics in archaeology are largely based on continuity and change in the design of tools used by men; in North America these consist largely of hafted bifaces, both projectiles and other bifacial tools associated with hunting activity.

While hafted bifaces comprise the primary diagnostic artifacts for early North American prehistory, pottery types replace bifaces as the chief time markers during late prehistory. Cross-cultural evidence allows us to safely assume that women made and used most of the pottery in these prehistoric societies (Arnold, 1985:108). It follows, then, that late prehistory is subdivided temporally by variation in technology usually attributed to women.

The significance of this observation becomes apparent when we consider the distinct disposal patterns of hafted bifaces versus pottery, and how these differences predetermine the distribution of associated archaeological remains (Figure 1). Specifically, hafted bifaces used in hunting are discarded at some domestic sites (where tools are replaced; represented in Figure 1 by the intersection of male and female activity loci), and at hunting-related and quarry-related locations used exclusively by men. In contrast, pottery is discarded at most, if not all, domestic sites and perhaps also at some locations where women conducted specialized activities. In short, the archaeological record of the preceramic period consists almost exclusively of locations at which hafted bifaces were discarded, while the ceramic period record consists largely of locations at which pottery was discarded. Inasmuch as the sexual division of labor ensures that these locations are not completely isomorphic, the preceramic and ceramic period archaeological records represent distinct samples of settlement variation. Our disregard for gender roles in this respect renders comparisons of the preceramic and ceramic periods untenable. As a result, observed differences in the records of these periods are interpreted as the result of anything other than gender.

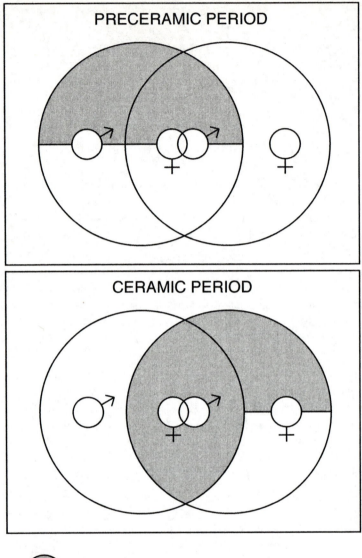

 Locations at which primary diagnostic
artifacts enter archaeological context

Figure 1 Model of the spatial relationships between the sexual division of labor and distributions of diagnostic artifacts in preceramic and ceramic period contexts

I must interject at this point that the model I propose applies to the hunting of
solitary game such as white-tailed deer, but not herd or migratory species such
as bison, reindeer, and caribou. In hunting the latter, entire co-resident groups

relocate to kill sites after a successful hunt. Under these circumstances, we should not anticipate spatial separation of men's and women's activities at the intersite level of analysis. Unfortunately, equivalent analogs for the organization of white-tailed deer hunting are not available. I can only assume that some of the intersite assemblage variability observed in the archaeological record of temperate forest hunter-gatherers reflects a spatial (and sexual) dichotomy in the logistical organization of deer hunting. Even if this dichotomy is exaggerated, the addition of pottery to the archaeological record of temperate forest hunter-gatherers assures that we are focused on locations at which women worked. This alone creates a potential bias in the way we perceive functional differences between preceramic and ceramic period sites.

Such gender bias is illustrated in recent models for the apparent shift from formal to expedient core reduction in flaked stone industries. Because it seemingly reflects a degeneration of the art of flintknapping, the change is sometimes referred to as "devolutionary" (Torrence, 1989:58). What is interesting about the change is that it occurs in so many different places across the globe, and at similar junctures in the histories of local prehistoric populations. Two models have been developed to account for these broad patterns. One developed by Torrence (1989) points to changes in the risk avoidance strategies of hunters as societies become increasingly dependent on agricultural production. An alternative articulated by Parry and Kelly (1987) focuses on the diminishing need for portable bifacial cores as the residential mobility of hunter-gatherers decreased through time. Both arguments are logically sound and supported by evidence. However, because the technological change coincides with the adoption of pottery in many parts of the globe, our perceptions of it are partly shaped by a shift in focus from men's roles to women's roles in stone tool production and use. If we include gender in the extant models of this technological change, we not only eliminate this bias, but also introduce a variable that accounts for more of the variation in the design, use, and discard of lithic stone tools cross-culturally.

Stone tools and risk avoidance

Robin Torrence (1989) proposes that cross-cultural variation in design and use of stone tools can be understood as a function of the risk avoidance strategies of hunter-gatherers. Of particular relevance is the short-term risk involved in capturing food. The abundance of a food resource at a particular point in space and time is an essential component of such risk, but the greatest risk arises when there is a dependence on mobile prey for food (Torrence, 1989:59). Conversely, relatively little short-term risk is expected when there is dependence on foods that are stationary, particularly plant foods. Torrence concludes that "the percentage of plant versus animal resources in the diet can be taken as a very rough indication of the strength of a potential risk faced by a hunter-gatherer group" (Torrence, 1989:60).

To illustrate the role of risk avoidance in tool design, Torrence draws a contrast between *instruments* on the one hand, and *weapons* and *facilities* on the other. She shows that instruments dominate the tool assemblages of hunter-gatherers whose diets consisted mainly of plant foods, while weapons and facilities characterize the technologies of groups dependent on mobile game (see Torrence, 1983). She further describes how hunting technology consists of complex, formalized tools designed for long-lasting, reliable service (see Bleed, 1986). That is, hunting tools are ready when needed, unlikely to fail, and easy to repair. These properties, Torrence argues, avert much of the uncertainty of hunting by minimizing the chance of technological failure.

In contrast, the instruments of the more vegetarian hunter-gatherers need not be maintainable or reliable because the timing and severity of risk are insignificant. Instruments are thus simple in design and rarely maintained for continuous or long-term use. In this regard, instruments are equivalent to the *expedient* technology described by Lewis Binford (1979).

Torrence (1989) employs this model to explain the shift from complex to simple lithic technology that characterizes archaeological sequences throughout the world. In eastern North America, the change is characterized as a decrease in the use of formal bifaces (weapons), and an increase in the use of informal, expedient tools (instruments). Torrence claims that the technological change coincides with the shift in subsistence from hunting and gathering to food production. As a consequence of this fundamental subsistence change, she argues, the nature of short-term risk changed. Hunting no longer occupied a risk-prone position in the economy, and thus did not require the application of elaborate and costly technology to avert failure.

My criticism of Torrence's model is that it downplays the importance of plant foods in nonagricultural economies, and thus portrays the technological change from formal to expedient core technology as abrupt. To be fair, Torrence confesses to the oversimplification of her model and points out that most assemblages will reflect a mix of technological responses to risk avoidance. The challenge, she suggests, is to determine how particular tool forms, not entire technologies, are subject to different levels and types of risk.

Her challenge offers a point of departure for addressing gender roles. If we can develop predictions about the types of subsistence activities men and women respectively perform and relate these to the timing and severity of risk, we can begin to refer the bridging arguments Torrence makes between risk and tool design to gender-specific technology. We can expect, as Torrence notes, that the risks of hunting mobile game are different than the risks of collecting plant foods, and that tools will be designed and used accordingly. That hunting and gathering were conducted simultaneously through a sexual division of labor suggests that technologies will indeed contain a mix of formal and expedient core technology. The co-occurrence of these distinct core types will depend on local factors such as the organization of land-use, duration of occupation, and site reoccupation, as well as the availability of raw materials. In more general terms, however, the relative contributions that formal and amorphous core technology make to hunter-gatherer technology can be a gauge to the relative contribution of women to subsistence production.

In eastern North America, bifaces and other formalized core tool forms dominate assemblages dating to the late Pleistocene and early Holocene. Many of these assemblages also contain expedient cores that were used for on-site flake production, and these lend indirect support to the increasing awareness that plant foods comprised a significant portion of Paleoindian and Early Archaic diet (Meltzer and Smith, 1986). Expedient tool technology becomes increasingly important over subsequent millennia, at times eclipsing biface technology. The manufacture of formal unifacial tools likewise abates. Following Torrence, these changes probably reflect the waning need for risk-averting technology, presumable due to the increasing importance of plant foods and, presumably, women's contribution to production. However, hunting did not cease, and, indeed, it probably intensified in areas of high population density. Nor did biface technology disappear altogether. Changes are evident in the design and production of bifaces and, at certain times and places, the production of bifaces and expedient cores converged. It is important to keep in mind that these trends are nonlinear. Because they appear to fluctuate from region to region, and at different rates, we should be able to track changes in the relative contributions of men and women through changes in flaked stone technology. Importantly, the model that Torrence provides, with its emphasis on hunting technology, permits us to view changes in men's technology as a response to changes in the subsistence activities of women, and this indeed is a promising avenue for future research.

Stone tools and mobility

An alternative to Torrence's model is an argument posed by William Parry and Robert Kelly (1987) on the relationship between flaked stone technology and hunter-gatherer mobility. Building upon the work of several authors (Binford, 1977, 1979; Goodyear, 1979; Kelly, 1988; Nelson, 1987), they look at biface technology as an adaptive solution to the spatial and temporal incongruity between tool production and tool use. This relates not only to the constraints of tool function and tool design, but also to "behavioral variables which mediate the spatial and temporal relations among activity, manufacturing, and raw material loci" (Kelly, 1988:717). They consider mobility to be the key behavioral factor that mediates these relations. Because there is no necessary relationship between geologic sources of rock and the locations of other resources people require, particularly food and water, stone tools have to be transported (see also Shott, 1986). And, because the functional requirements for stone tools cannot always be predicted, stone tool technology must also be flexible (see also Goodyear, 1979). Thus, mobility simultaneously dictates access to raw material, tool needs, and portability. Throughout prehistoric North America, bifacial core technology was used to meet the organizational contingencies of mobility.

Several authors have commented on the advantages of bifacial core technology to mobile hunter-gatherers (Goodyear, 1979; Kelly, 1988; Nelson, 1987; Parry and Kelly, 1987). For instance, Kelly (1988) suggests that formalized bifacial technology was selected whenever mobile settlement systems included occupations in areas lacking lithic raw material. Under these conditions, bifaces served as portable cores that could be reduced for usable flakes and shaped into formal tools that were flexible, maintainable, and recyclable. As this was a long-term, planned reduction strategy that hinged on one's ability to predictably flake stone, good-quality raw material was obviously a must (Goodyear, 1979). Parenthetically, the need to utilize good quality rock perpetuated the need for biface technology. That is, because sources of good material generally have spotty distributions, a reliance on these sources by mobile peoples created spatial incongruity between locations of procurement and locations of tool use.

Like the dichotomy set up by Torrence, Parry and Kelly (1987) juxtapose bifacial core technology with expedient core technology. They argue that the transition from bifacial to expedient core technology in several parts of North America coincided with the rise of sedentism. Residential stability, they argue, allowed tool makers to stockpile rock for immediate use. They further suggest that the tool-using activities of sedentary people were largely restricted to residential bases, so there was little spatial incongruity between raw material and tool use. It follows that there was little need to make formal bifaces for the anticipated needs of a lithic-poor environment.

In contradiction to the argument posed by Parry and Kelly are numerous examples of expedient core technology throughout eastern North America by mobile hunter-gatherers who also employed formal biface technology. These cases have been attributed by a number of authors to the luxury of local raw material abundance (Bamforth, 1986; Custer, 1987; Johnson, 1986). Here a mixed strategy of biface technology for anticipated needs and expedient technology for immediate needs seems to be the case.

The other problem with Parry and Kelly's argument is that groups that spent long periods of time at bases, and/or reoccupied bases on a seasonal basis continued to practice logistical mobility, ostensibly for hunting game. Thus, the need for bifacial core technology, both as weapons and as cores, continued.

How do the shortcomings of Parry and Kelly's thesis play themselves out in the sexual division of labor? To begin, we need to disentangle the different types of mobility embedded in the seasonal rounds of hunter-gatherers. Parry and Kelly (1987) consider residential mobility — the mobility of entire coresident groups — to be the critical consideration in technological design. Alternatively, I agree with Torrence (1989:62) that the relevant amount of mobility for the transport of tools is the distance travelled by the tool-user. In this sense, the distances and patterns of mobility of men and women differ. Thus, the sexual division of labor is a variable that potentially accounts for combinations of formal and expedient core technology in terms of the mobility parameters spelled out by Parry and Kelly. Rather than seeing the two technologies as being mutually exclusive, we should expect the use of these to be complementary and interdependent.

In terms of production, for example, bifacial and expedient core technologies varied from being independent to being interdependent. When occupying non-source areas, portable tools provided all of the raw material needs of stone tool-uses. Insofar as men were responsible for producing bifacial cores, women may have had little direct access to usable flakes, and instead depended on the by-products of men's work. In contrast, at residential bases near source areas, both men and women could have procured, manufactured, and used tools. Bifacial cores still comprised an important male technology for hunting forays into areas with either uncertain or unreliable raw material sources. Under these conditions, the production of bifaces remained distinct from the production of flakes from expedient cores irrespective of the availability of raw material at domestic sites.

The two strategies of tool production converged when bifaces were made from flakes removed from expedient cores at residential sites. This occurred in parts of the Southeast during the Early Woodland, and continued into late prehistory. The strategy can be partly explained by changes in biface technology itself, not the least of which was the adoption of bow and arrow technology in the Late Woodland period. In addition, though, we need to consider how women's uses of flaked stone helped to support the shift from bifacial to expedient core technology within men's technology. In this respect, the celebrated trends toward increased residential stability that mark the Woodland period had immediate and significant ramifications for women's work. As residential mobility became more difficult to maintain, a variety of other strategies was engaged to cope with the economic stresses that constraints on fissioning imposed. Many, if not most, of the economic changes associated with this trend are implicitly attributed to women: the adoption of pottery and the expansion of the food base to include starchy seeds, shellfishing, and incipient horticulture. As Cheryl Claassen (1991) observes, if we consider all the innovations and changes that we implicitly attribute to women, we have written into prehistory a time and energy crisis for women.

If this depiction of women's labor is correct, and I believe it may be, it goes without saying that women experienced a greater need for technology, including flaked stone technology. I think it is reasonable to propose that women sought raw materials and reduced rock for their own purposes. It is unrealistic to think that women depended solely on the by-products of men's flintknapping. Instead, women had intimate knowledge of the local landscape and were able to locate and exploit sources of rock that otherwise may have been ill-suited for biface manufacture. Women also had ample opportunity and motive for scavenging the lithic refuse of abandoned sites (Sassaman and Brooks, 1990). Both sources of raw material would have been well-suited to the needs of food processing and maintenance activities at residential bases.

Eventually, the roles that formal bifaces played in men's hunting activities were filled by more expedient forms made from flakes, and finally by bow and arrow technology that required only small modified flakes for tipping arrows. This change from long-lived, curated bifaces to short-lived, throw-away bifaces marks a significant change in the technology of men's hunting weapons, but it does not necessarily reflect a major organizational change in the men's activities *per se*. Rather, the change in men's technology may in part reflect the increased contribution of women to raw material procurement and core reduction at domestic sites. The removal of flakes for immediate on-site use and for the manufacture of projectiles for hunting now fell under a single production trajectory. It is likely that women, as well as men, participated in expedient core reduction. In any event, the process was simplified so that the steps of production no longer required spatial, temporal, technological or sexual differentiation.

Whatever became of the ill-fated formal biface? Across Eastern North America well-made formal bifaces do not disappear altogether, but they do seem to be relegated to special functions within society. Ceremonial uses of bifaces, including mortuary offerings, persisted well into late prehistory. It is tempting to suggest that formal bifacial technology remained under the domain of males and became relegated to ceremonial functions as an expression of male control over certain resources and productive processes. This idea might be further substantiated if we allow that within the secular world, flaked stone had developed into an androgynous technology, bearing little to no differentiation along lines of gender. Male rituals involving formal biface technology might therefore embody a form of male resistance to the changing conditions of technology.

Summary and conclusion

The sexual division of labor that we accept as a basic feature of hunter-gatherer organization obviously contributed to the patterns of technological variation we read in the archaeological record. The extant models for explaining the shift from formal biface to expedient core technology stand to gain from a consideration of gender. The changes in risk avoidance strategies that Torrence identifies, and the effects of sedentism on tool design that Parry and Kelly identify, can be recast to include the sexual division of labor. If we deny women a role in stone tool production and use, a stance that now seems wholly unfounded, then the attention on division of labor may seem extraneous. However, the decisions men make about the design, production, and use of flaked stone tools obviously have some bearing on the overall opportunities and constraints of the entire economy; so we should expect that changes in men's technology will reflect changes in the organization and success of women's activities.

Thus, models of the organization of hunter-gatherer technology need to be expanded to account for the social units that comprise divisions of labor involving stone tools. Perhaps separate models need to be developed for men and women (cf. Jochim, 1988). But we should also focus attention on variation in the integration or interdependence of male – female tool-using activities. Given the basic dichotomy we have between hunting and gathering, many of the well-developed bridging arguments of technological organization lend themselves to this problem. If we include gender in the models, we may begin to account for variation that cannot be fully explained by tool function, raw material constraints, or group mobility.

The goal, of course, is not to define particular men and women in the record, but to look for variation in gender relations and roles that can help us to model processes of culture change and continuity. I have no doubt that stone tools hold answers to these issues, and, the lack of ethnographic analogs notwithstanding, significant gains in these areas can be made if serious attention is brought to the subject. This is not an issue of politics; rather it is simply a natural part of the ongoing process of improving our abilities to describe and explain human variation. It is unfortunate, though explicable (Wylie, 1989), that the question of gender has taken so long to enter archaeological analysis (especially lithic studies), but it is fundamental to human organization and requires our further consideration.

■ ■ ■

References

Amick, D. S. 1987 *Lithic Raw Material Variability in the Central Duck River Basin: Reflections of Middle and Late Archaic Organizational Strategies*, Report of Investigations 46, Department of Anthropology, University of Tennessee, Knoxville.

Arnold, D. E. 1985 *Ceramic Theory and Cultural Process*, Cambridge University Press, Cambridge.

Bamforth, Douglas B. 1986 Technological Efficiency and Tool Curation, *American Antiquity*, 51, pp. 38–50.

Binford, Lewis R. (1977) Forty-seven Trips: A Case Study in the Character of Archaeological Formation Processes, in *Stone Tools as Cultural Markers: Change, Evolution and Complexity*, R. V. Wright (ed.), pp. 24–36, Australian Institute of Aboriginal Studies, Canberra.

—— (1979) Organization and Formation Processes: Looking at Curated Technologies, *Journal of Anthropological Research*, 35, pp. 255–273.

Bird, C. F. M. (1988) Women and the Toolmaker: Evidence of Women's Use and Manufacture of Flaked Stone Tools in Australia and New Guinea, paper presented at the Second New England Conference on Technological Analysis in Australian Archaeology.

Bleed, P. (1986) The Optimal Design of Hunting Weapons: Maintainability or Reliability, *American Antiquity*, 51, pp. 737–747.

Claassen, Cheryl (1991) Shellfishing and the Shellmound Archaic, in *Engendering Archaeology: Women in Prehistory*, J. M. Gero and M. W. Conkey (eds), pp. 276–300, Blackwell, Oxford.

Clark, J. E. (1987) Politics, Prismatic Blades, and Mesoamerican Civilization, in *The Organization of Core Technology*, J. K. Johnson and C. A. Morrow (eds), pp. 259–284, Westview Press, Boulder, Colorado.

Cross, J. R. (1990) *Craft Specialization in Nonstratified Society: An Example from the Late Archaic in the Northeast*, PhD dissertation, Department of Anthropology, University of Massachusetts, Amherst.

Custer, Jay F. (1987) Core Technology at the Hawthorne Site, New Castle County, Delaware: A Late Archaic Hunting Camp, in *The Organization of Core Technology*, J. K. Johnson and C. A. Morrow (eds), pp. 45–62, Westview Press, Boulder, Colorado.

Gero, J. M. (1989) Assessing Social Information in Material Objects: How Well Do Lithics Measure Up?, in *Time, Energy and Stone Tools*, R. Torrence (ed.), pp. 92–105, Cambridge University Press, Cambridge.

—— (1991) Genderlithics: Women in Stone Tool Production, in *Engendering Archaeology: Women in Prehistory*, J. M. Gero and M. W. Conkey (eds), pp. 163–193, Blackwell, Oxford.

Goodyear, Albert C. (1979) *A Hypothesis for the Use of Cryptocrystalline Raw Materials Among Paleo-Indian Groups in North America*, Research Manuscript Series 165, South Carolina Institute of Archaeology and Anthropology, University of South Carolina, Columbia.

Jefferies, R. W. (1982) Debitage as an Indicator of Intraregional Activity Diversity in Northwest Georgia, *Midcontinental Journal of Archaeology*, 7, pp. 94–132.

Jochim, M. A. (1988) Optimal Foraging and the Division of Labor, *American Anthropologist*, 90, pp. 130–136.

Johnson, Jay K. (1986) Amorphous Core Technologies in the Midsouth, *Midcontinental Journal of Archaeology*, 11, pp. 135–151.

Kelly, Robert L. (1988) The Three Sides of a Biface, *American Antiquity*, 53, pp. 717–731.

Lurie, R. (1989) Lithic Technology and Mobility Strategies: The Koster Site Middle Archaic, in *Time, Energy and Stone Tools*, R. Torrence (ed.), pp. 46–56, Cambridge University Press, Cambridge.

Meltzer, David J. and B. D. Smith (1986) Paleoindian and Early Archaic Subsistence Strategies in Eastern North America, in *Foraging, Collecting and Harvesting: Archaic Period Subsistence and Settlement in the Eastern Woodlands*, S. W. Neusius (ed.), pp. 3–31, Occasional Papers 6, Center for Archaeological Investigations, Southern Illinois University, Carbondale.

Myers, A. (1989) Reliable and Maintainable Technological Strategies in the Mesolithic of Mainland Britain, in *Time, Energy and Stone Tools*, R. Torrence (ed.), pp. 78–91, Cambridge University Press, Cambridge.

Nelson, M. C. (1987) The Role of Biface Technology in Adaptive Planning, paper presented at the 27th Annual Meeting of the Northeastern Anthropological Association, Amherst, Massachusetts.

—— (1991) The Study of Technological Organization, in *Archaeological Method and Theory*, Vol. 3, M. B. Schiffer (ed.), pp. 57–100, University of Arizona Press, Tucson.

Parry, William J. and Robert L. Kelly (1987) Expedient Core Technology and Sedentism, in *The Organization of Core Technology*, J. K. Johnson and C. A. Morrow (eds), pp. 285–304, Westview Press, Boulder, Colorado.

Raab, L. Mark, R. F. Cande, and D. W. Stahle (1979) Debitage Graphs and Archaic Settlement Patterns, *Midcontinental Journal of Archaeology*, 4, pp. 167–182.

Sassaman, Kenneth E. and Mark J. Brooks (1990) Cultural Quarries: Scavenging and

Recycling Lithic Refuse in the Southeast, paper presented at the Southeastern Archaeological Conference, Mobile, Alabama.

Shott, M. J. (1986) Technological Organization and Settlement Mobility: An Ethnographic Examination, *Journal of Anthropological Research*, 42, pp. 15–52.

Torrence, Robin (1983) Time-Budgeting and Hunter-Gatherer Technology, in *Hunter-Gatherer Economy in Prehistory: A European Perspective*, G. Bailey (ed.), pp. 11–22, Cambridge University Press, Cambridge.

—— (1989) Re-tooling: Towards a Behavioral Theory of Stone Tools, in *Time, Energy and Stone Tools*, R. Torrence (ed.), pp. 57–66, Cambridge University Press, Cambridge.

Wylie, A. (1989) Feminist Critiques and Archaeological Challenges, paper presented at the Chacmool Conference, Calgary.

Chapter 10

THE DEVELOPMENT OF HORTICULTURE IN THE EASTERN WOODLANDS OF NORTH AMERICA: Women's Role

Patty Jo Watson and Mary C. Kennedy

Introduction

We begin with the words of some famous anthropologists:

> The sound anthropological position is that certain sex-linked behaviors are biologically based, although subject to cultural modifications within limits.
>
> (Hoebel 1958: 391)

> A limited number of sex-associated characteristics also appear to be transmitted at the genetic level, such as an apparent tendency shared with many other animals for dominance and passivity in the male and female, respectively . . .
>
> (Keesing 1966: 75)

> The community recognizes that women must be accompanied by their babies wherever they go; hence they cannot hunt or fish as efficiently as the unencumbered males. Males are therefore free to be mobile and active while females have been accorded, by nature, a prior responsibility or obligation to rear additional members of the community in the only way this can be done. Hence the community assigns work involving more mobility to men and work involving less mobility to women.
>
> (Jacob and Stern 1952: 145–6)

> Man, with his superior physical strength, can better undertake the more strenuous physical tasks, such as lumbering, mining, quarrying, land clearance, and housebuilding. Not handicapped, as is woman, by the physiological burdens of

pregnancy and nursing, he can range farther afield to hunt, to fish, to herd, and to trade. Woman is at no disadvantage, however, in lighter tasks which can be performed in or near the home, e.g., the gathering of vegetable products, the fetching of water, the preparation of food, and the manufacture of clothing and utensils. All known human societies have developed specialization and cooperation between the sexes roughly along this biologically determined line of cleavage.

(Murdock 1949: 7)

Up to about nine thousand years ago all human populations lived by hunting and most of them also by fishing, supplemented by the picking of berries, fruits and nuts, and the digging of roots and tubers. Perhaps the first division of labor between the sexes was that the male became the hunter and the female the food-gatherer.

(Montagu 1969: 134)

Even in those societies where there are no professional or semi-professional artisans, all ordinary manufactures are delegated either to men or to women. Moreover, this sex division of labor is much the same wherever it occurs. Such universal patterns derive from universally present facts, such as the greater size and strength of the male, and his greater activity based on the differing roles of the two sexes in connection with the production and care of children. These factors unquestionably led to the earliest differentiation in food gathering activities. This must have begun at an extremely remote period. The males became the main providers of animal foods, since they were able to run down their prey and engage it in combat. The females being hampered throughout most of their adult lives by the presence either of infants *in utero* or in arms, were unable to engage in such active pursuits, but were able to collect vegetable foods and shell fish. . . . Thus to this day in the American family dinner the meat is placed in front of the father to be served and the vegetables in front of the mother. This is a folk memory of the days when the father collected the meat with his spear and the mother the vegetables with her digging stick.

(Linton 1955: 70–1)

Thus, the sexual division of labor is neatly laid out, and simply and cogently explained. Men are strong, dominant protectors who hunt animals; women are weaker, passive, hampered by their reproductive responsibilities, and hence, consigned to plant gathering. Not only is that the case for every ethnographically observed society, but it is carried back to "extremely remote" periods. This received view could be schematized as:

men>hunt>animals>active
women>gather>plants>passive

All the introductory texts from which these excerpts were taken were written before the women's movement and the reorganization of contemporary American life that made women working outside the domestic sphere an inescapable reality.

Introductory texts are much more cautious these days. Conspicuously absent is the explicit male/active, female/passive dichotomy (e.g. Harris 1987: 127; Oswalt 1986: 104–5; Peoples and Bailey 1988: 254–60). Current texts acknowledge that in every known society there is a sexual division of labor; that men hunting and women gathering seems almost always to be the case, but that beyond this there is tremendous variation in which labors a particular society assigns to a particular sex. The received view today is that in foraging societies:

men>hunt>animals
women>gather>plants

For purposes of argument we accept this premise and attempt to formalize this very division of labor for a particular time, region, and cultural historical process: the origin and early development of plant cultivation and domestication in the Eastern Woodlands of North America. We draw upon three lines of evidence: archaeological data, ethnohistoric data, and general schemes of human social organization derived from ethnography.

Data sources and arguments of relevance

Archaeological and archaeobotanical data

The time period relevant to the origin and early development of horticulture in the Eastern Woodlands is approximately 7000–2000 BP. Primary evidence for plant use during these five millennia comes from a variety of archaeological contexts, but only two basic categories: charred and uncharred plant remains. Charred plant remains are usually recovered by flotation/water separation systems; uncharred plants are recovered from dry caves and rockshelters; both categories are then analysed by paleoethnobotanists (Hastorf and Popper 1988; Pearsall 1989).

The evidence to date suggests three different episodes of domestication in the Eastern US (Smith 1987a; Watson 1989; Yarnell 1986). The first began about 7000 BP when a gourd-like cucurbit (*Cucurbita* sp.; perhaps *C. pepo*, perhaps *C. texana*, or even *C. foetidissima*) and bottle gourd (*Lagenaria siceraria*) begin to appear in archaeological deposits in the Eastern US. The second is from 3500 BP onward when domesticated forms of the weedy plants sumpweed, chenopod, and sunflower begin to appear. The third is the development of varieties of maize specific to the requirements of the Eastern US, a process that took place between 2000 and 1000 BP.

We are in the pioneer phase of knowledge expansion about prehistoric plant use. One characteristic of this pioneer phase is a scramble by interested scholars to synthesize the new data as they become accessible, not only in annotated inventories of the primary evidence (Yarnell 1977, 1983, 1986, forthcoming), but also in comparative discussions of regional developments (Asch and Asch 1985; Chapman and Shea 1981; Watson 1985, 1988, 1989), and in more general theoretical formulations (e.g. Chomko and Crawford 1978; Crites 1987; Lathrap 1987; Smith 1987a, 1987b). It seems desirable to launch an inquiry at yet another level: that of the women and men involved in the events and processes. While a great deal is being written about the evidence, it is, for the most part, gender-neutral writing; when actors are mentioned they are "people," or "humans," or "individuals". These accounts tend to be discussions of the archaeological evidence, the plant remains, rather than the people who manipulated the plants. We depart from that pattern here.

The ethnohistoric record

Although the archaeological record of plant use has only recently been sought, information about plant use by living peoples in the Eastern Woodlands has been available since the time of European entry in the sixteenth century. Thus, one source of data is historical or ethnohistorical such as that provided by Dye (1980), Hudson (1976), Le Page du Pratz (n.d.), Parker (1968), Swanton (1948), Will and Hyde (1917), Willoughby (1906), Wilson (1917), and Yarnell (1964). For example, in an often-quoted passage, Le Page du Pratz (n.d.: 156–7) describes the planting of *choupichoul* (Smith 1987c), an Eastern Woodlands cultigen being grown in Louisiana by the Natchez at the time of European entry into the Southeast: "I have seen the Natchez, and other indians, sow a sort of grain, which they called Choupichoul, on these dry sand-banks. This sand received no manner of culture; and the *women and children* covered the grain any how with their feet, without taking any great pains about it" (emphasis added). Throughout the ethnohistoric and ethnographic literature of the Eastern US are similar examples of women planting, reaping, collecting, and processing plants.

License to use the ethnographic and ethnohistorical information for archaeological inference would presumably be granted because it fulfills the criteria for the use of ethnographic analogy (the most comprehensive recent discussion is Wylie 1985, but see also Ascher 1961; Salmon 1982: 57–83; Watson, LeBlanc, and Redman 1971: 49–51, 1984: 259–63). That is, the information in question comes from the same or a very similar physical environment, and from people who are closely related physically and culturally. Therefore, the ethnographic/ethnohistoric information carries a certain degree of prior probability, of plausibility or likelihood, with respect to the archaeological materials. That does not mean, however, that it is to be accepted uncritically.

Social organization

There is another necessary source, and that is the more abstract and theoretical literature in anthropology about the organization and functioning of human groups at various levels of technological complexity. For present purposes we are content to evoke Fried (1967), Friedl (1975), Murdock and Provost (1973), Sahlins (1963, 1968), Service (1962, 1971), Steward (1948), and White (1959) and refer to them in general as the authority for some basic assumptions:

1   In small-scale, non food-producing, egalitarian societies, subsistence activities are divided on the basis of age and sex.
2   For biological reasons relating to gestation and lactation, adult women are primarily responsible for nourishing and socializing infants and small children, although various others can assist in these tasks.
3   For biological reasons relating to greater physical strength and hormone levels, adult men are charged with the primary responsibility for safeguarding the social units in which children are born and reared, and – in general – with tasks that require sudden bursts of energy, such as running after game.
4   Because of these biological constraints on men and women, groups tend to divide labor between the sexes so that women are responsible for activities that do not interfere with childcare and that can be performed near the habitation – cooking and "domestic activities" – as well as the collecting of stationary resources such as plants and firewood. Men are responsible for exploiting mobile resources, primarily the hunting of game, as well as for defense, and a variety of other such tasks.

Using these assumptions about the sexual division of labor, as well as evidence from the archaeological record and the ethnohistoric/ethnographic record, we depart from the usual gender-neutral perspective to discuss one of the most recent and most comprehensive theoretical treatments we know for the development of horticulture in the Eastern Woodlands: Bruce Smith's (1987a) paper, "The Independent Domestication of Indigenous Seed-Bearing Plants in Eastern North America."

The domestication of plants

Women and coevolution in the Eastern Woodlands:
weedy plant domestication

Smith's interpretive formulation may be rendered schematically as follows: at about 8000 BP, the beginning of the Middle Archaic period, human populations in the Eastern Woodlands are thought to have been small, few, and dispersed rather widely across the landscape. Their subsistence systems – hunting-gathering-foraging with some emphasis on deer and several kinds of nuts, especially hickory and acorn – were further characterized by residential mobility, probably cycling through similar or the same series of locales, season after season, year after year. Occupation sites were small, although summer camps on river terraces or levees were probably considerably larger than winter residential units in the uplands.

Geological studies indicate significant changes in Mid-Holocene (8000–5000 BP) fluvial systems throughout the East, partly as a result of a long drying trend, the Hypsithermal. Rivers stabilized and aggraded so that previously ephemeral or rare features such as meanders and oxbow lakes, bars and shoals, sloughs and backwater lagoons became much more common and long-lasting than in the previous post-Pleistocene millennia. As a result of these changes, human subsistence-settlement patterns also changed. When slackwater habitats, shoals, etc. took shape as relatively permanent features, then the abundant flora (edible bulbs, rhizomes, shoots, seeds) and fauna (many different kinds of fish, amphibians, mollusks, and waterfowl) characterizing them became readily accessible on a predictable, seasonal, long-term basis. Human settlements – in the form of base camps occupied from late spring to summer and on through fall, and oriented to these resource points – increased in size and were permanently occupied for at least four to five months each year for hundreds of years. This process resulted in the first recognizable anthropogenic locales in the archaeological record of the Eastern US; i.e. these sites represent the first long-lasting impact on this physical environment produced by human activity. Archaic shell mounds and midden mounds are then the scene where the rest of the story unfolds: these "domestilocalities", as Smith calls them, are the crux of his formulation.

The mounds and middens are significant and long-lived disturbed areas, highly congenial to the weedy species ancestral to the earliest cultivated and domesticated food plants. Smith discusses a series of four important factors in the coevolutionary interplay between human and plant populations at the domestilocalities: sunlight, fertile soil, continually disturbed soil, and continual introduction of seeds. He also stresses that some of the selective pressures operating on the weedy plants colonizing such locales are congruent with the best interests of humans who harvest them for food, most significantly big seeds and thin seed coats.

Intense competition among pioneer species in these rich openings favors seeds that sprout quickly and grow quickly. These traits translate botanically into seeds with reduced dormancy (a thin seed coat is one good means of effecting reduced dormancy) and large endosperm (food reserves to sustain rapid, early spring growth), the two morphological characteristics enabling identification of the earliest domesticate food plants: sumpweed and sunflower (bigger seeds than in wild populations) and *Chenopodium berlandieri* ssp. *jonesianum* (seeds with thinner seed coats than in wild *C. berlandieri*).

Finally, Smith outlines the main stages or steps in the general coevolutionary trajectory between *ca.* 6500 and 3500 BP in numerous places in the Eastern Woodlands.

At about 6500 BP. In the first stage, domestilocalities are inhabited by humans and by a series of weedy, colonizing, or pioneering plant species for several months during each growing season. Natural selective pressures operate on the plants in the directions just noted to produce big seeds and thin seed coats.

In the second stage, humans tolerate the useful edible species, but ignore, or even occasionally remove the useless or harmful species.

In stage three, humans actively encourage the useful species (which have gradually become even more useful), and while systematically harvesting them also systematically remove competing non-useful plants. Thus, the incidental gardens of stage 2 become true managed gardens, the proceeds of which are stored to augment the winter and early spring diet.

In stage four, humans deliberately plant seeds of the useful species each year, carefully tending and caring for the resulting crops.

At about 3500 BP. In stage five, plants emerge that are clearly recognizable morphologically as domesticates.

The entire process is quite low-key, and there is no drastic alteration in the diet as a result of it, but there is an increase in dependable plant resources.

If we populate Smith's evolutionary stages with gendered human beings chosen to accord with the four operating assumptions for the division of labor already noted, and with the ethnographic record for the Eastern Woodlands, then we must conclude that the adult women are the chief protagonists in the horticultural drama of the domestilocalities. Although the entire human group contributes to the sunlight and soil fertility factors, it is the women who are primarily responsible for soil disturbance and continual introduction of seeds. Smith lists as examples of disturbance: the construction of houses, windbreaks, storage and refuse pits, drying racks, earth ovens, hearths. Most of these probably represent women's work as do the majority of other examples he mentions: primary and secondary disposal of plant and animal debris, and a "wide range of everyday processing and manufacturing activities."

As to the continual introduction of seeds, Smith notes harvesting plants for processing and consumption at the domestilocality. Seed loss during processing, storage, and consumption (plus defecation subsequent to consumption) continually introduce seeds to the fertile soil of the domestilocality. Once again — although everyone joins in consumption and defecation — it is the women who are responsible for processing, and for food preparation and storage.

Have we not then definitively identified woman the gatherer, harvester, and primary disturber of domestilocalities in the prehistoric Eastern Woodlands as woman the cultivator and domesticator? Yes, we have. But anyone persuaded by Smith's or similar coevolutionary constructions would doubtless respond "So what?" Our conclusion, with which they would probably readily agree, is at best anticlimactic because the coevolutionary formulation downplays stress, drive, intention, or innovation of any sort on the part of the people involved, in this case the women. The coevolutionary formulation highlights gradualness; the built-in mechanisms adduced carry plants and people smoothly and imperceptibly from hunting-gathering-foraging to systematic harvesting to at least part-time food production with little or no effort on anyone's part. The plants virtually domesticate themselves.

While a number of the initial and ongoing selective pressures acting on these plants within such disturbed habitats were clearly related to human activities, these activities were unintentional and "automatic" rather than the result of predetermined and deliberate human action toward the plant species in question.

. . . It is this simple step of planting harvested seeds, even on a very small scale, that if sustained over the long-term marks both the beginning of cultivation, and the onset of automatic selection within affected domestilocality plant populations for interrelated adaptation syndromes associated with domestication.

. . . This continuing evolutionary process did not require any deliberate selection efforts on the part of Middle Holocene inhabitants of domestilocalities in the Eastern Woodlands. All that was needed was a sustained opportunistic exploitation and minimal encouragement of what were still rather unimportant plant food sources.

(Smith 1987a: 32, 33, 34)

This is in keeping not only with the current scheme for division of labor

women>gather>plants,

but also with the earlier (Keesing, Linton, et al.) scheme

women>gather>plants>passive.

Are we to be left with such a muted and down-beat ending to the Neolithic Revolution in the Eastern Woodlands?

Shaman the cultivator: gourd domestication

The domestication of the native cultigens described by Smith was apparently preceded by introduction of another type of domesticate, *Cucurbita* gourd and bottle gourd, in various parts of the Eastern US beginning about 7000 years ago. In an article entitled, "The Origins of Plant Domestication in the Eastern United States: Promoting the Individual in Archaeological Theory," Guy Prentice (1986) constructs a scenario for that earlier transformation.

Prentice first details the evidence for the tropical squash, *Cucurbita pepo*, in archaeological deposits dating from 7000–3500 BP, some of the earliest evidence for domesticated plants in Eastern North America. Investigators agree that *Cucurbita pepo* fruits would have been used primarily as containers, or perhaps as rattles, rather than food (Prentice 1986:104). He then argues (*ibid.*: 106) that the species was probably introduced through some form of trade with the tropical areas in which it grows naturally. The sites at which the earliest evidence for *Cucurbita pepo* is found are those of Archaic period, hunting and gathering, band-level societies. He notes that authoritarian controls in such societies would have been weak, and that shamans and headmen were probably exercising the strongest control within these groups (*ibid.*: 107). Prentice presents information from studies indicating that change is not an automatic process in human societies, that certain conditions must be met before an innovation is accepted (*ibid*.: 108–11). An innovation will take hold if it is introduced by an individual of high status, a specialist, an ambitious person who is in contact with outsiders and who is oriented toward commerce rather than subsistence:

> By postulating a ritual use for cucurbits during the Archaic period, one is led to conclude that it would be the shaman who would be most likely to adopt cucurbit agriculture. He would be the one most interested in new religious paraphernalia. He would have the greatest knowledge of plants. He would have been in communication with other shamans and probably exchanging plants and plant lore. If gourds were introduced as magical rattles and ritualistic containers for serving stimulants and medicines, he would have gained a very impressive "medicine" in the eyes of his patients. In fact, the gourd itself may have provided the medicine.
>
> (Prentice 1986: 113)

Here is an instance in which at least one archaeologist is not arguing for

women>gather>plants

Why not? Perhaps because this is a discussion of innovation, and

women>gather>plants>passive

– although it might lead to dinner – would not lead to *innovation*. Rather, this is a scenario for

man>trade>ceremony>active>innovation>cultivation>domestication

Perhaps it really was like that (see Decker 1988 and Smith 1987a for alternative views on the development of *Cucurbita* cultivation in eastern North America), but we are leary of explanations that remove women from the one realm that is traditionally granted them, as soon as innovation or invention enters the picture.

Women and maize agriculture in the Eastern Woodlands: the creation of northern flint

Maize was the most important domesticate among the horticultural societies of North America at the time of European contact. Although there was enormous variety among the indigenous subsistence economies in the Eastern and Western United States, wherever crops were grown maize was central, often being literally deified (e.g. Cushing 1974; Hudson 1976; Munson 1973; Stevenson 1904; Swanton 1948). Yet, as the latest evidence makes clear (Chapman and Crites 1987; Conard et al. 1984; Doebly, Goodman, and Stuber 1986; Ford 1987; Yarnell 1986), maize is a rather late entrant into the Eastern Woodlands, probably introduced from the Southwest, and appearing about 1800 BP. The development of horticulture in the Southwest seems to have been very different from that in the East (Minnis 1985, 1992; Wills 1988), and maize is much earlier there, apparently present by *ca.* 4000 BP.

There is great unclarity in the literature about the exact definitions and time-space distributions of contemporary maize varieties, but there is some consensus that the earliest kinds known in the East (and grown together with sunflower, sump-weed, chenopod, maygrass, knotweed, etc.) are of a type with 10 to 12 rows of kernels, and called Chapalote, Tropical Flint, North American Pop, and/or Midwestern 12-row. These varieties were developed from the earliest maize, which was originally created from wild populations occurring in Mesoamerica, Central America, or South America (or all three), but exactly where and how has been hotly debated for some 20 years (e.g. Galinat 1985b; Lathrap 1987).

Our concern here, however, is with the transition in the more northerly Eastern Woodlands from the early, higher row-number maize to a lower row-number variety variously known as Maiz de Ocho, Northern Flint, or Eastern 8-row maize, which appeared in the Northeast around AD 800–900, became quite standardized, and was the dominant agricultural crop of this region from approximately AD 1000 to historic times (Wagner 1983, 1987). There are at least three alternatives as to how this happened: (1) Eastern 8-row was created in the Eastern Woodlands from the Earlier Midwestern 12-row varieties; or (2) it, like the older form itself, was developed somewhere south of the Border and later diffused to the Eastern US; or (3) both (1) and (2) are too simple, and the origin of Northern Flint/Eastern 8-row involved more complicated combinations of both southerly (the Tropical Flint or Chapalote type) and northerly (the Northern Flint/Eastern 8-row type) maize varieties originating in several parts of northern, central, and southern America. Lathrap (1987) provides a comprehensive presentation of the second alternative (see also Upham *et al.* 1987), and Bruce Smith favors the third (Smith 1992). Although there is now a very solid corpus of information on Fort Ancient maize (Wagner 1983, 1987), primary evidence about Middle Mississippian maize is only beginning to be available (Blake 1986; Fritz 1986; Scarry 1986), so it is not yet possible to assess definitively the relative merits of these three suggestions.

At the moment one can suggest, without contravening the scanty available evidence and in fact remaining congruent with it, that the original form of Northern Flint (Eastern 8-row) was developed from a Chapalote (Midwestern 12-row, Tropical Flint) type of maize at one or several places in the northerly portions of Eastern North America. The earliest date now known for Northern Flint is *ca.* AD 800–900 from one site in western Pennsylvania and two near the north shore of Lake Erie (Blake 1986; Blake and Cutler 1983; Stothers 1976). Northern Flint is present by AD 1000 in the cultural context called Fort Ancient located in the Ohio River drainage of southern Ohio and Indiana, northern Kentucky, and northern West Virginia (Wagner 1983, 1987). On the present evidence, robust forms of Northern Flint appear later or not at all as one moves west and south from Fort Ancient territory (Blake 1986; Fritz 1986; Johannessen 1984; Scarry 1986). Thus, we believe we are justified in accepting, at least for purposes of our argument here, that the Northern Flint variety of maize was developed indigenously in northeastern North America from an older, Chapalote form that came into the east 1800 or 1900 years ago.

We assume that the first Chapalote or Chapolote-like forms of this tropical cultigen to enter northern latitudes in the Eastern US were not well suited to that physical environment, even if the plant diffused northward gradually from Mesoamerica. Day-length, annual temperature and moisture cycles, growing-season length, and substrate characteristics probably all differed significantly from those of the locales where Chapalote was initially grown. Hence, the Middle Woodland groups who planted and hoped to harvest this novel crop in the most northerly North American regions may have had more failures and near failures than successes. Lower row numbers on maize cobs are thought to be a botanical reflection of poor growing conditions such as short growing seasons, drought, or even unchecked competition from weeds (Blake and Cutler 1983: 83–4). Thus, it is possible that adverse climate was compounded by neglect in the development of Northern Flint.

We think it more likely, however, that cultivators in the northeasterly portions of North America actively encouraged, against environmental odds, the new starchy food source. Accepting the AD 800–900 dates from the Lake Erie and western Pennsylvania sites as the first establishing of Northern Flint, and noting the rapidity with which Northern Flint agriculture spread throughout the central Ohio River drainage (Fort Ancient) area immediately thereafter, we conclude that deliberate nurturing of maize in an inhospitable environment is a more plausible interpretation than is neglect in the development of this hardy variety.

Two points are implied from the above discussion: (1) maize acceptance and cultivation north of the Border was purposeful and deliberate; and (2) it was surely the women sunflower-sumpweed-chenopod gardeners in Middle and Late Woodland communities who worked (with varying success and interest) to acclimatize this imported species, by planting it deeper or shallower, earlier or later, in hills or furrows, and who crossed varieties to obtain or suppress specific traits. From *ca.* AD 1100–1200 to the time of European contact in the sixteenth century, Northern Flint was the main cultivated food of the hamlets, villages, towns, and chiefdoms that arose in the Ohio River Valley and the vast region north to the Great Lakes. To the west and south, in the Mississippi River and its tributary drainages, Northern Flint was also sometimes grown but in combination with other varieties having higher row-numbers (Blake 1986; Fritz 1986; Johannessen 1984; Scarry 1986; Smith 1992) Thus Northern Flint, together with pumpkins, squashes, sunflowers, and a long list of other cultigens, planted, tended, harvested, and processed by the women agriculturalists (Hudson 1976; Parker 1968; Swanton 1948; Will and Hyde 1917; Willoughby 1906; Wilson 1917), supported many thousands of people each year for hundreds of years. The accomplishments of these women cultivators is even more impressive when one realizes that their creation, Northern Flint, is the basis (together with Southern Dent, a maize variety that entered the southeastern

United States somewhat later) for all the modern varieties of hybrid "Corn Belt Dent" maize grown around the world today (Doebley *et al.* 1986; Galinat 1985a).

Conclusions

We close with a few further thoughts about the first women gardeners in the Late Archaic domestilocalities. Their contribution of domesticated sumpweed, sunflower, and chenopod (and possibly maygrass as well) to the diet and the archaeological record of initial Late Holocene human populations in the Eastern Woodlands may not have been so automatic a process with so insignificant a result as the coevolutionary formulation makes it out to be.

In the first place, the natural history, natural habitat and distribution, ecology, and genetic structure of most of the Late Archaic/Early Woodland cultigens and domesticates are not well understood. On closer inspection, it may turn out to be the case that some if not all the species initially domesticated would have required special, self-conscious, and deliberate treatment to convert them to garden crops, and to cause the very significant and progressive changes in seed size that at least two of them (sumpweed and sunflower) exhibit. Sunflower and maygrass were apparently being grown outside their natural ranges by 3000–2500 BP, and this must have been done purposefully.

Secondly, the best and most comprehensive dietary evidence for the early horticultural period comes from the long series of human paleofecal and flotation derived remains in Salts Cave and Mammoth Cave, west central Kentucky. The fecal evidence dates to 2800–2500 BP and is quite clear and consistent: over 60 per cent of the plant foods consumed were seeds of indigenous domesticates and cultigens: sunflower, sumpweed, and chenopod (Gardner 1987; Marquardt 1974; Stewart 1974; Watson and Yarnell 1986; Yarnell 1969, 1974, 1977, 1983, 1986, forthcoming). If maygrass, whose status is uncertain but which is here beyond its natural range, is added, then the total proportion of indigenous cultigens rises to well over two-thirds. This single and well-established datum for a period relatively early in the history of the indigenous domesticates might be taken to cast some doubt on the generalization that the addition of the domesticate species had only a slight dietary impact. The doubt is strengthened by corroborating evidence from Newt Kash (Jones 1936; Smith and Cowan 1987), Cloudsplitter (Cowan 1985), and Cold Oak (Gremillion 1988; Ison 1986; Ison and Gremillion 1989) shelters in eastern Kentucky (see also Smith 1987b).

A third matter to think about is the fact that – quite apart from all other considerations – the women plant collectors and gardeners of 3500–2500 BP were the first to devise and use techniques of tilling, harvesting, and processing the new domesticates. These same techniques must have been in use throughout the later periods, and were then applied to the production and processing of maize as well as the older cultigens. As Bruce Smith (1987a) points out, more than 60 years ago

Ralph Linton described significant differences in the tools and techniques used for maize production and processing in Eastern North America vs. those of the Southwest and Mexico, and suggested that in the East maize "was adopted into a preexisting cultural pattern which had grown up around some other food or foods" (Linton 1924: 349).

The fourth and last point is somewhat more tenuous, but we think it is important to consider the implications of one issue unanimously demonstrated by all the relevant ethnographic and ethnohistorical literature: the extensive and intensive botanical and zoological knowledge possessed by people in hunting-gathering-foraging societies. Botanical knowledge is (and would have been in prehistory) greatest among the women who gather, collect, harvest, and process plant resources. Such knowledge goes far beyond foodstuffs to include plants and plant-parts useful for dyes and for cordage and textile manufacture, as well as a vast array of medicinal leaves, bark, roots, stems, and berries. The ethnographically-documented women who exploited these various plant resources knew exactly where and when to find the right plant for a specific purpose. Surely their prehistoric predecessors controlled a similar body of empirical information about their botanical environments, and were equally skilled at using it for their own purposes. Viewed against such a background, the image of unintentional and automatic plant domestication by Late Archaic women pales considerably.

We think that archaeologists operate under at least two different schemes for explaining gender and labor in prehistoric foraging groups. The first is based upon the assumption that women are seriously encumbered and disadvantaged by their reproductive responsibilities and that men are unencumbered by theirs. In this scheme, these physical limitations are combined or conflated with certain personality traits that are thought by some to apply universally to the sexes. This is the scheme of Linton, Montagu, Hoebel, Keesing, etc.; in it women cannot be responsible for culture change because they are not men and therefore they are not active:

men>hunt>animals>active
women>gather>plants>passive

The second scheme is based upon a universal sexual division of labor for hunter-gatherers derived from available ethnographic evidence, but does not suppose that any innate psychological characteristics or activity levels separate males and females:

men>hunt>animals
women>gather>plants

We do not know who domesticated plants in the prehistoric Eastern Woodlands, but faced with a choice between an explanation that relies on scheme number one and one that relies upon scheme number two, we prefer the alternative we have presented: based on available ethnographic evidence for the Eastern United States in particular and the sexual division of labor in general, women domesticated plants. We would like to think that they domesticated them on purpose because they were bored, or curious, or saw some economic advantage in it; that they acted consciously with the full powers of human intellect and that their actions were a significant contribution to culture change, to innovation, and to cultural elaboration. We prefer this explanation because it makes explicit a formulation that anyone who has ever studied anthropology has to some degree absorbed, i.e. that food plants in foraging societies are women's business. Neither Prentice nor Smith argues that women did *not* domesticate plants in prehistoric North America, yet Prentice does argue that a particular group of men were responsible for this major innovation and Smith argues that the innovation was not consciously achieved. It may be the case that shamans were responsible for the introduction of horticulture. It may be that the invention of horticulture was largely unintentional, or passive. But until there is convincing evidence for either of these hypotheses, we prefer to pursue a third alternative: prehistoric women were fully capable not only of conscious action, but also of innovation.

■ ■ ■

References

Asch, David L. and Nancy B. Asch (1985). "Prehistoric Plant Cultivation in West-Central Illinois." In *Prehistoric Food Production in North America*. Richard Ford, ed. Ann Arbor: University of Michigan Museum of Anthropology, Anthropological Papers No. 75, 149–204.

Ascher, Robert (1961). "Analogy in Archaeological Interpretation." *Southwestern Journal of Anthropology* 17: 317–25.

Blake, Leonard (1986). "Corn and Other Plants from Prehistory into History in the Eastern United States." In *The Protohistoric Period in the Mid-South: 1500–1700. Proceedings of the 1983 Mid-South Archaeological Conference*, D. Dye and R. Bristler, eds. Mississippi Department of Archives and History, Archaeological Report 18, 3–13.

Blake, Leonard and Hugh C. Cutler (1983). "Plant Remains from the Gnagey Site (36SO55)." Appendix II, in R. George, "The Gnagey Site and the Monongahela Occupation of the Somerset Plateau." *Pennsylvania Archaelogist* 53: 83–8.

Chapman, Jefferson and Gary Crites (1987). "Evidence for Early Maize (*Zea mays*) from the Icehouse Bottom Site, Tennessee." *American Antiquity* 52: 352–4.

Chapman, Jefferson and Andrea Brewer Shea (1981). "The Archaeological Record: Early Archaic to Contact in the Lower Little Tenneessee River Valley." *Tennessee Anthropologist* 6: 64–84.

Chomko, Stephen A. and Gary W. Crawford (1978). "Plant Husbandry in Prehistoric Eastern North America: New Evidence for its Development." *American Antiquity* 43: 405–8.

Conard, N., D. Asch, N. Asch, D. Elmore, H. Gove, M. Rubin, J. Brown, M. Wiant, K. Farnsworth and T. Cook (1984). "Accelerator Radiocarbon Dating of Evidence of Prehistoric Horticulture in Illinois." *Nature* 308: 443–6.

Cowan, C. Wesley (1985). "From Foraging to Incipient Food-Production: Subsistence Change and Continuity on the Cumberland Plateau of Eastern Kentucky." Unpublished Ph.D. dissertation, University of Michigan.

Crites, Gary (1987). "Human–Plant Mutualism and Niche Expression in the Paleoethno-
    botanical Record: A Middle Woodland Example." *American Antiquity* 52: 725–40.

Cushing, Frank H. (1974). *Zuni Breadstuff*. New York: Museum of the American Indian
    Heye Foundation, Indian Notes and Monographs 8 (reprint edn).

Decker, Deena (1988). "Origin(s), Evolution, and Systematics of *Cucurbita pepo*
    (Cucurbitaceae)." *Economic Botany* 42: 4–15.

Doebley, J., M. Goodman and C. Stuber (1986). "Exceptional Genetic Divergence of
    Northern Flint Corn." *American Journal of Botany* 73: 64–9.

Dye, David (1980). "Primary Forest Efficiency in the Western Middle Tennessee Valley."
    Ph.D. dissertation, Department of Anthropology, Washington University, St. Louis.

Ford, Richard I. (1987). "Dating Early Maize in the Eastern United States." Paper read at
    the 10th Annual Conference of the Society of Ethnobiology, Gainesville, FL.

Fried, Morton H. (1967). *The Evolution of Political Society*. New York: Random House.

Friedl, Ernestine (1975). *Women and Men: an Anthropologist's View*. New York: Holt, Rinehart,
    and Winston. Reprinted 1984 by Waveland Press, Prospect Heights, IL.

Friedman, J. and M. J. Rowlands, eds (1977). *The Evolution of Social Systems*. London:
    Duckworth.

Fritz, Gayle (1986). "Prehistoric Ozark Agriculture: The University of Arkansas Rockshelter
    Collections." PhD dissertation, Department of Anthroplogy, University of North
    Carolina, Chapel Hill.

Galinat, Walton C. (1985a). "Domestication and Diffusion of Maize." In *Prehistoric Food
    Production in North America*, Richard Ford, ed. Ann Arbor: University of Michigan
    Museum of Anthroplogy, Anthropological Papers No. 75, 245–78.

—— (1985b). "The Missing Links between Teosinte and Maize: A Review." *Maydica* 30:
    137–60.

Gardner, Paul S. (1987). "New Evidence Concerning the Chronology and Paleoethnobotany
    of Salts Cave, Kentucky." *American Antiquity* 52: 358–67.

Gremillion, Kristin J. (1988). "Preliminary Report on Terminal Archaic and Early Woodland
    Plant Remains from the Cold Oak Shelter, Lee County, Kentucky." Report submitted
    to Cecil R. Ison, USDA Forest Service Station, Stanton Ranger District, Stanton,
    Kentucky.

Harris, Marvin (1987). *Cultural Anthropology*, 2nd edn. New York: Harper & Row.

Hastorf, Christine and Virginia Popper, eds (1988). *Current Paleoethnobotany: Analytical
    Methods and Cultural Interpretations of Archaeological Plant Remains*. Chicago: University
    of Chicago Press.

Hoebel, E. Adamson (1958). *Man in the Primitive World: An Introduction to Anthropology*. New
    York: McGraw-Hill.

Hudson, Charles (1976). *The Southeastern Indians*. Knoxville: University of Tennessee Press.

Ison, Cecil R. (1986). "Recent Excavations at the Cold Oak Shelter, Daniel Boone National
    Forest, Kentucky." Paper presented at the Kentucky Heritage Council Annual
    Conference, Louisville.

Ison, Cecil R. and Kristin J. Gremillion (1989). "Terminal Archaic and Early Woodland
    Plant Utilization Along the Cumberland Plateau." Paper presented at the Society for
    American Archaeology Annual Meeting.

Jacobs, Melville and Bernhard Stern (1952). *General Anthropology*. New York: College Outline
    Series, Barnes and Noble. Reprinted 1964.

Johannessen, Sissel (1984). "Paleoethnobotany." In *American Bottom Archaeology*, C. Bareis and J. Porter, eds. Urbana and Chicago: University of Chicago Press, 197–214.

Jones, Volney (1936). "The Vegetal Remains of Newt Kash Hollow Shelter." In *Rock Shelters in Menifee County, Kentucky*, William Webb and W. Funkhouser, eds. Lexington: University of Kentucky, Reports in Archaeology and Anthropology 3.

Keesing, Felix M. (1966). *Cultural Anthropology: The Science of Custom*. New York: Holt, Rinehart, and Winston.

Lathrap, Donald W. (1987). "The Introduction of Maize in Prehistoric Eastern North America: The View from Amazonia and the Santa Elena Peninsula." In *Emergent Horticultural Economies of the Eastern Woodlands*, William Keegan, ed. Carbondale: Center for Archaeological Investigations, Southern Illinois University, Occasional Paper No. 7, 345–71.

Le Page du Pratz, Antoine Simon (n.d.). *The History of Louisiana*. Pelican Press, Inc.

Linton, Ralph (1924). "The Significance of Certain Traits in North American Maize Culture." *American Anthropologist* 26. 345–9.

—— (1955). *The Tree of Culture*. New York: Alfred A. Knopf.

Marquardt, William H. (1974). "A Statistical Analysis of Constituents in Paleofecal Specimens from Mammoth Cave." In *Archaeology of the Mammoth Cave Area*, Patty Jo Watson, ed. New York: Academic Press, 193–202.

Minnis, Paul (1985). "Domesticating Plants and People in the Greater American Southwest." In *Prehistoric Food Production in North America*, Richard Ford, ed. Ann Arbor: Museum of Anthroplogy, University of Michigan, Anthropological Papers No. 75, 309–40.

—— (1992). "Earliest Plant Cultivation in Desert North America." In *Agricultural Origins in World Perspective*, Patty Jo Watson and C. W. Cowan, eds. Washington, DC: Smithsonian Institution Press, 101–19.

Montagu, Ashley (1969). *Man, His First Two Million Years: A Brief Introduction to Anthropology*. New York: Columbia University Press.

Munson, Patrick J. (1973). "The Origins and Antiquity of Maize-Beans-Squash Agriculture in Eastern North America: Some Linguistic Implications." In *Variation in Anthropology; Essays in Honor of John C. McGregor*, D. Lathrap and J. Douglas, eds. Urbana: Illinois Archaeological Survey, 107–35.

Murdock, George P. (1949). *Social Structure*. New York: The Free Press.

Murdock, George P. and Caterina Provost (1973). "Factors in the Division of Labor by Sex: A Cross-cultural Analysis." *Ethnology* 12: 203–25.

Oswalt, Wendell H. (1986). *Life Cycles and Lifeways: An Introduction to Cultural Anthropology*. Palo Alto, CA Mayfield Publishing.

Parker, Arthur C. (1968). "Iroquois Uses of Maize and Other Plant Foods." In *Parker on the Iroquois*, W. Fenton, ed. Syracuse: Syracuse University Press, 1–119.

Pearsall, Deborah (1989). *Paleoethnobotany: Reconstructing Interrelationships Between Humans and Plants from the Archaeological Record*. San Diego, CA: Academic Press.

Peoples, James and Garrick Bailey (1988). *Humanity: An Introduction to Cultural Anthropology*. St. Paul, MN: West Publishing.

Prentice, Guy (1986). "Origins of Plant Domestication in the Eastern United States: Promoting the Individual in Archaeological Theory." *Southeastern Archaeology* 5: 103–19.

Sahlins, Marshall (1963). "Poor Man, Rich Man, Big-Man, Chief: Political Types in Melanesia and Polynesia." *Comparative Studies in Society and History* 5: 285–303.

—— (1968). *Tribesmen*. Englewood Cliffs, NJ: Prentice-Hall.

Salmon, Merrilee (1982). *Philosophy and Archaeology*. New York: Academic Press.

Scarry, C. Margaret (1986). "Change in Plant Procurement and Production During the Emergence of the Moundville Chiefdom." PhD dissertation, Department of Anthropology, University of Michigan, Ann Arbor.

Service, Elman (1962). *Primitive Social Organization*. New York: Random House.

—— (1971). *Primitive Social Organization*, 2nd edn. New York: Random House.

Smith, Bruce D. (1987a). "The Independent Domestication of the Indigenous Seed-Bearing Plants in Eastern North America." In *Emergent Horticultural Economies of the Eastern Woodlands*, William Keegan, ed. Carbondale: Center for Archaeological Investigations, Southern Illinois University, Occasional Paper No. 7, 3–47.

—— (1987b). "Hopewellian Farmers of Eastern North America." Paper presented at the 11th International Congress of Prehistoric and Protohistoric Science, Mainz, West Germany.

—— (1987c). "In Search of Choupichoul, the Mystical Grain of the Natchez." Keynote Address, 10th Annual Conference of the Society of Ethnobiology, Gainesville, Florida.

—— (1992). "Prehistoric Plant Husbandry in North America." In *Origins of Agriculture in World Perspective*, Patty Jo Watson and C. W. Cowan, eds. Washington, DC: Smithsonian Institution Press, 121–41.

Smith, Bruce D. and C. Wesley Cowan (1987). "The Age of Domesticated *Chenopodium* in Prehistoric North America: New Accelerator Dates from Eastern Kentucky." *American Antiquity* 52: 355–7.

Stevenson, Matilda C. (1904). *The Zuni Indians*. Washington: Annual Report of the Bureau of American Ethnology 1901–1902, vol. 23.

Steward, Julian (1948). *Patterns of Cultural Change*. Urbana: University of Illinois Press.

Stewart, Robert B. (1974). "Identification and Quantification of Components in Salts Cave Paleofeces, 1970–1972." In *Archaeology of the Mammoth Cave Area*, Patty Jo Watson, ed. New York: Academic Press, 41–8.

Stothers, David M. (1976). "The Princess Point Complex: A Regional Representative of the Early Late Woodland Horizon in the Great Lake Area." In *The Late Prehistory of the Lake Erie Drainage Basin*, David Brose, ed. Cleveland: Cleveland Museum of Natural History, 137–61.

Swanton, John R. (1948). *The Indians of the Southeastern United States*. Washington: Bureau of American Ethnology Bulletin 137. Reprinted 1979 by Smithsonian Institution Press.

Upham, S., R. S. MacNeish, W. C. Galinat and C. M. Stevenson (1987). "Evidence Concerning the Origin of Maiz de Ocho." *American Anthropologist* 89: 410–19.

Wagner, Gail E. (1983). "Fort Ancient Subsistence: The Botanical Record," *West Virginia Archaeologist* 35: 27–39.

—— (1987). "Uses of Plants by Fort Ancient Indians." Ph.D. dissertation Department of Anthropology, Washington University, St. Louis.

Watson, Patty Jo (1985). "The Impact of Early Horticulture in the Upland Drainages of the Midwest and Midsouth." In *Prehistoric Food Production in North America*. Richard Ford, ed. Ann Arbor: University of Michigan Museum of Anthropology, Anthropological Papers No. 75, 73–98.

—— (1988). "Prehistoric Gardening and Agriculture in the Midwest and Midsouth." In *Interpretation of Culture Change in the Eastern Woodlands During the Late Woodland Period*, R. Yerkes, ed. Columbus: Ohio State University, Department of Anthropology, Occasional Papers in Anthropology No. 3, 38–66.

—— (1989). "Early Plant Cultivation in the Eastern Woodlands of North America." In *Foraging and Farming: the Evolution of Plant Exploitation*, D. Harris and G. Hillman, eds. London: Allen and Hyman, 555–70.

Watson, Patty Jo and Richard A. Yarnell (1986). "Lost John's Last Meal." *Missouri Archaeologist* 47: 241–55.

Watson, Patty Jo, Steven A. LeBlanc, and Charles L. Redman (1971). *Explanation in Archaeology: An Explicitly Scientific Approach*. New York: Columbia University Press.

—— (1984). *Archaeological Explanation: The Scientific Method in Archaeology*. New York: Columbia University Press.

White, Leslie (1959). *The Evolution of Culture*. New York: McGraw-Hill.

Will, George F. and George E. Hyde (1917). *Corn Among the Indians of the Upper Missouri*. Lincoln: University of Nebraska Press.

Willoughby, Charles C. (1906). Houses and Gardens of the New England Indians. *American Anthropologist* 8: 115–32.

Wills, W. H. (1988). *Early Prehistoric Agriculture in the American Southwest*. Sante Fe, NM: School of American Research Press.

Wilson, Gilbert L. (1917). *Agriculture of the Hidatsa Indians, an Indian Interpretation*. University of Minnesota Studies in the Social Sciences 9. Reprints in Anthropology 5 (May 1977), J&L Reprint Co. Lincoln, NB.

Wylie, Alison (1985). "The Reaction Against Analogy." In *Advances in Archaeological Method and Theory*, vol. 8, Michael Schiffer, ed. Orlando, FL: Academic Press, 63–111.

Yarnell, Richard A. (1964). *Aboriginal Relationships Between Culture and Plant Life in the Upper Great Lakes Region*. Ann Arbor: University of Michigan, Museum of Anthropology, Anthropological Papers No. 23.

—— (1969). Contents of Human Paleofeces. In *The Prehistory of Salts Cave, Kentucky*, Patty Jo Watson, ed. Springfield: Illinois State Museum. Reports of Investigations No. 16, 41–54.

—— (1974). "Plant Food and Cultivation of the Salt Cavers." In *Archaeology of the Mammoth Cave Area*, Patty Jo Watson, ed. New York: Academic Press, 113–22.

—— (1977). "Native Plant Husbandry North of Mexico." In *Origins of Agriculture*, C. Reed, ed. The Hague: Mouton, 861–75.

—— (1983). "Prehistory of Plant Foods and Husbandry in North America." Paper presented at the Annual Meeting of the Society for American Archaeology, Pittsburgh.

—— (1986). "A Survey of Prehistoric Crop Plants in Eastern North America." *The Missouri Archaeologist* 47: 47–59.

—— (forthcoming). "Sunflower, Sumpweed, Small Grains, and Crops of Lesser Status." In *Handbook of North American Indians*, W. Sturtevant, ed. Washington, DC: Smithsonian Institution Press.

PART IV

From sexual divisions to gender dynamics

INTRODUCTION

Can gender, not merely sex, be recognized in the archaeological record? The papers presented and recommended in this section continue to question our Euro-centric stereotypes about sex differences, and our conflation of gender with sex. They also question whether gender roles and the visual signaling of gender identity with material culture are always important, whether they change, and whether sex is always the most important variable in the construction of gender categories and roles.

Patricia Galloway notes that "anthropological studies suggest that menstrual seclusion may be an important correlate of social organization" and that contemporary archaeologists claim social organization as an important area of study. She asks, "Where Have All the Menstrual Huts Gone?" (chapter 11). Although archaeologists study architectural remains as correlates of some aspects of social organization, and Native Americans of the Southeast region are known to have practiced menstrual seclusion historically, "where are the menstrual huts" in this area? Use of the term "huts" is part of the problem, not part of the solution, Galloway argues. The topic of menstruation in Western cultures is, if not avoided altogether, trivialized. Other cultures have different notions of what it means to menstruate, perhaps even of what it means to be a woman. Menstruating women may not be confined to flimsy, expedient "huts" at all, but rather to a variety of kinds of structures, depending on particular cultural values and practices. Galloway uses ethnographic literature and oral traditions about women and menstruation together with archaeological data to explore larger issues of gender ideology in the prehistory of the southeastern United States.

Sharisse D. McCafferty and Geoffrey G. McCafferty bridge the archaeological study of labor and that of symbolic meanings in "Spinning and Weaving as Female Gender Identity in Post-Classic Mexico" (chapter 12). They focus not only on the economic importance of women's textile production, but on spinning and weaving as metaphors for sexuality and female procreative powers, and the basis for women's power and identity in male-dominated complex societies of the Post-Classic period in Mesoamerica.

In the final article in this section, "Identifying Gender Representation in the Archaeological Record: A Contextual Study" (chapter 13), Liv Gibbs employs multiple lines of archaeological evidence including burial offerings, ritual caches of artifacts called hoards, figurines, rock art, and settlement patterns to explore how ancient Scandinavians created gender identities with material goods and art. Her study is an excellent example of archaeology's unique ability to trace *changes* in gender identities and gender relations. Like Galloway, she takes on questions about the visibility of gender identity, asking not only when are differences visible or invisible to archaeologists because of our prior conceptions, but when did prehistoric peoples make gender visible through deliberate acts of marking difference with material culture?

Some archaeologists, recognizing that in living societies gender is not always a simple binary masculine/feminine categorization, have identified cross-gender categories. Mary K. Whelan (1991), for example, has brought together burial data, historic records, and ethnographic material to explore gender identities in a historic U.S. Plains population. She questions whether gender identity is always based on biological sex, and notes the burial of a biological female with artifacts otherwise associated with males. She argues that this female probably functioned as a man in Dakota society, a practice documented in many North American Indian tribes for both males and females. She also questions the binary masculine/feminine classification and finds evidence for more than two genders, arguing for example that children were not accorded the same gender identities as adults. Papers by Grete Lillehammer (1989) and Kathleen Bolen (1992) discuss children and their varied social identities in depth.

■ ■ ■

Further reading

Barber, Elizabeth Wayland (1994)
Bolen, Kathleen M. (1992)
Costin, Cathy Lynne (1996)
Duke, Philip (1991)
Lillehammer, Grete (1989)
Mills, Barbara J. (1995)
Whelan, Mary K. (1991)

■ ■ ■

References

Barber, Elizabeth Wayland (1994) *Women's Work, The First 20,000 Years: Women, Cloth, and Society in Early Times*, New York: W. W. Norton & Co.
Bolen, Kathleen M. (1992) "Prehistoric Construction of Mothering," in C. Claassen (ed.) *Exploring Gender Through Archaeology: Selected Papers of the 1991 Boone Conference*, Madison, Wisconsin: Prehistory Press, pp. 49–62.
Costin, Cathy Lynne (1996) "Exploring the Relationship between Gender and Craft Production in Complex Societies: Methodological and Theoretical Issues of Gender Attribution," in R. P. Wright (ed.) *Gender and Archaeology*, Philadelphia: University of Pennsylvania Press, pp. 111–140.
Duke, Philip (1991) "Recognizing Gender in Plains Hunting Groups: Is It Possible or Even Necessary?," in D. Walde and N. Willows (eds) *The Archaeology of Gender: Proceedings*

of the 22nd Annual Chacmool Conference, Calgary: The Archaeological Association of the University of Calgary, pp. 280–283.

Lillehammer, Grete (1989) "A Child Is Born. The Child's World in an Archaeological Perspective," *Norwegian Archaeological Review* 22: 91–105.

Mills, Barbara J. (1995) "Gender and the Reorganization of Historic Zuni Craft Production: Implications for Archaeological Interpretation," *Journal of Anthropological Research* 51: 149–172.

Whelan, Mary K. (1991) "Gender and Historical Archaeology: Eastern Dakota Patterns in the 19th Century," *Historical Archaeology* 25: 17–32.

Chapter 11

WHERE HAVE ALL THE MENSTRUAL HUTS GONE? The Invisibility of Menstrual Seclusion in the Late Prehistoric Southeast

Patricia Galloway

Overture

> . . . she invariably had three things with her on the ledge of her ground-floor box: her opera-glass, a bag of sweets, and a bouquet of camellias. For twenty-five days of the month the camellias were white, and for five they were red; no one ever knew the reason for this change of colour, which I mention though I can not explain it.
>
> (Alexandre Dumas fils)

"She," of course, was Alexandre Dumas fils's Camille, the Lady of the Camellias, a very expensive Parisian courtesan who renounced everything for love. Today the best-selling line of French "sanitary napkins" is brand-named "Camellia," but then that is the kind of mildly smutty public discourse that straitlaced Americans would expect from the French. And it is a far cry, indeed, from a high-flown literary allusion to the grubby term "menstrual hut" – or is it? Both terms were coined by Western cultures, and both share the tendency to hide female practices accommodating the "wound that does not heal." As archaeologists we are deluding ourselves if we think our own professional practice is unaffected by that same tendency. If the most basic move toward engendering archaeology is finding women in the archaeological record, the search for evidence of menstrual practices is about as direct a way to do it as there could be. Yet it is a search that pretty clearly has not been made. This is unfortunate, since anthropological studies suggest that menstrual seclusion may be an important correlate of social organization, and social organization is just what researchers concerned with the late prehistoric Southeast have all been claiming to be interested in.

Literature Review

The term "menstrual hut" is already very evocative; why not "house" or simply "structure"? We know in a general way that in historic period Southeastern nonstate societies women subject to rules of ritual seclusion during menses withdrew to specific structures for the duration of their period of "pollution." But Southeastern archaeologists do not find menstrual huts routinely, even when investigating settlements; they have apparently assumed that the structures reserved for that purpose were too squalid and temporary to leave evidence worth looking for, and the term "hut" is an index of that assumption. But why have such assumptions been made? Is this really the reliable import of the ethnographic literature?

In the first place, "the ethnographic literature" for the early historic period in the Southeast is almost exclusively limited to the work of John R. Swanton. We should remember in dealing with the information he provides that this is the same John Swanton who presented the explicit sexual material in *Myths and Tales of the Southeastern Indians* (1929) in Latin, and his reticence in dealing with reproductive matters with most of his contemporary informants is reflected in the fact that his sources on the topic of menstruation are mostly limited to the fortuitous testimonies of eighteenth-century male European missionaries and colonists and (for the Creeks) other ethnologists of his own time. Neither Swanton nor his colleagues obtained information about menstrual huts from female informants, so all that we have regarding this matter, even now, amounts to external observation at best. A sample of Swanton's evidence for menstrual practices and taboos follows:

1   *Timucua*: fish and venison food restrictions, prohibition of fire kindling; similar food restrictions after childbirth (Swanton 1946:713). Note that Swanton's source for making of "a separate fire" by women during menses is its listing as a superstitious sin in the 1613 *Confessionario of Francisco Pareja* (Milanich et al. 1972:25).

2   *Creek*: menstrual seclusion in house "by herself" for four days (as at childbirth); utensils for food preparation and consumption reserved for use during menses; prohibition on consumption of meat from large animals and on presence in garden; bathing required downstream from men, prohibition on presence upwind of men; required bath and change of clothes for purification at the end of menses. Early-twentieth-century informants and ethnologists referred to "a house," a "seclusion lodge," "a separate tent or house," and "a small house near some spring or stream" (Swanton 1928a:358–360, 1946:714).

3   *Chickasaw*: menstrual huts, built far from dwellings but near enough to the village to be safe from enemies, used monthly and at childbirth; required bath and change of clothing afterward; food restrictions during pregnancy, also *couvade* practices (abstention from work, avoidance by other men) by the husband after birth. Adair refers to the relevant structures as "small huts" (Swanton 1928a:358–359, 1946:715–716).

4   *Choctaw*: small cabin "apart" monthly and for childbirth; food restrictions at childbirth; *couvade* practices (food restrictions) (Swanton 1946:716). Note that this comes from only one source, the *ca.* 1730s French "Anonymous Relation."

5   *Natchez*: A brief remark taken from the descriptions of marriage by the missionary Father Le Petit notes that during menstruation there was a prohibition on marital intercourse; Swanton notes nothing further for the Natchez on this subject (1911:97).

Thus where information is available for Southeastern Indian groups, it all definitely points to ritual seclusion during menses carried out publicly, generally in a structure specifically reserved for the purpose, with accompanying taboos. It is relevant that where such ritual seclusion took place for menstruation, it was also required along with many of the same taboos for childbirth, often apparently in the same structure. Unfortunately the evidence is rather vague on the details of such structures, suggesting that many of those who reported them may not have seen one. The overwhelming evidence for such structures makes it all the more curious that none has been found by archaeologists.

The anthropology of menstruation

The topic of menstrual practices has served along with female puberty initiations and childbirth practices as a hobbyhorse for nearly every strain of anthropological thought (see Buckley and Gottlieb 1988b). Lately, as a result of attention from feminists, menstrual practices have come in for a good deal of popularizing "anthropological" and "psychological" treatment, being linked with the old notion of primal matriarchies and the New Age "goddess" movement in several popular books (cf. Delaney et al. 1976; Shuttle and Redgrove 1978; even Weideger 1976 overgeneralizes from very poor anthropological evidence). However praiseworthy a clear-eyed look at menstruation as experienced by modern women is, these books have not clarified matters by viewing menstrual seclusion as "universal" and a "cruelty" imposed by patriarchal authority jealous of "women's mysteries," and in any case they all virtually ignore prehistoric cultures.

Several relatively recent serious anthropological studies are, I think, much more helpful in thinking about prehistory because they grapple with the problem of how menstrual seclusion works within cultures and its possible correlation with social organization. Paige and Paige (1981) have treated the topic as part of an analysis of the sociopolitical functioning of "fraternal interest groups" under a version of exchange theory; Douglas (1966) and Schlegel (1972) have analyzed menstrual seclusion as part of cross-cultural studies of pollution and male domination, respectively; several of the essays edited by Buckley and Gottlieb (1988a) focus on the experience of the practice itself and on its advantages to women; while Martin's

(1992) work on Western female embodiment stresses the usefulness of menstrual taboos to modern women. These rather heterogeneous studies appear to agree that menstrual seclusion and its accompanying practices are advantageous to women and are characteristic of societies where husbands and males in general are not particularly dominant, especially matrilineal societies where residence rules are generally matrilocal. Paige and Paige (1981) go on to generalize that such societies – societies with "weak fraternal interest groups" – are characterized by a subsistence base that is not valuable enough to require defense, such as shifting agriculture with hunting and gathering. This is not inappropriate as a description of the historic tribes of the Southeast, but it is more problematic as a characterization of the rather aggressive chiefdom model now accepted for the late prehistoric societies that preceded them.

Kinship and residence in Mississippian societies have been more assumed about than understood. Knight (1990) has recently discussed the relation of kinship to sociopolitical structure in some detail, foregrounding the problematic nature of ethnohistorically attested kinship forms in the early colonial Southeast, but concludes that archaeological correlates "are yet to be worked out." And although Paige and Paige (1981:121) argue generally that matrilineal, matrilocal societies do not have an abundant and rich resource base, they have discussed one example of an advanced agricultural society, the Nayar of India (which is matrilineal and matrilocal), that practices menstrual seclusion and is even characterized by nonresident husbands.

Clearly much more work remains to be done in understanding whether menstrual seclusion does actually correlate reliably with matrilineality/matrilocality, since the cross-cultural sample used by Paige and Paige (1981) was based on largely androcentrically biased ethnographies and coding practices (cf. Buckley 1988:192–193). It is, for example, quite possible that matrilineality/matrilocality in the Southeast was an artifact of the protohistoric disease holocaust period: Harris (1988:34–37) suggests that warfare or other disruption is a strong pressure for matrilocality, and it stands to reason that since matrilineages would select for female children to expand the lineage and attract bridewealth, they would also favor population increase and prove an ideal vehicle for post-catastrophe population recovery.

Still, it is not beyond the bounds of possibility that the known population expansion of the Mississippian period might also be explained in this manner; that the Natchez model, at least for matrilines, is correct for the Mississippian period; and that Mississippian societies might thus be characterized by the same practices – which should be marked materially by the presence of "menstrual huts." If, on the other hand, Mississippian societies did not practice menstrual seclusion, it is quite possible that their kinship organization was not matrilineal, and their residence practice not matrilocal. If that possibility is admitted, then a thorough reexamination of our dependence on post-contact ethnographies is in order. The point is that the correlation between menstrual seclusion and matrilineal kinship seems to be good enough that it should be possible to test for matrilineal kinship archaeologically if we can just figure out what a "menstrual hut" ought to look like in the ground.

Menstrual taboos and modern archaeology

If the ethnographic evidence and the matrilineal model are correct, there must have been thousands of menstrual huts constructed in the Southeast, just from the colonial period from which they are certainly attested. Yet so far no menstrual hut has been reliably reported from a Southeastern archaeological context. The few identifications from elsewhere are unfortunately problematic. J. Heilman's identification of a "women's house" (House II/77) at the Fort Ancient Sunwatch site is the right period, but it remains unpublished and details are lacking (J. Heilman, personal communication, 1992); furthermore, the structure in question is located within the village, which would contradict the need for spatial separation. Robson Bonnichsen (1973:281) suggested a "menstrual retreat" as one possible explanation for apparently female-occupied tent remains at a contemporary multiple-structure Cree camp, but this and the other two candidate explanations proved false when the camp owner was interviewed. Finally, Lewis Binford's halfhearted identification of a possible menstrual hut in the Hatchery West report (1970:40–41) was based solely on the fact that it was a small and anomalous structure. Why "anomalous"? Perhaps simply because menstruation is marked as "polluting" and "dangerous" in our own society's dominant male discourse, and that prejudice is transferred to other societies, including prehistoric ones, without much reflection. I am suggesting, in short, that the influence of modern taboos on ethnocentric archaeologists, whether male or female, should not be ignored; just as women rarely menstruate in Western literature, so menstruation is generally ignored in considering women's lives archaeologically, as though women in all times and places similarly hid the condition of menstruation – indeed hid it so effectively that it became invisible in the archaeological record.

The symptoms of this ethnocentricity are not far to seek. Charles Hudson, in his influential normative summary of Southeastern menstrual seclusion practices in 1976, matter-of-factly drew on uniformitarian generalization when he offered the following assertion, now discounted by cross-cultural studies (Hudson's reference in this passage is to Paige's 1973 popular article, which was actually about how Western women are *socialized* to suffer during menstruation):

> The Southeastern Indians may have recognized at least implicitly some sound social and psychological principles. Psychologists have amply verified what folk knowledge tells us about menstruation, namely that women become depressed, hostile, anxious, and even socially disruptive just before and during menstruation.

> (Hudson 1976:320)

There is very good reason for anthropologists and archaeologists enculturated in Western societies to believe assertions like Hudson's and to experience "negative affect" associated with the very topic of menstruation, despite mounting evidence for the social origin of most of the negative behavioral correlates observed in

Western societies (Martin 1992:92–138). Because Western societies practice the hiding of menstruation (as do many "primitive" societies like the Manus of New Guinea [Mead 1939: 157–158]), the topic itself is treated with reticence by females, discomfited derision by males, and with pollution anxieties, in many instances, by both. Being seen in public to bleed from the vagina is still one of the most profound humiliations a Western female can experience, despite the fact that at least a majority of American women value their menstrual periods as a sign of their identity as women and of their continuing fertility (Martin 1992).

Beginning with the commodification of disposable "sanitary" supplies in 1921, advertisements for them have stressed invisibility, security of protection from stain-ing, and suppression of menstrual odor, without once using the word "menstruation." These advertisements have frequently featured women wearing white or light-colored clothing (though white clothing is the very last thing a menstruating Western woman would choose to wear) or especially the expensive formal clothing worn on highly public (and therefore dangerously exposed) occasions. Even in the 1990s, very little has changed in terms of the language used (menstruation and blood are almost never mentioned explicitly), although much more frankness in the portrayal of the product (particularly comparative photographs of sanitary napkins, for example) is evident. The fact remains that despite all the pop-psychology discussion of premen-strual syndrome, or PMS, menstruating Western women are still not supposed to betray the fact in public and may still be subject to specific restrictions in private on grounds of religious or other belief (Martin 1992: 97–98). And although most Western males do not go so far as John Milton, whose wife had to sleep on the floor while menstruating rather than pollute the marriage bed, many are reluctant to have sexual intercourse with menstruating women.

This is not a trivial issue. The whole topic of menstruation in modern Western cultures is still so avoided by women through shame, or trivialized by men through PMS jokes (even scientific ones), that our discomfort with it may blind us even to paying attention to its significance in other cultures or in subcultures within our own. Modern Miccosuki women use paper plates and plastic utensils in the tribal cafeteria during their periods, while men and nonmenstruating women use china and stainless steel (Pat Kwachka, personal communication, 1992), and the same practice is followed in conservative Creek households (Bell 1990: 334). Orthodox Jewish women around the world are forbidden to prepare food while menstruating and are required to take a ritual bath at the termination of the menstrual cycle. I suggest, therefore, that discomfort with the topic and its resulting erasure from scientific discourse are the simple reasons that no one has proposed a model for the archaeological correlates of menstrual seclusion practices.

Cultural practices that deal with areas of life that the dominant culture does not mark as shameful (and that are the domain of men and, therefore, "unmarked") can be looked at in public, and this is nowhere more graphically obvious than in the treatment of blood: we have become accustomed to gallons of blood and gore from wounds inflicted by (generally male) violence, whether on the evening news or in our entertainment, and even we as archaeologists have exhibited endless fascination with evidence for wounds on skeletal remains. Yet advertisements depicting the absorptive capabilities of "sanitary" supplies prudishly use a thin *blue* liquid for demonstration. Examples of treatment of blood from the female genital area in current entertainment media include horror films (both *Carrie* and *The Exorcist* treat the alleged enormously magnified telekinetic powers of young girls at menarche) and decidedly unusual European films (in both Ingmar Bergman's *Cries and Whispers* and the soft-porn French film *Going Places*, women mutilate their vaginas, in the first case possibly to simulate menstruation and avoid intercourse, and in the second to recover menstrual function lost during a prison sentence). In none of these films is menstruation treated as something that happens ordinarily to every woman, and in the very few television shows that have treated it so (*All in the Family, Cosby Show, I'll Fly Away*), the theme is taken up only once or twice, and blood has been notable for its invisibility.

Considerations for an archaeological model

The same kind of gender discrimination, I suggest, carries over into the treatment of archaeological features. Features created by male-dominated or gender-neutral activities, even if they were designed for purification from ritual pollution, do not suffer from invisibility. Indeed several instances of putative sweat lodges are reported in the Southeastern literature (for example, the Fredericks site sweat lodge reported in Ward and Davis 1988). Yet for at least half of the population, the so-called menstrual huts were equally important for ritual purification, both monthly and after childbirth. This helps make an argument for their being more than flimsy "huts."

To suggest something of the possible existential force of the taboos connected with the menstrual-seclusion practice in the prehistoric Southeast, let me offer a specific example from the early eighteenth century, in which a male adult Creek was observed to vomit the *sagamité* he had eaten before learning that it had been prepared by a menstruating woman; he then claimed to see red specks in the remaining food in the pot (Swanton 1931). His European guest thought he was overreacting, but the nineteenth- and twentieth-century Creek materials that Swanton presented and that Bell has confirmed by recent fieldwork — which indicate persistent beliefs that menstruating women should not touch men or gardens and that it was dangerous for men to smell menstruating women, to bathe downstream of them, or to walk where they had walked — indicate that this was likely normal behavior, however androcentrically interpreted. If people in Southeastern societies indeed believed that menstruating women were capable of introducing disruption and disaster at frequent and regular intervals, it was cost-effective for the societies to be serious about their precautions and to provide substantial structures for containing the danger, as other societies have done.

Because of this fear of pollution, the location where menstruating women should be secluded, according to all the testimony offered, had to be at a distance from where men carried on their ordinary activities, and ought to have been downstream from the primary village or hamlet water source (Swanton 1928a). Restrictions on contact with males and with agricultural fields dictated that historic period menstrual huts were placed on the outskirts of the villages, at what might be seen as the village/fields boundary, and the taboo was observed no matter what. In the 1750s, Chickasaw women who so isolated themselves in the face of attacks by pro-French enemies were recognized as valorous, because their action helped to preserve their husbands' virility (Bossu 1962: 171). This locational practice can be compared with an example from the South Seas, the Ulithi, who placed the communal menstrual structure parallel to the shore (Paige and Paige 1981: 213), thus also at the village/subsistence-source boundary.

Another issue that needs to be addressed when considering how many menstrual huts there were, and how substantial they were, is the average frequency of menstruation for late prehistoric Southeastern women. There is still great difficulty in addressing the issue of birth regulation archaeologically, but modern studies of women without access to medicalized birth control measures show that women can and do regulate birth frequency by means of extended lactation after a birth and complex socially institutionalized practices of abstention from intercourse. Although it is finally being recognized that the Western frequency of regular menstrual periods is unusual and perhaps unprecedented, it is not true that fertile non-Western women were always pregnant. Thus it is possible that if menstrual seclusion was practiced in the late prehistoric Southeast, at any given time as many as one-eighth to one-tenth of the fertile adult female population might have been so secluded. What the women did during their ritual seclusion from village life should be of interest, both because it would suggest what kind of structure was involved and because it would account for a significant expenditure of time. Pollution restrictions would have meant that there were many things menstruating women could not do (evidence for which would therefore not be found): produce household necessities like pottery or cloth, work at cultivation, perhaps take care of children, or cook for the household. With a wide range of activities barred, most of them the very activities that constituted the enormous visible economic contribution of women to Southeastern societies, what was left?

Although, most frequently, "menstrual huts" were also used for all the other activities related to female biological reproduction – including puberty rituals, childbirth, and the purification rituals following it – details of what went on inside them are noticeably missing for the colonial period Southeast as elsewhere (cf. Buckley and Gottlieb 1988b: 12–13). Yet it is unlikely that fertile women spent one-fourth to one-fifth of their time while not pregnant or lactating sleeping or looking at the wall. Part of that notion may arise from the general assumption that women were alone in their huts.

There is another possibility worth considering, which is that more than one woman from the same household might be spending the same time in ritual seclusion. The tendency of women who live together or work together in close proximity to synchronize menses is now widely attested medically as well as anecdotally (see McClintock 1971 for the *locus classicus*; Knight 1988: 233 lists references from recent medical literature; Knight 1991 builds an entire theory of the origins of culture on the phenomenon). Menstrual synchrony would surely have been experienced by the menstruating women, all of them related, in the extended matrilineage households postulated as the dominant residential mode in the late prehistoric Southeast. The ethnographic evidence from historic Southeastern tribes is not at all clear on how many of these huts there were at any given time, but the possibility of menstrual synchrony suggests that perhaps each lineage had its own women's house, a structure as substantial as any other. [Author's note: Strassmann's recent (1997) arguments against real menstrual synchrony nevertheless attest to the statistical likelihood of apparent near-synchrony by chance and do not materially affect the argument for women's house institutions.]

Much has been made of the hard and unremitting work of women in the aboriginal agricultural Southeast, as opposed to the episodic hunting and defense activities of men. Although that picture is surely skewed, no one who works hard is going to mind getting up to a week off once a month, as Hudson has suggested (1976: 320; cf. Martin 1992:98). But it is likely that such time would be spent doing something. Even if societies themselves articulate the male-segregated activities as "sacred" and the female-segregated activities as "polluting" (though this is usually attributable to a Western reading of the evidence), that does not mean that there are no activities at all. Instead, it would seem reasonable to suggest that a similar range of activities might take place in the structures dedicated to both and that archaeological correlates might be suggested for them. Buckley's (1988) work on Yurok menstrual practices suggests that they could be seen as directly parallel to the male purification activities aimed at the accumulation of spiritual power, and that the structures used for menstrual seclusion could be as important as men's houses.

Since male ethnographers have been invited to partake of the activities in "men's houses," we do know something of what goes on in them. Men carry out ritual activities or preparation for ritual activities, tell stories about hunting and women, sleep, and make ceremonial items, weapons or boats, or items of personal adornment. Although not restricted to the interior of the men's house by pollution restrictions, the ceremonial items are frequently restricted to use within the men's house because of secrecy requirements. And because male ethnographers are telling the tale, the talking that goes on is usually dignified as instructive for younger men or as reinforcing societal conventions (or, in case the stories go beyond societal conventions, as encouraging innovation). It is rarely trivialized as gossip.

If activities in the women's house paralleled such men's house activities, certainly women must have spent time resting as men did; certainly they also spent time talking and telling stories that could be similarly dignified as instruments of societal regulation. Other social activities, such as gambling, are documented ethnographically (Underhill 1936). We know they ate, because there is evidence that they had to use special vessels that could not be used elsewhere; indeed the Beng women of the Ivory Coast prepare a particularly prized and delectable dish only when menstruating (Gottlieb 1988: 71–72). Because they did bleed, they may have had bloodstained breechcloths or other absorbent materials to dispose of by burning or burial. Is there any reason why it would have been unlikely that they partici-pated in ritual activities? Certainly the sun worship that dominated Southeastern ritual practice is connected with fertility, and women in their period of ritual seclu-sion would at a minimum be concerned with the continuing fertility that their very seclusion proclaimed.

At this point I take a side trip into Southeastern myth to emphasize the connec-tions between women, blood, and fertility by retelling the common story from the region of the origin of corn, with its overtones of the dominance of hunting-gath-ering by agriculture. In this tale there is a family consisting of a father, Hunter; a mother, Corn; and two boys, one a son of Hunter and Corn and one an adopted son who had been made from discarded deer's blood. After the boys had in mischief released game animals from the secret place where their father kept them, thereby making them scarce and hard to find, they became interested in how it was that their mother was able to provide corn and beans for them to eat instead. One day they spied on her activities within the storehouse and discovered that the corn and beans came from her body. Thinking her a witch, they decided to kill her. Seeing them refuse the food she offered, which they now considered polluted, she guessed their plan and instructed them on how they should do it: clear a large piece of ground and drag her dead body over it seven times. The boys killed her after having cleared only small patches of ground and then dragged her body over it only twice. As a result, corn sprang up only where her blood touched the cultivated earth, and it would make only two crops per year ever after (paraphrased from the Cherokee version as presented in Lankford 1987:148–151; cf. Bell 1990:335 for the relevance of this myth to Creek social reproduction).

This is as clear a connection as could be desired between female fertility, of which blood is the sign, and agricultural fertility, of which female blood is the cause. I would suggest that it may even include a mythical explanation of the origin of menstrual seclusion in the Southeast. I take the liberty of imagining that this connection would have been celebrated and ritualized somehow and, further, that it must have been part of at least some rites connected with the "women's house." It seems to me that the widespread attestation of the existence of "women's languages" in the Southeast (cf. Bell 1990:341 n. I), correlated as it is with the practice of menstrual seclusion from the community, may also argue for the exis-tence of a "women's house" institution with ritual characteristics that has simply been missed in the ethnohistorical literature for the reasons suggested above.

What might this possibility of ritual activity mean for archaeological correlates? We have had a hard time trying to decide how to identify other structures connected with Southeastern ritual; temple structures are known not only by their division into multiple rooms and the presence of a hearth, but almost indispensably by location on a mound. Clearly a "women's house" would be distinguished by the locational considerations I have discussed, and structurally it would require a hearth, because women would be staying there for several days, but little else of a structural nature can be suggested.

The story would, however, be different with reference to artifacts. If ritual artifacts such as statuettes or pipes or everyday items like pottery vessels, which might have been specially decorated to ensure their recognition and avoidance by others, were used inside the women's house, pollution restrictions would keep them there, where they would likely be found.

Archaeological implications

What we have to look for, therefore, would be much like any other Mississippian house of wattle and daub or thatch. It would be spatially distinguished because it would be at whatever distance from living areas and field or forest that ritual purity demanded. The pattern of its location might select for nearness to running water because of its requirement for ritual cleansing. It would be downstream from the village or hamlet. If the disposal of soiled garments or pads had to be provided for by burning or burial – as we know was the case with the placenta – evidence of such disposal would be found within the house or nearby. Furthermore, if we reconceive the "menstrual hut" as a "women's house," then the complex of artifactual evidence would be much expanded to include ritual elements – structures, artifacts – and more of the long-term requirements of daily life. The presence of artifacts symbolically associated with females, fertility, and agriculture would fit this scenario, as would a distinctive ceramic assemblage with limited distribution. Both sorts of evidence are habitually assigned to (male) ritual contexts, as at the BBB Motor site (Emerson 1989; Pauketat and Emerson 1991) and the Sponemann site (Jackson *et al*. 1992) in the American Bottom, but in light of this discussion it might be worth reevaluating the evidence to see if another explanation might deal equally parsimoniously with the evidence.

I am suggesting, of course, that the red bauxite Birger and Keller figurines at the BBB Motor site, portraying kneeling women occupied in agricultural pursuits, and the similar Sponemann, Willoughby, and West figurines from Sponemann may be a clue that there is another possible interpretation not only for the "temple" complexes on both sites but for Ramey ceramics as well. Emerson's (1989:65) interpretation of Ramey motifs as "involving fertility and life forces" could hardly be more apposite to such an interpretation. Pauketat and Emerson interpret the symbolism of the Ramey jar, seen from above, as the cosmos (the decorative field) surrounding an orifice symbolizing the Underworld, such that the contents of the jar were seen as "associated with feminine life forces – earth, fertility, Under World – or female activities (e.g., agriculture, food preparation)" (Pauketat and Emerson 1991:933). But why not then see the orifice as the vaginal opening, and the contents of the pots (perhaps that dangerous red-flecked *sagamité*?) as coming from the body of the Corn Mother? Certainly pottery with "broad, simple designs . . . highly visible at a distance" (Pauketat and Emerson 1991:922) would be easily avoidable; designs "meant for a special purpose rather than simply being decorations for the elite" (Emerson 1989:63) could be meant to warn of pollution. The care taken in the execution of Ramey pottery, which Emerson (1989:66–67) argues was by "potters who were associated with each specific lineage/community ritual group," would be appropriate to a ware made by women not burdened by daily tasks (note that there is enough variation in Ramey ceramics that highly restricted specialist production is not suggested), and its relative scarcity fits well with a ware used for periodic seclusion. Such a "'utilitarian' ritual ware" (Emerson 1989:65) might well be included in mortuary offerings (especially for childbirth deaths), would appear in midden and garbage deposits, and would be distributed through all levels of the social hierarchy (since all women menstruate and most give birth).

It is worth noting that the BBB Motor site also exhibited other finds that could be reinterpreted in the direction of women's house practices: systematically reex-cavated pit features; red ocher pigment and a large quartz crystal with a dramatic red impurity (which Emerson compares to a Cherokee story of a man who regu-larly fed such a crystal with blood!); and *Datura stramonium*, which could have been used for abortion or difficult childbirths. Finally, the site was separated from the surrounding land by water and marshes during the period of its use. None of this evidence is conclusive, but I suggest that it is worth a thorough revaluation, espe-cially the sexing of the burials.

The occurrence of figurines similar to those at BBB Motor made a "ceremonial" interpretation inevitable for the Sponemann "Ceremonial Complex" of architectural and pit remains, which includes a "temple" and an adjoining structure interpreted as the temple-keeper's lodging. Because the figurines were evidently intentionally "killed" by being broken into fragments, and because the spread of those fragments coincides closely with the burned "temple," Fortier argues that the figurines had been broken outside the structure and most of the fragments placed within it before its intentional destruction by fire. This destruction supposedly marked a final "purifi-cation" step in an episode of "busk" ceremonialism focused on this "household temple" structure, which Fortier identifies by analogy with temples described by Du Pratz for the Natchez (Jackson *et al.* 1992: 52–70).

Again, however, it would seem that an alternative interpretation connected with women's house ceremonialism and especially purification practices might be appro-priate, at least for the "Ceremonial Complex" portion of the site. Fortier suggests that the destruction of the figurines and the "temple" building was part of a ritual act terminating a "year-end busk celebration" and representing "a symbolic act of regeneration and perhaps purification of the sacred busk complex." Further, he suggests that the "sanctity of this act and the busk ground itself" is signified by the fact that the site was not reoccupied after the destruction episode (Jackson *et al.* 1992: 303). Yet if the "temple" and adjoining "lodging" were interpreted as a women's house complex accommodating menstrual-seclusion facilities and fertility ceremonialism, it would seem that abandonment might be as much the product of notions of pollution as of sacredness, and the apparently inauspicious location of the site in a low clayey swale (Jackson *et al*. 1992: 49) would then suggest that it was chosen because of its proximity to water needed for purification.

In both the "ceremonial" and "residential" precincts of the Sponemann site small quantities of Ramey ceramics were found, although the concentration of small sherds in pits, especially in the "ceremonial" precinct, gave Fortier grounds for the suggestion that they were part of assemblages that represented the sweeping out of structures as another part of a "purification" practice. Certainly this kind of distribution for Ramey ceramics – whether associated with menstrual practices or not – helpfully raises the question of whether a possible distinctive "menstrual ware" might not also appear in an ordinary domestic setting, where vessels might be stored or used to obtain cooked foods destined for women in menstrual seclusion. This last surmise shows that finding evidence of distinctive women's houses will not be uncomplicated, but it will not be done at all unless we ask the questions.

There is no way we are going to understand late prehistoric Southeastern cultures until we come to grips with the basic issues of kinship organization and the role of women. Nor can we completely ignore a substantial portion of Southeastern women's lives, particularly one so strikingly connected with the central arcana of Mississippian ceremonialism. Ethnohistorical evidence can only take us so far back; after that, archaeology must serve as time machine. Here, however, ethnographic analogy gives us an actual structure to look for, and it is time we stopped being too ethnocentric to do so.

■ ■ ■

References

Bell, Amelia Rector (1990) "Separate People: Speaking of Creek Men and Women." *American Anthropologist* 92: 332–345.

Binford, Lewis R. (1970) "Archaeology at Hatchery West." *Memoirs of the Society for American Archaeology* 24.

Bonnichsen, Robson (1973) "Millie's Camp: An Experiment in Archaeology." *World Archaeology* 4: 227–291.

Bossu, Jean-Bernard (1962) *Travels in the Interior of North America, 1751–1762*. Translated and edited by Seymour Feiler. Norman: University of Oklahoma Press.

Buckley, Thomas (1988) "Menstruation and the Power of Yurok Women." In *Blood Magic*, edited by Thomas Buckley and Alma Gottlieb, 188–209. Berkeley: University of California Press.

Buckley, Thomas and Alma Gottlieb (eds) (1988a) *Blood Magic: The Anthropology of Menstruation*. Berkeley: University of California Press.

—— (1988b) "A Critical Appraisal of Theories of Menstrual Symbolism." In *Blood Magic*, edited by Thomas Buckley and Alma Gottlieb, 3–50. Berkeley: University of California Press.

Delaney, Janice, Mary Jane Lupton and Emily Toth (1976) *The Curse: A Cultural History of Menstruation*. New York: E. P. Dutton.

Douglas, Mary (1966) *Purity and Danger*. London: Pelican.

Emerson, Thomas E. (1982) *Mississippian Stone Images in Illinois*. Champaign-Urbana: Illinois Archaeological Survey Circular No. 6.

—— (1989) "Water, Serpents, and the Underworld: An Exploration into Cahokian Symbolism." In *The Southeastern Ceremonial Complex: Artifacts and Analysis*, edited by Patricia Galloway, 45–92. Lincoln: University of Nebraska Press.

Gottlieb, Alma (1988) "Menstrual Cosmology among the Beng of Ivory Coast." In *Blood Magic*, edited by Thomas Buckley and Alma Gottlieb, 55–74. Berkeley: University of California Press.

Harris, Marvin (1988) *Culture, People, Nature: An Introduction to General Anthropology*. 5th ed. New York: Harper and Row.

Hudson, Charles (1976) *The Southeastern Indians*. Knoxville: University of Tennessee Press.

Jackson, Douglas K., Andrew C. Fortier and Joyce A. Williams (1992) *The Sponemann Site 2: The Mississippian Oneota Occupations (11-Ms-S17)*. American Bottom Archaeology, FAI-270 Site Reports, No. 24. Urbana: University of Illinois Press.

Knight, Chris (1988) "Menstrual Synchrony and the Australian Rainbow Snake." In *Blood Magic*, edited by Thomas Buckley and Alma Gottlieb, 232–255. Berkeley: University of California Press.

—— (1991) *Blood Relations: Menstruation and the Origins of Culture*. New Haven, Conn.: Yale University Press.

Knight, Vernon James (1990) "Social Organization and the Evolution of Hierarchy in Southeastern Chiefdoms." *Journal of Anthropological Research* 46: 1–23.

Lankford, George (1987) *Native American Legends*. Little Rock: August House.

Martin, Emily (1992) *The Woman in the Body: A Cultural Analysis of Reproduction*. 2nd ed.: Boston: Beacon Press.

McClintock, Martha K. (1971) "Menstrual Syndrome and Suppression." *Nature* 229 (5282):244–245.

Mead, Margaret (1939) *From the South Seas: Studies of Adolescence and Sex in Primitive Societies*. New York: William Morrow and Company.

Milanich, Jerald, William C. Sturtevant, and Emilio Moran (eds and trans) (1972) *Francisco Pareja's 1613 Confessionario: A Documentary Source for Timucuan Ethnography*. Tallahassee: Florida Division of Archives, History, and Records Management.

Paige, Karen Ericksen (1973) "Women Learn to Sing the Menstrual Blues." *Psychology Today* 7:41–46.

Paige, Karen Ericksen, and Jeffrey M. Paige (1981) *The Politics of Reproductive Ritual*. Berkeley: University of California Press.

Pauketat, Timothy R., and Thomas E. Emerson (1991) "The Ideology of Authority and the Power of the Pot." *American Anthropologist* 93:919–941.

Schlegel, Alice (1972) *Male Dominance and Female Autonomy*. New Haven, Conn.: HRAF Press.

Shuttle, Penelope, and Peter Redgrove (1978) *The Wise Wound: Eve's Curse and Everywoman*. New York: Richard Marek.

Strassmann, Beverly, I. (1997) The Biology of Menstruation in *Homo Sapiens*: Total Lifetime Menses, Fecundity, and Nonsynchrony in a Natural-Fertility Population. *Current Anthropology* 38(1):123–29.

Swanton, John R. (1911) *Indians of the Lower Mississippi Valley and Adjacent Coast of the Gulf of Mexico*. Bureau of American Ethnology Bulletin 43. Washington, D.C.

—— (1928a) "Social Organization and Social Usages of the Indians of the Creek Confederacy." Bureau of American Ethnology 42nd annual report (1925), 43–472. Washington, DC.

—— (1928b) "Sun Worship in the Southeast." *American Anthropologist* 30: 206–213.

—— (1929) *Myths and Tales of the Southeastern Indians*. Bureau of American Ethnology Bulletin 88. Washington, DC.

—— (1931) *Source Material for the Social Ceremonial Life of the Choctaw Indians*. Bureau of American Ethnology Bulletin 103. Washington, DC.

—— (1946) *Indians of the Southeastern United States*. Bureau of American Ethnology Bulletin 137. Washington, DC.

Underhill, Ruth (1936) *The Autobiography of a Papago Woman*. Memoir 46, American Anthropological Association.

Ward, Trawick, and Steve Davis (1988) "Archaeology of the Historic Occaneechi Indians." *Southern Indian Studies* 36–37.

Weideger, Paula (1976) *Menstruation and Menopause: The Physiology and Psychology, the Myth and Reality*. New York: Knopf.

Chapter 12

SPINNING AND WEAVING AS FEMALE GENDER IDENTITY IN POST-CLASSIC MEXICO

Sharisse D. McCafferty and
Geoffrey G. McCafferty

Introduction

Spinning and weaving are traditional activities specific to the female domestic sphere in indigenous Mexican society. Evidence from ethnohistoric sources, including Spanish accounts and pre-Columbian codices, indicates that spinning and weaving were also important in Central Mexico immediately prior to the Spanish Conquest as both functional and symbolic activities. Finished textiles played an important role in the economy and tribute of Post-Classic Mexico. As costumes, they also served to communicate status, rank, ethnic affiliation, and gender.

In addition to these functional qualities, spinning and weaving acted symbolically in defining and reifying female identity. In this chapter we discuss how spinning and weaving acted as metaphors for sexuality, childbirth, and female life-cycles in Post-Classic Mexico; and how these activities served as a means of initiation into female ideologies. Finally, we suggest that the symbolism surrounding spinning and weaving defined female identity as one source of control over reproduction and thus as a basis of female power. The changing symbolic role of these activities during the Late Post-Classic and Early Colonial periods allows interpretations of the construction and transformation of female gender ideologies and the negotiation of gender relations.

Symbolic archaeology and the study of gender

Spinning and weaving were traditionally considered women's work in pre-Columbian Central Mexico (Hellbom 1967). Although functional aspects of these activities have been described by anthropologists, the possibility of a symbolic significance has been largely overlooked. In Mesoamerica, Cecilia Klein (1982) has addressed the relationship between spinning and weaving symbolism and the metaphor of the loom as a structuring principle of the Mesoamerican worldview. For the Aztecs of Central Mexico, June Nash has interpreted spinning and weaving in gender terms as a "metaphor for subordination and humility" (1978: 356). She supports this with the example of Tezozomoc, king of Azcapotzalco, who sent a shipment of cotton to the king of Texcoco in 1410, allegedly as an insult to his masculinity (see also Bernal 1976). Nash goes on to suggest diachronic changes in gender relations during the Post-Classic period, emphasizing specific arenas of female participation but concluding that male monopoly of military and bureaucratic spheres limited female access to wealth and prestige (1978: 361) and was supported through a state ideology of male dominance.

In contrast to the paradigm of male dominance, this chapter employs a model in which the symbolism of spinning and weaving acted within an alternative, female discourse, operating apart from, even in resistance to, the dominant male ideology. Symbols helped to define female identity and delimit an arena within which female power could be negotiated. While evidence supports Nash's contention of a dominant socio-political position for Aztec males, it must not be assumed that other groups were without access to power. Several recent studies have addressed the issue of pre-Columbian gender relations from the perspective of women as an active interest group negotiating status through strategic decision-making (Brumfiel 1991; Kann 1989; Kellogg 1988; G. McCafferty and S. McCafferty 1989a, b; S. McCafferty and G. McCafferty 1988; see also Silverblatt 1978, 1987 for examples from South America).

A comparable use of symbolism in female discourse has been illustrated in the ethnoarchaeological studies of the Ilchamus of Baringo, Kenya (Hodder 1982, 1986), where women decorate calabash gourds used for feeding milk to children. While the ethnographic study of the Ilchamus indicated that women had little overt power in the public arena, "covertly, . . . the decoration defines and emphasizes the reproductive importance of women in a society in which reproduction (of children and of the cattle that produce milk) is the central pivot of male power" (Hodder 1986: 109). Women have adopted a strategy of emphasizing the source of their power in resistance to the pattern of male behavior. We assert that a comparable female discourse existed in pre-Columbian Mexico, as women expressed their control over reproduction and domestic production through symbolic representations of spinning and weaving.

Recognizing gender differences in the past is complicated by the androcentric bias that permeates anthropological research (Conkey and Spector 1984). The male bias that characterizes Western science has traditionally emphasized male activities while peripheralizing female activities. This is particularly true of the documentary records from the Spanish conquest (Brown 1983; Leacock and Nash 1977). The inherent androcentrism of early Colonial period ethnohistoric records – written by priests and *conquistadores* using a medieval mind-set – conforms to the culture historical model used in anthropological convention: an emphasis on political history, economics, technology, and the masculine elements of the native religious pantheon. Women, women's activites, and female cultural elements were dealt with superficially and stereotypically.

To study past gender relationships it is necessary to critically appraise potential biases that affect interpretation at every stage of analysis. In our investigations of pre-Columbian Mexican spinning and weaving we have used a variety of sources. However, in addition to relying on literal textual references, this study also considers the pictorial representations of spinning and weaving and their associated tools in different contextual situations. In so doing we adopt methodologies from historical archaeology and material culture studies, which indicate that biases existing in textual records are often less pronounced when referring to material culture (Deetz 1977). An example of this principle in Colonial Mexican texts is found in the *Florentine Codex*, where the Spanish priest Bernardino de Sahagún noted that women had little influence in the marketplace; yet in the accompanying illustrations women are shown selling an assortment of goods (Hellbom 1967: 134; Sahagún 1950–1982, Book 10: 61–62, cf. plates 119 and 120).

The approach we use presumes an active role for material culture and its encoded symbols in the creation and transformation of society (Hodder 1982). On one level, symbols act as a form of communication, mediating social relationships while establishing group identity and maintaining boundaries (Wobst 1977). On another level, meanings vary depending on situational contexts, and symbols help to create these contexts (Bourdieu 1977; Hodder 1986). For instance, material culture – in this case spinning and weaving implements – will have different meanings within the different contexts in which it appears. These contexts can vary widely, based on who and what other factors are involved, when and where the activity takes place, and how all of the factors are integrated into the total context.

Another critical factor is the identification of historical antecedents, or traditions, for particular types of behavior. When contextual patterns are culturally prescribed, elements of material culture acquire symbolic properties that can evoke meaning regardless of context. The symbols are meaningful to those participants familiar with the patterned behavior. In this way symbols can be transmitted, but as symbolic information becomes invested in material culture it can also be controlled and manipulated. By studying symbols diachronically, we have a means of monitoring relationships not otherwise observable in the historical record.

The ethnoarchaeology of spinning and weaving

Central Mexico had a well-developed weaving industry incorporating a wide range of materials, motifs, colors, and forms. This was noted by the early Spanish chroniclers (Cortés 1986; Díaz del Castillo 1963; Durán 1971; Motolinía 1951; Sahagún 1950–82) and has been well documented by Patricia Anawalt (1981).

Pre-Columbian weaving was done on the backstrap loom, a highly portable device where one end is attached to a tree or post, while the other end is wrapped around the weaver who maintains tension on the warp using body weight (figure 1a). Spinning techniques included both drop- and supported spinning methods, depending on the material being spun and the desired quality of the thread (Hochberg 1980). Drop-spinning is done with a heavy whorl on the spindle shaft, where the rotating spindle is repeatedly dropped to draw out and twist the raw fiber. Drop-spinning can be done virtually anywhere, and ethnographic accounts describe women spinning with this technique as they walk to the fields or in the marketplace (Granberg 1970:13–16; Starr 1908). Supported spinning is done with the tip of the spindle shaft resting in a small bowl or on a flat surface. It provides greater control over the spinning process and results in a finer-quality thread (figure 1b). Drop-spinning can only be done with relatively long staple fibers, such as maguey, while cotton is best suited for supported spinning.

Cotton in particular was a valuable trade and tribute commodity associated with elite status (Berdan 1982:30–31; Rodriguez Vallejo 1976). Maguey fiber was another commonly spun material and, depending on the species used and the number of production steps, it could produce either coarse or high-quality thread. Additional materials used for spinning included human and animal hair (rabbit and dog), feathers, and vegetable fibers such as milkweed and *chichicastle*, a fibrous nettle native to Southern Mexico, also known as *mala mujer* (García Valencia 1975:61–62).

Education in spinning and weaving techniques began at an early age, and by adolescence girls were learning the rudiments of weaving (Codex Mendoza, plates LIX-LXI, described in Hellbom 1967:110–115) (figure 2). The primary weaver in

Figure 1a   Aztec noblewoman weaving on backstrap loom in patio of house (After Sahagún 1950–1982, book 10: figure 58). Drawing by Sharisse McCafferty

Figure 1b Aztec woman spinning with spindle supported in small bowl (after Codex Mendoza, vol. 3, folio 68r). Drawing by Sharisse McCafferty

a household was the wife, who had the responsibility of making clothing and other woven goods for the household (Durán 1971:423). Thread was often spun by other family members, especially young girls and old women, and occasionally by males depending on production needs and end use.

In addition to domestic use, spinning and weaving provided a means for women to participate in the market economy (Sahagún 1950–82, Book 8:69; Hellbom 1967:299). Woven goods produced in the household could be sold in the market or used as tribute. Capes and blankets were regularly presented as gifts at different ceremonies and were an important means for gaining social status (Sahagún 1950–82, Book 6:196). A woman's skill as a weaver was considered a positive asset in this pursuit. The practice of polygamy by the Aztecs was credited in part to the need for the elite to maintain a large labor pool of women for producing textiles

Figure 2 Aztec woman instructing daughter in weaving technique (after Codex Mendoza, vol. 3, folio 60r). Drawing by Sharisse McCafferty

for ritual gift-giving (Motolinía 1951: 202, 246). In temple compounds, spinning and weaving of fine textiles produced costumes, cotton armor, and incense bags for distribution as emblems of rank and for religious and state ceremonies (Anawalt 1981; Motolinia 1951). Finally, capes and *quachtlis* (small woven cloths) were used as standards of value in the pre-Columbian economy and were exchanged at a rate regulated by the Aztec state administration (Sahagún 1950–82, Book 9:48; Book 3:6–7; Berdan 1982:44).

Spinning and weaving were important functional tasks in Mesoamerican society, but it is our contention that they were equally important ideologically in structuring patterns of female identity. The female experience could be described as an analogue of spinning and weaving activities, "interwoven" throughout daily practice by myth, folklore, gossip, and jokes. The metaphor of spinning and weaving is used in many cultures to explain the world (Eliade 1975:45–46; Klein 1982; Schaefer 1989; Wilbert 1974). There is ample evidence that this was the case in Post-Classic Central Mexico, as has been noted by Thelma Sullivan (1982:14):

> Spinning goes through stages of growth and decline, waxing and waning, similar to those of a child-bearing woman. The spindle set in the spindle whorl is symbolic of coitus, and the thread, as it winds around the spindle, symbolizes the growing fetus, the woman becoming big with child. . . . Weaving, too, the intertwining of threads, is symbolic of coitus, and thus spinning and weaving represent life, death, and rebirth in a continuing cycle that characterizes the essential nature of the Mother Goddess.

The metaphor of spinning and weaving is demonstrated in the Nahuatl riddle "What is it that they make pregnant, that they make big with child in the dancing place?" Answer: "Spindles" (Sahagún 1950–82 Book 6:240; paraphrased in Sullivan 1962:14). The "dancing place" was the bowl in which the spindle was set. Contemporary spinners in Mexico still refer to the spindle as dancing (*bailando*) in a bowl during supported spinning (García Valencia 1975:60).

Indoctrination into female ideology began at an early age in a dedication ceremony involving spindles, fiber, whorls, looms, needles, and cooking utensils as symbols of female gender identity (Sahagún 1950–82, Book 6:201) (figure 3). The Aztec ceremony involved the presence of a midwife/priestess of the Mother Goddess, who read the astrological destiny and gave the child its calendrical name (Hellbom 1967:39). The priestess then took the umbilical cord of the girl child and buried it by the hearth, and "thus she signified that woman was to go nowhere. Her very task was the home life, life by the fire, by the grinding stone . . . She was to prepare drink, to prepare food, to grind, to spin, to weave" (Sahagún 1950–82, Book 6:171).

Spinning and weaving were an essential part of the moral upbringing of young girls. They were associated with high status, but were taught as desirable skills for all "good" girls. Young girls began learning to spin by the age of four and learned to weave clothing by the age of fourteen (Hellbom 1967:167; Codex Mendoza 1964; Zorita

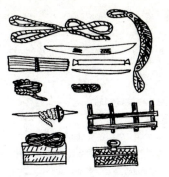

Figure 3   Spinning and weaving implements (After Sahagún 1950–1982, Book 8, figure 78). Drawing by Sharisse McCafferty

1963:137). Since spinning and weaving were activities practiced predominantly in the household, it was taught that this was the female domain, with weaving ability a characteristic of a "proper wife" and thus a favorable trait for obtaining a husband:

> Pay heed to, apply yourself to, the work of women, to the spindle, to the batten.
> Watch carefully how your noblewomen, your ladies, our ladies, the noblewomen, who are artisans, who are craftswomen, dye [the thread], how they apply the dyes [to the thread], how the heddles are set, how the heddle leashes are fixed . . .
> It is not your destiny, it is not your fate, to offer [for sale] in people's doorways, greens, firewood, strings of chiles, slabs of rock salt, for you are a noblewoman.
> [Thus], see to the spindle, the batten . . .
> [Sahagún 1950–82, Book 6:96, quoted in Sullivan 1982:13–14]

The combined tasks of spinning and weaving were symbolic of the changes in the female life cycle, with spinning an activity of young girls and old women, while a married woman had the responsibility of weaving to supply clothing for the family, especially her husband and children. A common metaphor for infertility was one who spun but never wove (Sullivan 1982:19), as in the myth of *cihuapipiltin*, deified women who died in childbirth. A contemporary myth from the state of Chiapas relates how witches in the mountains spend their time endlessly spinning, with the implication that "spinning without weaving is a futile and unproductive occupation" (Cordry and Cordry 1968:42).

The sexual symbolism of spinning and weaving is also incorporated into the Christmas ceremony of the Tzotzil Maya of Chiapas (Bricker 1973:19). Men dressed as "grandmothers" give the young women a lesson in spinning and weaving full of sexual metaphors on the importance of pleasing their husbands by fulfilling their female duties.

The symbolism of spinning and weaving as an emblem of female identity is richly demonstrated in ethnohistory and folklore. In addition, its significance pervades the mythology surrounding the Central Mexican goddesses.

Mythology and gender identity

Symbols of female gender identity were transmitted through religious beliefs incorporating the female deities to create active social roles. In pre-Columbian Mexico religion was not an abstract set of norms but an active factor in prescribing behavior. The myths that surrounded the goddesses were a means for enculturation, as mythology was used to transmit and justify gender ideologies (Taggart 1983). The metaphors expressed in mythology served to transform the natural into the supernatural, creating an ideological mystification of gender relationships and defining a female identity.

Mesoamerican religion was complex, and the Aztec pantheon in particular incorporated deities from neighboring lands as a result of imperial conquest and diverse cultural composition. As a consequence, isolating a specific deity associated with spinning and weaving is difficult. The traits extend beyond any one goddess and blend into many, until we see an archetypal pattern with multiple identities. The three main deities associated with spinning and weaving were Tlazolteotl, Xochiquetzal, and Mayahuel. A fourth, Toci, was also closely linked to the patterns embodied by the Mother Goddess and, by extension, to female identity. A brief description of each will present their individual traits and will demonstrate their overlapping attributes.

Tlazolteotl was known as the "Great Spinner and Weaver," and probably originated among the Huaxtecs of northern Veracruz (Sullivan 1982). She was associated with childbirth, the moon, menses, and purification; sexuality, witchcraft, and healing. She was also the *Tlaelquani*, "Eater of Filth," who absolved the sins of both men and women before death. Since it was believed that a child came into the world coated in the sins of its parents, Tlazolteotl (in the guise of her priestesses/midwives) received and purified the new-born (Sahagún 1950–82, Book 6:175). Another name for Tlazolteotl, Ixcuina, is a reference to her relationship to cotton (*ixcatl*), used in spinning but also important as an abortive, a lactogenic, and for absorbing menstrual flow (i.e., "eating filth") (Sullivan 1982:19). Tlazolteotl was often depicted in the four-part nature of the female life cycle: first young and immature, then in full sexual bloom, later as a mother and center of the household, and finally as an old woman wise with experience (Sahagún 1950–82, Book 1:23; Sullivan 1982:12).

Tlazolteotl was often portrayed in the codices wearing a headband of unspun cotton and with cotton draped from her earspools (figure 4). Spindles with whorls were thrust into her hair as decoration or carried as a staff or weapon. Black bitumen (*chapopote*) was used to decorate her face as further indication of gender

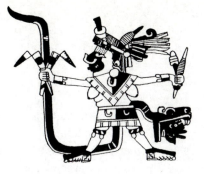

Figure 4   Mexican goddess, Tlazolteotl, with spindles in headband and hand (after Codex Laud: 39). Drawing by Sharisse McCafferty

identity. Another diagnostic emblem of Tlazolteotl was the crescent shape, which signified the moon, and which decorated her clothing and *yacametztli* nose ornament. Tlazolteotl's skirt and/or *quechquemitl* were occasionally divided into red and black halves, symbolic of the structural oppositions incorporated in her character.

Tlazolteotl was associated with snakes, dogs, and centipedes (Sullivan 1982: 17–18), all symbolic of fertility and the earth. Dogs were regarded as "eaters of filth" because they were commonly found foraging in garbage dumps. Centipedes are also found in areas of decomposing trash and were associated with the transformation of waste into productive humus. The essence of female ideology was embodied in Tlazolteotl, with the metaphor of spinning and weaving symbolic of the ongoing process of generation and regeneration.

Xochiquetzal, or "Precious Flower," was in many ways the Nahua equivalent of Tlazolteotl and shared many of her attributes. She was associated with flowers, artisans, and sexuality, both as the goddess of the marriage bond and as patroness of harlots (Brundage 1982; G. McCafferty and S. McCafferty 1989a). Xochiquetzal was reputed to have introduced the knowledge of spinning and weaving and to have provided the creative initiative for painting, carving, and music (Heyden 1985). These were occupations of the elite, especially of the children of the nobility who would not succeed to political posts (Sahagún 1950–82, Book 8:45). Hummingbirds, butterflies, and flowers were glyphic elements identifying her as protector of the earth and its vegetation and the souls of the dead. The quetzal bird, dual locks of hair or twin upright tassels, a gold butterfly nose ornament, and a blue dress were other visual means of identifying Xochiquetzal (Duran 1971). Another aspect of the goddess, Itzpapolotl, or "Obsidian Butterfly," was a goddess of war and death in combat (Berlo 1983). While she was a protector or male warriors, Xochiquetzal was especially sensitive to women in labor, "since childbirth itself was likened to death and to battle" (Klein 1972:40).

Mayahuel was known as Lady Maguey because of her association with the agave plant, one of the fundamental elements of Mexican culture. Virtually every portion

of the plant was used, including fiber for weaving, juice for the fermentation of
pulque, and spines for ritual blood-letting (Gonzales de Lima 1956; Sullivan
1982:24–25). Although spun *maguey* did not have the elite status of cotton, it was
more versatile in many ways and thus was more widely used. Mayahuel was a
goddess of weaving; she was also associated with healing, female productivity, and
reproduction. *Pulque*, the fermented juice of the maguey, was used ceremonially
throughout Central Mexico. Like Tlazolteotl, Mayahuel shared the characteristic
headband of unspun fiber, in this case probably maguey, with spindles thrust into
it (Sullivan 1982). Mayahuel was the embodiment of female productivity, often
depicted with bare breasts as a symbol of her nurturing character. In the *Codex
Vaticanus A* (21v) she is portrayed with 400 breasts (a metaphor for "prolific") in
reference to her fecundity (Sullivan 1982:24; another possible example of this is
found in the *Codex Nuttall* 27:I).

Finally, the goddess Toci, or Teteo-innan, was associated with the bath house,
an area of healing, illicit sexual union, and childbirth. She was referred to as "Our
Grandmother," a protector of women and source of wisdom. Her symbols were
the broom and the shield, relating to her role in women's work and healing, and
also as a warrior and protector. Toci was also known as Ilamatecuhtli, "the Mother
of the Gods," and as such was a central figure in Mesoamerican mythology
(Nicholson 1971). As part of the ritual calendar, the "Feast of the Sweeping"
(*Ochpaniztli*) was dedicated to Toci, in which a goddess impersonator was sacrificed
after performing her symbolic roles as a woman (Durán 1971:232–3):

> [The impersonator] was delivered to the old women who brought her a bundle
> of maguey fiber. They made her comb it, wash it, spin it, and weave a cloth
> of it. At a certain hour she was led out of the temple to a place where she
> was to perform the act [of weaving]. . . . When the eve of the feast arrived,
> the woman, who had finished her weaving (which was a skirt and blouse of
> maguey fiber), was led by the old women to the marketplace. They made
> her sit there and sell the things she had spun and woven, thus indicating that
> the mother of the gods had been engaged in that occupation in her time to
> make a living, spinning and weaving garments of maguey fiber, going to the
> markets to sell them, thus providing for herself and her children.

As spinning and weaving were attributes of the Mother Goddess complex, they
were linked symbolically to the authority of the goddesses and metaphorically to
fertility and reproduction. Priestesses of the female deities were skilled midwives
and adept at herbal and magical methods for inducing conception and contracep-
tion (Sahagún 1950–82, Book 1:4–5; Hellbom 1967:36). This implies control over
reproduction, one of the most important sources of female power, and therefore
a potential arena for gender competition.

Evidence for the multiplicity of symbolic meanings surrounding spinning and
weaving can be found in the pre-Columbian codices, where the presence of spindles and spindle whorls were characteristic traits for identifying the female deities

and their priestesses. In the *Codex Nuttall* (e.g., pages 43:III and 48:IV) they were used to denote place names, perhaps as a means of identifying female domains or specific activity areas. Spindles, with or without whorls or thread, were also used as hair adornments in the codices, serving as an emblem of gender identity. Spindles are still worn in the hair in weaving communities of the Mixteca de la Costa, Oaxaca, where they are diagnostic of *malacateras*, or "spinners."

An additional use of spinning and weaving symbolism in the codices was the use of weaving tools, especially battens, as weapons or as staffs of authority to represent female power (G. McCafferty and S. McCafferty 1989b; Sullivan 1982). In the feast of *Atemoztli*, images of mountain fertility deities were made out of amaranth dough, sacrificed using weaving battens, and then eaten (Sahagún 1950–82, Book 2:29; Anawalt 1981:14). This suggests that the weapons of the female deities were the same domestic tools that served to define female identity.

Conclusion

The symbolism of spinning and weaving served to define female identity in the sense that it created a set of meaningful associations that united women as an interest group. Spinning and weaving were gender specific activities that took place in the household, an area in which female power was concentrated. They were tasks that were practiced by virtually all women, regardless of class or age, and were taught as a fundamental part of the female gender role. The primary female goddesses associated with spinning and weaving were also linked with reproduction, and this theme was related metaphorically in the folklore surrounding spinning and weaving. The relationship between weaving materials (such as cotton and maguey) and fertility further reinforces the concept that female power was closely related to control over reproduction. The tools of spinning and weaving (spindles, whorls and battens) acted as symbols of this power, with the women represented in the codices that bore these tools – be they goddesses, priestesses, sacrificial impersonators, or mortals – identified as women with access to resources of female power.

The archaeology of gender identity

This chapter has developed out of our study of archaeological spindle whorls from Cholula, Puebla. Spindle whorls were usually made of baked clay and acted as flywheels to maintain inertia for the rotating spindle while twisting fiber into thread (Hochberg 1980; Smith and Hirth 1988). In Post-Classic Mexico (AD 900–1520) spindle whorls were often decorated with mold-made or incised designs, and occasionally they were painted or coated with bitumen. Interestingly, whorls are rare from earlier and later time periods, suggesting that permanent baked clay whorls may have had a symbolic role in addition to their functional utility. In contrast to highland Mexico, at the site of Matacapan in central Veracruz, spindle whorls *were* found in Classic period contexts (Hall 1989) and can possibly be related to increased status of women associated with textile production (Kann 1989).

In comparing archaeological assemblages from Post-Classic Cholula, striking differences are apparent in the decorative motifs on spindle whorls that probably relate to cultural changes through time. From an excavated household compound (the UA-1 site on the campus of the Universidad de las Americas) dating to the Early Post-Classic period (*ca.* AD 1000–1200) (G. McCafferty 1986, 1993), whorls displayed diverse decorative motifs, including complex geometric and zoomorphic patterns (figures 5a-f), and many have a bitumen coating over the mold-impressed designs (14%, n = 51).

Bitumen-covered whorls have been associated with the Gulf Coast region based on archaeologically recovered examples from sites in Veracruz (Ekholm 1944; Parsons 1972:57). Functional explanations for bitumen as a covering are unsatisfactory, and instead we suggest a symbolic interpretation, particularly as it relates to the cult of Tlazolteotl. While the Gulf Coast affiliation of the goddess would support the identification of bitumen-covered whorls as trade goods, it is not conclusive. At the UA-1 excavation at Cholula, five whorls were found with identical molded patterns, suggesting that they were produced in the same mold, and two were covered with bitumen. This suggests that the bitumen covering was probably applied onsite.

In another assemblage from the same area (UA-79), dating to the Late Post-Classic period (*ca.* AD 1350–1520), many of the previous motifs are nearly absent as is the use of bitumen. Instead, the whorls are often decorated with floral patterns, possibly depicting marigolds (figures 5g-j). Flowers were closely associated with the Mother Goddess complex, especially Xochiquetzal and Toci, and the marigold was used in special rituals by priestess/midwives (Sahagún 1950–82, Book 2:19; Heyden 1985).

The stylistic differences between the two assemblages occurred over a period of about 200–400 years, during which time the documentary sources record the conquest of Cholula by the Tolteca-Chichimeca ethnic group (Historia Tolteca Chichimeca; Olivera and Reyes 1969). The historical evidence for ethnic change, from the original Olmeca-Xicallanca group (with ties to the Gulf Coast) to the Tolteca-Chichimeca, is supported by changes in the material culture (McCafferty 1989a, b). The evidence from this spindle whorl analysis suggests that spinners were initially affiliated with the cult of Tlazolteotl, using symbolic elements such as bitumen to identify with her power. By the Late Post-Classic period this affiliation had been transferred to the cults of Xochiquetzal and Toci as evidenced by the predominance of floral motifs. What effect this religious change may have had on gender relations remains to be explored further, although the similarities between the goddesses suggest that the structural differences may have been minimal.

Figures 5a-f Archaeological spindle whorls from UA-1 (Cholula, Puebla) showing complex geometric and zoomorphic design motifs. Drawings by Sharisse McCafferty

Another symbolic association relates whorl patterns and shield decorations. Decorated shields are represented in the pictorial manuscripts, with different motifs relating to regional identity and military rank (Peñafiel 1985). Patterns identical to those found on shields were also found on spindle whorls, particularly those from the UA-1 household context. Whorls decorated with hatched semicircles, for example, may relate to the *teueuelli* ("sacrificial shield") carried by the goddess Toci and the Aztec patron Huitzilopochtli. Susan Kellogg (1988) has discussed the conceptual similarities between warfare and childbirth as a "structural equivalence"

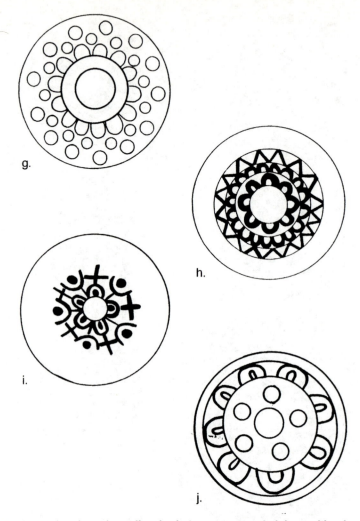

Figures 5g-j   Archaeological spindle whorls from UA-79 (Cholula, Puebla) showing floral motifs. Drawings by Sharisse McCafferty

linking male and female genders. This may be one explanation for the use of shield patterns on whorls, relating to the exhortation of the midwife to "take up the little shield" during childbirth (Sahagún 1950–82, Book 6:154, 161; G. McCafferty and S. McCafferty 1989b). On a more practical level, it can be speculated that a sharp spindle through a whorl would have been a formidable female weapon, the Mesoamerican equivalent of a long hat pin.

Spindle whorls *do* play a functional role in spinning, but they do not need to be as elaborately made as the Post-Classic Cholula whorls. Contemporary spinners often use spindles with sun-baked clay whorls applied directly to the shaft, resulting in an efficient system that would rarely leave a trace in the archaeological record.

Since whorls are not recovered from Classic period contexts, yet woven garments are depicted in mural paintings, it is likely that a similar, impermanent spindle whorl was used.

We suggest that the symbolic importance of decorated spindle whorls emphasized affiliation with the female deities and therefore promoted a group identity. Spindles with whorls worn in the hair may have been an emblem of status as is still the case among the Mixtecs of the Oaxaca coast. As a talisman of the deity, spindle whorls may have been used in fertility rites (Durán 1971: 264–5, 269). The act of spinning itself, which was practiced throughout the day in varied situations, could almost be interpreted as a form of worship in the sense of symbolic bonding with the Mother Goddess(es).

Based on ethnohistoric evidence and supported by the archaeological spindle whorls from Cholula, female power during the Post-Classic period was expressed through the metaphor of spinning and weaving. Following the Spanish Conquest, the ideological system of Mesoamerica was fundamentally altered and consequently so were gender relationships (Nash 1980). The authority of the female deities was transferred to the cult of the Virgin and any overt control over reproduction was discouraged by the Church. Effectively, female power rapidly declined. And although technological change did not alter the indigenous weaving industry, the use of decorated and baked spindle whorls was quickly abandoned.

The use of archaeological methods to study ideology, through symbols and material culture, provides a methodology for studying change in the relations between and within social groups. Group relationships are continuously redefined as strategies for control over power are negotiated. Changing symbols of group identity can relate to these changing relationships and thereby indicate the arenas of interaction. In the example from Post-Classic Mexico, control over reproduction was one focus of gender competition, symbolized in the myths of spinning and weaving. That these symbols were abandoned following the Spanish Conquest does not necessarily mean that the competition was also abandoned but only that gender identities were redefined with other symbols of identity taking their place.

References

Anawalt, Patricia R. (1981) *Indian Clothing Before Cortes: Mesoamerican Costumes, from the Codices.* Norman: University of Oklahoma Press.

Berdan, Frances F. (1982) *The Aztecs of Central Mexico: An Imperial Society.* New York: Holt, Rinehart and Winston.

Berlo, Janet Catherine (1983) The Warrior and the Butterfly: Central Mexican Ideologies of Sacred Warfare and Teotihuacan Iconography. In *Text and Image in Pre-Columbian Art,* edited by J. C. Berlo, pp. 79–118. Oxford: BAR International Series 180.

Bernal, Ignacio (1976) Tenochtitlán es una isla. Mexico, DF: Utopia, Companía Editorial.

Bourdieu, Pierre (1977) *Outline of a Theory of Practice.* Cambridge: Cambridge University Press.

Bricker, Victoria (1973) *Ritual Humor in Highland Chiapas.* Austin: University of Texas Press.

Brown, Betty Ann (1983) Seen but not Heard: Women in Aztec Ritual – The Sahagún Texts. In *Text and Image in Pre-Columbian Art*, edited by J. C. Berlo, pp. 119–154. Oxford: BAR International Series 180.

Brumfiel, Elizabeth (1997) Weaving and Cooking: Women's Production in Aztec Mexico. In *Engendering Archaeology: Women and Prehistory*, edited by J. Gero and M. Conkey. Oxford: Basil Blackwell.

Brundage, Burr Cartwright (1982) *The Phoenix of the Western World: Quetzalcoatl and the Sky Religion*. Norman: University of Oklahoma Press.

Codex Mendoza (1964) Codex Mendoza, Bodleian Library, Oxford: In *Antigüedades de México basadas en la recopilación de Lord Kingsborough*, edited by Jose Corona Nuñez. México, D.F.: Secretaría de Hacienda y Crédito Público.

Codex Nuttall (1975) *The Codex Nuttall. A Picture Manuscript from Ancient Mexico*. The Peabody Museum Facsimile, edited by Zelia Nuttall (introduction by A.G. Miller). New York: Dover Publications, Inc.

Codex Vaticanus A (1964) Codex Vaticanus A (3738), Biblioteca Apostolica Vaticana, Rome. In *Antigüedades de México basadas en la recopilación de Lord Kingsborough*, edited by Jose Corona Nuñez. México, DF: Secretaría de Hacienda y Crédito Público.

Conkey, Margaret, and Janet Spector (1984) Archaeology and the Study of Gender. In *Advances in Archaeological Method and Theory*, Vol. 7, edited by M.B. Schiffer, pp. 1–38. New York: Academic Press.

Cordry, Donald, and Dorothy Cordry (1968) *Mexican Indian Costumes*. Austin: University of Texas Press.

Cortés, Hernán (1986) *Letters from Mexico* (translated and edited by A. Pagden). New Haven and London: Yale University Press. (Originally written from 1519–1526.)

Deetz, James (1977) *In Small Things Forgotten*. New York: Doubleday.

Díaz del Castillo, Bernal (1963) *The Conquest of New Spain* (translated by J.M. Cohen). Middlesex: Penguin Books. (Originally written in the 1560s.)

Durán, Diego (1971) *The Book of the Gods and Rites and the Ancient Calendar* (translated by F. Horcasitas and D. Heyden). Norman: University of Oklahoma Press.

Ekholm, Gordon F. (1944) Excavations at Tampico and Panuco in the Huasteca, Mexico. *Anthropological Papers* 38(5). New York: American Museum of Natural History.

Eliade, Mircea (1975) *Rites and Symbols of Initiation: The Mysteries of Birth and Rebirth* (translated by W.R. Trask). New York: Harper and Row.

García Valencia, Enrique Hugo (1975) *Textiles: Vocabulario sobre materias primas, instrumentos de trabajo, y técnicas de manufactura*. Cuadernos de Trabajo, No.3, Museo Nacional de Antropología, Seccion de Etnografía. México, DF: INAH.

Gonzales de Lima, Oswaldo (1956) *El maguey y el pulque en los Códices mexicanos*. México, DF: Fondo de Cultura Económica.

Granberg, Wilbur J. (1970) *People of the Maguey: The Otomi Indians of Mexico*. New York: Praeger Publishers.

Hall, Barbara (1989) Spindle Whorls and Textile Exchange at Matacapan, Veracruz. Paper presented at the Annual Meeting of the American Anthropological Association, Washington, DC.

Hellbom, Anna-Britta, (1967) La participación cultural de las mujeres: Indias y mestizas en el México precortesiano y postrevolucionario. Monograph Series, Publication No. 10. Stockholm: The Ethnographical Museum.

Heyden, Doris (1985) *Mitología y simbolismo de la flora en el México pre-hispanico*. Mexico, DF: Universidad Nacional Autónoma de México.

Historia Tolteca-Chichimeca (1976) *Historia Tolteca-Chichimeca* (edited and translated by P. Kirchhoff, L. Odena G., and L. Reyes G.). México, DF: Instituto Nacional de Antropología e Historia.

Hochberg, Bette (1980) *Handspindles*. Santa Cruz: B. and B. Hochberg.

Hodder, Ian (1982) *Symbols in Action*. Cambridge: Cambridge University Press.

—— (1986) *Reading the Past*. Cambridge: Cambridge University Press.

Kann, Veronica (1989) Late Classic Politics, Cloth Production, and Women's Labor: An Interpretation of Female Figurines from Matacapan, Veracruz. Paper presented at the Annual Meeting of the Society for American Anthropology, Atlanta, GA.

Kellogg, Susan (1988) Cognatic Kinship and Religion: Women in Aztec Society. In *Smoke and Mist: Mesoamerican Studies in Memory of Thelma D. Sullivan*, edited by J. K. Josserand and K. Dakin, pp. 666–681. Oxford: BAR International Series 402.

Klein, Cecilia (1972) The Face of the Earth: Frontality in Two-Dimensional Mesoamerican Art. New York: Garland Series, Outstanding Dissertations in the Fine Arts.

—— (1982) Woven Heaven, Tangled Earth: A Weaver's Paradigm of the Mesoamerican Cosmos. In *Ethnoastronomy and Archaeoastronomy in the American Tropics*, edited by A. F. Aveni and G. Urton, pp. 1–35. New York: Annals of the New York Academy of Sciences, vol. 385.

Leacock, Eleanor, and June Nash (1977) Ideology of Sex: Archetypes and Stereotypes. New York: *Annals of the New York Academy of Sciences*, vol. 285.

McCafferty, Geoffrey G. (1992) The Material Culture of Postclassic Chohula, Mexico: Contextual Analysis of the UA-1 Domestic Compounds. PhD Dissertion, SUNY, Binghamton.

—— (1986) The Material Culture of Early Post-Classic Cholula and the "Mixteca-Puebla" Problem. Paper presented at the Annual Meeting of the Society for American Archaeology, New Orleans, LA.

—— (1989a) Ethnic Boundaries and Ethnic Identity: Case Studies from Post-Classic Mexico. Unpublished MA thesis, Dept. of Anthropology, SUNY Binghamton, Binghamton, NY.

—— (1989b) Ethnic Identity in the Material Culture of Post-Classic Cholula. Paper presented at the Annual Meeting of the Society for Historical Archaeology, Baltimore, MD.

McCafferty, Geoffrey G., and Sharisse D. McCafferty (1989a) Xochiquezal: Images of the Goddess in Aztec Society. In *Collected Papers from the Conference "The Goddess as Muse to Women Artists,"* edited by Mary Kelley, SUNY Cortland.

—— (1989b) Weapons of Resistance: Material Metaphors of Gender Identity in Post-Classic Mexico. Paper presented at the Annual Meeting of the American Anthropological Association, Washington, DC.

McCafferty, Sharisse D., and Geoffrey G. McCafferty (1988) Powerful Women and the Myth of Male Dominance in Aztec Society. *Archaeological Review from Cambridge* 7:45–59.

Motolinia, Toribio de (1951) *History of the Indians of New Spain* (translated and annotated by F. B. Steck). Washington, DC: Academy of American Franciscan History. (Originally written ca. 1536–1543.)

Nash, June (1978) The Aztecs and the Myth of Male Dominance. *Signs: Journal of Women in Culture and Society* 4(2):349–362.

—— (1980) Aztec Women: The Transition from Status to Class in Empire and Colony. In *Women and Colonization: Anthropological Perspectives*, edited by M. Etienne and E. Leacock, pp. 134–148. New York: Praeger Publishers.

Nicholson, Henry B. (1971) Religion in Pre-Hispanic Central Mexico. In *Handbook of Middle American Indians, Vol. 10: Archaeology of Northern Mesoamerica*, Part 1, edited by R. Wauchope, G. F. Ekholm, and I. Bernal, pp. 395–446. Austin: University of Texas Press.

Olivera, Mercedes, and Cayetano Reyes (1969) Los Choloques y los Cholultecas: Apuntes sobre las relaciones etnicas en Cholula hasta el siglo XVI. *Anales del INAH*, Epoca 7a, Tomo I, 1967–68, México, DF.

Parsons, Mary H. (1972) Spindle Whorls from the Teotihuacan Valley, Mexico. In *Miscellaneous Studies in Mexican Prehistory*, edited by M. W. Spence, J. R. Parsons, and M. H. Parsons, pp. 45–80. *Anthropological Papers*, No. 45. Ann Arbor: Museum of Anthropology, University of Michigan.

Peñafiel, Antonio (1985) *Indumentaria antigua: Armas, vestidos guerreros y civiles de los antiguos Mexicanos*. México, DF. Editorial Innovación.

Rodriguez Vallejo, Jose (1976) *Ixcatl: El algodon mexicano*. México, DF: Fondo de Cultura Económica.

Sahagún, Bernadino de (1950–1982) *Florentine Codex: General History of the Things of New Spain*. Trans. C. E. Dibble and A. J. D. Anderson. Salt Lake City and Santa Fe: University of Utah Press and School of American Research. (Originally written by 1569.)

Schaefer, Stacy B. (1989) The Loom as a Sacred Power Object in Huichol Culture. Paper presented at the Annual Meeting of the American Anthropological Association, Washington, DC.

Silverblatt, Irene (1978) Andean Women in the Inca Empire. *Feminist Studies* 4:36–61.

—— (1987) *Sun, Moon, and Witches: Gender Ideologies and Class in Inca and Colonial Peru*. Princeton: Princeton University Press.

Smith, Michael E., and Kenneth G. Hirth (1988) The Development of Pre-Hispanic Cotton-spinning Technology in Western Morelos, Mexico. *Journal of Field Archaeology* 15:349–358.

Starr, Frederick (1908) *In Indian Mexico*. Chicago: Forbes and Company.

Sullivan, Thelma (1982) Tlazolteotl-Ixcuina: The Great Spinner and Weaver. In *The Art and Iconography of Late Post-Classic Central Mexico*, edited by E. H. Boone, pp. 7–36. Washington, DC: Dumbarton Oaks.

Taggart, James (1983) *Nahuat Myth and Social Structure*. Austin: University of Texas Press.

Wilbert, Johannes (1974) *The Thread of Life: Symbolism of Miniature Art from Ecuador*. Studies in Pre-Columbian Art and Archaeology 12. Washington, DC. Dumbarton Oaks.

Wobst, Martin (1977) Stylistic Behavior and Information Exchange. In *Papers for the Director: Research Essays in Honor of James B. Griffin*, edited by C. E. Cleland. pp. 317–342. Anthropological Papers, No. 61. Ann Arbor: Museum of Anthropology, University of Michigan.

Zorita, Alonso de (1963) *Life and Labor in Ancient Mexico* Trans. B. Keel. New Brunswick: Rutgers University Press. (Originally written in 1570s or 1580s.)

Chapter 13

Gibbs

IDENTIFYING GENDER REPRESENTATION
IN THE ARCHAEOLOGICAL RECORD:
A Contextual Study

Liv Gibbs

Archaeological views about the role of women in past
societies are necessarily affected by archaeologists' assumptions about the role of women in their own society. Gibbs
argues that gender relations cannot be determined solely
by the biological distinctions between men and women.
Rather, they are culturally constructed in a variety of ways.
Instead of imposing uncritically our own gender perceptions
on the past, Gibbs attempts to identify changing gender
relations in the prehistory (Mesolithic to Bronze Age) of
Zealand, Denmark by considering contextually varied sets of
data. In comparing the representation of women in hoards,
burials, settlements, art and figurines, Gibbs notes that in
different types of data of different time periods females may
be highly visible or invisible. Also, a symbolic association
between males, agriculture, woodwork and warfare decreased
through time, but an association between females and agriculture increased. These varied trends are interpreted in
terms of the changing representation and misrepresentation
of female roles as women negotiate their positions in a
changing society.

Introduction

There is virtually no systematic work on the archaeological
study of gender . . . [nor] archaeological work in which an
author explicitly claims that we can *know* about gender in the

past as observed through the archaeological record, who then proceeds to demonstrate that knowledge, or to describe *how* we can know.

(Conkey and Spector 1984, p. 2)

This article is a response to the situation noted above.[1] It will attempt to outline the importance of the archaeological study of gender, arguing that inferences about gender roles and relations *can* be made on the basis of material culture patterning and demonstrating this through a case study of N.E. Zealand, Denmark (Gibbs 1985).

"Gender" is a complex, major topic of research in the social sciences (cf. MacCormack 1980) and for this reason a simple definition is difficult to achieve. However, as a starting point the difference between "gender" and "sex" should be noted. "Sex" is a physiological distinction (woman/man), whereas "gender" (female/male)[2] is purely a social and cultural construct, comprising the roles given to, and identities perceived by, men and women in a particular society.

It has been increasingly realized that gender roles and relations are crucial in determining social structures and practices (Edholm *et al.* 1977, p. 126; La Fontaine 1978), yet to date, archaeological studies have failed to recognize the importance of gender in structuring past social relations and material culture, concentrating instead principally on aspects of stratification and power (e.g. Levy 1979; Kristiansen 1984; Tilley 1984). Furthermore, ethnographic studies have shown that in many societies, gender differences are the cause of considerable tension and negotiation for power which often affect, and are represented in, material culture patterning (e.g. Braithwaite 1982; Hodder 1982c). This suggests that, by its very nature, the archaeological record has great potential for identifying past, intangible social relations across time through an examination of their material residues.

A second reason for examining gender in its own right in the archaeological record is that it increases our awareness of the fact that all interpretation is socially conditioned at a very basic level, thus pointing to the need to be conscious of, and try to overcome, the inherent assumptions and biases which have been common in the archaeological literature for over a century: for example, in the late nineteenth century Lubbock and Morgan (cf. O'Kelly 1980, pp. 5–6) argued for a progressive change from matrilineal to patrilineal (and therefore patriarchal) society, and the traditional "Man the Hunter" model (Washburn and Lancaster 1968) is still often accepted unquestioningly. Likewise, the practice of defining women by their reproductive capacity and men by their social roles (e.g. Faris 1983) and the continued acceptance of the idea of the domestic/public split (Rosaldo 1974) illustrate the androcentric, ethnocentric view of gender roles, which is still perpetuated in many archaeological studies (e.g. Bouzek *et al.*, 1966, p. 111). The aim here is not to adopt a radically feminist stance, but to argue firstly that archaeologists should consider the great variety of possible roles which might have been played by women as well as men in the past (as suggested by ethnographic studies), and secondly that they should look at the actual archaeological record for evidence of gender roles and relations in each particular society, rather than assuming a natural, universal division of labour in time and space.

Ethnographic work is used here as an heuristic device, that is, to generate ideas and possibilities (cf. Hawkes 1954, p. 162; Ucko 1969, p. 162): as such, it suggests that gender roles and relations may be represented in material form in the settlement and burial contexts (e.g. Hodder 1982c and 1984); archaeological data from the particular area studied here (Denmark) point to hoards, figurines and rock carvings as further contexts of gender representation. It should be emphasized that the implication is *not* that material culture is necessarily a direct reflection of gender roles: it is actively constructed and as such can be used in gender relations and their representation. It is argued that convincing hypotheses about the social implications of gender representation can be made by drawing on a number of contexts in which gender associations are recognized (e.g. burials, hoards, rock carvings) and then using them to construct a form of "relational analogy" (Hodder 1982b, pp. 16–24) in which a sufficient number of *interrelated* associations (in terms of gender) is recognized to justify an assertion. In this way the relationships between the contexts can be made clear.

The data

The small size of the study area for burials and hoards (N.E. Zealand), inevitably adds to the problems created both by the paucity of excavated and published settlement evidence (particularly from Zealand: cf. Coles 1982, p. 267; Jensen 1982, p. 151), and by the small number of figurines and rock carvings known from this area. Consequently, for these three classes of data, evidence from the whole of Denmark has been considered in order to ensure a more representative sample as the basis for inference. The results of the burial and hoard analyses for N.E. Zealand (Gibbs 1985) supported the trends postulated in more general studies of the whole of Denmark (e.g. Broholm 1943–9; Kristiansen 1984; Levy 1982), so the inferences made on the basis of N.E. Zealand's data appear not to be invalidated by the size of the sample.

Specific problems encountered in the analyses included firstly the inability to examine the distribution and internal arrangements of male and female burials and hoards on the basis of present published evidence. Secondly, very few burials of women with grave goods are known from the Neolithic period, Period 1 of the Bronze Age and the Later Bronze Age. In the Neolithic period, although a reasonable number of skeletons from the tombs have been sexed, the muddled nature of the multiple inhumations and the lack of firm associations between these definitely sexed burials and particular grave goods have created difficulties in identifying those items which are recurrently female associated. For Period 1 of the Bronze Age no female burials, sexed or inferred, are known at present from Denmark (Randsborg 1974, p. 46). For the Later Bronze Age, when cremations are predominant, sexing of these burials is only in its early stages (Pia Bennicke, personal communication) and no results are available yet. Since all such cremations seem to have been accompanied either by diagnostically male-associated items or by items found with both men and women in the Earlier Bronze Age, and furthermore no diagnostically female-associated items (ornaments) appear with these cremations, the picture created is one in which female burials are apparently "invisible" or undetected. At the very least, the way of representing females appears to have altered considerably by the Later Bronze Age. The result of such problems in recognizing female burials is that inferences concerning sex ratios are precluded, although it should be remembered that the burials in megalithic tombs and under barrows are not necessarily a direct reflection of the composition of Danish society (contra Broholm 1944, pp. 257f.).

This study has followed the common practice (e.g. Levy 1982; Randsborg 1974) of categorizing items according to their presumed rather than known functions (Tables 1 and 2) as a useful, although obviously highly subjective, analytical device.

Inferring gender from burials and hoards: towards a methodology

The problems and assumptions involved in the interpretation of mortuary, and by extension, hoard data, are well rehearsed in the literature (e.g. Hodder 1982b, pp. 139–46; Parker Pearson 1984, pp. 63–94). If, however, one wishes to make any inferences from such data, some "leaps of faith" are necessary. One major leap of faith made in this study concerns the way in which a gender is assigned to depositions. Very little anthropological sexing of Danish prehistoric burials has been carried out to date (cf. Albrethsen and Brinch Petersen 1976; Hansen et al. 1973; Bröste et al. 1956; Broholm 1947), yet this is the only way of establishing a firm link between sex (woman/man) and material culture, from which gender associations (female/male) in unsexed burials can then be extrapolated. Traditionally, however, artefacts in burials or on settlements have usually been classified as male- or female-associated solely on the basis of the interpreter's own ethnocentric and androcentric preconceptions about past gender roles (e.g. Clarke 1972).

This study began by recording the items associated with anthropologically sexed skeletons in burials, revealing that there were mutually exclusive associations of artefacts with men and women (Table 1). A few items were common to both sexes. On the basis of the similarities between the artefacts in anthropologically sexed burials and the items in unsexed burials, the latter were classified as female or male (i.e. the *gender* represented in a burial by the grave goods; cf. Table 1). This method of assigning a gender to burials was applied to both inhumations and cremations, although at present all inferences about gender for cremations have to rely on the associations of artefacts with sexed inhumations (see above), and are thus very tentative.

The "hoards" of Denmark ("accumulations of . . . [items] buried together in apparent isolation": Bradley 1982, p. 110) have traditionally been classified as "ritual" or "non-ritual" (e.g. Levy 1982) on the basis of their contents and location. The "non-ritual" or secular hoards, which comprised predominantly scrap material, mint or incomplete items, have been variously interpreted (e.g. as founders' or merchants' hoards; cf. Bradley 1982): it is argued here that is is inappropriate to attach a particular gender to such depositions, since their contents do not appear to have been selected on the basis of their gender association. In contrast, the so-called ritual hoards are characterized by their apparently strong gender associations. The items in inhumations and hoards were very similar throughout the timespan considered here, and mutually exclusive collections of apparently female- or male-associated items seem to have been buried together in hoards in the same way as they were deposited in burials. It can therefore be argued that it is appropriate to ascribe a gender (female/male) to such hoards on the basis of their contents (Table 2).

In the following sections, each of the different types of data will be considered in terms of gender representation and the trends, their interrelationships and possible implications will be explored.

Gender representation in N.E. Zealand's burials and hoards

Throughout the timespan under consideration here (Late Mesolithic to the end of the Bronze Age), female burials numbered fewer than male burials. From the Late Mesolithic to Period 3 of the Bronze Age the number of male and female inhumations increased, but then decreased dramatically in the Later Bronze Age. The first cremations appeared in Period 2: male cremations then increased considerably, but by the Later Bronze Age female cremations were no longer identifiable in the archaeological record on the basis of the artefacts buried with them.

The sources used in this study mentioned no ritual hoards for the Late Mesolithic or for Period 3 of the Bronze Age in this area. The number of male-associated hoards (for the sake of brevity only, male hoards) decreased from the *Trichterbecherkultur* (TRB) period to Period 4, and then disappeared from "visibility" in the archaeological record. Female hoards did not appear until Period 2 of the Bronze Age, from which time they increased in number. Thus from Period 2 to Period 4, in which both female and male hoards existed, the ratio of male to female hoards changed from 2.5:1 to 1:2.

From the above it seems that as the number of male burials increased, the number of male hoards decreased. Conversely, as the number of female burials decreased or became "invisible", the number of female hoards increased.

Diversity of artefact-types among objects

To calculate the diversity of artefact-types (Kintigh 1984), for each burial (or hoard) the number of objects was plotted against the number of artefact-types. Best-fit lines were worked out using the formula for linear regression (Texas Instruments 1979, V, 37), the diversity being the gradient of those lines.

Table 1 The categorization of artefacts from burials in NE Zealand

Period	Weapons		Tools		Jewellery	
	Male	*Female*	*Male*	*Female*	*Male*	*Female*
Late Meso.	bone dagger*		flint knife* flint flake* flint axe* antler axe* stone axe* bone spatula* & awl	flint knife*	ochre* tooth bead* antlers*	ochre* tooth bead* antlers*
TRB	bone arrowhead* flint arrowhead		flint flake* flint axe* flint chisel* flint sickle* stone axe* clay pot*		amber bead* bone bead* bone ornament*	
Late Neol.	flint arrowhead* flint dagger* flint spearhead*		flint flake* flint knife* flint axe* & saw* flint chisel* flint sickle* flint scraper* flint firestone* stone axe* clay pot*	bone bodkin*	amber bead* bronze arm-ring* br. spiral finger-ring*	bone bead* tooth bead* slate pendant*
Earlier Bronze Age	bronze sword* bronze dagger* bronze spearhead	br. dagger*	bronze knife* bronze palstave* bronze tweezers*	bronze awl* bronze knife* clay pot*	bronze buckle* br. fibula* & pin* br. belt-clasp*	bronze buckle* bronze fibula* & pin br. arm-ring* & -band

Table 1 continued

Period	Weapons		Tools		Jewellery	
	Male	Female	Male	Female	Male	Female
Earlier Bronze Age	flint dagger		bronze razor*	bark bowl*	bronze arm-ring	bronze neck-collar*
	flint arrowhead		br. axe & awl	horn comb*	bronze arm-band	bronze neck-ring*
	bone flanged axe		br. fish-hook		br. spiral f.-ring	bronze belt-plate*
			bronze sickle		bronze ring	br. spiral f.-ring*
			bronze chisel		bronze disc	bronze ear-ring*
			flint firestone*		br. 2-axe ornamt.	bronze ankle-ring
			flint flake		br. double-button*	br. double-button
			flint sickle		horn double-button*	br. spiral arm-ring
			flint scraper		gold arm-ring*	br. hanging vessel
			clay pot*		gold sp. finger-ring	gold ear-ring*
			bark box*		gold ring & disc	gold spiral f.-ring
			horn comb*		amber bead*	gold ring
					blue glass bead	gold spiral arm-ring
						amber bead*
						blue glass bead*
Later Bronze Age	bronze sword		bronze knife		bronze arm-ring	
	bronze dagger		bronze sickle		br. spiral f.-ring	
	bronze spearhead		br. awl & saw		br. ring & button	
	bronze arrowhead		bronze needle		br. double-button	
			bronze tweezers		br. fibula & pin	
			bronze razor		bronze buckle	
					mini. br. sword	
					amber bead	

* = items found in Danish sexed burials

Table 2 The categorization of artefacts from hoards in NE Zealand

Period	Weapons		Tools		Jewellery	
	Male	*Female*	*Male*	*Female*	*Male*	*Female*
TRB	flint dagger		flint flake			
			flint chisel			
			flint sickle			
			flint axe			
			stone shaft-hole axe			
			greestone axe			
			slate axe			
			bone chisel			
			clay pot			
Late Neol.	flint dagger		flint sickle			
	flint spearhead		flint scraper			
			stone shaft-hole axe			
Period 1	bronze spearhead		bronze flanged axe			
Period 2	bronze sword		bronze palstave	bronze sickle	bronze ankle-ring	bronze neck-collar
	bronze spearhead		bronze celt	bronze knife		bronze belt-plate
						bronze tutulus
						bronze spiral arm-ring
Period 3						
Period 4					(bronze helmet)	bronze neck-ring
						bronze belt-plate
						bronze spiral arm-ring
						bronze arm-band
						br. hanging vessel

Table 2 continued

Period	Weapons		Tools		Jewellery	
	Male	Female	Male	Female	Male	Female
Period 5				bronze sickle		bronze neck-ring
						bronze belt-plate
						bronze spiral arm-ring
						bronze arm-ring
						bronze ring
						bronze fibula
						bronze pin
						br. hanging vessel
						belt ornament
						belt
Period 6				bronze celt		bronze neck-ring
						bronze arm-ring
						bronze arm-band
						bronze pin
						br. spiral finger-ring

The diversity of artefact-types in male burials (male artefact diversity) increased more than three-fold from the TRB to the Late Neolithic, but then remained stable (Fig. 1). Female artefact diversity in burials, however, increased steadily through time, roughly doubling with each new period. Male artefact diversity was always greater than female artefact diversity: one possible explanation for this is that, whilst both women and men were buried with jewellery, men always had tools and weapons as well. To assess the validity of this idea, the diversities of jewellery-types for female and male burials were calculated for the periods when both occurred: if these diversities proved to be very similar, it would indicate that the data fit the hypothesis, although they may have fitted others too. The results (Table 3) showed that in Periods 2 and 3 the jewellery diversities were indeed fairly similar; in the Late Mesolithic the diversities were not very similar, although they could be influenced by the small sample size for this period.

In the hoards, male artefact diversity was likewise always greater than female artefact diversity (Fig. 2), but there were insufficient data to enable the application of the "jewellery diversity test". Although the sample size was limited, it seems that male artefact diversity increased until Period 2, but in Period 4 there was only one hoard. In contrast, female artefact diversity decreased from Period 2 to 5, but increased slightly in Period 6.

From the above it appears, therefore, that male artefact diversity in burials and hoards was always greater than female artefact diversity in similar contexts. In addition, the diversity in hoards was consistently lower than that in burials.

Most frequent artefact category and specific artefact type

The types of artefact found in female burials and hoards were very similar throughout the timespan, and consisted pre-dominantly of forms of jewellery (cf. Tables 1 and 2); for example, in Period 2 in both contexts the most frequently occurring female associated artefact-types were the bronze belt-plate and bronze neck collar; in Later Bronze Age female hoards these were replaced by the

Table 3 The degree of similarity between jewellery diversities in male and female burials (NE Zealand)

Period	% Difference in diversity
Late Meso.	88
TRB	—
Late Neol.	—
Period 1	—
Period 2	18
Period 3	23
Later Bronze Age	—

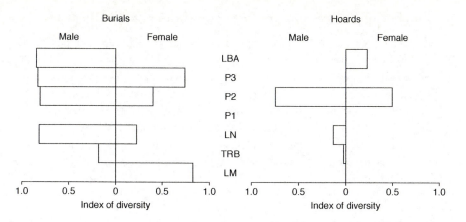

Figure 1 The diversity of artefact-types in burials from NE Zealand

Figure 2 The diversity of artefact-types in hoards from NE Zealand

bronze neck-ring (cf. Montelius 1885, plates 2–6). Tools occurred very rarely in female depositions, namely in only one burial and hoard per period. Bronze knives, however, were found in 31% of female burials in Period 3, and in both of the Period 2 female hoards. Weapons did not occur in female hoards in this area, but were found in 15% of Period 2 and 8% of Period 3 female burials in the form of a bronze dagger (e.g. in the Period 2 Ølby burial; Aner and Kersten 1973, no. 299).

Throughout the timespan, male burials consistently contained tools, weapons and jewellery, whereas male hoards only had tools and weapons (Tables 1 and 2). In both contexts, from the Neolithic to the end of the Earlier Bronze Age the most frequently occurring male-associated artefact-type was either a tool or a weapon: in Period 2 the bronze sword was prevalent, occurring in 64% of male burials and 60% of male hoards. In Period 3 this figure rose to 72% for male burials, but no male hoards from NE Zealand have been published which date to this period.

As mentioned above, by the Later Bronze Age it seems that only male-associated items or those found with both men and women were buried with cremations, and no cremations of this period have been recovered containing female-associated ornaments resembling those deposited in Earlier and Later Bronze Age hoards and Earlier Bronze Age burials. A change also seems to have occurred in the sort of items placed in burials (cremations) in the Later Bronze Age: many examples of miniature versions of grave goods from earlier periods now appeared. By far the most frequent types of artefact buried with cremations in this period, however, were dress-fittings (buttons and pins), knives and toilet equipment (tweezers and razors). The only possibly male hoard from NE Zealand is that from Vikso (Levy 1982, no. 96), which contained two Period 4 ornamented, beaten bronze helmets, similar to those worn by the supposedly male figurines in the Grevensvaenge hoard (see below).

The number of objects and artefact-types in burials and hoards

The number of objects and artefact-types in each burial and hoard per period was recorded in order to ascertain whether there were significant differences according to gender-association. The results indicated that the number of objects most regularly found in a burial was the same (one or two) for females and males until the end of the Earlier Bronze Age, but this number was always less than that in female and male hoards. Both male and female burials and male hoards produced a similar number of artefact-types per deposit. It is noticeable, however, that in female hoards the most frequent number of objects and artefact-types was consistently larger than in any other context.

Tools, agriculture and gender: the evidence

Although sickles (see below) and fish-hooks occurred in a few male depositions suggesting fishing and cultivation, the majority of tools in these contexts (Tables 1 and 2) were probably used for hide-work (e.g. scrapers, knives, awls and bodkins: cf. Coles 1979, p. 197; Morris 1984) and woodwork (e.g. palstaves, chisels, axes and flint flakes: cf. Coles 1979, p. 101; Coles and Orme 1985; Morris 1984). The other main set of tool-types found in male burials was toilet equipment (tweezers and razors) which, however, was noticeably absent, in conjunction with jewellery, from male hoards. On the basis of this difference in the types of artefact deposited in male burials on the one hand, and in male hoards on the other, it is possible that this distinction reflects the different forms of statement being made in the two contexts (see below). In terms of possible gender roles, however, both the burial and hoard consumption contexts point to the existence of a symbolic association between males, hide- and wood-work and agriculture in the Late Mesolithic, Neolithic and Earlier Bronze Age, but in the Later Bronze Age – when male hoards apparently ceased – in the burial context the emphasis was then mainly on items associated with personal appearance and hide-work.

Two forms of evidence link agriculture and gender. Firstly sickles, which in NE Zealand occurred in male burials and hoards, but in decreasing numbers through time. Sickles were not apparently found in female burials in this area, although the validity of this possible characteristic needs to be tested on burials from a wider area. Since the sickles in female hoards constituted one of the very few tool-types associated with females throughout the Bronze Age, and furthermore these tools had a known function (cf. Coles 1979, pp. 29–30; Steensberg 1943), the analysis of hoards with sickles was extended to the whole of Denmark to ascertain whether the gender associations still held. This supported the observation from NE Zealand that the number of male hoards with sickles decreased through time; furthermore, it showed that female hoards with sickles outnumbered their male counterparts in Period 2 and then continued to increase in number in the Later Bronze Age. Thus whilst the symbolic association between males, agriculture and wood-work decreased through time, the association between sickles found in hoards and females increased.

The second form of evidence linking agriculture to gender concerns ards; Glob (1951) has argued that in the Later Bronze Age unused, worn, wooden or simplified ards and ard-parts were carefully deposited in the same types of bog as were hoards. Furthermore, some of the ard-shares were accompanied by women's hair-plaits (Brøndsted 1939, pp. 276–7; Eskildsen and Lomborg 1976, p. 26). This therefore strengthens the symbolic association between females and agriculture in the Later Bronze Age.

Gender representation and the domestic context: an analysis of the Danish settlement evidence

The term "settlement" as used here refers to residential or habitation sites. Ethnographic work has pointed to two aspects of settlement evidence which are directly related to gender. Firstly, in many societies there is a close cultural identification of women/females (usually as mothers) with the "domestic sphere" and men/males with a "public sphere" (Harris 1981; Rosaldo 1974). Instead of assuming that this is a universal condition in time and space, the evidence should be examined for clues about gender roles in each particular cultural context.

An analysis of the burial and hoard data from NE Zealand suggested the existence of a strong symbolic association between males, the economy and fighting from the Late Mesolithic to the end of the Earlier Bronze Age, whereas such a link between females, the economy and fighting was very weak until female hoards with sickles and female burials with daggers appeared in the Earlier Bronze Age (see above). If these symbolic associations were related to gender roles in life, it might be argued – on the basis of the negative evidence for an association between females, the economy and fighting in the Late Mesolithic and Neolithic – that females were then related largely to the domestic sphere.

Such a suggestion is not very convincing without other evidence to support it; more positive evidence for an association between females and the domestic sphere occurred in the Bronze Age (when the links between females and the economy also increased), in the form of distinct similarities between designs found predominantly on female-associated artefacts in burials and motifs on the walls of some Later Bronze Age houses. This suggests that females may have been symbolized in, and were perhaps responsible for making the designs in the latter (and former?) context (see below). Furthermore, the existence of a Later Bronze Age figurine of a woman holding a bowl (Broholm 1947, p. 197) may indicate that females were involved in food preparation and/or pottery production and its decoration, although obviously not too much weight can be placed on theories based on one figurine alone. Nevertheless, it can be argued that there is some evidence that females were associated (at least symbolically) with the domestic context, its related activities and the economy too in the Bronze Age, whilst males were (at least symbolically) linked with the economy and fighting until the end of the Earlier Bronze Age. The implications of the changes in the types of artefact associated with cremations in the Later Bronze Age are more problematic.

The second feature illustrated by ethnographic work is the widespread link between the social position of females, gender tension and the symbolic elaboration of the domestic context and its associated artefacts (e.g. Braithwaite 1982; Hodder 1984a). An analysis of Danish domestic structures and their contents through time suggested that such an explanation may lie behind two distinct trends in the evidence, although it should be stressed that any trends postulated for the settlement (including domestic pottery) data are only tentative at present, given the paucity of excavated and published sites.

The first of these possible trends was that through time the domestic structures increased in size, complexity and elaboration. Although the evidence for Mesolithic structures is limited both at the permanent base camps and at the seasonally occupied special-purpose camps, traces of small, single-celled huts have been recovered, such as that at Maglemosegaard in NE Zealand (Albrethsen and Brinch Petersen 1976). Similarly, in the TRB period, structures identified with more certainty as dwellings also seem to have been small and single-celled, such as those at Lindebjerg (Liversage 1980) and Ørnekul (Becker 1952), both of which are in Zealand. Production areas in this period were set apart from the huts as was the case, for example, at Mosegaarden in Jutland (Madsen et al. 1982).

Very few Late Neolithic settlements have been excavated (Jensen 1982b), but that at Myrhøj in Jutland (Jensen 1972) suggests that some structures were larger (up to 20 metres long), of sub-rectangular shape and bi-cellular; moreover, weaving and tool production were now apparently taking place inside the structures. This trend towards greater complexity, elaboration and diversity of structure continued in the Earlier Bronze Age, for which period two types of dwelling have been identified: firstly, the turf-walled, small, single-celled C- or O-shaped type with one door and a hearth which occurs, for example, at Røjle Mose, on Fyn (Jaeger and Laursen 1983). The second type is the larger, more substantial, three-aisled, bi-cellular post-built longhouse with two doors. This type of structure has been recovered, for example, at Vadgaard in Jutland (Lomborg 1973). Whilst evidence of cooking has been recovered from the turf structures, in addition the longhouses have produced traces of weaving and the specialized production of flint tools in specific areas of the building. Such evidence has been recovered at Egehøj in Jutland (Boas 1983).

The data suggest that no major changes in the general structural form of longhouses occurred from the Earlier Bronze Age through to the Iron Age, but over the course of the first millenium BC an increasing number of longhouses seems to have had animal-stalling in their east ends. Traces of such stalling have been recovered at some Later Bronze Age sites such as Hovegaarde and Spjald in Jutland (Becker 1972).

A number of possible explanations may lie behind this increase in the size and internal complexity of domestic structures; for example, larger groups of people may have been living in them. However, the evidence suggests that the most likely explanation for this trend is that it was related to the increase in the number of activities performed inside the houses over the course of the Bronze Age. Furthermore, given the associations between females and the domestic context demonstrated above, and the evidence from the hoards that females may have been more actively involved in the agricultural element of the economy in the Bronze Age, the increase in the number of economic activities taking place within the domestic context may be further evidence of the greater female involvement in the economy.

The second possible trend in the settlement evidence, which may have been connected with gender tension and its representation, was the increase in decoration of the domestic context and of some domestic fine ware. Taking the artefactual aspect first, although examples of decorated antler and bone tools (S. H. Andersen 1980) and painted wooden paddles (Coles 1984, pp. 71–72) have been recovered from Mesolithic settlements and bogs, the settlement pottery and blubber lamps appear to have been sparsely decorated (Clark 1975, pp. 184–7). In the TRB period there was some decoration on settlement pottery (Ebbesen 1975); although limited, the published evidence for Late Neolithic and Earlier Bronze Age domestic pottery (Jensen 1972; Boas 1983) suggests that the quantity of decorated wares and the extent of the decoration itself were still only minimal or moderate. The small amount of pottery published so far from Later Bronze Age settlements suggests that some of the finer domestic pottery was then more highly decorated (e.g. at Jegstrup in Jutland: Davidsen 1982; at Voldtofte on Fyn: Berglund 1982 and Jensen 1967; and at Gevninge in Zealand: Jensen 1966). Furthermore, pieces of daub painted with specific designs suggest that the walls of some long-houses were also decorated (e.g. at Voldtofte on Fyn: Berglund 1982; and at Skamlebaek in Zealand: Lomborg 1979).

By the Later Bronze Age, therefore, the evidence points to an increased emphasis on the house as a domestic context and as a centre of economic activity, as is suggested by the house's interior elaboration, the decoration of some of its associated pottery and the occurrence of models in the form of house urns (Brøndsted 1939, pp. 249–50; Lomborg 1979).

Danish figurines and gender symbolism

Bronze anthropomorphic figurines have been included in this analysis on account both of their recognizably sexual characteristics and of their particular associations. Only one Earlier Bronze Age figurine is known, comprising a head of unknown sex on a razor from a Period 2 grave (Broholm 1947, p. 198, fig. 1). However, at least twelve figurines representing women, one representing a man and two others representing men or being "sexless" date to the Later Bronze Age. The figurine of a man from Viborg is crudely fashioned, nude and very weathered (cf. Brøndsted 1939, p. 238, fig. 225b). It is debatable whether two of the figurines from the Grevensvaenge hoard represent men or are sexless (cf. Glob 1974, p. 143, fig. 57 and p. 164, fig. 70); whatever the case, they are both wearing helmets similar to those found in the Period 4 hoard from Viksø, Zealand (cf. Levy 1982, no. 96 and plate 16).

Twelve figurines have been classified as being representations of women on the following grounds. Firstly, they have overt sexual characteristics (cf. the Viksø and Faardal examples; Broholm 1947), which are accentuated by the figurines' nudity or semi-nudity. It is possible, therefore, that women's sexuality was being emphasized, or perhaps this was merely the easiest way to make a figurine unmistakably that of a woman. Secondly, all the figurines are wearing jewellery in the form of neck- and ear-rings: these are among the items which identify women/females in burials and hoards. Finally, three of the figurines are clad in bronze versions of cord skirts similar to that of the Egtved woman (cf. Eskildsen and Lomborg 1976, p. 24), and one of the Grevensvaenge figures is wearing a long skirt like those of the Skrydstrup girl and the Borum Eshøj old woman (ibid., pp. 19 and 26).

Whilst three of the Later Bronze Age figurines representing women were integral parts of theoretically utilitarian items – a pin-head and two knife-handles, at least five were items of display found in hoards: for example, the deposition from Fangel Torp was classified as "non-ritual" by Levy (1982, no. 251), yet noticeably it contains a predominance of female-associated items and sickles. The Faardal "ritual" hoard (ibid., no. 290) also consists of female-associated artefacts in addition to the figurine of a woman.

Most considerations of these figurines have described them as "goddesses" and "gods" (e.g. Glob 1974, p. 165; Djupedal and Broholm 1952), the labels traditionally assigned to figurines of many shapes and materials from diverse areas and time periods (cf. Gimbutas 1982). However, as Ucko (1962, p. 47) has argued, the individual figurines themselves should be studied in detail with reference to their particular context. Following this policy, it seems that, among the Danish Later Bronze Age figurines there was considerable diversity in quality and shape; for example, the face on the Javngyde knife-handle is well modelled (cf. Brøndsted 1939, p. 224, fig. 211c), but the Faardal, Fangel Torp and Viksø figurines all have coarse, crude features. Furthermore, the latter three are stocky, whereas the Kaiserberg and Grevensvaenge figurines are thin (cf. Broholm 1947, pp. 198–9). Although there does not seem to be a simple equation between the shape, quality and attire of the figurines, it can be argued that in these Later Bronze Age figurines, "womanhood" (cf. Rice 1981) and those items which identified females, were being deliberately emphasized. This situation therefore contrasted strongly with the lack of recognizably female associations in the burial context of the same period.

The representation of gender in Danish rock carvings

The rock carvings of NE Zealand are typical of those from the whole of Denmark and date to the Bronze Age (cf. Glob 1969; Malmer 1981). It is not intended to provide a general summary of this evidence, but rather to point to aspects which pertain to gender representation.

Traditionally, the cup-mark – which constitutes the most frequently occurring design from the repertoire of engravings – has been interpreted as the symbol representing a woman when it appears between the legs of a human figure (cf. Glob 1969, p. 306). However, Malmer (1981, p. 76) has argued that although phallic figures are distinguishable as men, all other figures are to some extent ambiguous; for example, the short vertical line interpreted as representing a woman's sex organ on the Maltegaard engraved disc could also be regarded as a phallic symbol. Furthermore, although in rock carvings long hair has often been regarded as an indication that a figure represents a woman, some phallic figures have long hair (Malmer 1981, p. 76). For this reason, Malmer only refers to "phallic" and "non-phallic" figures. It seems, therefore, that whilst men are usually clearly identifiable and thus visible in the rock art, representations of women are either ambiguous or unidentifiable, and are thus essentially "invisible".

Whilst the relatively frequent occurrence of hands and feet in rock carvings suggests an emphasis on humans even though figures themselves are not very numerous (Malmer 1981, p. 104), and the meaning of some designs is far from clear (e.g. the circle with a cross inside it), other motifs are notable for their absence or paucity; for example, although weapons occur in male burials and hoards, they are not depicted in rock carvings. Furthermore, it is noticeable that there are apparently very few engravings in Denmark depicting agricultural scenes (Malmer 1981, p. 104), even though it was probably, on the whole, a rich area agriculturally (cf. Randsborg 1974). Finally, with regard to the location of the petroglyphs, according to Glob (1969) they are often associated with graves in a primary, or more usually a secondary, position.

To conclude, in terms of gender representation it can be regarded as significant that, whilst the symbolic association in hoards between females and agriculture was increasing over the course of the Bronze Age, agricultural representations in the rock carvings were apparently sparse, and depictions of women were either ambiguous or unidentifiable.

The social implications of gender representation in Danish prehistory: a theory

It was argued above that, through the identification of a series of interrelated trends or features in a number of contexts, it might be possible to recognize manifestations of gender tension in material culture patterning. Using ethnographic examples as heuristic devices, the evidence analysed in this study allowed such a venture.

Consciously selected items deposited in the ground can be regarded as intentional social statements. On this basis, in NE Zealand's burials and hoards a symbolic association between males, weapons, tools and agriculture seems to have been displayed overtly – particularly in burials – until the Later Bronze Age, when male-associated items in the latter consumption context changed to being related predominantly to aspects of personal appearance (dress fittings and toilet equipment), and male hoards apparently ceased. This suggests that in the Late Mesolithic,

Neolithic and Earlier Bronze Age a particular statement – perhaps establishing the importance of males in the economy and warfare and displaying their fine possessions (e.g. jewellery) – was being made publicly in burials. The male hoards, which contained only tools and weapons (no jewellery), can perhaps be interpreted as having been deposited by males who were reinforcing recognition of their importance in the roles connected with these artefacts. By the Later Bronze Age, however, a different message was being displayed in burials, in which economic and warfare elements were only minimally represented: perhaps this was related to changes in the division of labour by gender in life over the course of the Bronze Age.

This latter possibility is supported by the fact that these transformations in male consumption contexts coincided with the emergence of a visible symbolic relationship in hoards between females and agriculture. If this association was related to changes in life, it is possible either that the female role in agriculture was only now being represented materially for some reason, or that females were taking on an increasingly important or even new role in this aspect of the economy in the first millennium BC – a period which, it has been argued, saw the major cultivation of new areas (e.g. of sand) for the first time in conjunction with agricultural intensification (Coles and Harding 1979, p. 493; Kristiansen 1984, p. 92). In such a situation females, as economic producers, may have begun to try to negotiate for social position (Rosaldo 1974, p. 37), a potential source of gender tension.

It has been argued that "Women do not naturally disappear, their disappearance is socially created and constantly reaffirmed" (Edholm et al. 1977, p. 126). One explanation for female burials becoming "invisible" or ambiguous in the Later Bronze Age – in terms of the lack of identifiably female-associated items found with cremations – may be, therefore, that burying females without their diagnostic grave goods was one way of making a social statement which publicly emphasized males' control over females. Furthermore, the ambiguous nature or lack of depictions of women in rock art and the extreme paucity of agricultural representations – at a time when the female role in agriculture was possibly increasing – may have been part of the same process. It seems, therefore, that the social recognition of the increasing economic importance of females and their pre-existing roles may have been controlled in the workings of an essentially masculinist ideology through the concealment and misrepresentation of these roles in the burial context and rock carvings.

Ethnographic studies suggest that, in the face of such suppression, women (females) sometimes use various means to draw attention to their roles and thus carry on a silent discourse amongst themselves (Hodder 1982c, p. 69 and 1984, p. 62). This may explain some features of Later Bronze Age material culture patterning. Firstly, as mentioned above, ethnographically a link between the social position of women (females), gender tension and the symbolic elaboration of the domestic context and its associated artefacts has been recognized in a wide range of societies (e.g. Hodder 1984). It is possible, therefore, that the Later Bronze Age practice of decorating longhouse walls (cf. Berglund 1982) with painted motifs similar to those found predominantly on female-associated artefacts in Bronze Age burials and hoards was one way in which females were marking out their impor-tance in the domestic context as reproducers and producers. Given the similarity of motifs in the consumption and domestic contexts, it is possible that this deco-ration represented females symbolically (see above). Perhaps, therefore, it was the females who were decorating the domestic context with female symbols as a means of asserting their solidarity and value (cf. Rosaldo 1974, p. 38). Likewise, the more elaborate decoration on some domestic pottery in the Later Bronze Age may have been another form of silent discourse between females (cf. Hodder 1982c, pp. 68–9 and p. 146) and a means by which they drew attention to their role in food preparation and perhaps pottery production too; it is possible that decoration was also used to mark out particular types of vessels associated only with females or males (cf. Welbourn 1984).

A third possible manifestation of female protest and statement in the Later Bronze Age may lie in the unprecedented size of hoards of artefacts and certain other items deposited in bogs, all of which identified and symbolized females and their various roles: jewellery, figurines of women and the sickles, ard-shares and women's hair-plaits, which represented the female role in agriculture. Indeed, the latter two may be evidence that females were actively involved in ploughing as well as harvesting (cf. Boserup 1970, p. 38). This would contradict Goody's (1976) and Sherratt's (1981) equations of females with hoe and swidden agriculture, and males with plough and pastoralism. It would thus serve as a salutary reminder that each society constructs its own division of labour by gender.

Conclusion

Prehistoric social structure seen through a one-dimensional model in terms only of stratification and power should be superseded by models which also contain a second, more fundamental dimension of social organization and interactions, comprising relations between women and men. Gender differences, as various ethnographic studies have attested, are frequently the scene of tension and negoti-ation for social power which often affect, and are represented in, material culture patterning: they therefore deserve more attention from archaeologists than they have received to date.

In this study a number of different types of Danish prehistoric evidence (burials, hoards, figurines, settlement pottery, domestic structures and rock carvings) were analysed diachronically and the relationships between them in terms of gender representation were identified. It was noted that over the course of the Bronze Age a number of interrelated symbolic gender associations seem to have emerged (Table 4) such that by the Later Bronze Age there appears to have been a separa-tion of contexts in terms of gender and "visibility":

Visible/detected	female	= hoards
	male	= burials and rock art
Invisible/undetected	female	= burials and rock art
	male	= hoards

On this basis it was suggested that the predominance of female-associated items in hoards and in the bogs themselves, coupled with the elaboration of the domestic context and some of its associated pottery, were responses made by females to the concealment in the burial context and rock carvings of forms of representation which would show the importance of female roles in society. Gender representation or its absence, therefore, was an indication of, and a response to, gender tension.

This "contextual study" (cf. Hodder 1982a, p. 152) has shown that it *is* possible to identify and interpret gender representation in the archaeological record by establishing a firm association between sex and material culture in burials (and sometimes figurines) as a basis for inferring gender associations in other forms of evidence. The relationship between forms of gender representation in different contexts is established through the construction of a form of "relational analogy".

It is argued that the archaeological study of gender is valuable firstly because it takes into account the importance of gender relations in actively structuring not only social relations and practices, but also material culture patterning. This, in turn, points to the potential of the archaeological record for reconstructing past social relations from their material residues. Secondly, the archaeological study of gender increases awareness of the fact that all interpretations are socially and culturally conditioned at a very basic level, and thus highlights the need to recognize and avoid assumptions concerning past gender roles. In spite of the difficulties involved in the identification and interpretation of gender representation, the potential for studying prehistoric gender through its material manifestations is apparent. As yet, however, it is not fully realized.

Table 4   The symbolic associations of the Later Bronze Age

1 Female burials "invisible"/undetectable	1 Male cremations "visible"/detectable
2 Figures of women "invisible"/ambiguous in rock art	2 Phallic figures identifiable in rock art
3 Number of "female hoards" at its largest	3 No "male hoards"
4 Figurines of women with overt sexual characteristics	4 Very few figurines of men
5 Sickles in "female hoards"	5 Sickles buried with male cremations
6 Ard-shares and hair-plaits deposited together in bogs	
7 Decoration of the domestic context and some of its associated pottery	

■   ■   ■

Notes

1   The data for the Later Bronze Age burials and the Neolithic burials and hoards were kindly provided by K. Davidsen, Assistant Keeper of the National Museum of Denmark, Copenhagen. Mrs Bente Kuma helped with translation. I would like to thank the following for their advice and comments: Professor J. M. Coles, Nigel Holman, Mike Parker Pearson and Marie Louise Stig Sørensen. In particular I am grateful to Andy Brown, Sheena Crawford and Paul Lane for their help. Finally, I am indebted to Ian Hodder whose own work sparked off my interest in the archaeological study of gender – L. Gibbs.

2   Gibbs's use of these terms differs significantly from use by other authors in this volume. Elsewhere male/female refer to sex categories, and man/woman refer to gender identities – editors.

■ ■ ■

References

Abbreviations

Aarbøger = *Aarbøger for Nordisk Oldkyndighed og Historie*

Albrethsen, S. E. and Brinch Petersen, E. (1976) "Excavation of a Mesolithic cemetery at Vedbaek, Denmark", *Acta Archaeologica* 47: 1–28

Andersen, S. H. (1980) "Ertebøllekunst. Nye Østjyske fund af mønstrede Ertebølleoldsager", *Kuml*: 7–62 (With English Summary)

Aner, E. and Kersten, K. (1973) *Die Funde der Älteren Bronzezeit der Nordischen Kreises in Dänemark, Schleswig-Holstein und Niedersachsen. Band 1: Frederiksborg und Københavns Amt*, National-museum Københavan und Neumünster

Becker, C. J. (1952) "Ørnekul paa Nekselø. En Sjaellandsk Stenalderboplads med Hustomte", *Aarbøger*: 60–107 (With English Summary)

—— (1972) "Hal og hus i Yngre Bronzealder", *Nationalmuseets Arbejdsmark*: 5–16

Berglund, J. (1982) "Kirkebjerget: a Late Bronze Age settlement at Voldtofte, South-West Funen", *Journal of Danish Archaeology* 1: 51–63

Boas, N. A. (1983) "Egehøj, a settlement from the Early Bronze Age in East Jutland", *Journal of Danish Archaeology* 2: 90–101

Boserup, E. (1970) *Woman's Role in Economic Development*, Allen & Unwin, London

Bouzek, J. *et al.* (1966) *The Knovíz Settlement of North-West Bohemia*, Fontes Archaeologici Pragenses 10

Bradley, R. (1982) "The destruction of wealth in later prehistory", *Man* 17: 108–22

Braithwaite, M. (1982) "Decoration as ritual symbol: a theoretical proposal and an ethnographic study in Southern Sudan" in I. Hodder (ed.) *Symbolic and Structural Archaeology* (New Directions in Archaeology), Cambridge University Press, Cambridge

Broholm, H. C. (1943–9) *Danmarks Bronzealder*, Vols. 1 (1943), 2 (1944), 3 (1946), 4 (1949), Arnold Busck, Copenhagen

—— (1947) "Anthropomorphic Bronze Age figurines in Denmark", *Acta Archaeologica* 18: 196–202

Brøndsted, J. (1938–9) *Danmarks Oldtid* 1–2, Gyldendalske Boghandel Nordisk Forlag, Copenhagen

Bröste, K., Balslev Jørgensen, J., Becker, C. and Brøndsted, J. (1956) *Prehistoric Man in Denmark. A Study in Physical Anthropology*, Nordiske Fortidsminder 1–2, Copenhagen

Clark, G. (1975) *The Earlier Stone Age Settlement of Scandinavia*, Cambridge University Press, Cambridge

Clarke, D. L. (1972) "A provisional model of an Iron Age society and its settlement system" in D. Clarke (ed.) *Models in Archaeology*, Methuen, London

Coles, J. M. (1979) *Experimental Archaeology*, Academic Press, London

——— (1982) "The Bronze Age in Northwestern Europe: problems and advances", *Advances in World Archaeology* 1: 265–321, Academic Press, London

—— (1984) *The Archaeology of Wetlands*, Edinburgh University Press

Coles, J. M. and Harding, A. F. (1979) *The Bronze Age in Europe*, Methuen, London

Coles, J. M. and Orme, B. J. (1985) "Prehistoric woodworking from the Somerset levels: 3: roundwood" in J. M. Coles, B. J. Orme and S. E. Rouillard (eds) *Somerset Levels Papers* 11, Stephen Austin, Hertford

Conkey, M. W. and Spector, J. D. (1984) "Archaeology and the study of gender" in M. Schiffer (ed.) *Advances in Archaeological Method and Theory* 7: 1–38, Academic Press, London

Davidsen, K. (1982) "Bronze Age houses at Jegstrup, near Skive, Central Jutland", *Journal of Danish Archaeology* 1, 65–75

Djupedal, R. and Broholm, H. C. (1952) "Marcus Schnabel og Bronzealderfundet fra Grevensvaenge", *Aarbøger*: 5–59 (With English Summary)

Ebbesen, K. (1975) *Die Jüngere Trichterbecherkultur auf den Dänischen Inseln*, Arkaeologiske Studier Vol. 2, University of København

Edholm, F., Harris, O. and Young, K. (1977) "Conceptualising women", *Critique of Anthropology* 3: 101–30

Eskildsen, E. & Lomborg, E. (1976) "Giftetanker", *Skalk* 5: 18–26

Faris, J. C. (1983) "From form to content in the structural study of aesthetic systems", in D. Washburn (ed.) *Structure and Cognition in Art* (New Directions in Archaeology), Cambridge University Press, Cambridge

Gibbs, L. (1985) *"Identifying gender representation in the archaeological record: a contextual study of N.E. Zealand, Denmark"*, unpublished BA dissertation, Department of Archaeology, University of Cambridge

Gimbutas, M. (1982) *The Goddesses and Gods of Old Europe 6500–3500 BC*, Thames and Hudson, London, 2nd edition

Glob, P. V. (1951) *Ard og Plov i Nordens Oldtid*, Jysk Arkaeologisk Selskabs Skrifter Bind 1 (With English Summary), University of Aarhus

—— (1969) *Helleristninger i Danmark*, Jutland Archaeological Society Publications 7, København

—— (1974) *The Mound People*, Faber, London

Goody, J. (1976) *Production and Reproduction. A Comparative Study of the Domestic Domain*, Cambridge University Press, Cambridge

Hansen, U. L., Nielsen, O. V. and Alexandersen, V. (1973) "A Mesolithic grave from Melby in Zealand, Denmark, *Acta Archaeologica* 43: 239–49

Harris, O. (1981) "Households as natural units", in K. Young, C. Wolkowitz and R. McCullagh (eds) *Of Marriage and the Market*, CSE Books, London

Hawkes, C. (1954) "Archaeological theory and method; some suggestions from the Old World", *American Anthropologist* 56, 2(1): 155–68

Hodder, I. (1982a) "The identification and interpretation of ranking in prehistory: a contextual perspective" in C. Renfrew and S. Shennan (eds) *Ranking, Resource and Exchange* (New Directions in Archaeology), Cambridge University Press, Cambridge

—— (1982b) *The Present Past*, Batsford, London

—— (1982c) *Symbols in Action* (New Studies in Archaeology), Cambridge University Press, Cambridge

—— (1984) "Burials, houses, women and men in the European Neolithic" in D. Miller and C. Tilley (eds) *Ideology, Power and Prehistory* (New Directions in Archaeology), Cambridge University Press, Cambridge

Jaeger, A. and Laursen, J. (1983) "Lindebjerg and Røjle Mose: Two Early Bronze Age settlements on Fyn", *Journal of Danish Archaeology* 2: 102–17

Jensen, J. (1966) "Zwei Abfallgruben von Gevninge, Seeland, aus der jüngeren Bronzezeit", *Acta Archaeologica* 37: 187–203

—— (1967) "Voldtofte-fundet. Bopladsproblemer i yngre Bronzealder i Danmark", *Aarbøger:* 91–154 (with English Summary)

—— (1972) "Bopladsen Myrhøj: 3 hustomter med klokkebaegerkeramik", *Kuml:* 61–122 (With English Summary)

—— (1982) *The Prehistory of Denmark*, Methuen, London

Kintigh, K. W. (1984) "Measuring archaeological diversity by comparison with simulated assemblages", *American Antiquity* 49: 44–54

—— (1984) "Ideology and material culture: an archaeological perspective" in M. Spriggs (ed.) *Marxist Perspectives in Archaeology* (New Directions in Archaeology), Cambridge University Press, Cambridge

La Fontaine, J. S. (1978) *Sex and Age as Principles of Social Differentiation*, ASA Monograph 17, Academic Press, London

Levy, J. E. (1979) "Evidence of social stratification in Bronze Age Denmark", *Journal of Field Archaeology* 6: 49–56

—— (1982) *Social and Religious Organization in Bronze Age Denmark*, BAR International Series 124, Oxford

Liversage, D. (1980) "Neolithic monuments at Lindebjerg, Northwest Zealand", *Acta Archaeologica* 51: 85–152

Lomborg, E. (1973) "En landsby med huse og kulsted fra aeldre bronzealder", *Nationalmuseets Arbejdsmark*: 5–14

—— (1979) "Urnehuset", *Skalk* 3: 4–9

MacCormack, C. P. (1980) "Nature, culture and gender: a critique" in C. P. MacCormack and M. Strathern (eds.) *Nature, Culture and Gender*, Cambridge University Press, Cambridge

Madsen, T. and Jensen, H. J. (1982) "Settlement and land use in Early Neolithic Denmark", *Analecta Praehistorica Leidensia* 15: 63–86

Malmer, M. P. (1981) *A Chronological Study of North European Rock Art*, Kungl. Vitterhets Historie och Antikvitets Akadamien, Antikvariska Serien 42

Montelius, O. (1885) *Om tidsbestaemning inom Bronsaaldern med saerskildt afseende paa Skandinavien*. Kongl. Vitterhets Historie och Antiqvitets Akedemiens Handlingar 30, ny följd, 10: 1–328 (With French Summary)

Morris, G. (1984) "Microwear and organic residue studies on Sweet Track flints" in J. M. Coles, B. J. Orme and S. E. Rouillard (ed.) *Somerset Levels Papers* 10, Stephen Austin, Hertford

O'Kelly, C. G. (1980) *Women and Men in Society*, D. Van Nostrand Company, New York

Parker Pearson, M. (1984) "Social change, ideology and the archaeological record" in M. Spriggs (ed.) *Marxist Perspectives in Archaeology* (New Directions in Archaeology), Cambridge University Press, Cambridge

Randsborg, K. (1974) "Social stratification in Early Bronze Age Denmark: a study in the regulation of cultural systems", *Prähistorische Zeitschrift* 49: 38–51

Rice, P. C. (1981) "Prehistoric venuses: symbols of motherhood or womanhood", *Journal of Anthropological Research* 37: 402–14

Rosaldo, M. (1974) "Woman, culture and society: a theoretical overview" in M. Rosaldo and L. Lamphere (eds.) *Woman, Culture and Society*, Stanford University Press, Stanford

Sherratt, A. (1981) "Plough and pastoralism: aspects of the secondary products revolution", in I. Hodder, G. Isaac and N. Hammond (eds.) *Pattern of the Past*, Cambridge University Press, Cambridge

Steensberg, A. (1943) *Ancient Harvesting Implements*, The Commission House, København

Texas Instruments. (1979) *Personal Programming*, Bedford

Tilley, C. (1984) "Ideology and the legitimation of power in the Middle Neolithic of Southern Sweden" in D. Miller and C. Tilley (eds) *Ideology, Power and Prehistory* (New Directions in Archaeology), Cambridge University Press, Cambridge.

Ucko, P. J. (1962) "The interpretation of prehistoric anthropomorphic figurines", *Journal of the Royal Anthropological Institute* 92: 38–54

Washburn, S. and Lancaster, C. S. (1968) "The evolution of hunting", in R. Lee and I. DeVore (eds.) *Man the Hunter*, Aldine, Chicago.

Welbourn, A. (1984) "Endo ceramics and power strategies" in D. Miller and C. Tilley (eds.) *Ideology, Power and Prehistory* (New Directions in Archaeology), Cambridge University Press, Cambridge

PART V

Gender iconography and ideology

INTRODUCTION

In the previous section, several authors explored how divisions of labor and space help define the *meanings* of male and female in spiritual and symbolic as well as economic terms. Papers in this section explore past gender identities and roles by focusing on ritual, religion, and ideology – the use of religious and other symbolism for political and social purposes. Ideology is particularly important in the study of gender. This is because ideological systems often provide the conceptual basis for the belief that a particular sexual division of labor and system of gender classification are the natural order of things. Data consist primarily of visual arts – images by, for, and about men and women. "With art, ideology takes material form," writes Barbara Bender (1989: 88). Art is part of ideological imprinting, "part of a process of institutional-ization, not only of what is to be said and thought, but how it is to be said and who is to say it – part, therefore, of an on-going process of negotiation and re-negotiation of social relations."

In "The Paleolithic Mother-Goddess: Fact or Fiction?" (in chapter 14), Pamela Russell takes on the popular conception of an ancient Mother Goddess based on finds of ice age figurines in Europe. As the earliest known depictions of human bodies, these figurines have attracted a great deal of scholarly attention for over a century. Russell places this attention in historical context, examining not only the artifacts, but also who has said what about them, from "prudish Victorian" men, to contemporary members of the women's spirituality movement.

Ann Cyphers Guillén, in "Women, Rituals, and Social Dynamics at Ancient Chalcatzingo", studies gender iconography in complex societies – chiefdoms and states – in Latin America. The diversity in meanings and functions of female figurines in Latin America, and changes in figurine complexes over time, call into question the simple attributions of "fertility" and "great goddess" to female figurines here and in other parts of the world. Hers is one of a series of studies of figurines and other images of women in Latin American prehistory. Rosemary Joyce

(1992), for example, argues that for the Maya elite, making male and female images was an important part of maintaining their power base. Gender identities were based on complementary economic and ideological roles for men and women. These identities were actively constructed by the consistent pairing of male and female images with particular costumes, tools, and symbols, in public monuments. Leaders claimed authority by appropriating the symbols, as well as the labor, of both halves of this male–female complementary pair. Anna Roosevelt (1988) surveyed figurines from many parts of Latin America, from Mexico to South America. She argues that female figurines are most abundant and elaborate in garbage, house remains, burials and caches (and not in temples or shrines) in sites that represent emerging chiefdoms or early states with economies undergoing a transition to intensive production of staple food crops. Women may have "gained in status due to their roles in reproduction and food production" at times of economic and demographic growth, especially in societies that pass property and rank through the female line. Likewise, Ian Hodder (1992: 254) contends that in Neolithic Europe, "As domestication intensifies and settled villages are formed, so the elaboration of domestic symbolism, the numbers of female figurines and the subdivision and decoration of houses also increases."

■ ■ ■

Further reading

Bevan, Lynne (1995)
Braithwaite, Mary (1982)
Hays-Gilpin, Kelley A. (1996)
—— (in press)
Hodder, Ian (1984)
—— (1992)
Hurcombe, Linda M. and Moira Donald (eds) (1997)
Joyce, Rosemary (1992)
—— (1993)
Kehoe, Alice B. (1991)
Koehler, Lyle (1997)
Lesure, Richard G. (1997)
Malone, Caroline, *et al.* (1993)
McCafferty, Sharisse D. and Geoffrey G. McCafferty (1994)
Nelson, Sarah M. (1990)
Roosevelt, Anna Curtenius (1988)
Whitley, David S. (1994)
—— (in press)

■ ■ ■

References

Bender, Barbara (1989) "The Roots of Inequality," In D. Miller, M. Rowlands and C. Tilley (eds) *Domination and Resistance*, London: Unwin Hyman.

Bevan, Lynne (1995) "Powerful Pudenda: The Penis in Prehistory," *Journal of Theoretical Archaeology* 3/4:41–58, Glasgow: Cruithne Press.

Braithwaite, Mary (1982) "Decoration as Ritual Symbol," in I. Hodder (ed.) *Symbolic and Structural Archaeology*, Cambridge: Cambridge University Press, pp. 80–88.

Hays-Gilpin, Kelley A. (1996) "Anasazi Iconography: Medium and Motif," in P.R. Fish and J. J. Reid (eds) *Interpreting Southwestern Diversity: Underlying Principles and Overarching Patterns*, Anthropological Research Papers 48, Tempe, Arizona: Arizona State University, pp. 55–67.

—— (in press) "Conception and Birth in Puebloan Rock Art, Landscape, and Architecture" in D. S. Whitley (ed.) *Rock Art and Ethnography*, Albuquerque: University of New Mexico Press,

Hodder, Ian (1984) "Burials, Houses, Women and Men in the European Neolithic," in D. Miller and C. Tilley (eds) *Ideology, Power and Prehistory*, Cambridge: Cambridge University Press, pp. 51–68.

—— (1992) "Gender Representation and Social Reality," *Theory and Practice in Archaeology*, Oxford: Blackwell, pp. 254–61.

Hurcombe, Linda M., and Moira Donald (ed) (1997) *Gender and Material Culture: Representations of Gender from Prehistory to the Present*, Basingstoke: Macmillan.

Joyce, Rosemary (1992) "Images of Gender and Labor Organization in Classic Maya Society," in C. Claassen (ed.) *Exploring Gender Through Archaeology: Selected Papers from the 1991 Boone Conference*, Madison, Wisconsin: Prehistory Press, pp. 63–70.

—— (1993) "Women's Work: Images of Production and Reproduction in Pre-Hispanic Southern Central America," *Current Anthropology* 34:255–274.

Kehoe, Alice B. (1991) "No Possible, Probable Shadow of Doubt," *Antiquity* 65:129–131.

Koehler, Lyle (1997) "Earth Mothers, Warriors, Horticulturalists, Artists, and Chiefs: Women Among the Mississippian and Mississippian-Oneota Peoples, AD 1211–1750," in C. Claassen and R. A. Joyce (eds) *Women in Prehistory: North America and Mesoamerica*, Philadelphia: University of Pennsylvania Press, pp. 211–226.

Lesure, Richard G. (1997) "Figurines and Social Identities in Early Sedentary Societies of Coastal Chiapas, Mexico, 1550–800 BC," in C. Claassen and R. A. Joyce (eds) *Women in Prehistory: North America and Mesoamerica*, Philadelphia: University of Pennsylvania Press, pp. 226–248.

Malone, Caroline, Anthony Bonanno, Tancred Gouder, Simon Stoddart, and David Trump (1993) "The Death Cults of Prehistoric Malta," *Scientific American* December: 110–117.

McCafferty, Sharisse D. and Geoffrey G. McCafferty (1994) "Engendering Tomb 7 at Monte Alban," *Current Anthropology* 35: 143–166.

Nelson, Sarah M. (1990) "Diversity of the Upper Paleolithic 'Venus' Figurines and Archeological Mythology", in S. M. Nelson and A. B. Kehoe (eds) *Powers of Observation: Alternative Views in Archeology*, Archeological Papers of the American Anthropological Association Number 2, pp. 11–22.

Roosevelt, Anna Curtenius (1988) "Interpreting Certain Female Images in Prehistoric Art," in V. Miller (ed.) *The Role of Gender in Precolumbian Art and Architecture*, Washington, DC: University Press of America, pp. 1–34.

Whitley, David S. (1994) "By the Hunter, For the Gatherer: Art, Social Relations, and Subsistence Change in the Prehistoric Great Basin," *World Archaeology* 25(3): 357–372.

—— (in press) "Finding Rain in the Desert: Landscape, Gender and Far Western North American Rock Art," in C. Chippendale and P. S. Tacon (eds) *The Archaeology of Rock Art*, Cambridge: Cambridge University Press.

Chapter 14

THE PALAEOLITHIC MOTHER-GODDESS:
Fact or Fiction?

Pamela Russell

Since 1864 some 200 carvings dating from the Palaeolithic era and identified as human representations (Rice 1981:402) have been found right across Europe (Abramova 1967:88). Throughout this century they have been a source of enormous interest, not only to prehistorians, but also to many others who see these little figurines as a vital clue to the beliefs and customs of the first Europeans of our own species. A popular idea has emerged that they were intended to represent a pan-European female deity, the great Mother-Goddess of the late ice age (for example, Ucko 1968:xv).

Some of the earlier finds were, indeed, unmistakable models of women, obese, naked, with voluminous breasts, prominent stomachs and large buttocks and thighs, the most well-known example being the so-called Venus of Willendorf. Found in Austria in 1908 (Delporte 1979:137), she is popularly seen as the archetype of the whole collection: 11 cm high, she is, like all of them, small enough to be held in the hand (Abramova 1967:70). Her puny arms are folded above her breasts, and her legs taper to a point. Her head appears to be covered in ringlets or plaits and she has no facial features.

Most of the figurines are made of ivory or soft stone and some show the remains of red colouring (Bahn and Vertut 1988:84). Most are probably over 20,000 years old, and it is very likely that they were being made from perishable materials even before the date of the oldest known, 31,000 BP (Bednarik 1989:121).

On present evidence these objects are the first recorded attempts at representing the human body. Their general attraction is well demonstrated in the abundance of the literature that describes them, and they are frequently linked to, and compared with, other carved statuettes from later Neolithic sites – sites believed by their excavators to suggest the existence of goddess worship and an associated fertility cult (Ucko 1968:410).

One can understand, perhaps, the impact of the nude female representations on the men of the prudish Victorian age – for of course it was the men who were finding these fascinating objects, propounding theories about early social customs, and publicising these theories to the scholars of the day, also men.

In 1903 Saloman Reinach presented his new theory of Palaeolithic hunting magic, a theory that gained wide acceptance and which quickly developed into the idea that religion in the late ice age centred around a cult of animal and human fertility associated with the figurines (James 1959:13–17). Archaeology was flourishing in the late 1800s and the classical archaeologists were also finding Neolithic statuettes which they identified as representations of a prehistoric fertility goddess (Ucko 1968:409). They revived the theories of the Swiss lawyer Johann Bachofen who, in his 1856 lecture at Stuttgart, proposed the existence of prehistoric matriarchies and the cult of a female deity, the Earth- or Mother-Goddess (Hays 1958:60–1; Lowie 1937:40–3).

The scholars of the new century envisaged her as the fundamental mother-symbol, the faceless fertile being who would ensure a continuing supply of young humans and animals. As one writer wrote:

> The female ideal was conceived as a machine for giving birth and feeding efficiently, with enormous breasts . . . and an equally enormous, almost spherical volume for the stomach and hips, capable of sheltering a capacious, comfortable maternal womb.

The female statuettes were seen as the expression of the necessity to reproduce in early times, of "man's obsessive need for women who would bear him lots of children" (Berenguer 1973:51–2).

It is quite clear that while the prehistorians of the early 1900s saw the Mother-Goddess as an important divinity, this did not influence their assessment of the place of Palaeolithic women in general. Rather, it confirmed their view that they were simply producers of children and useful for their abilities in the domestic sphere.

This attitude persisted at least until the 1960s and, one suspects, even later. Reinach's paper generated many imaginative theories surrounding hunting magic and resulted, in spite of Bachofen, in the vision of a male-oriented religious system and a Goddess to whom the hunters could plead for assistance in their own pursuits. Religion and art (including the making of figurines) were seen as important aspects of Palaeolithic life in which only the men participated.

The carvings, described as symbols of "fertility, procreation and life" (Guilaine 1986:48), were thought to demonstrate, by their "swelling wombs and ample curves" (Bowra 1962:10) that prehistoric women were "essentially passive, child-bearing nurturers . . . regarded as divine in terms of the cults of fertility that were then practised" (Julien 1986:30). And the words of the Scriptures were cited as evidence that patriarchy was "the primeval condition of the human race" (Maine, cit. Bamberger 1974:264).

The figurines were often accepted as erotic objects – for the men, of course (for example, Luquet 1930:109–11). Eroticism in art, says one archaeologist, "was inevitably connected with male impulse and desire" (Mellaart 1967:202). This was "art by and for men", representing "a straight line from the ice-age to Rodin and the playboy bunnies of later days" (Kurtén 1986:113–14). Scholars waxed eloquent: "Woman was [the] Gate of Life . . . the Object of Desire; between these two poles have . . . [man's] emotions swung" (Laver 1948:2, cit. Seltman 1957:20).

Some writers have pointed to the emphasis on sexual characteristics (for example, Childe 1958:21) and to the sexually-inviting attitudes they detected in the carvings (Guthrie 1984:63–8), and one even believed that the shape of them showed how anxious Paleolithic women were to please their men: "These figures must indicate", he says, "what the men who produced them found interesting and desirable . . . woman is quick to respond in physical type to the admiration of man" (Seltman 1957:19) – presumably by over-eating, though he is not clear on this.

It was, and still is commonly accepted that many or most carvings represent pregnant women. Ardrey described Frau Willendorf as "heavily pregnant" (1976:165). Others see them as about to give birth (Duhard 1987:162), to have just given birth (Michiels 1926:53), or to have done so many times already (Berenguer 1973:51). And steatopygia was also identified, and linked with Darwin's discovery that Hottentot women tended to have large derrières, which Hottentot men found very attractive (1901:881). The case for and against Palaeolithic female steatopygia on the basis of the figurines was fiercely debated (see, for example, Atgier 1912:711; Regnault 1912:35–6).

With the 1960s came "women's liberation". Feminist ideas begin to be felt in the Western world and a new kind of anthropological literature emerged, growing in volume and insistence. The women moving into academia were starting to question some of the research methods and conclusions of their male mentors in the past.

Angered by the male chauvinism apparent in the literature of the previous decades, many women began to express in print their resentment at the bias they could clearly see. How, they wondered, could scholars continue to believe that Palaeolithic women had such a subordinate part to play in the life of these early gatherer-hunter people – that they were simply sex objects for the pleasure and use of men? Women writers, like the men, cited Bachofen's prehistoric Mother-Goddess theory, but they emphasised his study of primeval matriarchies and his belief that "mother-right" was important in early religion. Bachofen, they said, showed how the original matriarchies had been replaced by the patriarchies of later eras (Bamberger 1974:264). Feminists discovered in Bachofen's writing confirmation of the high status of prehistoric women, personified by the deity "revered as wise, valiant, powerful and just" (Stone 1976a:5). They seized upon the figurines and the concept of the Mother-Goddess as proof that a female supreme being had existed in Europe "as far into the past as . . . about 25,000 BC" (Stone 1976b:xii).

While the deity and her images were generally accepted by both male and female scholars as an important part of late Palaeolithic religion, each saw the goddess in a different light. To the men, she was the representation of ideal womanhood, from their point of view, and the symbol of fertility and procreation in a male dominated religious system. They generally remained, and remain, unconvinced of the high status of ice-age women relative to men. To the women, this point was crucial. The Upper Palaeolithic was the foundation period for *Homo sapiens sapiens* and for them it was important that misconceptions about these first societies should be put right.

The 1970s and 1980s have produced an influx of what might be called "goddess" books justifying the new feminist view (for example, Carmody 1981; Stone 1976a; Sjöo and Mor 1987; Gimbutas 1984, 1990). While much anthropological work on gender by women is well researched and succeeds in exposing the biased thinking of earlier times, some of the "goddess" contributions, in themselves, reveal new biases. Written largely by women unqualified in prehistory/archaeology (the authors of one are practising witches) (Farrar and Farrar 1987), these texts purport to prove, by using the evidence the "right" way, that the facts are already there to be interpreted properly.

The "goddess" books often veer off into the realms of the mystical – a mish-mash of cosmology, mythology and astrology. The authors delve into Freudian and Jungian psychology, presenting women in prehistory, through the figurines, as some kind of super-beings revered by submissive males for their femaleness and their ability to produce children. The archaeological evidence is, in some cases, distorted enough to make any careful prehistorian shudder. Instead of bringing some common sense to our thinking about Palaeolithic society there is as much or more of a bias in this new way of accepting unproven theories, suggestions, and opinions of the past.

Even the book of Genesis has been given a facelift. One learns that it contains all the recognisable elements of the religion of the ancient goddess, but that she underwent a sex-change. This feminist literature is based on the idea that the supreme deity, a female, was transformed into a male god by men for their own purposes, while she became merely the God's wife/consort.

This kind of unfounded information is unfortunately being absorbed by too many ordinary readers, who are led to believe that the authors have checked their facts. The "goddess" authors castigate "anthropological/archaeological/academic" establishments for ignoring literature which, they say, proves they are right. There is "almost total blindness", they insist, "vis-a-vis the obvious female orientation of the Upper Palaeolithic . . . every statue and painting we discover cries out to us . . . these early Stone Age people bequeathed to all humanity a foundation of ideas . . . the cave as the female womb; the mother as the pregnant earth; the magical fertile female as the mother of all animals" (Sjöo and Mor 1987:8, 79; Thompson 1981:102).

The new feminist authors distort the real archaeological evidence just as much as the early chauvinistic males did. They make misleading statements, for example:

> It is thoroughly known that the only "God-image" ever painted on rock, carved in stone, or sculpted in clay, from the Upper Palaeolithic to the Middle Neolithic . . . was the image of a human female.

> (Sjöo and Mor 1987:7)

This is not thoroughly known at all — in fact, it is quite untrue. And another statement: "Accumulated archaeological evidence affirms overwhelmingly that prehistoric peoples worshiped a female deity" (Gadon 1990:xii). Archaeology can merely occasionally suggest such a possibility: that such a goddess existed at all in the ice age is at the least questionable, and not founded on fact.

One suspects that Bachofen, the romantic Swiss juror described as a mystic (Lowie 1937:41, 51) would be very surprised to learn how his thoughts on the Earth/Mother Goddess have been interpreted and how far-reaching his ideas, based only on mythology, have become. He merely romanticised womanhood, nostalgically describing woman's "unblemished beauty . . . chastity and high mindedness" (Bachofen 1967:83). Given the age that he lived in, he is unlikely to have been a true upholder of women's rights. Indeed, it is apparent from his writings that he saw patriarchy as the logical and desirable apex of an evolutionary social pattern. As Joan Bamberger points out, "the Victorian vision of woman elevated her to the status of goddess", but Bachofen still saw women as dependent, and dominated by men (Bamberger 1974:265).

The concept of some kind of cult was generally accepted, but there is a subtle fundamental difference in the way that the male and female writers saw it. The men described a fertility cult, emphasising the importance of the end product (children or young animals): the women were more concerned with the mother cult and with the power of female fertility (for example, Gimbutas 1984:10). They have concentrated on the women themselves, and on their high status in society because of their ability to control its continuity by performing the miracle of giving birth. While apparently embracing the same Mother-Goddess principle, each group has retained its own idealisation of human society.

So who is right? What evidence exists to confirm, or negate, either view? What is clear is that the only valid evidence is that of the figurines themselves. Further examination suggests that even the identification of these objects as human is sometimes suspect. Many of the illustrations in definitive works on female images (for example, Delporte 1979) are so vague that they could represent almost anything. Maybe it is a case, at times, of seeing what one hopes to see.

And the figurines are not all female. In both Palaeolithic and Neolithic collections some are unequivocally male, some possibly male, and the largest proportion are of indeterminate or no sex (Ucko 1968; Hadingham 1980:223–4). Of the Palaeolithic female examples, many are slim and most would be regarded as normal in today's terms. So if the carvings were meant to represent a Great Mother-Goddess, was she sometimes imagined to be slim, even pencil-slim? In which case the idea of obesity equating with fertility has to be abandoned. Was there also a Father-God, and other hermaphrodite deities too? It is not a valid argument to identify only a few of the figurines as a great pan-European Goddess and ignore the rest.

The Neolithic Great Goddess is somewhat hypothetical too. The first excavators of Neolithic statuettes had come straight from classical archaeology, bringing their own preconceived theories about the meaning of naked female representations. Inevitably Neolithic and Palaeolithic figurines were compared, in spite of the large time-gap, and few questioned the Mother-Goddess/fertility explanations (Ucko 1968:409, 415–17). The early Neolithic site of Çatal Hüyuk is often described as a centre of Mother-Goddess worship, though the evidence here, as at Hacilar (Ucko 1968:437–8), is inconclusive. There were both male and female figurines at Çatal Hüyuk, and it looks as if a male Bull-God was frequently represented. Mellaart, however, identified all bumps on the wall as breasts and all the figures as female, though most appear to be sexless (Mellaart 1967:Chapter 6). He may well have been influenced by the prevailing background of Mother-Goddess ideas.

Perhaps one should regard such a goddess merely as one of a varied pantheon of male, female and sexless supernatural beings, assuming that this is what the stat-uettes actually represent. The authenticity of some of the extreme Palaeolithic examples has already been questioned (Clottes and Cerou 1970:436, 441), and one must likewise question both the existence of a Europe-wide fertility cult and the use of the figurines as confirmation of male or female dominance at this early stage. In spite of statements to the contrary, very few Palaeolithic figurines are extreme in shape (Bahn and Vertut 1988:138) or depicted as pregnant; genitalia are rarely shown (Bahn and Vertut 1988:136); true steatopygia is almost absent; and stat-uettes often have facial features. The heads "bowed in subservience, submissiveness and shyness" (Guthrie 1984:67), suggesting to some, perhaps, the proper attitude of women, and the erotic and sexually-inviting poses conjured up by others (for example, Guthrie 1984:63–70) all seem to be figments of the imagination – one could describe it as "wishful thinking" (Bahn and Vertut 1988:164). The name "Venus" has its own connotations too. It was given originally to the "Vénus impudique" (a slim figure) in 1864 (Delporte 1979:54–5): unfortunately it became a typological label for all contemporary anthropomorphous shapes.

Not all prehistorians, of course, are male chauvinists or ardent feminists. Many recognise the pressures of their own social conditioning and unconscious preju-dices. It is possible to discuss gender issues and to study figurines without "encountering castration anxieties in men and shouts of triumphant Amazon joy" in women (Thompson 1981:148).

What other explanations could there be for existence of the carvings? Many possibilities have been proposed which have nothing to do with fertility, obesity, or a Mother-Goddess. These include portraits of real or ancestral people (Abramova 1967:89; Piette in Delporte 1979:276, 290), initiation figures (Ucko 1968:425), good luck amulets (Hadingham 1980:225), puppets (Zamiatnine in Nougier

1984:281), priestesses (Delporte 1979:276, 290), witches (Ronen 1976: 57), or figures to scare away strangers (Von Koenigswald 1972:137 in Rice 1981:402). Perhaps they were used by women to ward off difficulties in childbirth (Augusta 1960:34), by men as a worry-stone, or by children as dolls (Von Koenigswald 1956:187; Ucko 1968:422). Or they may simply have been a protecting figure for the household, as in some Siberian dwellings today (Waechter 1976:124).

One argument against the human fertility cult theory is that Palaeolithic people, like other gatherer-hunter groups, may not have been interested in producing more children (Ucko 1968:412), in contrast to agricultural societies.

While it is probable that our Palaeolithic ancestors believed in the supernatural, and that superstition played a part in their daily lives, one must be cautious in assuming that their religion bore any resemblance to the monotheistic religions of today. The Great Mother-Goddess of ice-age Europe is a shadowy hypothetical being. She may even be pure fiction.

■ ■ ■

References

Abramova, Z. A. 1967 Palaeolithic art in the USSR. *Arctic Anthropology* 4(2):1–179.

Ardrey, R. (1976) *The Hunting Hypothesis*. Fontana/Collins.

Atgier, (Dr) (1912) La Stéatopygie en France. *Bulletins et Mémoires de la Société d'Anthropologie de Paris*, pp. 7, 11.

Augusta, J. (1960) *Prehistoric Man*. London: Hamlyn.

Bachofen, J. J. (1967) *Myth, Religion and Mother-Right*. London: Routledge and Kegan Paul.

Bahn, P. G. and J. Vertut (1988) *Images of the Ice Age*. Leicester: Windward.

Bamberger, J. (1974) The myth of matriarchy. In M. Z. Rosaldo and L. Lamphere (eds) *Woman, Culture and Society*, pp. 263–80. Stanford University Press.

Bednarik, R. G. (1989) The Galgenberg figure from Krems, Austria. *Rock Art Research* 6(2): 118–25.

Berenguer, M. (1973) *Prehistoric Man and His Art*. London: Souvenir Press.

Bowra, C. M. (1962) *Primitive Song*. London: Weidenfeld and Nicholson.

Campbell, J. (1967) Introduction in J. J. Bachofen, *Myth, Religion and Mother-Right*, London: Routledge and Kegan Paul.

Carmody, D. L. (1981) *The Oldest God*. Nashville: Abingdon.

Childe, V. G. (1958) *The Prehistory of European Society*. Harmondsworth: Penguin.

Clottes, J. and E. Cérou (1970) La statuette feminine de Monpazier (Dordogne). *Bulletin de la Société Préhistorique Française* 67. Etudes et Travaux 2:435–44.

Darwin, C. (1901) *The Descent of Man*. London: John Murray.

Delporte, H. (1979) *L'Image de la Femme dans L'Art Préhistorique*. Paris: Picard.

Duhard, J.-P. (1987) La statuette de Monpazier représente-t-il une parturiente? *Bulletin de la Société Préhistorique Ariège Pyrénées* XLII: 155–63.

Farrar, J. and S. Farrar (1987) *The Witches' Goddess*. London: Robert Hale.

Gadon, E. W. (1990) *The Once and Future Goddess*. New York: Aquarian Press.

Gimbutas, M. (1984) *The Goddesses and Gods of Old Europe*. London: Thames and Hudson.

—— (1990) *The Language of the Goddess*. New York: Harper Row.

Guilaine, J. (1986) Religious cults and concepts. In J. Hughes (ed.) *World Atlas of Archaeology, Encyclopaedia Universalis*, pp. 48–9.

Guthrie, R. D. (1984) Ethological observations from Palaeolithic art. In H. Bandi *et al.* (eds), *La Contribution de la Zoologie et de l'Ethologie a l'Interpretation de l'Art des Peuples Chasseurs Préhistoriques*. 3e Colloque de la Société Suisse des Sciences Humaines, Sigriswil. Fribourg: Editions Universitaires, pp. 35–74.

Hadingham, E. (1980) *Secrets of the Ice Age*. London: Heinemann.

Hays, H. R. (1958) *From Ape to Angel*. London: Methuen.

James, E. O. (1959) *The Cult of the Mother-Goddess*. London: Thames and Hudson.

Julien, M. (1986) Woman in the Palaeolithic age. In J. Hughes (ed.) *World Atlas of Archaeology, Encyclopaedia Universalis*, pp. 30–1.

Kurtén, B. (1986) *How to Deep Freeze a Mammoth*. New York: Columbia University Press.

Laver, J. (1948) *Homage to Venus*. London: Faber.

Lowie, R. H. (1937) *The History of Ethnological Theory*. New York: Rinehart.

Luquet, G. H. (1930) *The Art and Religion of Fossil Man*. Cit. G. R. Levy, (1948), *The Gate of Horn*, p. 58. London: Faber.

Mellaart, J. (1967) *Çatal Hüyuk*. London: Thames and Hudson.

Michiels, G. (1926) *De L'obésite Partialle*, p. 53. Paris.

Nougier, L.-R. (1984) *Les Premiers Éveilles de l'Homme*. Lieu Commun.

Regnault, F. (1912) La representation de l'obésite dans l'art historique. *Bulletins et Mémoires de la Société d'Anthropologie de Paris*, pp. 35–6.

Rice, P. C. (1981) Prehistoric Venuses: Symbols of motherhood or womanhood? *Journal of Anthropological Research* 37(4): 402–14.

Ronen, A. (1976) *Introducing Prehistory*, London: Cassell.

Seltman, C. (1957) *Women in Antiquity*. London: Pan Books.

Sjöo, M. and B. Mor (1987) *The Great Cosmic Mother*. New York: Harper Row.

Stone, M. (1976a) *The Paradise Papers*. London: Virago Press.

—— (1976b) *When God was a Woman*. San Diego: Harcourt Brace Jovanovich.

Thompson, W. I. (1981) *The Time Falling Bodies Take to Light*. New York: St. Martin's Press.

Ucko, P. J. (1968) *Anthropomorphic Figurines*. London: Andrew Szmidla.

Von Koenigswald, G. H. R. (1956) *Meeting Prehistoric Man*. London: Thames and Hudson.

—— (1972) Cit. P. C. Rice (1981) Prehistoric Venuses: Symbols of motherhood or womanhood? *Journal of Anthropological Research* 37(4): 402–14.

Waechter, J. (1976) *Man Before History*. Oxford: Phaidon Press.

Chapter 15

WOMEN, RITUALS, AND SOCIAL DYNAMICS AT ANCIENT CHALCATZINGO

Ann Cyphers Guillén

Female figurines from the Cantera phase at Chalcatzingo, Morelos, depict stages of the life cycle: puberty, pregnancy, and child rearing. Contextual data indicate that the figurines were used in female-focused life-crisis ceremonies that created a web of social rights and obligations validated by reciprocal exchanges. These rights and obligations were the means by which power and influence were created, directed, and controlled by particular households. Thus, these figurines and their contexts permit a better understanding of the role of women in the dynamics of social-hierarchy formation at Chalcatzingo, and how the formation of social bonds and patterns of exchange were important in the accumulation of power.

Ancient peoples of highland Mexico developed significant degrees of social complexity during the Early and Middle Preclassic periods (2300–400 BC) and instituted the processes that led to state development and urbanism in the Late and Terminal Preclassic periods. The way in which archaeologists have traditionally diagnosed the level of overall complexity had been to search for salient traits, typical of some ideal form of prestate organization. Wolf (1990) emphasizes a trend to shift away from static trait categorizations to consideration of specific social processes. As part of this trend, diagnostic traits used by archaeologists are being reexamined for universality of application (Earle 1987; Feinman and Neitzel 1984; Peebles and Kus 1977). The association of significant and diagnostic criteria with the actual nature of developmental diversity should be sought within the archaeological record.

In line with this approach the present investigation examines women's roles and positions in Middle Preclassic society at the important regional center of Chalcatzingo, Morelos, with regard to the development of social complexity and power accumulation in terms prestate political economy. Cantera phase (700–500 BC) residential groups and their domestic rituals are interpreted from structural remains and from small clay figurines that generally depict women (Guillén 1987a, 1988, 1989). An emerging picture of Middle Preclassic social dynamics in Chalcatzingo society is related to and clarifies aspects of trade and its consequences, the formation of gender hierarchy, the tendency toward the institutionalization of hierarchical kin-ordered relationships, and the organization, operation, and manipulation of reciprocal systems in that society.

This study examines the archaeological contexts of the figurines and the figurines themselves, which are discussed with regard to head typologies, thematic analyses, and distributional data. The explanation of figurine use presented here emphasizes the continually changing configurations of interpersonal and intergroup relations, and how this activity can be used by an emerging central authority.

Chalcatzingo: an overview

Located in the center of the highland alluvial valley of the Río Tenango in eastern Morelos, the site of Chalcatzingo lies on the piedmont of two impressive granodiorite hills known locally as the Cerro de la Cantera and Cerro Delgado (Figure 1). The archaeological settlement is located in order to take maximum advantage of the different ecological zones in the valley (Bugé 1987).

Initial occupation dates to the Amate phase, 1500–1100 BC and surface indications and stratigraphic information point to a size of 6 ha (Hirth 1987). Salient characteristics include the practice of maize agriculture and the construction of monumental architecture. The first construction phase of the 70-m-long mound in the Plaza Central (Structure 4) dates to this phase as does a stone-faced low platform structure on Terrace 6 (Grove and Guillén 1987). Architectural and artifactual diversity points to the existence of well-developed social differences even though the 10 regularly spaced Amate-phase sites in the valley do not configure a clear settlement hierarchy (Hirth 1987), probably because early occupation is obscured by later settlements.

The ceramics somewhat resemble those of the Río Cuautla area (Grove 1974) and Basin of Mexico sites like Tlatilco (Guillén 1987b; Piña Chan 1958; Porter 1955). However the "Tlatilco style" of ceramics, principally the complex of stirrup spouts and composite bottles deriving stylistically from West Mexico (Kelly 1974, 1980; Oliveros 1974), is notably absent at Chalcatzingo, contrasting markedly with a strongly patterned distribution of these bottle forms along the Río Cuautla. Indeed Chalcatzingo appears to be outside the sphere of cultural interaction marked by the distribution of these artifacts. Although Grove (1987a, 1989) believes that this

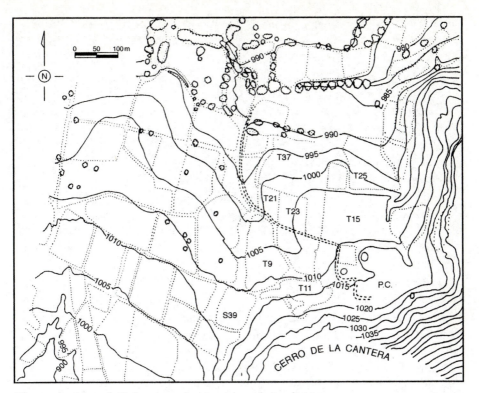

Figure 1 Map of Chalcatzingo showing internal site divisions

is due to a sampling problem at Chalcatzingo, stemming from a dearth of Amate-phase burials, it seems more likely that the trail of bottles down the Río Cuautla corresponds to a localized trade route passing through central Morelos and into northern Guerrero to obtain the highly prized cinnabar reported from the areas around Huahuaxtla and Huitzuco (Fries 1960; González 1944).

Local ceramics correspond to the widespread Early Preclassic red-on-brown style. At the end of this phase, or at the beginning of the Barranca phase, locally made ceramics reminiscent of Calzadas Carved (Coe and Diehl 1980) appear in minor quantities. It is important to note that the neighbouring site of Las Bocas, located across the pass into Puebla, with its purported assemblage of ceramics with Olmec motifs, probably dates to this time period; the "Tlatilco style" is notably absent there also.

The distributions of West Mexican and the Olmec-style ceramics clearly follow trade and communication routes. Chalcatzingo's Middle Preclassic importance, in fact, may be largely locational and perhaps a consequence of Cuicuilco's control of the eastern Ixtapalapa communication route leading out of the Basin of Mexico (Charlton 1984).

Even though human burials were not recovered from Amate-phase contexts at Chalcatzingo, it is important to note that, during the Early Preclassic in the central highlands, figurines are frequently used as mortuary offerings (Piña Chan 1958;

Porter 1955). Figures depicting women, men, children, animals, acrobats, shamans, and ball players, among others, were ritually interred with the deceased, and the use of these objects in death rites underscores the complex social activity accompanying life-crisis moments. A possible functional change in figurine use occurred following the Early Pre classic period (Guillén 1988), and this change coincides with evidence for regional population growth (Hirth 1987), and probable subsequent agricultural intensification (Boserup 1965), as part of the processes of social differentiation (Price 1984). A shift seems to occur in figurine use, from ritually deposited mortuary offerings to objects used in other life-cycle rituals and then discarded as garbage. With an increasing emphasis on rituals dedicated to the living, there is heightened formalization of the rituals celebrating social bonds and a clear diversification of social and economic opportunities by increasing the number of life-cycle moments celebrated. During the Middle Preclassic, figurines tend not to be placed in burials either in the Basin of Mexico (Vaillant 1930, 1935) or in Morelos (Grove 1974; Guillén 1987a).

During the Barranca phase (1100–700 BC), as Chalcatzingo doubled or tripled in size, reaching a spatial extent of 13 ha with a population of 130–325 persons (Hirth 1987), internal site planning began to include some terrace construction. In the valley system, regional settlement doubled with 22 sites composing three population clusters (Hirth 1987).

Testimony for trade and exchange within the macro-region includes obsidian from Otumba and Paredón (Charlton et al. 1987c) and fine-paste ceramics imported from the Izucar de Matamoros Valley (Guillén 1987b, 1987c; Guillén and Grove 1987). Light and/or direct contact with the Gulf Coast Olmec center of San Lorenzo is suggested by the sporadic occurrence of kaolin ceramics and the emulation of Calzadas Carved pottery. At this time there is no clear indication that extra-regional contact was the stimulus for the development of societal complexity. Rather, social inequality seems to have developed as a result of local or regional tendencies possibly founded on the differential control of scarce resources in the area. Chalcatzingo functioned as an important center in eastern Morelos before the advent of Olmec interest in it.

During the Cantera phase, 700–500 BC, the site attained a maximum size of 43 ha with 433–1,081 inhabitants (Hirth 1987). Interregional trade with the Olmec heartland came late (Grove et al. 1976), but was a key developmental characteristic (Grove 1968, 1987a; Hirth 1987). As a gateway community, Chalcatzingo was the major regional and ceremonial center, at the head of a well-developed sociopolitical hierarchy of 49 valley sites (Hirth 1978, 1987).

Intrasite functional diversity is manifested not only by habitational structures and burials reflecting clear wealth and status differences (Merry de Morales 1987; Prindiville and Grove 1987), but also in planned monumental and public architecture (Grove and Guillén 1987). Low, stone-faced platforms functioning as bases for high-status residential structures may have had public functions, as indicated by the erection of stelae in front of them. Significant differences among ceremonial constructions are illustrated by the 70-m-long platform (Plaza Central Structure 4) and the altar/throne/tomb construction (Monument 22) on Terrace 25. The construction and maintenance of two water-control systems (Terrace 15, Structure 1; El Rey Drainage), suggest that these were public efforts to control and harness hill runoff and protect the artificial terraces.

Single-craft workshop areas have been identified for obsidian on Terrace 37 (Burton 1987) and for ceramics on S39A (Grove and Guillén 1987; Guillén 1987a). In Structure 2 of the Plaza Central, figurines, greenstone, and iron ore were all worked at one time, though the intensity of specialization is unknown. Because this particular workshop forms a unit with a high-status domestic structure (Plaza Central Structure 1–1), it seems highly likely that control of such specialized production may be correlated with, and perhaps partly responsible for, the high status of this residential group.

Stylistically, Cantera ceramics signal participation in the widespread whiteware horizon of Middle Preclassic Mesoamerica, although Chalcatzingo developed its own regional preferences in certain forms and decorations (Guillén 1987b). Other ceramics show emulation of styles from the Gulf Coast and southern Mesoamerica (Guillén 1982). Regionally restricted types such as Peralta Orange and Xochitengo polychromes are excellent markers for the extent of Chalcatzingo's immediate sphere of influence.

Imported objects are more abundant at this time than ever before. Stingray spines, shell, and a small jadeite figure may have been obtained from the Gulf Coast, and iron-ore mirrors were imported from Oaxaca (Grove 1987b). Some serpentine and jadeite beads and ear spools may derive from the same rock sources used by La Venta (Thomson 1987). The surprising presence of turquoise (Grove 1987b) points to contacts far to the northwest.

Monumental art indicates that contact with Gulf Coast Olmec peoples enhanced existing social differences, as the inhabitants adopted the Olmec belief system that may have functioned to legitimize genealogical descent from the gods and ancestors (Guillén 1984). Taken together with data from the archaeological structures suggesting increasing corporateness, these observations permit the inference of a probable increased emphasis on genealogical descent during the Cantera phase.

During Cantera times the regional status of the site grew, and the doors to further economic opportunities probably opened. The reasons for Olmec contact have been postulated by various authors as commercial (Coe 1965; Grove 1968), military (Coe 1965), and colonization (Bernal 1969). The results of the Chalcatzingo Project (Grove, ed. 1987) favor trade as perhaps the most important factor among a constellation of important forces in operation.

Figurines

Small clay figurines usually depicting naked or partially clothed women are ubiquitous in Mesoamerica. The nudity represented in the figurines and the occasionally depicted pregnancy were points of departure for noting the undeniable procreative powers of women and proposing that a "fertility cult" existed (Barba de Piña Chan 1956, 1980; Piña Chan 1955). For biological and social reproduction, the obvious importance of women's fertility and procreative powers makes the "fertility-cult" idea so general as to be lacking in specific empirical content. No evidence for specific fertility-cult behavior is provided in these interpretations. Purportedly, figurines were buried in agricultural fields; however, the finding of Preclassic figurines in modern agricultural fields is unconvincing evidence for cult ceremony. Following a similar line of reasoning, Spinden (1928) once used the general distribution of female clay figurines throughout the Americas as evidence for the diffusion of agriculture.

Interpretations of Early and Middle Preclassic Oaxacan figurines have relied on context to aid in explanation as in the ritual group of figurines of Middle Preclassic date excavated in San José Mogote (Drennan 1976). Both Flannery (1976) and Drennan (1976) postulate the existence of Preclassic dance societies in Oaxaca. As these authors indicate, there are few data on context that provide a basis for clarifying figurine function.

The clay figurines in this study come from intensive excavations conducted by the Project Chalcatzingo (Grove (ed.) 1987), which recovered more than 8,000 figurine fragments from controlled and definable archaeological contexts, constituting one of the largest Preclassic figurine collections from a single Mesoamerican site. All fragments, whether heads, limbs, or torsos, were meticulously classified. Over 4,000 fragments derive just from Cantera-phase contexts (700–500 BC). In contrast to previous studies (Grove and Gillespie 1984; Harlan 1975, 1979, 1987), the present analysis deals with the complete corpus of excavated figurines in relation to their stratigraphic and cultural contexts. Because the thematic and quantitative information on the Cantera-phase figurines has already been reported (Guillén 1987a, 1988), only a brief summary of these data is presented here as necessary background for the following discussion.

At Chalcatzingo, as at most sites, the figurine collections have a highly fragmented character. Despite interpretations of ritual destruction of figurines by breaking off the heads (Angulo 1987; Grove 1987c; Harlan 1987), other body parts are also broken off. Inherent structural weakness in the articulation of limbs and heads may be a more acceptable explanation in the absence of clear evidence for ritual breakage. Few figurine fragments have complete heads and torsos, and even fewer are completely intact figures, a state reflecting a casual discard habit. The head classification used here explicitly defines types often loosely defined in Vaillant's classic typology (1930, 1931, 1935). The spatial distribution of head types in relation to bodies and with regard to internal site features is presently under analysis and will be forthcoming.

The careful study of the corpus of figurine bodies shows that female figurines predominate with 92 per cent of the sample while males occur about 3 per cent of the time and children 5 per cent. Clearly defined themes represented by the female bodies are based on physiology, clothing, adornment, and activity. The most salient theme is pregnancy, which is represented in three notable stages. The prominence of the abdomen defines the stages as well as a vertical incised line representing the gray line, an actual physiological trait most visible during the third trimester of pregnancy and caused by the increased production of progesterone (Vargas 1971). Nonpregnant female bodies may represent adolescents. It is possible that these figurines were used in curing rites and life-cyle rites such as menarche, marriage, and childbirth. Less frequent are figurines that carry children, animals, or objects. The absence of old women is notable. The fertile stages of the female life cycle are emphasized with representations of puberty, stages of pregnancy (Figure 2), and child rearing.

Common head types at Chalcatzingo fall in the "C" tradition (C2, C5, C8) (Figures 3 and 4), and the "Ch" type defined by Harlan (1987), all of which are locally made. The "Ch" figurines are a figurine-head style specific to Chalcatzingo (Harlan 1975, 1987) (Figure 5). Reyna's (1971) work on figurines points to the existence of localized figurine styles and their association with societal identities. Population interaction involving life-cycle ceremonies may account for the diversity of figurine styles present at a site in addition to the local and predominant style. The "Ch" figurines at Chalcatzingo are, for example, characteristic of the site and are found in greatest abundance there. Their presence at other sites in minor quantities may reflect the kinds of human and material exchanges mentioned for life-cycle celebrations.

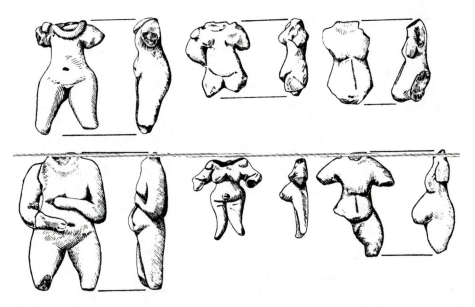

Figure 2   Female figurine bodies from the Cantera phase showing the representation of pregnancy

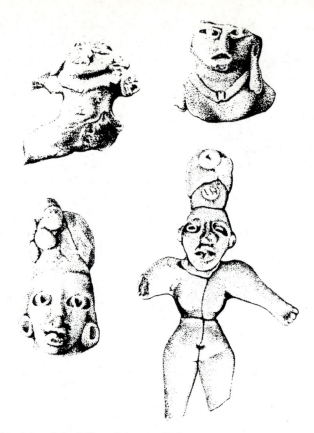

Figure 3   Figurines of the "C" tradition in Chalcatzingo

The type C8 was originally defined by Vaillant (1930) at El Arbolillo in the Basin of Mexico (Figure 4). Yet helmeted, cross-eyed figurines of this type appear at Gulf Coast Olmec sites such as La Venta and Tres Zapotes, where they seem to predominate in the figurine-head assemblages. (Some Gulf Coast style-figurines were classed as Type A by Vaillant [1930].) The introduction of C8-style figurines into the central highlands correlates with increasing contact with the Gulf Coast Olmec area. In Chalcatzingo, the C8s form approximately 30 per cent of the Cantera-phase figurine heads and closely parallel their Olmec counterparts in the fineness of manufacturing technique, the use of helmets as headdresses, eye treatment and convergent strabismus, and the distinctive representation of pregnant women with the gray line.

In contrast to studies emphasizing just the C8 heads (Grove 1987c, Grove and Gillespie 1984), this study of all heads and bodies, as well as the frequencies of heads to bodies, suggests that most C8s were probably women (Guillén 1987a, 1988, 1989). Because 92 per cent of all identifiable bodies are female, and 30 per cent of all heads are C8s, there is a high probability that virtually all C8 heads originally belonged to female bodies; it is also significant that the paste and surface finish of C8 heads coincides with that of female bodies. Analyses also indicate that

Figure 4   Figures of the "C8" tradition in Chalcatzingo

Figure 5   Figures of the "Ch" tradition in Chalcatzingo

female bodies of the Cantera phase, including those originally attached to C8 heads, show major themes related to life-cycle rituals: adolescence, stages of pregnancy, and child rearing.

The importance of C8s in the Cantera phase coincides not only with Chalcatzingo's greater participation in long-distance trade, but also with maximum population growth in the valley. The emulation of Olmec elites in the use of ritual and sumptuary goods is clearly a consequence of new economic relationships. Thematically and typologically similar to C8 heads from Chalcatzingo, figurines from Olmec sites may also have been used in transition or life-cycle rites. Long ago, Weiant (1943) perceptively asked if body physiology, clothing, and adornments of Tres Zapotes figurines could have been related to age or civil status.

The C8 figurines, so overwhelmingly female, imply a close relationship with the Gulf Coast Olmec, centering on human and material exchanges. If, as noted above, these figurines – like the other styles – are also associated with the female life cycle, the celebration of such rituals permeated with Olmec symbolism among the Olmec-influenced sector of Chalcatzingo's population (although, clearly, not necessarily exclusively in this sector) permits the inference of increased corporateness, with its emphasis on descent and its consequence that alliance relationships between and among household and supra-household groups assume increasing socioeconomic significance.

As discussed below in relation to all Cantera-phase female figurines, such relationships are often initiated or intensified in the celebration of life-crisis rituals of the members of the respective groups. The associated ritual process almost inevitably entails exchanges between or among the groups, exchanges that may be reciprocal or redistributive but which serve to cement and perpetuate social bonds (Firth 1939, 1951; Meillassoux 1981).

These interpretations contrast markedly with the "cult of the ruler" hypothesis (Grove and Gillespie 1984), in which C8 bodiless heads are not only identified as males, but as actual portraits of male rulers. It is implicit that authority and power vested in male rulers developed as a consequence of Olmec contact, and furthermore, that the production of C8 figurines was destined for use by a governing elite. As is demonstrated here, tags such as "cult of the ruler" or "fertility cult" give static descriptions for objects used in dynamic social rituals in which human and material resources could be maneuvered to advantage by those persons seeking to accumulate power. The role of women as highly visible actors in the dynamics of social-hierarchy formation and accentuation is also obscured by "cult" explanations.

Archaeological contexts and figurine associations

Ceramic figurines of the Middle Preclassic are rarely found as dedicatory offerings. Their less formal use and discard contrast with the more elaborate activities associated with small stone figurines. For example, the deliberate arrangement and burial of the stone figurines in Offering 4 at La Venta (Drucker *et al.* 1959) define a formal ceremonialism involving ritual dedication. Figurine distribution was tested at Chalcatzingo by examining and contrasting the occurrence of ceramic figurines in domestic, craft, and public/ceremonial contexts. No figurines were found in direct association with the public/ceremonial context (Terrace 25, Monument 22), and in one of the two elite burials in the long platform mound (Plaza Central, Structure 4) a single figurine head (Merry de Morales 1987) could be an offering or simply redeposited fill. As a consequence, the present investigation concentrated on the domestic and craft contexts, where figurines were most abundant. Figurines tend to cluster in domestic spaces where evidence for food preparation occurred (carbon, ground-stone artifacts, hearths, braziers, and ubiquitous domestic pottery). In my analyses of the structures, I found that stages in the domestic cycle produce adjustments such as room expansion and additions, with orientation and major structural features remaining intact. When major features are maintained in successive rebuildings on the same site, corporateness may be indicated (Guillén 1987a), another indicator of increasing social complexity during the Cantera phase.

The contexts analyzed were rigorously controlled for floor and feature associations, and it is thought that these represent largely primary deposition since *in situ* artifacts are found on the use surfaces. However, even if secondary depositions of figurines were present, the association of figurines with household deposits still remains strong, with figurines entering into household deposits just as do food-processing artifacts and other debris. In either case, figurines are associated with household activities, although perhaps not necessarily directly with the houses in which they are found. In contrast, the absence of figurines in ceremonial activities including mortuary rituals is a general rule for the Cantera phase.

Structure 1 of the Plaza Central shows a sequence of three distinct constructions spanning several centuries. Periodic construction and reconstruction, intentional superposition, and identical alignment of the constructions demonstrate a temporal and ideational continuity implying the existence of a corporate group with well-defined economic, political, social, and ceremonial functions. In all three constructions, figurines are found in proximity to cooking areas. Of particular interest is a small pit feature containing a high figurine count as well as a portable stone carving (Grove 1987d: 338, Figure 20.12), which may be evidence for some type of ritual activity.

A particularly large structure on Terrace 11, unfortunately disturbed by 11 looters' pits, yielded some original use surfaces with *in situ* artifacts on the floor. Figurines tend to cluster near a possible kitchen area defined by the presence of groundstone artifacts, pottery vessels, and brazier fragments.

The Terrace 23 domestic unit represents a highly complex sequence of buildings and rebuildings, suggesting the alteration/expansion, contraction, and conflation of interior spaces according to changes in the size of the resident domestic unit over time. The highest figurine frequencies are observed in and around hearth areas and in association with groundstone artifacts.

Two areas of specialized craft production at Chalcatzingo, including figurine manufacture, merit comment. The first is located in the southwest corner of the Plaza Central, where Structure 2 and Structure 1 to the east, together with a probable third structure, are believed to have formed part of an elite household compound. Remains such as greenstone drill cores, iron-ore dust, and fragments, and an extraordinary abundance and variety of figurines types from the patio area to the north indicate that several kinds of craft activities were conducted here. More than 1,400 figurine fragments come from this structure and associated patio, and the majority are found outside the structure or in one room. Clustered in one room, more than 125 figurine fragments were associated with five polishing stones and quantities of red pigment. C8 and Ch1 head types predominate here. In general, Structure 2 indicates that craft production in several local and nonlocal materials was controlled and centralized by an elite, and perhaps corporate group.

The second workshop context, located on S39 near the southwestern edge of the site, does not exhibit evidence of habitation along with craft activity. A high concentration of figurines occurs in conjunction with the most important evidence for ceramic manufacture, the tools.

Evidence from S39 and Plaza Central Structure 2 suggests that figurines at Chalcatzingo were not manufactured by every household, but rather in specialized workshops. The geographical restriction of the Chalcatzingo style of figurines indicates the production of figurines was for local consumption and not for export. The elite production of figurines contrasts markedly with craft production that is pervasive in all domestic units because, in the latter case, exchange value of products tends to be items equally available to all members of the society. When a craft is linked directly to an elite group, the organization of craft production and distribution changes, and other values enter into exchange consideration. The exchange value of figurines produced and controlled by an elite Chalcatzingo domestic group may have been particular resources or products that the group wished to control. In this way, the elite's control of figurines for life-cycle rituals, needed by everyone, may have permitted them to manipulate aspects of regional redistribution.

In contrast with the nonresidential areas such as Plaza Central Structure 4, Terrace 25, and Terrace 37, a much higher frequency of figurines is noted in domestic contexts. Within domestic spaces, important clusters of figurines are found in and around food-processing areas. The high frequencies of figurines with ceramic tools in workshop contexts most probably point to figurine manufacture. It is interesting that only in the workshops were figurines found as burial offerings, and in both cases, in an infant burial.

The existence of animal depictions in the figurine repertoire of Chalcatzingo is significant for their consistent association with the female figurines. Di Castro (1988) has shown that animals were depicted as full-body figurines, as part of effigy vessels, and as headdresses for human figurines. Wild animals such as ducks, coatimundis, tapirs, and coyotes, among others, were represented, but the dog was predominant in animal figurines and represented a domesticated source of protein. It is well known that the Aztecs kept dogs as pets and for table fare during the Late Postclassic period (Aguilera 1985). Present in archaeological deposits since early times at Chalcatzingo, dog remains are the most abundant of all faunal remains during the Cantera phase (Grove 1987e). It is possible that dogs were one valuable food source consumed perhaps not on a daily basis but on festive occasions when ostentatious protein consumption could have been important. Dog representations in clay and dog skeletal remains are found in association with figurines in domestic refuse. Even though the representation of female figurines carrying dogs could be interpreted as a human–pet relationship, the economic importance of the dog as a domesticated protein source should not be forgotten.

Social bonds and economic exchange in life-cycle rituals

Various lines of evidence presented above have suggested a context for the Chalcatzingo figurines that sets forth a web of social rights and obligations linking household with household, supra-household group with supra-household group. One such unit acts as host and other units participate as guests; through time each group will play each role *vis-à-vis* other groups. Such participation and the consequent web of rights and obligations would have been validated by economic exchanges. I suggest that Cantera-phase life-cycle rituals may have triggered this sort of continuing social action. The figurine data document such rituals based on the female life cycle; comparable events for males may have existed as well, but if so, the evidence from the figurines does not offer confirmation. Thus, the two important linked characteristics of these rituals, the formation of social bonds and the establishment of patterns of exchange, are critical to the accumulation of power in increasingly differentiated societies through the effective manipulation of human resources by an emerging centralized authority. The following discussion examines this in more detail insofar as it is reasonable to suggest that these processes occurred at ancient Chalcatzingo.

Relationships established among or between people at life-cycle ceremonies can affect the structure and dynamics of their lives until they die. Considerable thought and planning is given to the selection of baptismal *compadres*, for example, in modern Mexican society where such bonds begin a lifetime of obligations. Ritual moments when non-kin bonds are formalized can be categorized as scarce resources to be used to establish advantageous social relations that extend beyond the normal responsibilities and rights associated with kinship (Almagor 1978). The birth of a child, especially the first-born, offers an opportunity for the establishment of special social relationships. Important social bonds formed among participants in age grades are formed generally during transition or initiation rites (Steward 1977). Initiation rites associated with menarche signal and emphasize the sexual/reproductive receptivity of young females, and many times they indicate the age of marriageability. Where bridewealth and dowry are customary in marriage rites, the initial exchange of goods and services is the beginning of a long-term set of exchanges among affinal kin (Eliade 1958, 1964, 1969; Firth 1939; Turner 1969; Van Gennep 1960).

Another special characteristic of life-cycle rituals is that social relationships formed at such times probably are initiated with some form of economic exchange, usually labeled as "reciprocal." An integral part of the rituals or ceremonies associated with life-transition moments is the exchange of food (Sahlins 1972:187). The passage of food creates obligations to reciprocate. An imbalance in the flow of food or related goods and services creates indebtedness. Reciprocity is the predominant, characteristic mechanism that creates, symbolizes, and perpetuates obligations among individuals, groups, and communities. Standardized quantities and qualities of foods and services are a measure of that interdependence; and some form of accounting or tabulation of reciprocity is usually kept on the balance of debt.

Economic exchanges are begun during the ritual activity that celebrates the formalization of the relationship, but do not end there. They imply not only an immediate and reciprocal exchange of something, but also indicate the flow of goods and services between individuals, between groups, and between producers and consumers. The quantity, quality, direction, and manner of exchange of these goods and services are obviously affected by religious, moral, and aesthetic considerations and values (Mayer 1974:1–3). These social and economic relationships continue after the special life-cycle moment has passed and are a social resource for the participants who extend their web of obligations and responsibilities to include people outside their kinship network. For example, with the creation of affinal relations through marriage, formalized exchange relationships may facilitate the operation of other economic mechanisms. This is particularly true of marriage alliances between elite families. The acquisition of one or several women, often young females, constitutes a competitive process in which sexual/reproductive value acquires a certain prestige and possible economic advantages, depending on the position and power of the family. Polygyny is obviously one possible route to the accumulation of power via the use and manipulation of affinal relations in order to obtain access to certain resources (Almagor 1978).

In agricultural communities where production occurs at the household level, domestic self-sufficiency is generally the major goal; the critical factor in reciprocal exchanges tends to be social labor or services (Meillassoux 1978). Mutual help in production is a potentially accumulable service in the inherently unbalanced structure of the reciprocal-exchange system. Control of social labor would considerably enhance the production and accumulation potential of an emerging central authority. In discussing the emergence of chiefly redistribution, it has been noted that the advantage gained in economic imbalances formed during reciprocal exchanges may have served as "starting mechanisms" in the formation of rank (Gouldner 1960, in Sahlins 1972:207).

Although reciprocity stands on the dyadic contract (Wolf 1966), it extends itself beyond individuals to encompass increasingly larger groups. To successfully articulate many sizes and types of organizations requires the skilled exercise of social power that surpasses the elastic constraints of reciprocity. When reciprocity can no longer maintain group cohesion, mediating institutions appear (Mayer 1974:362).

Following Sahlins (1972), institutionalized group integration through reciprocity, and probably redistribution, extends beyond the community and perhaps regional level. Interestingly, as social and kinship distance increase, there seems to be a tendency for balanced reciprocal exchange to be transformed into more advantageous, less moral, or even commercial transactions. In contemporary peasant societies, Sahlins points out that exchanges on a larger scale and between more distant groups may be characterized by barter and purchasing.

In summary, in the process of increasing differentiation, the status of the members of the emerging social entities, such as lineages, increases relative to each other, and entire lineages may attain differential status. Reciprocal exchanges become increasingly redistributive and unequal. As the size of the exchanging groups increases, balanced reciprocal exchanges may be largely restricted to lineage heads within the community and beyond it to key members of foreign groups (in the case of Chalcatzingo, extending perhaps to the Gulf Coast). The more powerful and influential lineage heads would maintain a greater number of such ties. Lower-status lineage members would derive their supplies of exotica from those persons. This suggests a dynamic in which, despite an ideology of kinship, the relationship is probably shifting to one resembling that between patron and client.

Unbalanced reciprocity characterizes the nature of patron–client exchange of goods and services, due to the unequal status of the participants. The balance of debt may be maintained in the types of goods and services exchanged or in the way that these are handled, thus conserving a debt favorable to the patron and a continual obligation on the part of the client. Patron–client relationships are thought to set the stage for well-defined social classes (Santley 1984:48–49).

Concluding observations

Even though many theories have placed early women's roles in a subordinate position, the active roles played by women in Chalcatzingo society are emphasized here as well as the manner in which these contribute to the accumulation of political power. For the Preclassic period, it is unfortunately not known if men or women were the political decision makers, what type of residence pattern was common, or how filiation and descent operated. In fact, even the sex of the food producers in this society remains a mystery. Thus, the emphasis on female depictions in the figurines constitutes our first real glimpse into Preclassic gender roles and relations in the social hierarchy and in the political economy of this early society.

Cantera-phase themes and archaeological contexts provide a point of departure for interpretations of the figurines. Their use in rites of passage associated with puberty/marriage, pregnancy, and childbirth/childcare are an obvious interpretation. Another possible complementary interpretation involves figurine use in curing rites. Use in rituals associated with age grades or sodalities could be another possibility even though potentially supporting ethnohistoric evidence for the existence of such social institutions in later Mesoamerica is not available. With regard to marriage, certainly the key role of women in the formation of ties between lineages has been shown in the Maya area, as well as their important genealogical position in the legitimation of ranked positions within lineage hierarchies (Kelley 1962; Proskouriakoff 1963, 1964; Schele and Miller 1986). In fact, it is likely that this same mechanism was once commemorated in monumental art at Chalcatzingo (Guillén 1984), and also by the Chalcatzingo figurines that emphasize feminine sexuality and reproduction as part of a social preoccupation regarding the availability of, access to, and control of these attributes.

Formal life-crisis rituals, such as those proposed for figurine use, would epitomize the inseparability of social and economic spheres since such occasions generally bring economic exchanges to the forefront. The individual female's social position would have been closely intertwined with all symbols and activities associated with life-cycle ceremonies when important social bonds are established and economic exchanges are initiated.

In the analysis of Cantera-phase figurines, the emphasis on women's physiological state and/or age as related to the female life cycle must be considered in conjunction with archaeological contexts, which indicate that figurine use and discard predominate in domestic areas in and around food-processing areas and containing domestic refuse. The archaeological record rarely permits the definition of gender-specific artifacts, but the combination of female preeminence in figurines along with the household context leads me to believe that women were the social actors who used the figurines in life-cycle rituals. It is important to note, however, that women may not have been the only participants in these rituals.

The figurines stimulate the formulation of abstract analytic questions about social integration during the Cantera phase. Through ethnographic analogy regarding a nearly universal association of life-cycle rituals, food and wealth displays, and exchanges, it is possible to propose that life-cycle rituals involving figurine use were associated with exchanges. Nevertheless, the association of figurines, feasting rituals, and exchanges requires archaeological demonstration at the empirical level. The kinds of supporting evidence for the proposed association are less obviously manifested by material remains than in the case of ethnographic observation. A review of ethnographic reports shows that no material testimony of these events is commonly left. Nevertheless, it is possible that life-cycle rituals could leave tenuously associated vestiges of feasting such as ovens used for food preparation and garbage pits following the cleanup; special protein-rich foods are likely to be consumed in significant quantities, but, as ethnographic accounts consistently show (Firth 1963; Newman 1965; Rappaport 1968), the economically important distribution of these foods throughout the society scatters the material remains of the feast. Some ceremonies may be characterized by the burial of caches of objects, such as amulets, musical instruments, fetishes, adornments, and the like, but this does not occur in all societies. Sometimes ceremonies may be conducted in a special area or structure set aside for that purpose.

Related archaeological information suggests a positive correlation. Cantera-phase figurines are found discarded in food-processing areas along with domestic refuse and were not placed in ritual caches. Figurines are associated with hearths and pit features, and consistent distributions occur with dog remains at the domestic level. Further evidence for figurine association with food and wealth is thematic – the portrayal of female figurines holding animals, predominantly dogs (Di Castro 1988). Dogs were clearly an important protein source and surely were consumed on festive occasions.

The operation of exchange is clearly inferred from the adoption of figurine styles from other participating groups, such as the Olmec and other highland groups.

The degree of social differentiation based on division of labor by age, sex, and kinship is unclear during the Amate and Barranca phases, but by the Cantera phase, contact through trade considerably enhanced previously existing social differences. It may be proposed that Chalcatzingo's intense participation in interregional trading spheres coincided with significant internal social dynamics affecting the development of sociopolitical complexity, such as the appearance of hierarchically ordered corporate groups and elite control of domestic craft production (Guillén 1987a). Closely related to these could be the organization and operation of reciprocal systems that stimulated the accumulation of goods and services, leading to the formation of patron–client relationships.

Thus, it is possible to interpret the Middle Preclassic female figurines at Chalcatzingo as the material manifestations of a reciprocal exchange system revolving around the celebration of female life-cycle transitions. In accord with ethnographic data, the manipulation of reciprocity provided a basis for the accumulation of goods, services, and social labor, and hence, of power, by an emerging central authority. Clearly, at Chalcatzingo, the introduction of foreign, Olmec-style figurines may indicate not only intermarriage with the Olmec and the subsequent descent and genealogical calculation of kin and social distance, but also the increased size of the exchanging groups.

■ ■ ■

References

Aguilera, C. (1985) *Flora y fauna mexicana, mitología y tradiciones.* Editorial Everst, León, España.

Almagor, U. (1978) Gerontocracy, Polygyny and Scarce Resources. In *Sex and Age As Principles of Social Differentiation,* edited by J. S. La Fontaine, pp. 139–158. Academic Press, New York.

Angulo, J. (1987) The Chalcatzingo Reliefs: An Iconographic Analysis. In *Ancient Chalcatzingo,* edited by D. C. Grove, pp. 132–158. University of Texas Press, Austin.

Barba de Piña Chan, B. (1956) Tlapacoya, un sitio preclásico de transición. *Acta Antropológica*, época 2, tomo I, no. 1. Escuela Nacional de Antropología e Historia, México, D.F.

—— (1980) *Tlapacoya, los principios de la teocracia en la cuenca de Mexico.* Biblioteca Enciclopédica del Estado de México, México, D.F.

Bernal, I. (1969) *The Olmec World.* University of California Press, Berkeley.

Boserup, E. (1965) *The Conditions of Agricultural Growth: The Economics of Agrarian Change Under Population Pressure.* Aldine, Chicago.

Bugé, D. (1987) Plant Ecology and Paleoecology. In *Ancient Chalcatzingo*, edited by D. C. Grove, pp. 14–20. University of Texas Press, Austin.

Burton, S. (1987) Obsidian Blade Manufacturing Debris on Terrace 37. In *Ancient Chalcatzingo*, edited by D. C. Grove, pp. 321–328. University of Texas Press, Austin.

Charlton, T. (1984) Production and Exchange: Variables in the Evolution of a Civilization. In *Trade and Exchange in Early Mesoamerica*, edited by K. G. Hirth, pp. 17–43. University of New Mexico Press, Albuquerque.

Charlton, T., D. C. Grove and P. K. Hopke (1978) The Paredon, Mexico, Obsidian Source and Early Formative Exchange. *Science* 201:807–809.

Coe, M. D. (1965) The Olmec Style and Its Distributions. In *Archaeology of Southern Mesoamerica*, pt. 2, edited by G. R. Willey, pp. 739–775. Handbook of Middle American Indians, vol. 3, R. Wauchope, general editor. University of Texas Press, Austin.

Coe, M. D., and R. A. Diehl (1980) *In the Land of the Olmec.* 2 vols. University of Texas Press, Austin.

Di Castro, A. (1988) *Representaciones zoomorfas, de cerámica de Chalcatzingo*, Morelos. Unpublished tesis de licenciatura, Escuela Nacíonal de Antropología e Historia, México, D.F.

Drennan, R. D. (1976) Religion and Social Evolution in Formative Mesoamerica. In *The Early Mesoamerican Village*, edited by K. V. Flannery, pp. 345–363. Academic Press, New York.

Drucker, P., R. F. Heizer, and R. J. Squier (1959) *Excavations at La Venta, Tabasco, 1955.* Bulletin No. 170. Bureau of American Ethnology, Smithsonian Institution, Washington, DC.

Earle, T. (1987) Chiefdoms in Archaeological and Ethnohistorical Perspective. *Annual Review of Anthropology* 16: 279–308.

Eliade, M. (1958) *Rites and Symbols of Initiation, The Mysteries of Birth and Rebirth.* Harper and Row, New York.

—— (1964) *Shamanism, Archaic Techniques of Ecstasy.* Princeton University Press, Princeton, New Jersey.

—— (1969) *The Quest, History and Meaning in Religion.* University of Chicago Press, Chicago.

Feinman, G. and J. Neitzel (1984) Too Many Types: An Overview of Sedentary Prestate Societies in the Americas. In *Advances in Archaeological Method and Theory*, vol. 7, edited by M. B. Schiffer, pp. 39–101. Academic Press, New York.

Firth, R. (1939) *Primitive Polynesian Economy.* Routledge, London.

—— (1951) *Elements of Social Organization.* Watts, London.

—— (1963) *We, The Tikopia: A Sociological Study of Kinship in Primitive Polynesia.* Beacon Press, Boston.

Flannery, K. V. (1976) Contextual Analysis of Ritual Paraphernalia from Formative Oaxaca.

In *The Early Mesoamerican Village*, edited by K. V. Flannery, pp. 333–344. Academic Press, New York.

Fries, C., Jr. (1960) *Geología del estado de Morelos y de partes adyacentes de México y Guerrero, región central meridional de México*. Boletín No. 60. Instituto de Geología, Universidad Nacional Autónoma de México, México, DF.

González, J. (1944) *Minería y riqueza minera de México*. Monografías Industriales No. 2. Banco de México, México, DF.

Goulder, A. (1960) The Norm of Reciprocity: A Preliminary Statement. *American Sociological Review* 25:161–178.

Grove, D. C. (1968) The Preclassic Olmec in Central Mexico: Site Distribution and Inferences. In *Dumbarton Oaks Conference on the Olmec*, edited by E. Benson, pp. 179–185. Dumbarton Oaks Research Library and Collection, Washington, DC.

—— (1974) *San Pablo, Nexpa, and the Early Formative Archaeology of Morelos, Mexico*. Publications in Anthropology No. 12. Vanderbilt University, Nashville, Tennessee.

—— (1987a) Chalcatzingo in a Broader Perspective. In *Ancient Chalcatzingo*, edited by D. C. Grove, pp. 434–442. University of Texas Press, Austin.

—— (1987b) Raw Materials and Sources. In *Ancient Chalcatzingo*, edited by D. C. Grove, pp. 376–386. University of Texas Press, Austin.

—— (1987c) Comments on the Site and Its Organization. In *Ancient Chalcatzingo*, edited by D. C. Grove, pp. 420–433. University of Texas Press, Austin.

—— (1987d) Ground Stone Artifacts. In *Ancient Chalcatzingo*, edited by D. C. Grove, pp. 329–342. University of Texas Press, Austin.

—— (1987e) Faunal Analysis. In *Ancient Chalcatzingo*, edited by D. C. Grove, Appendix J, pp. 547–549. University of Texas Press, Austin.

—— (1989) Chalcatzingo and Its Olmec Connection. In *Regional Perspectives on the Olmec*, edited by R. J. Sharer and D. C. Grove, pp. 122–147. Cambridge University Press, New York.

Grove, D. C. (editor) (1987) *Ancient Chalcatzingo*. University of Texas Press, Austin.

Grove, D. C. and S. Gillepsie (1984) Chalcatzingo's Portrait Figurines and the Cult of the Ruler. *Archaeology* July/August:27–33.

Grove, D. C. and A. C. Guillén (1987) The Excavations. In *Ancient Chalcatzingo*, edited by D. C. Grove, pp. 21–55. University of Texas Press, Austin.

Grove, D. C., K. G. Hirth, D. Bugé and A. Cyphers (1976) Settlement and Cultural Development at Chalcatzingo. *Science* 192:1203–1210.

Guillén, A. C. (1982) The Implications of Dated Monumental Art From Chalcatzingo, Morelos, Mexico. *World Archaeology* 13:382–393.

—— (1984) The Possible Role of a Woman in Formative Exchange. In *Trade and Exchange in Early Mesoamerica*, edited by K. G. Hirth, pp. 115–124. University of New Mexico Press, Albuquerque.

—— (1987a) *Las figurillas de Chalcatzingo, Morelos: Estudio de arte y antropología*. Unpublished PhD dissertation, Facultad de Filosofía y Letras, Universidad Nacional Autónoma de México, México, DF.

—— (1987b) Ceramics. In *Ancient Chalcatzingo*, edited by D. C. Grove, pp. 200–251. University of Texas Press, Austin.

—— (1987c) Estudio petrográfico de dos cerámicas importadas de Chalcatzingo, Morelos. *Antropología y Técnica* 2:85–98. Universidad Nacional Autónoma de México, México, DF.

—— (1988) Thematic and Contextual Analyses of Chalcatzingo Figurines. *Mexicon* X:98–102.

—— (1989) Las figurillas C8 de Chalcatzingo, Morelos. In *Ensayos de alfarería prehispánica e histórica de Mesoamérica, homenaje a Eduardo Noguera Auza*, edited by M. C. Serra and C. Navarrete, pp. 85–96. Universidad Nacional Autónoma de México, México, DF.

Guillén, A. C., and D. C. Grove (1987) Chronology and Cultural Phases at Chalcatzingo. In *Ancient Chalcatzingo*, edited by D. C. Grove, pp. 56–62. University of Texas Press, Austin.

Harlan, M. E. (1975) *Prehistoric Exchange at Chalcatzingo, Morelos, Mexico*. Unpublished Ph.D. dissertation, Department of Anthropology, University of Arizona, Tucson.

—— (1979) An Inquiry into the Development of Complex Society at Chalcatzingo, Morelos, Mexico: Methods and Results. *American Antiquity* 44:471–493.

—— (1987) Chalcatzingo's Formative Figurines. In *Ancient Chalcatzingo*, edited by D. C. Grove, pp. 252–263. University of Texas Press, Austin.

Hirth, K. G. (1978) Interregional Trade and the Formation of Prehistoric Gateway Communities. *American Antiquity* 43:35–45.

—— (1987) Formative Period Settlement Patterns in the Río Amatzinac Valley. In *Ancient Chalcatzingo*, edited by D. C. Grove, pp. 343–367. University of Texas Press, Austin.

Kelley, D. H. (1962) Glyphic Evidence for a Dynastic Sequence at Quirigua, Guatemala. *American Antiquity* 27:323–335.

Kelly, I. (1974) Stirrup Pots from Colima: Some Implications. In *The Archaeology of West Mexico*, edited by B. Bell, pp. 206–211. Sociedad de Estudios Avanzados del Occidente de México, Ajijic, Jalisco.

—— (1980) *Ceramic Sequence in Colima: Capacha, an Early Phase*. Anthropological Papers No. 37. University of Arizona Press, Tucson.

Mayer, E. (1974) *Reciprocity, Self-sufficiency and Market Relations in a Contemporary Community in the Central Andes of Peru*. Unpublished Ph.D. dissertation, Department of Anthropology, Cornell University, Ithaca, New York.

Meillassoux, C. (1978) "The Economy" in Agricultural Self-sustaining Societies: A Preliminary Analysis. In *Relations of Production: Marxist Approaches to Economic Anthropology*, edited by D. Seddon, pp. 127–157. Frank Cass, London.

—— (1981) *Maidens, Meal and Money, Capitalism and the Domestic Community*. Cambridge University Press, New York.

Merry de Morales, M. (1987) Chalcatzingo Burials as Indicators of Social Ranking. In *Ancient Chalcatzingo*, edited by D. C. Grove, pp. 95–113. University of Texas Press, Austin.

Newman, P. L. (1965) *Knowing the Gururumba*. Holt, Rinehart & Winston, New York.

Oliveros, J. A. (1974) Nuevas exploraciones on El Opeño, Michoacan. In *The Archaeology of West Mexico*, edited by B. Bell, pp. 182–201. Sociedad de Estudios Avanzados del Occidente de México, Ajijic, Jalisco.

Peebles, C., and S. Kus (1977) Some Archaeological Correlates of Ranked Societies. *American Antiquity* 42:421–448.

Piña Chan, R. (1955) *Las culturas preclásicas de la cuenca de México*. Fondo de Cultura Económica, México, DF.

—— (1958) *Tlatilco*. Serie Investigaciones Nos. 1–2. Instituto Nacional de Antropología e Historia, México, DF.

Porter, M. (1955) *Tlatilco and the Preclassic Cultures of the New World*, Viking Fund Publication in Anthropology No. 19 Wenner-Gren Foundation for Anthropological Research, New York.

Price, B. J. (1984) Competition, Productive Intensification, and Ranked Society: Speculations from Evolutionary Theory. In *Warfare, Culture and Environment*, edited by R. B. Ferguson, pp. 209–240. Academic Press, New York.

Prindiville, M. and D. C. Grove

—— (1987) The Settlement and Its Architecture. In *Ancient Chalcatzingo*, edited by D. C. Grove, pp. 63–81. University of Texas Press, Austin.

Proskouriakoff, T. (1963) Historical Data in the Inscriptions of Yaxchilan, Part 1. *Estudios de Cultura Maya* 3: 149–167.

—— (1964) Historical Data in the Inscriptions of Yaxchilan, Part 2. *Estudios de Cultura Maya* 4: 177–202.

Rappaport, R. A. (1968) *Pigs for the Ancestors, Ritual in the Ecology of a New Guinea People*. Yale University. Press, New Haven, Connecticut.

Reyna, R. M. (1971) Las figurillas preclásicas. Unpublished tesis de maestría, Escuela Nacional de Antropología e Historia, Mexico, DF.

Sahlins, M. (1972) *Stone Age Economics*. Tavistock, London.

Santley, R. (1984) Obsidian Exchange, Economic Stratification, and the Evolution of Complex Society in the Basin of Mexico. In *Trade and Exchange in Early Mesoamerica*, edited by K. Hirth, pp. 43–86. University of New Mexico Press, Albuquerque.

Schele, L., and M. E. Miller (1986) *The Blood of Kings: Dynasty and Ritual in Maya Art*. Kimbell Art Museum, Fort Worth.

Spinden, H. (1928) *Ancient Civilizations of Mexico and Central America*. American Museum of Natural History, New York.

Steward, F. H. (1977) *Fundamentals of Age-Group Systems*. Academic Press, New York.

Thomson, C. (1987) Chalcatzingo Jade and Fine Stone Objects. In *Ancient Chalcatzingo*, edited by D. C. Grove, pp. 295–304. University of Texas Press, Austin.

Turner, V. (1969) *The Ritual Process: Structure and Anti-Structure*. Aldine, Chicago.

Vaillant, G. C. (1930) *Excavations at Zacatenco*. Anthropological Papers Vol. 32, Pt. 1. American Museum of Natural History, New York.

—— (1931) *Excavations at Ticoman*. Anthropological Papers Vol. 32, Pt. 2. American Museum of Natural History, New York.

—— (1935) *Excavations at El Arbolillo*. Anthropological Papers Vol. 35, No. 2. American Museum of Natural History, New York.

Van Gennep, A. (1960) *The Rites of Passage*. University of Chicago Press, Chicago.

Vargas, L. A. (1971) *Pigmentation cutanée et cycle menstruel*. Unpublished PhD dissertation, La Faculté des Sciences de Paris, Paris.

Weiant, C. W. (1943) *An Introduction to the Ceramics of Tres Zapotes, Veracruz, Mexico*. Bulletin No. 139. Bureau of American Ethnology, Smithsonian Institution, Washington, DC.

Wolf, E. R. (1966) *Peasants*. Prentice-Hall, Englewood Cliffs, New Jersey.

—— (1990) Distinguished Lecture: Facing Power. *American Anthropologist* 92: 586–596.

PART VI

Power and social hierarchies

INTRODUCTION

In the 1970s, feminists turned to anthropologists for answers to some basic questions: what accounts for women's oppression? Is male dominance a universal? Do women have lower status in all societies or just certain kinds? Early on, anthropologists recognized that hunter-gatherers tend to have egalitarian social systems, including equality between men and women. Sedentary agriculturalists, in contrast, tend to be characterized by gender hierarchies, although the status of women varies tremendously. Did gender hierarchy that accords lower status to women arise with the beginnings of agriculture, with the rise of the state, or was it always there? Given that women and men are in some ways biologically different, does difference always lead to hierarchy; that is, to differences in prestige, autonomy, or power? A debate emerged between those who followed Engels in situating the oppression of women in the rise of state-level societies (for example, Eleanor Leacock, Karen Sacks, and Christine Gailey), and those who argued that gender asymmetry favoring men was a human universal (for example, Sherry Ortner, Michelle Rosaldo, and Louise Lamphere). In this second view, women's oppression was born in the early emergence of a constrained domestic sphere for women that contrasted with men's public sphere. Some argue that although women exercise authority within the domestic sphere, they ultimately lose power through separation then domination by the more encompassing domain of men. Archaeology is uniquely able to address these issues with its long-term perspective, but as noted by Conkey and Gero, archaeologists joined the anthropological debates about gender only recently.

By the time archaeologists got involved in gender studies, other anthropologists (including most of those involved in the original debate) had for the most part given up questions about origins and universals. Relative ranking of men and women is difficult to assess, because dominance, status, and power are all multidimensional. Differential access to food, sex, wealth, esoteric knowledge, political office, and freedom of movement may vary independently of one another. Societies may place different values on such factors. Euro-americans value political power highly, for example, but in some societies, political office is considered a burden rather than a privilege. Anthropologists now examine a multiplicity of questions about "gender hegemonies" – the dominant gender relations in a society, which can be characterized by gender complementarity and gender parallelism as well as hierarchy. Some have proposed the term "heterarchy" to describe societies with multiple realms of status and power. Archaeologist Janet Levy (1995), for example, argues that heterarchy based on ritual power is apparent in Danish Bronze Age hoards and burials. Both men and women had access to such power and status, but women's rituals emphasized deposits of artifacts in watery places, perhaps referencing fertility, while men were involved in ritual processions and combat. At the same time, settlement evidence suggests a relatively egalitarian society. Diversity, ambiguity, and fluctuation, rather than rigid rankings by gender and wealth, apparently characterized interpersonal relationships in this culture.

Ethnohistorian Irene Silverblatt (1987, 1991b) describes a *parallel* descent, inheritance, ritual, and status system for the Inca, prior to the Spanish Conquest. Elite women exercised power and authority in their domain, as elite men did in theirs. Many researchers have questioned the assumption that states always weaken kin groups, and focus on historical trajectories of change that lead to profound differences among complex societies in different parts of the world. In addition, the explicit study of resistance to gender hegemonies is emerging. For example, Elizabeth Brumfiel studied ceramic figurines in the Basin of Mexico made at the time of Aztec expansion. She finds that "The striking differences between official and popular images of the female subject suggest that hinterland populations did not accept the elite ideology. In fact, the popular images provide evidence of an ideology of resistance that sharply contested the official gender ideology of the state" (Brumfiel 1996:155). In addition, several authors have documented clashes between the gender systems of Native Americans and Spanish colonists (McEwan 1992, Silverblatt 1987, Trocolli 1992). No situation better demonstrates the fact that sex and gender are culturally constructed than circumstances like these, where what is thought be the "natural order of things" collides with another view of natural order. These studies, and others, contribute to more complicated and more informative understandings of power and hierarchy.

In "Skeletal Evidence for Sex Roles and Gender Hierarchies in Prehistory" (chapter 16), Mark Cohen and Sharon Bennett examine biological evidence for differences between males and females in health, nutrition, and work load. Sarah Nelson, in chapter 17, "Gender Hierarchy and the Queens of Silla," traces the history of the debate about gender hierarchies and the rise of the state. She demonstrates that when kinship is an important part of status differentiation, women may hold positions of prestige and power. Liv Helga Dommasnes' "Women, Kinship, and the Basis of Power in the Norwegian Viking Age" (chapter 18) provides a detailed case study of women in strong kin groups within a stratified society maintaining a high degree of economic autonomy.

■ ■ ■

Further reading

Bender, Barbara (1989)
Brumfiel, Elizabeth M. (1991)
—— (1996)
Cucchiari, Salvatore (1981)
Lesko, Barbara S. (ed.) (1989)

Levy, Janet E. (1995)
McEwan, Bonnie G. (1992)
Nash, June (1978)
Ortner, Sherry B. (1978)
—— (1996)
Stalsberg, Ann (1991)
Silverblatt, Irene (1987)
—— (1991a)
—— (1991b)
Trocolli, Ruth (1992)

■ ■ ■

References

Bender, Barbara (1989) "The Roots of Inequality," in D. Miller, M. Rowlands, and C. Tilley (eds) *Domination and Resistance*, London: Unwin Hyman, pp. 83–95.

Brumfiel, Elizabeth M. (1991) "Weaving and Cooking: Women's Production in Aztec Mexico," in J. M. Gero and M. W. Conkey (eds) *Engendering Archaeology: Women and Prehistory*, Oxford: Basil Blackwell, pp. 224–251.

—— (1996) "Figurines and the Aztec State: Testing the Effectiveness of Ideological Domination," in R. P. Wright (ed.) *Gender and Archaeology*, Philadelphia: University of Pennsylvania Press, pp. 143–166.

Cucchiari, Salvatore (1981) "The Gender Revolution and the Transition from Bisexual Horde to Patrilocal Band: The Origins of Gender Hierarchy," in S. B. Ortner and H. Whitehead (eds), *Sexual Meanings: The Cultural Construction of Gender and Sexuality*, Cambridge: Cambridge University Press, pp. 21–79.

Lesko, Barbara S. (ed.) (1989) *Women's Earliest Records from Ancient Egypt and Western Asia*, Proceedings of the Conference on Women in the Ancient Near East, Brown University, Providence, Rhode Island. Atlanta, Georgia: Scholars Press.

Levy, Janet E. (1995) "Heterarchy in Bronze Age Denmark: Settlement Pattern, Gender, and Ritual," in R. M. Ehrenreich, C. L. Crumley and J. E. Levy (eds) *Heterarchy and the Analysis of Complex Societies*, Archeological Papers of the American Anthropological Association Number 6, Washington, DC: American Anthropological Association, pp. 41–53.

McEwan, Bonnie G. (1992) "The Archaeology of Women in the Spanish New World," *Historical Archaeology* 25(4):33–41.

Nash, June (1978) "The Aztecs and the Ideology of Male Dominance," *The Journal of Women in Culture and Society* 4:21:349–362.

Ortner, Sherry B. (1978) "The Virgin and the State," *Feminist Studies* 45(3):19–35 (also reprinted in *Making Gender*, below).

——(1996) "Gender Hegemonies," in S. B. Ortner *Making Gender: The Politics and Erotics of Culture*, Boston: Beacon Press, pp. 139–172.

Stalsberg, Ann (1991) "Women as Actors in North European Viking Age Trade," in R. Samson (ed.) *Social Approaches to Viking Studies*, Glasgow: Cruithne Press, pp. 76–84.

Silverblatt, Irene (1987) *Moon, Sun, and Witches: Gender Ideologies and Class in Inca and Colonial Peru*. Philadelphia: University of Pennsylvania Press.

——(1991a) "Women in States," *Annual Review of Anthropology* 17:427–460.

——(1991b) "Interpreting Women in States: New Feminist Ethnohistories," in M. DiLeonardo (ed.) *Gender at the Crossroads of Knowledge: Feminist Anthropology in the Postmodern Era*, Berkeley and Los Angeles: University of California Press, pp. 140–171.

Trocolli, Ruth (1992) "Colonization and Women's Production: The Timucua of Florida," in C. Claassen (ed.) *Exploring Gender Through Archaeology: Selected Papers of the 1991 Boone Conference*, Madison, Wisconsin: Prehistory Press, pp. 95–102.

SKELETAL EVIDENCE FOR SEX ROLES AND GENDER HIERARCHIES IN PREHISTORY

Mark Nathan Cohen and Sharon Bennett

Comparisons among human societies provide recognition of cross-cultural regularities in the relationship between gender roles or gender hierarchies and other aspects of society such as the mode of production (see review articles by Lamphere 1977; Quinn 1977; Rapp 1979; Atkinson 1982; Mukhopadhyay and Higgins 1988). Such studies enable us to move outside the cultural stereotypes of our own society, to see something of the range of cultural variations on gender themes, and to begin to discern the degree to which gender differences are grounded in biology or defined by cultural roles.

Despite the importance of these contributions, cross-cultural studies on contemporary human groups are limited in several respects. Contemporary societies represent only a fraction of the cultural variations with which human beings have experimented; moreover by the time they are witnessed by contemporary observers such societies are often heavily influenced by participation in the world market or by Western values and role expectations (Leacock 1978; Anderson 1985). At least until 1970, such societies have been represented to anthropologists primarily by male informants and witnessed and interpreted primarily by male Western observers who not only were accustomed to visualizing relations between the sexes from a male perspective but were often excluded in the field from areas of female activity and power. Rosaldo (1980) has argued that modern ethnographers (of either sex), who come from a culture in which attention focuses on male activities, simply have not known what questions to ask about women. Sacks (1976) warns that observers familiar with state-level societies may be blind to sexual equality in other contexts.

The problem is further complicated by the fact that the meaning of the concept of "gender hierarchy" is diffuse, embracing a number of measures including prestige, power, access to and control of economic goods, and "gender ideology" which are not necessarily congruent with one another (see chapter 17 by Nelson, this volume). Measurement problems abound. As Rapp (1979) and Lamphere (1977) point out, we do not readily distinguish gender "asymmetry," gender "complementarity," and gender "subjugation." We lack consistent measures of status or of hierarchy which are valid across cultures and can be applied in a comparative manner from case to case.

The appeal to archaeological information can help resolve some of these problems. Archaeological samples expand the range of cultures which can be considered, and they help to guarantee that we witness cultures which are uninfluenced by Western values. Skeletons of prehistoric individuals provide some of the most useful archaeological data for gender studies. Well-preserved adult skeletons can be sexed with an accuracy in excess of 95 per cent, and even fragmentary human remains can often be sexed with an accuracy of 85 per cent or more (Buikstra and Mielke 1985). Sex is more difficult to determine in children's skeletons, but since the adult skeleton records childhood events in a number of ways it is theoretically possible, even in the absence of associated artifacts, to make significant statements about sex-related differences in the experience of childhood. Furthermore, skeletal data are comparatively immune to distortion by the gender-role expectations of the observer, since much of the analysis can be done in testing procedures that are sex-blind (the known sex of the skeleton can be withheld from individuals making other analyses).

Information on gender roles and hierarchies provided by the sketetal record can be acquired in two ways. The first is to look at the design and construction of tombs and cemeteries as overt clues to social status of the individuals studied (see chapter 17). Differences in the quality of artifacts accompanying individuals in death, in the construction of tombs, or in the spatial placement of tombs afford clues to the overt social rules which govern hierarchies of all kinds including gender hierarchy. Such patterns of burial have been used not only to identify upper-class individuals and royalty but also – in combination with types of skeletal analysis described below – to determine whether status is ascribed or achieved, whether or not high status is associated with genetic or ethnic distinctions, and whether it results in differential access to basic resources. Patterning of skeletons in cemeteries along with studies of genetic traits in the skeleton may even reveal which sex leaves home at marriage (Haviland 1967; Swedlund and Armelagos 1976; Chapman, Kinnes, and Randsborg 1981; Buikstra 1976, 1984; Goldstein 1976; Blakely and Beck 1982; Koch 1983; Cook 1984; Konigsberg 1986, 1987).

In this chapter, we bypass the wealth of information available from spatial and contextual analysis of burial patterns and focus instead on analysis of the skeletons themselves, noting techniques summarized by various authorities (Brothwell 1981; Steinbock 1976; Ubelaker 1978; Ortner and Putschar 1981; Buikstra and Cook

1980; Huss-Ashmore *et al.* 1982; Cohen and Armelagos 1984; Gilbert and Mielke 1985). Information in large quantity from skeletal analysis is relatively new and is less familiar and intuitively less accessible to non-specialists than burial data. Moreover, the skeletal information is directly revealing of health, nutrition, activity, physical stress or workload, risk, and mortality – aspects of status and hierarchy which analysis of formal and overt social markers may miss. At the same time, the skeletal data may challenge conclusions about hierarchy derived from more symbolic modes of analysis. Analysis of skeletons provides data about biological well-being which can be objectively measured and compared across cultures, thus bypassing the problem of definition and comparability that plagues studies of gender hierarchy cross-culturally. The same point must also be put in a more negative way, however. Measures of health and activity may not provide direct clues to "power" or "authority" or other more symbolic aspects of hierarchy. At the very least, however, the juxtaposition of explicit measures of health and activity with other measures of hierarchy and status raises issues about the definition of the latter.

The major problem or limitation of skeletal data is that few such data are yet available. Quantitative or population-based work in paleopathology that has been done involves samples unevenly distributed in time and space. There is a particular paucity of samples from mobile hunter-gatherers who often do not collect their dead in a single location. Nevertheless, even the available data are richly indicative of gender hierarchies in the distant past.

Applications of skeletal data to gender issues

This chapter presents a "sampler," based on a review of the literature, of applications of skeletal analysis to issues of gender inequality. We divide the presentation into seven sections: physical injury, trauma, and violence; physical stress and workload; infection and disease; nutrition; childhood stress; reproduction; and mortality. Examples are provided for prehistoric populations as well as for some twentieth-century groups.

Physical injuries, trauma, and violence

Paleopathologists can assess the nature of physical health risks experienced by members of each sex through the analysis of wounds, fractures, and dislocations observable in skeletal populations. Such analysis provides a picture of the overall frequency of trauma, its distribution by age and sex, and the pattern of limbs at risk. In many cases the cause of injury can be determined and the distinction made between accidental injury and interpersonal violence. As a result, hypotheses about the distribution of gender-related violence can theoretically be tested. For example, an analysis of the large American Indian population from the Late Woodland Libben site (*c* AD 800–1100) in Ohio, revealed a high incidence of fractures – 45 per cent of skeletons had at least one. But most fractures appeared to have resulted from accidents, predominantly falls. The authors discovered no significant sex-related differences in the distribution of fractures, except that males were more likely to have fractured a femur than were females. Fractures were extremely rare among small children. Apparently neither domestic violence nor traumatic child abuse was characteristic of the culture. The incidence of fractures was instead a simple function of age or years at risk, suggesting that fracture was a random risk not associated with specific activities of different age groups.

The early colonial period Mayan population of Tipu, comprising about 600 individuals who died in the sixteenth and early seventeenth centuries, displays a much lower rate of trauma; fewer than 10 per cent of individuals display a fracture (Armstrong 1985). Here, too, most traumas appear to be accidental in origin and random in distribution through the population, although there are two clear cases of violence directed toward children. In contrast, Eisenberg (1986), working with a prehistoric Mississippian period American Indian population from the Averbuch site (AD 1275–1400), suggests that most traumas were intentionally inflicted and that traumas show a different age distribution and a different skeletal distribution in males and females. Swedlund and Armelagos (1976) report a disproportionate increase in fractured bones in female skeletons dating to the Christian period (after AD 550) in Nubia which they consider indicative of the comparatively low status of women at the time.

These isolated examples tell us little about the factors which govern the frequency of pathology. Until the examples become far more numerous, a more promising approach is the comparative analysis of sequential populations at one archaeological site or a collection of closely related sites in the same area. Ideally such comparisons enable us to evaluate changes in sex roles and gender status, associated with defined changes in economy or politics, with other aspects of culture held relatively constant. Cohen and Armelagos (1984) recently collected studies on the changes in skeletal pathology in archaeological series spanning the transition from hunting and gathering to intensive farming in different parts of the world in an attempt to gain a cross-cultural perspective on the impact of farming on human health. Few of the studies, however, or other sources of data, provide good comparative, quantitative evidence on the frequency of trauma, and trauma data differentiated by sex are even more unusual.

In one case, Goodman et al. (1984) analyzed the archaeological sequence from the Dickson Mounds site in Illinois (AD 950–1300) where the frequency of fractures in adults increased as a hunting and gathering population adopted and intensified its agriculture and became increasingly involved in a larger political network. The trend toward increasing trauma was more pronounced for adult males, suggesting that the new economic/political regime intensified physical risk for men more than for women. Similarly, Perzigian, Tench, and Braun (1984) discovered an increase in intentional trauma to males, presumably due to an increase in warfare, during the intensive agricultural Fort Ancient period in Ohio (after c AD 1000).

Physical stress and workload

Paleopathologists can assess the quality and quantity of the physical stress imposed on individuals by different lifestyles and thus assess the distribution of the workload by sex. The skeleton provides two major clues to physical stress and workload: degenerative arthritis (Jurmain 1977; Steinbock 1976) and the robusticity of the skeleton (Larsen 1984). Degenerative arthritis or degenerative joint disease (DJD), which reflects the wear on particular joints, is displayed either as the polishing of joint surfaces through friction or as the development of extra bony growths on joint margins. Robusticity reflects the response of bone shafts to biomechanical stress as well as the enlargement of muscle attachment areas and joint surfaces associated with use. The pattern of either DJD or robusticity in the skeleton can provide clues to the activities in which individuals engaged; and quantitative changes in frequency and severity of DJD can provide clues to changing distribution of the workload.

In their analysis of twentieth-century black Americans from Arkansas, Rose and co-workers (1985) discovered markedly high rates of arthritis for adults of both sexes, compared even to prehistoric populations with which they had worked. They suggest that the pattern of work was different for the two sexes: men were likely to display arthritis of the long bones, while women seem to have made particularly strenuous use of their hands. At the prehistoric Mississippian period Averbuch site in Tennessee, American Indian males had much higher rates of arthritis than females as well as a higher frequency of back injuries (Eisenberg 1986).

The attempt by Cohen and Armelagos (1984) to establish patterns of change in physical stress and workload associated with the origins of agriculture and thus to assess theories about the evolution of human workload incorporates only a few studies with explicit reference to gender-specific patterns. Goodman et al. (1984) report that at Dickson Mounds both DJD and osteophytosis (arthritic changes in the spine) increased through time, suggesting an increase in physical stress with the adoption of agriculture, and they note that these forms of arthritis, like trauma, displayed more severe increase for males than for females. This finding suggests that it was primarily males at this site who bore the brunt of the increased workload. Cassidy (1984), however, contrasting hunter-gatherers with later farmers in Kentucky (the Archaic period Indian Knoll population, c 2500 BC, and the Mississippian period Hardin Village site, c AD 1550) found that vertebral arthritis was less pronounced for men in the later group, suggesting that they enjoyed a reduced workload. But the same condition increased or remained steady, depending on the age of individuals, among women. Arthritis of the joints also increased more consistently among women than among men with the adoption of agriculture. In this population farming seems to have resulted in a significant redistribution of the workload by sex.

Cook (1984) also reports changing patterns of arthritis with the adoption of agriculture in Illinois (a sequence of populations from 6000 BC to AD 1200).

Arthritis became more severe in women in the later populations, but there was no change in the pattern of arthritis in the skeleton. Men displayed no increase in the severity of arthritis, but displayed a change in the pattern of arthritic joints. The evidence suggests that women may have experienced an intensification of their existing activity pattern, men a change in activities. Hamilton (1982), cited by Cook (1984), reports a disproportionate increase in deltoid tuberosity (an area of muscle attachment on the upper arm) in women associated with the intensification of food production in these same populations. Similarly, Bridges (1982, 1983), working with populations from Alabama spanning roughly the same periods and the same economic transition, found robusticity to increase through time particularly in female skeletons. Larsen (1984) reports that in Georgia arthritis was reduced after the adoption of agriculture (c AD 1150), but the greater reduction in arthritis occurred among male skeletons.

Infection and disease

Paleopathologists can assess patterns of infection in prehistoric populations. Most analysis of infection deals with undifferentiated infection – infection of unspecified etiology – which is referred to as periostitis when it afflicts only the surface of the bone or as osteomyelitis when it invades the bone cortex. The most frequent causes of such infection are common staphylococcus and streptococcus bacteria. In addition, several diseases, most notably treponemal infection (yaws and/or syphilis) and tuberculosis can be diagnosed specifically in the skeleton (Steinbock 1976; Ortner and Putschar 1981). When mummies are available for analysis a much larger range of specific infections can be identified. Unfortunately, mummified specimens – although they may enable us to make comparisons of health among sequential populations in some specific locations (see, for example, Allison 1984) – are not yet common enough to be useful for identifying cross-cultural patterns.

The relationship between patterns of infection and gender hierarchy is less obvious than with other classes of pathology. The distribution of an infectious agent within a population is less subject to conscious or even unconscious cultural control than are other forms of stress, so the link between disease distribution and cultural patterns may not be self-evident. As with other types of pathology some attention must also be paid to possible sex differences in natural susceptibility to specific diseases as well as differences in behavior. A number of known diseases are associated with specific human activities and their distribution is therefore a good index of the sexual division of labor. For example, a number of human diseases, such as toxoplasmosis and tularemia, are associated with handling animals or meat. Unfortunately, few of these diseases leave diagnostic scars on the skeleton.

Rates of infection, however, may tell something else about the sexual division of labor. There is a clear positive association between rates of infection and sedentism and/or large population aggregates (Cohen and Armelagos 1984). To the extent that their activities were more domestic, hence more closely tied to sedentary living, members of one sex might well display higher rates of "village" diseases. There is evidence from skeletal populations for sex-differentiated rates of infection although as yet the meaning of most of these data is not clear. For example, men were significantly more infection prone than women in the agricultural Fort Ancient population from Kentucky (Cassidy 1984). In Georgia, females experienced a slightly greater increase in frequency of infection than did males with the adoption of agriculture – a pattern which suggests that women were more sedentary than men in the new economy (Larsen 1984).

Nutrition

Paleopathologists and bone chemists can assess the quality and quantity of the nutrition available to individuals. Several specific vitamin and mineral deficiencies can be at least tentatively identified, including shortage of iron (anemia), zinc (anemia), calcium (poor bone mineralization), vitamin C (scurvy), and vitamin D (rickets) (see Steinbock 1976; Ortner and Putschar 1981). Protein calorie malnutrition is evident in bone cortical area and bone remodeling (Martin, Goodman, and Armelagos 1985). In addition a number of different aspects of the skeleton – stature and robusticity of the skeleton, diameter of the pelvic inlet, and the height of the base of the cranium – provide clues to the overall adequacy of nutrition, particularly the adequacy of protein and calorie intake (Angel 1984).

Assessing sex-related differences in nutrient intake through skeletal analysis can be tricky. We know on the one hand that the two sexes differ in some degree in their utilization of nutrients: for example, women lose more iron than men. Similarly, there is clearly sexual dimorphism in bone cortical maintenance based on demand for calcium through pregnancy and lactation, and on levels of estrogen, but we do not know to what extent those differences are universal and constant in a quantitative sense across cultures.

It is not surprising that porotic hyperostosis and cribra orbitalia, the skeletal symptoms of anemia, are often more common in adult female than male skeletons just as anemia is more common in contemporary women than men. For example, 13 per cent of adult women but only 5 per cent of adult males in an early historic period population from British Columbia display cribra orbitalia (Cybulski 1977). Signs of anemia are more common in female skeletons than male skeletons in prehistoric cultures in Iran (Rathbun 1984). What is surprising is that male/female differences are often not as pronounced as contemporary clinical experience would suggest. Walker (1985), for example, finds no significant differences between the sexes in prehistoric populations from the American Southwest. Stuart-Macadam (1985), citing the rather small difference between the sexes in most prehistoric populations, argues that the visible scars may be primarily the unremodeled remains of childhood malnutrition.

It is also difficult to determine whether such differences as do occur reflect the better quality of the male (adult or child) diet, the greater susceptibility of women to iron loss, or even different experience with parasites since parasitization of one form or another can be an important factor in the observed anemias. Our best clues, therefore, will lie not so much in the uncorrected quantitative comparison of male and female skeletons within a particular population, but in an assessment of changes in sex-related differences which occur as cultures change. In assessing the pattern of nutritional changes associated with the transition from hunting and gathering to agriculture in various parts of the world, Cohen and Armelagos (1984) demonstrated that various skeletal indicators most commonly suggested a decline in nutrition as a concomitant of incipient or intensified agriculture. The frequency of anemia increased almost universally. Where reported, bone cortical area often declined at least temporarily. And retarded growth in childhood became more common.

Where the data are appropriately broken down, sex-related differences in nutrition are often apparent as are sex-specific trends in the quality of nutrition over time. Cassidy (1984) reports that anemia was more pronounced in the agricultural Fort Ancient population in Kentucky than in an earlier hunting and gathering group, but symptoms of anemia were more pronounced in adult women than in adult men during the later period, suggesting that women (or perhaps female children?) had suffered a disproportionate decline in the quality of the diet. Martin et al. (1984), reporting on the archaeological sequence from Nubia, note that young females in agricultural societies displayed nutritional problems evidenced by pathological bone loss to a degree which they considered not simply a function of aging. Smith and co-workers (1984) found premature osteoporosis in populations in the Levant, particularly concentrated among women, but also particularly concentrated among women of later (Roman and Arab) periods. Early paleolithic and mesolithic populations in the Levant showed no such pattern of bone loss or showed significantly less loss. Apparently changes in diet and/or fertility associated with later agricultural economies exerted a disproportionately negative effect on the nutritional status of women in this part of the world.

Dental caries rates also provide a clue to changes in diet. Caries are rare in early human populations and increase almost universally with the adoption of agriculture and the preparation of soft sticky foods (Turner 1979; Powell 1985). The sexes may be affected unequally by the transition because they obtain a different dietary balance. Larsen (1983, 1984) reports that among Indians in Georgia women suffered a greater increase in dental caries than men as a result of the adoption of agriculture, a pattern which he believes represents economic and dietary specializations similar to those reported for some ethnographic groups.

The proportions of meat and vegetables, and of seafood in the diet can also be assessed through trace element analysis, particularly the analysis of strontium and the ratio of strontium to calcium, and the analysis of stable isotopes, particularly those of carbon and nitrogen (see Sillen and Kavanaugh 1982; Norr 1984; Nelson et al. 1986; Klepinger 1984; Gilbert 1985; Schoeninger 1979, 1982). Several studies have attempted to use strontium analysis to suggest gender differences in access to meat — roughly speaking, a high strontium content translates as a low meat diet, other things being equal. Schoeninger (1979) suggests that the higher strontium levels of women in a prehistoric Mesoamerican population indicate women's low status and low meat consumption. Similarly Angel (1984) reports that at the bronze age Karatas site in Greece women had lower zinc levels than men which might indicate lower meat intake. It has now been recognized, however (by Schoeninger herself among others; see also Gilbert 1985), that we must first factor-out sex differences in skeletal utilization of strontium and perhaps other elements. Women may store more strontium than men in their skeletons on the same diet. Pregnant and lactating women screen their infants from normal strontium intake, storing the excess in their own skeletons. So, absolute differences in levels of strontium or other trace elements between men and women may not be socially meaningful.

In the terminal Woodland period in the Illinois Valley (AD 800–1000), during the transition to agriculture, strontium analysis shows a greater sex differential than in earlier periods, possibly reflecting a relative decline in women's access to animal protein (Buikstra 1984; Lambert, Szpunar, and Buikstra 1977). Conversely, at Dickson Mounds (referred to above) the difference in trace element content between male and female skeletons declined through time suggesting that the adoption of agriculture tended to make male and female diets more equal (Gilbert 1985).

Changes in body size, particularly in stature, may be indicative of changes in nutrition, although changes in activity patterns may also be implicated. Changes in sexual dimorphism – the ratio of average male to average female dimension – provide clues to the relative nutrition, and activity patterns, of the two sexes.

Haviland (1967) reported some years ago that Mayan stature declined through the Classic period of Maya civilization, a pattern that has been observed also by Saul (1972) and Nickens (1976). Declining nutrition is implicated, but Haviland also noted that female stature was less affected than male stature by the trend.

Frayer (1980, 1981) and Mieklejohn et al. (1984) document a decline in sexual dimorphism associated with declining stature for both sexes during the European mesolithic period. This trend may be indicative of a decline in nutrition which had a greater impact on men than on women. Frayer, however, interprets this pattern as reflecting declining physical demands on the male with the decline of big game hunting. He argues that the greater similarity of male and female dimensions indicates the increasing similarity of their workloads.

Angel (1984) also reports a decline in stature from the paleolithic through the neolithic periods in the region of the Mediterranean, but one shared by both sexes. Combining stature with other measures, Angel suggests that the trend reflected a decline in nutrition. Smith, Bar-Yosef, and Sillen (1984) found that Levantine populations had similar percentage dimorphism throughout the sequence, except that they displayed slightly lower dimorphism in the Natufian terminal hunting and gathering phase, now thought to be a period of nutritional stress, and a time of very short stature for both sexes. In Ecuador there were parallel trends in stature for the two sexes through the known archaeological sequence (Ubelaker 1984). On the other hand, in Nubia, females showed less variation over time in femur length (an estimator of stature) than did males (Martin *et al.* 1984). In the Caddoan region of the south-central United States the adoption of agriculture resulted in increased size (measured on the head of femur) for both males and females – but females in particular increased dramatically in size, suggesting that they participated disproportionately in an improvement in nutrition which accompanied the transition (Rose *et al.* 1984). Conversely, in the Mississippi Valley, sexual dimorphism increased with the origins of agriculture because both males and females got smaller but women decreased in size more dramatically than men. In the latter case, not only did nutrition apparently decline but women's share in available nutrients also was reduced. In Georgia, both sexes became smaller with the adoption of agriculture, but females showed the greater size reduction (Larsen 1981, 1984). Larsen suggests that there was a greater reduction in female workload with the adoption of agriculture as noted above, but also a relative as well as absolute decline in women's access to protein. Conversely, Bridges (1985 cited in Frayer and Wolpoff 1985) reports that sexual dimorphism declined over the transition to agriculture in Alabama because female body size increased more than male as a function of a greater increase in their workload.

Childhood stress episodes

Paleopathologists can provide a quantitative assessment of episodes of stress in childhood. The human skeleton records episodes of stress or growth disturbances during the growth period of the child in two major ways: in the formation of Harris lines in the shafts of long bones (lines of high bone density that appear as opaque lines in radiographs) and in macroscopic or microscopic lines of irregular enamel formation in teeth referred to as enamel hypoplasia and Wilson bands. Harris lines are thought to reflect relatively transient stress episodes while macroscopic hypoplasia are considered to represent more severe or long-lasting stresses (Martin, Goodman, and Amelagos 1985). Of the two indicators, Harris lines are the more controversial since many authorities consider them an indication of the ability to recover from stress rather than of the frequency of stress *per se* (Murchison, Owsley, and Riopelle 1983; Cohen and Armelagos 1984). Defects of tooth enamel are now widely used as indicators of comparative stress frequency. Because both Harris lines and enamel defects occur at age-specific positions on bones and teeth, the pattern of defects can be used to determine both the age at which stress occurs and the time-pattern of stresses. It is possible, for example, to distinguish between annual, seasonal, and irregular stresses (Cassidy 1984; Goodman *et al.* 1984). Because these indicators, particularly those in teeth, survive into adulthood in the skeleton it is possible to identify patterns of childhood stress in individuals whose sex can be determined. As a result it is possible to identify sex-specific rates of stress or sex-related differences in the age distribution of stresses.

Danforth (1988) reports that microscopic dental defects of teeth (Wilson bands) are far more common among males than females in the Tipu colonial period Mayan population. In the Late Woodland Libben population from Ohio (referred to above) males and females typically display different ages of formation of Wilson bands which are tentatively interpreted as indicative of different weaning patterns for male and female children (Rose, Boyd, and Condon 1981; Rose, Condon, and Goodman 1985).

The interpretation of sex differences, however, is complicated by the possibility that the sexes may be inherently different either in the degree to which the body buffers stress episodes or in the manner in which stress is recorded. Some authorities consider the female body to be more resilient (less prone to growth disruption) than the male body. As a result, there is some tendency to view lower stress rates in females as natural, and lower stress rates in males as a reflection of disproportionate cultural protection to male children. It is also possible that the sexes differ in the periods of growth during which they are more or less resilient. Clearly much more work is needed before we can establish the "natural" background pattern of sex differences in stress markers against which culturally induced patterns of stress can be measured. As with other indicators already discussed, absolute differences between the sexes for these stress markers in any one culture are less important than evidence of changes in relative frequency of stress.

The two indicators commonly yield conflicting patterns when hunter-gatherers are compared with farmers in any one region (Cohen and Armelagos 1984). Harris lines were often more common in hunter-gatherers; enamel hypoplasia and Wilson bands were almost universally more common in farming populations. Cohen and Armelagos conclude (following a suggestion in Cassidy 1984) that the pattern might be interpreted as showing that the neolithic revolution represented a trade off of one kind of stress for another, such as bouts of seasonal hunger traded for periodic starvation and epidemics. They also note that, since Harris lines denote healthy recovery rather than stress *per se*, the two indicators together might point to a greater frequency of stress among farmers, better recovery from stress among hunter-gatherers, in accordance with other signs that hunter-gatherers were comparatively well nourished.

Unfortunately, few studies have differentiated the data by sex. Goodman *et al.* (1984) do report differences in the frequency of Harris lines by sex at Dickson Mounds, and they also found differences between the sexes in the age distribution of lines. Females were commonly more stressed during the adolescent growth spurt; males more often in ages one to seven years. Goodman, Armelagos, and Rose (1980) report that women in the earliest hunting and gathering population at Dickson Mounds showed more enamel hypoplasia than men although rates of hypoplasia for the two sexes were equal in the later Mississippian farming population at the site. They suggest that male children received preferential treatment in the earlier population but not in the later. Cook (1984) found that Harris lines showed different trends in the two sexes, associated with the transition from hunting and gathering to agriculture in Illinois, suggesting that the transition had very different effects on the health of male and female children. Cook also discovered that microscopic dental indicators of stress occurred with similar frequency in the two sexes in the earlier Woodland period hunting and gathering population but were significantly more frequent in men than in women during the later Mississippian period farming population. This result suggests a relative decline in the protection afforded male children at the later site.

In the burials of children, and particularly those skeletons retaining their decid-uous teeth, it is possible to identify periods of stress which occurred *in utero* or in the first few months of life, during which time nursing would have been nearly universal in prehistoric cultures. Such stress markers provide indirect evidence about maternal health and nutrition. Cassidy (1984), for example, reports that children in the agricultural Fort Ancient sample (but not in her Archaic hunter and gath-erer sample) displayed significant numbers of enamel defects of deciduous teeth suggesting severe stress both *in utero* and during the first months of life – a pattern which may represent severe maternal malnutrition in the later population. Working with prehistoric populations from Ohio, Sciulli (1977) has also found more enamel defects of deciduous teeth in agricultural groups than in hunter-gatherer groups. Storey (1985), reporting on the population from one ward of Teotihuacan, the urban metropolis in prehistoric Mesoamerica, similarly has identified a high frequency of deciduous tooth enamel hypoplasia, as well as of still birth, late fetal death, and late fetal growth retardation (bones whose lengths are below expecta-tions based on aging the infant by the development of its teeth). She suggests this pattern is indicative of severe maternal malnutrition.

Reproduction

Paleopathology offers a number of approaches to identifying changes in parity and maternal behavior in prehistory. This work bears on the interpretation of the inter-action between reproductive behavior and gender hierarchies. It may be possible to estimate directly the number of children that a given woman has borne or at least the number of pregnancies that she has experienced by identifying and quan-tifying "parturition scars" on the pelvis (Angel 1969, 1971, 1984). The method is controversial and not widely accepted (Buikstra and Mielke 1985; Green, Suchey, and Gokhale 1979). Since, as discussed below, the quantitative representation of children in prehistoric cemeteries is also suspect, attempts to determine changing rates of fertility directly have proved unsatisfactory. Charles *et al.* (1987) have proposed that it may be possible to identify the effects of pregnancy on annular rings of tooth cementum which are now known to form throughout life – a tech-nique which, if successful, may permit us to identify individual patterns of reproduction including an individual's age at first pregnancy, number of pregnan-cies, and interval between pregnancies.

Sillen (Sillen and Smith 1984) has pioneered a method of estimating the average age of weaning or, more precisely, the average age of cereal or vegetable food supplementation of children's diets in prehistoric populations. The method is based on the fact that breast milk is very low in strontium content, cereals very high. Sillen suggests that once correction is made for changes in the growing child's own systemic discrimination against absorption and deposition of strontium, this difference in diet can be recognized. Identification of the age at which a shift in levels of strontium occurs when a number of infants in a cemetery are compared can provide an estimate of the average age of supplementation in a population. This technique potentially can help sort out the controversy surrounding interpretation of the impact of the neolithic revolution on nursing patterns and fertility (Lee 1980) and can also bear on the hypotheses of Kolata (1974) and Draper (1975) relating nursing and fertility to men's workload and women's status.

We are currently working on a technique to evaluate changes in strontium content along the axis of growth of a single tooth which should permit us to identify the age of weaning (Cohen and Bennett 1987). Since this technique can be applied to adult teeth, whose formation spans the range of probable weaning ages, it should be possible to determine whether male and female infants were treated differently in any given population.

Mortality

The most controversial area of skeletal analysis concerns the determination of age at death and the construction of mortality profiles and other descriptive statistics about mortality experience. Everyone involved in skeletal analysis recognizes that cemetery populations may not be complete or representative samples of the living population from which they have been culled. All agree that the methods of determining the age at death, particularly among adults, are imprecise, although whether the imprecision is sufficient to call the results into question is a matter of debate (Van Gerven and Armelagos 1983; Bocquet-Appel and Masset 1982, 1985). Finally, there is growing recognition that even when cemeteries are complete death assemblages, they can provide a misleading picture of the living population from which they are derived (see especially Sattenspiel and Harpending 1983).

Where gender issues are concerned there are further potential sources of error. First, sex is an obvious potential bias in the selection of people for burial in a cemetery. Second, at least two of the most reliable aging techniques now employed – age estimation from the auricular surface of the pelvis and from the pubic symphysis – involve areas of the body in which sexual dimorphism is an obvious and large, but imperfectly measured, source of error. Hence, for the time being, conclusions about lifespan need to be made with caution. Cementum annulation of teeth, briefly mentioned above, may provide a more accurate means of assessing age at death (Condon et al. 1986; Charles et al. 1986, 1987). These caveats notwithstanding, skeletal data may offer some useful observations. Particularly of interest are cases in which a single investigator or team sees changes in the relative ages at death between the sexes. Such comparisons within the work of individual scholars minimize the risk that apparent differences reflect differences in the techniques of age determination that are applied.

One common pattern in prehistoric groups is that, contrary to contemporary Western experience (but like the experience of some non-industrial nations, see United Nations 1978), men often appear to have had higher average ages at death than women (Acsadi and Nemeskeri 1970; Angel 1984; Owsley and Bass 1979; Rathbun 1984; Blakely 1971; Buikstra and Mielke 1985 who cite also Milner 1982). The explanation frequently cited is that women experience higher mortality during child-bearing years. An alternative finding is that of Lovejoy *et al.* (1977) who suggest that higher young-adult mortality among males at the Libben site results from warfare. It is clear that the relative life expectancy of the two sexes is at least partially a culturally controlled variable which can be used as one measure of gender hierarchy. Demographic profiles can also determine how the patterns of death differ between the sexes, displaying different modal ages at death (Owsley and Bass 1979; Owsley and Bradtmiller 1983).

As is true of other skeletal indicators, the most interesting results involve change in relative levels of mortality when sequential populations are compared. Cassidy (1984), for example, argues that life expectancy at all ages was higher for men than for women in the Archaic period culture in Kentucky. In the agricultural Fort Ancient population, female life expectancy was higher than male life expectancy for all ages, suggesting that the adoption of agriculture and associated social and political changes had a more profound negative effect on male lifespan than on female lifespan.

Mortality profiles in a cemetery may also contribute indirectly to the interpretation of other social patterns. Benfer, working with the Paloma site in Peru (*c* 6000 to 2500 BC), suggests that the distribution of ages at death may permit the identification of marital patterns. Starting with the assumption that the peak of adult female mortality represents death in childbirth, and noting that the peak of female ages at death at Paloma is comparatively late, Benfer suggests that the Paloma data indicate a pattern of delayed marriage and late childbirth.

Cemetery profiles may also yield information on socially induced patterns of mortality. Cassidy (1984) concludes explicitly that the overall distribution of health and death in the Archaic population in Kentucky points to a sexually egalitarian society. In contrast, Benfer (1984) suggests that gender-specific age distributions at death point to socially induced mortality among female infants at Paloma in Peru.

Summary

Although skeletal data are scant and scattered, their study can contribute powerfully to the elucidation of gender issues. These data provide evidence of changing sex-associated differentials in workload, physical risk, disease, nutrition, reproductive patterns, childhood stress, and mortality. They provide fairly concrete indices of relative biological status and health which should help to refine our measurement of gender hierarchy – and to which other, more symbolic measures of status and gender hierarchy must always be compared. The data supplement ethnographic studies and enlarge the observed range of cultural variation. They permit us to observe the effects of specific economic or social transitions on the relative well-being of the two sexes in contexts clearly removed from Western influence. And they allow expanded tests of hypotheses generated by studies of the ethnographic present. Substantial additional information of the type reviewed in this chapter can be obtained by increased attention to existing skeletal populations and by continued excavation. Future studies will help cut through some of the complexities and controversies involved in the interpretation of gender hierarchy.

References

Acsadi, Gyorgy and J. Nemeskeri (1970) *History of Human Lifespan and Mortality*. Budapest: Akademei Kiado.

Allison, Marvin (1984) Paleopathology in Peruvian and Chilean Populations. In *Paleopathology at the Origins of Agriculture*. Mark N. Cohen and George J. Armelagos, eds, pp. 515–30. New York: Academic Press.

Anderson, Karen (1985) Commodity Exchange and Subordination: Montagnais-Naskapi and Huron Women 1600–1650. *Signs* 11:48–62.

Angel, J. Lawrence (1969) The Bases of Paleodemography. *American Journal of Physical Anthropology* 30:427–37.

—— (1971) Early Neolithic Skeletons from Çatal Hüyük: Demography and Pathology. *Anatolian Studies* 21:77–98.

—— (1984) Health as a Crucial Factor in the Changes from Hunting to Developed Farming in the Eastern Mediterranean. In *Paleopathology at the Origins of Agriculture*. Mark N. Cohen and George J. Armelagos, eds, pp. 51–74. New York: Academic Press.

Armelagos, George J. and Dennis P. Van Gerven (1980) Sexual Dimorphism and Human Evolution: An Overview. *Journal of Human Evolution* 9:437–46.

Armstrong, Carl (1985) Pathology and Measure of Robusticity in the Long Bones of the Tipu Population. Paper presented at the annual meeting of the Northeast Anthropological Association.

Atkinson, Jane M. (1982) Anthropology. *Signs* 8:236–58.

Benfer, Robert (1984) The Challenges and Rewards of Sedentism: The Preceramic Village of Paloma, Peru. In *Paleopathology at the Origins of Agriculture*. Mark N. Cohen and George J. Armelagos, eds, pp. 531–58. New York: Academic Press.

Blakely, Robert (1971) Comparison of the Mortality Profiles of Archaic, Middle Woodland, and Middle Mississippian Skeletal Populations. *American Journal of Physical Anthropology* 34:43–54.

Blakely, Robert and Lane Beck (1982) Trace Elements, Nutritional Status, and Social Stratification at Etowah, Georgia. *Annals of the New York Academy of Sciences* 376:417–31.

Bocquet-Appel, J. P. and C. Masset (1982) Farewell to Paleodemography. *Journal of Human Evolution* 11:321–33.

—— (1985) Paleopathology: Resurrection or Ghost. *Journal of Human Evolution* 14:107–11.

Bridges, Patricia S. (1982) Postcranial Dimensions in the Archaic and Mississippian Cultures of Northern Alabama: Implications for Prehistoric Nutrition and Behavior. *American Journal of Physical Anthropology* 57:172–3.

—— (1983) Subsistence Activities and Biomechanical Properties of Long Bones in Two American Populations. *American Journal of Physical Anthropology* 60:177.

—— (1985) A Biomechanical Analysis of Two Prehistoric Amerind Groups: Changes in Habitual Activities and the Division of Labor with the Transition from Hunting and Gathering to Agriculture. Ph.D. dissertation, University of Michigan.

—— (1987) Osteological Correlates of Prehistoric Activities. Paper presented at the annual meeting of the American Anthropological Association.

Brothwell, Don R. (1981) *Digging Up Bones: The Excavation, Treatment and Study of Human Skeletal Remains.* 3rd edition. Ithaca, NY: Cornell University Press.

Buikstra, Jane (1976) *Hopewell in the Lower Illinois Valley: A Regional Study of Human Biological Variation and Prehistoric Mortuary Practices.* Northwestern University Archeological Program Scientific Papers 2. Evanston, IL: Northwestern University.

—— (1984) The Lower Illinois River Region: A Prehistoric Context for the Study of Ancient Diet and Health. In *Paleopathology at the Origins of Agriculture.* Mark N. Cohen and George J. Armelagos, eds, pp. 217–36. New York: Academic Press.

Buikstra, Jane and Della C. Cook (1980) Paleopathology: An American Account. *Annual Review of Anthropology* 9:433–70.

Buikstra, Jane and James Mielke (1985) Demography, Diet and Health. In *The Analysis of Prehistoric Diets.* Robert I. Gilbert, Jr and James H. Mielke, eds, pp. 359–422. New York: Academic Press.

Cassidy, Claire M. (1984) Skeletal Evidence for Prehistoric Subsistence Change in the Central Ohio River Valley. In *Paleopathology at the Origins of Agriculture,* Mark N. Cohen and George J. Armelagos, eds, pp. 307–46. New York: Academic Press.

Chapman, Robert, Ian Kinnes, and Klaus Randsborg, eds. (1981) *The Archaeology of Death,* New York: Cambridge University Press.

Charles, Douglas K. *et al.* (1986) Cementum Annulation and Age Determination in *Homo sapiens.* I. Tooth Variability and Observer Error. *American Journal of Physical Anthropology* 71:311–20.

—— (1987) Age Estimation and Differential Diagnosis. Paper presented at the annual meeting of the Northeast Anthropological Association.

Cohen, Mark N. (1989) *Health and the Rise of Civilization.* New Haven, CT: Yale University Press.

Cohen, Mark N. and George J. Armelagos, eds. (1984) *Paleopathology at the Origins of Agriculture.* New York: Academic Press.

Cohen, Mark N. and Sharon Bennett (1987) Analysis, Seriation and Age-Determination of the Maya of Tipu. Proposal to the National Science Foundation.

Condon, Keith, Douglas Charles, James Cheverund, and Jane Buikstra (1986) Cementum Annulation and Age Determination in *Homo sapiens.* II. Estimates and Accuracy. *American Journal of Physical Anthropology* 71:321–30.

Cook, Delia C. (1984) Subsistence and Health in the Lower Illinois Valley: Osteological Evidence. In *Paleopathology at the Origins of Agriculture.* Mark N. Cohen and George J. Armelagos, eds, pp. 237–70. New York: Academic Press.

Cybulski, Jerome S. (1977) Cribra Orbitalia, a Possible Sign of Anemia in Early Historic Native Populations of the British Columbia Coast. *American Journal of Physical Anthropology* 47:31–40.

Danforth, Marie (1988) Comparison of Health Patterns in Late Classic and Colonial Mayan Populations Using Enamel Microdefects. PhD Dissertation, Indiana University.

Draper, Patricia (1975) !Kung Women: Contrasts in Sexual Egalitarianism in the Foraging and Sedentary Contexts. In *Toward an Anthropology of Women*. Rayna Reiter, ed., pp. 77–109. New York: Monthly Review Press.

Eisenberg, Leslie (1986) The Pattern of Trauma at Averbuch: Activity Levels and Conflict During the Late Mississippian Period. Paper presented at the annual meeting of the American Association of Physical Anthropologists.

Frayer, David (1980) Sexual Dimorphism and Cultural Evolution in the Late Pleistocene and Holocene of Europe. *Journal of Human Evolution* 9:399–413.

—— (1981) Body Size, Weapon Use and Natural Selection in the European Upper Paleolithic and Mesolithic. *American Anthropologist* 83:57–73.

Frayer, David and Milford Wolpoff 1985 Sexual Dimorphism. *Annual Review of Anthropology* 14:429–74.

Gilbert, Robert I. Jr (1985) Stress, Paleonutrition and Trace Elements. In *The Analysis of Prehistoric Diets*. Robert I. Gilbert Jr and James H. Mielke, eds, pp. 339–58. New York: Academic Press.

Gilbert, Robert I. Jr and James H. Mielke, eds. (1985) *The Analysis of Prehistoric Diets*. New York: Academic Press.

Goldstein, Lynne (1976) Spatial Structure and Social Organization: Regional Manifestation of Mississippian Society. Ph.D. dissertation, Northwestern University.

Goodman, Alan, George J. Armelagos, and Jerome Rose (1980) Enamel Hypoplasias as Indicators of Stress in Three Prehistoric Populations from Illinois. *Human Biology* 52:515–28.

Goodman, Alan, Debra Martin, George J. Armelagos, and George Clark (1984) Health Changes at Dickson Mounds, Illionis (AD 950–1300). In *Paleopathology at the Origins of Agriculture*, Mark N. Cohen and George J. Armelagos, eds., pp. 271–306. New York: Academic Press.

Gray, J. Patrick and Linda D. Wolfe (1980) Height and Sexual Dimorphism of Stature among Human Societies. *American Journal of Physical Anthropology* 53:441–56.

Green, Richard, Judy M. Suchey, and D. Gokhale (1979) Analysis of Dorsal Pitting on the Pubis in an Extensive Sample of Modern American Females. *American Journal of Physical Anthropology* 51:317–40.

Hamilton, Margaret E. (1982) Sexual Dimorphism in Skeletal Samples. In *Sexual Dimorphism in Homo sapiens: A Question of Size*. Roberta L. Hall, ed., pp. 107–63. New York: Praeger.

Haviland, William (1967) Stature at Tikal: Implication for Ancient Maya Demography and Social Organization. *American Antiquity* 35:316–25.

Hubbert, William T., William F. McCulloch, and Paul Schurrenberger (1975) *Diseases Transmitted from Animals to Man*. Springfield, IL: Thomas.

Hudson, Charles, Ronald Butler, and Dennis Sikes (1975) Arthritis in the Prehistoric Southeastern United States: Biological and Cultural Variables. *American Journal of Physical Anthropology* 43:57–62.

Huss-Ashmore, Rebecca, Alan Goodman, and George J. Armelagos (1982) Nutritional Inference from Paleopathology. *Advances in Archaeological Theory and Method* 5:395–474.

Jurmain, Robert D. (1977) Stress and the Etiology of Osteoarthritis. *American Journal of Physical Anthropology* 46:353–65.

Klepinger, Linda (1984) Nutritional Assessment from Bone. *Annual Review of Anthropology* 13:75–96.

Koch, Joan K. (1983) Mortuary Behavior Patterns and Physical Anthropology in Colonial St. Augustine. In *Spanish St. Augustine: The Archaeology of a Spanish Creole Community*. Kathleen A. Deagan, ed. with contributions by Joan K. Koch, pp. 187–226. New York: Academic Press.

Kolata, Gina Bari (1974) !Kung Hunter-Gatherers: Feminism, Diet, and Birth Control. *Science* 185:932–4.

Konigsberg, Lyle (1986) Skeletal Lineages and Biological Distance. Paper presented at the annual meeting of the American Association of Physical Anthropologists.

—— (1987) A Formal Basis for the Analysis of Osteological Indicators of Residential Practices. Paper presented at the annual meeting of the American Association of Physical Anthropologists.

Lambert, Joseph, Carol Szpunar, and Jane Buikstra (1977) Chemical Analysis of Excavated Human Bone from Middle and Late Woodland Sites. *Archaeometry* 21:115–29.

Lamphere, Louise (1977) Anthropology. *Signs* 2:612–17.

Larsen, Clark (1981) Functional Implications of Post-Cranial Size Reduction on the Prehistoric Georgia Coast, USA. *Journal of Human Evolution* 10:489–502.

—— (1983) Behavioral Implications of Temporal Change in Cariogenesis. *Journal of Archaeological Science* 10:1–8.

—— (1984) Health and Disease in Prehistoric Georgia: The Transition to Agriculture. In *Paleopathology at the Origins of Agriculture*. Mark N. Cohen and George J. Armelagos, eds., pp. 367–92. New York: Academic Press.

Leacock, Eleanor (1978) Women's Status in Egalitarian Society: Implications for Social Evolution. *Current Anthropology* 19(2):247–75.

Lee, Richard B. (1980) Lactation, Ovulation, Infanticide and Women's Work: A Study of a Hunter-Gatherer Population. In *Biosocial Mechanisms of Population Regulation*. Mark N. Cohen, R. S. Malpass and H. G. Klein, eds, pp. 321–48. New Haven, CT: Yale University Press.

Lovejoy, C. Owen, and K. G. Heiple (1981) The Analysis of Fractures in Skeletal Populations with an Example from the Libben Site, Ottowa Co., Ohio. *American Journal of Physical Anthropology* 55:529–42.

Lovejoy, C. Owen, R. S. Meindle, T. R. Pryzbeck, T. S. Barton, K. G. Heiple, and D. Kotting (1977) Paleobiology at the Libben Site, Ottowa Co., Ohio. *Science* 198:291–3.

Martin, Debra, George J. Armelogos, Alan H. Goodman, and Dennis Van Gerven (1984) The Effects of Socioeconomic Change in Prehistoric Africa: Sudanese Nubia as a Case Study. In *Paleopathology at the Origins of Agriculture*. Mark N. Cohen and George J. Armelagos, eds., pp. 193–216. New York: Academic Press.

Martin, Debra, Alan Goodman, and George J. Armelagos (1985) Skeletal Pathologies as Indicators of Diets. In *The Analysis of Prehistoric Diets*. Robert I. Gilbert Jr and James H. Mielke, eds, pp. 227–79. New York: Academic Press.

Meiklejohn, Christopher, Catherine Schentag, Alexander Venema, and Patrick Key (1984) Socioeconomic Changes and Patterns of Pathology and Variation in the Mesolithic and Neolithic of Western Europe: Some Suggestions. In *Paleopathology at the Origins of Agriculture*. Mark N. Cohen and George J. Armelagos, eds, pp. 75–100. New York: Academic Press.

Milner, G. (1982) Measuring Prehistoric Levels of Health: A Study of Mississippian Period Skeletal Remains from the American Bottom, Illinois. PhD dissertation, Northwestern University.

Mukhopadhyay, Carol C. and Patricia J. Higgins (1988) Anthropological Studies of Women's Status Revisited: 1977–1987. *Annual Review of Anthropology* 17: 461–95.

Murchison, M. A., Douglas Owsley, and A. J. Riopelle (1983) Transverse Line Formation in Protein Deprived Rhesus Monkeys. Paper presented at the annual meeting of the Paleopathology Association.

Nelson, David R., Malcolm McCulloch, and Shen-su Sun (1986) Effects of Diagenesis on Strontium, Carbon, Nitrogen and Oxygen Concentrations and Isotopic Composition of Bone. *Geochemica et Cosmochemica Acta* 50: 1941–9.

Nickens, Paul (1976) Stature Reductions as an Adaptive Response to Food Production in Mesoamerica. *Journal of Archaeological Science* 3: 31–41.

Norr, Lynette (1984) Prehistoric Subsistence and Health Status of Coastal Peoples from the Panamanian Isthmus of Lower Central America. In *Paleopathology at the Origins of Agriculture*, Mark N. Cohen and George J. Armelagos, eds, pp. 463–90. New York: Academic Press.

Ortner, Donald J. and Walter G. Putschar (1981) *Identification of Pathological Conditions in Human Skeletal Remains*. Smithsonian Contributions to Anthropology 28. Washington, DC.

Owsley, Douglas and William Bass (1979) A Demographic Analysis of Skeletons from the Larson Site (39ww2), Walworth County, South Dakota: Vital Statistics. *American Journal of Physical Anthropology* 51: 145–54.

Owsley, Douglas and Bruce Bradtmiller (1983) Mortality of Pregnant Females in an Ankara Village: Osteological Evidence. *American Journal of Physical Anthropology* 61: 331–8.

Perzigian, Anthony J., Patricia Tench, and Donna J. Braun (1984) Prehistoric Health in the Ohio River Valley. In *Paleopathology at the Origins of Agriculture*. Mark N. Cohen and George J. Armelagos, eds, pp. 347–66. New York: Academic Press.

Powell, Mary L. (1985) Dental Wear and Caries in Dietary Reconstruction. In *Analysis of Prehistoric Diets*. Robert I. Gilbert Jr and James H. Mielke, eds, pp. 307–38. New York: Academic Press.

Quinn, Naomi (1977) Anthropological Studies on Women's Status. *Annual Review of Anthropology* 6: 181–225.

Rapp, Rayna (1979) Anthropology. *Signs* 4: 497–513.

Rathbun, Ted A. (1984) Skeletal Pathology from the Paleolithic through the Metal Ages in Iran and Iraq. In *Paleopathology at the Origins of Agriculture*. Mark N. Cohen and George J. Armelagos, eds, pp. 137–68. New York: Academic Press.

Rosaldo, Michelle Zimbalist (1980) The Use and Abuse of Anthropology: Reflections on Feminism and Cross Cultural Understanding. *Signs* 5: 389–417.

Rose, Jerome, Barbara A. Barnett, Michael S. Nassaney, and Mark W. Blaeuer (1985) *Gone to a Better Land*. Research Series 25. Fayetteville: Arkansas Archaeological Survey.

Rose, Jerome, L. F. Boyd, and Keith W. Condon (1981) Enamel Microdefects and Subadult Infections. *American Journal of Physical Anthropology* 54: 270.

Rose, Jerome, Keith W. Condon, and Alan H. Goodman (1985) Diet and Dentition: Developmental Disturbances. In *The Analysis of Prehistoric Diets*. Robert I. Gilbert Jr and James H. Mielke, eds, pp. 281–305. New York: Academic Press.

Rose, Jerome *et al.* (1984) Paleopathology and the Origins of Maize Agriculture in the Lower Mississippi Valley and Caddoan Culture Areas. In *Paleopathology at the Origins of Agriculture*. Mark N. Cohen and George J. Armelagos, eds, pp. 393–424. New York: Academic Press.

Sacks, Karen (1976) State Bias and Women's Status. *American Anthropologist* 78: 565–9.

Sattenspiel, Lisa and Henry Harpending 1983 Stable Populations and Skeletal Age. *American Antiquity* 48: 489–98.

Saul, Frank P. (1972) *The Human Skeletal Remains of Altar de Sacrificios*. Papers of the Peabody Museum of Archaeology and Ethonology 63(2). Cambridge, MA.

Schoeninger, Margaret J. (1979) Diet and Status at Chalcatzingo: Some Empirical and Technical Aspects of Strontium Analysis. *American Journal of Physical Anthropology* 51: 295–310.

—— (1982) Diet and Evolution of Modern Human Form in the Middle East. *American Journal of Physical Anthropology* 58: 37–52.

Sciulli, Paul W. (1977) A Descriptive and Comparative Study of the Deciduous Dentition of Prehistoric Ohio Valley Amerindians. *American Journal of Physical Anthropology* 48: 71–80.

Sillen, Andrew and Maureen Kavanaugh (1982) Strontium and Paleodietary Research: A Review. *Yearbook of Physical Anthropology* 25: 69–90.

Sillen, Andrew and Patricia Smith (1984) Weaning Patterns are Reflected in Strontium–Calcium Ratios of Juvenile Skeletons. *Journal of Archaeological Science* 11: 237–45.

Smith, Patricia, Ofer Bar-Yosef, and Andrew Sillen (1984) Archaeological and Skeletal Evidence for Dietary Change during the Late Pleistocene/Early Holocene in the Levant. In *Paleopathology at the Origins of Agriculture*. Mark N. Cohen and George J. Armelagos, eds, pp. 101–36. New York: Academic Press.

Steinbock, R. Ted (1976) *Paleopathological Diagnosis and Interpretation: Bone Diseases in Ancient Human Populations*. Springfield, IL: Thomas.

Stini, William (1969) Nutritional Stress and Growth: Sex Differences in Adaptive Response. *American Journal of Physical Anthropology* 31:417–26.

—— (1985) Growth Rates and Sexual Dimorphism in Evolutionary Perspective. In *The Analysis of Prehistoric Diets*. Robert I. Gilbert Jr and James H. Mielke, eds, pp. 191–226. New York: Academic Press.

Storey, Rebecca (1985) An Estimate of Mortality in a Pre-Columbian Urban Population. *American Anthropologist* 87:519–35.

Stuart-Macadam, Patty (1985) Porotic Hyperostosis: Representative of a Childhood Condition. *American Journal of Physical Anthropology*, 66:391–8.

Swedlund, Alan and George J. Armelagos (1976) *Demographic Anthropology*. Boston: William C. Brown.

Tanner, Nancy and Adrienne Zihlman (1976) Women in Evolution. Part I: Innovation and Selection in Human Origins. *Signs* 1:585–608.

Turner, Christy (1979) Dental Anthropological Indicators of Agriculture among the Jomon
    People of Central Japan. *American Journal of Physical Anthropology* 51:619–35.
Ubelaker, Douglas H. (1978) *Human Skeletal Remains: Excavation, Analysis, Interpretation.*
    Chicago, IL: Aldine Publishing Company.
—— (1984) Prehistoric Human Biology of Ecuador: Possible Temporal Trends and Cultural
    Correlations. In *Paleopathology at the Origins of Agriculture.* Mark N. Cohen and George
    J. Armelagos, eds, pp. 491–514. New York: Academic Press.
Ullrich, H. (1975) Estimation of Fertility by Means of Pregnancy and Childbirth Alterations
    of the Pubis, Ilium, and Sacrum. *Ossa: International Journal of Skeletal Research* 2:23–39.
United Nations (1978) *Statistical Yearbook 1977.* New York: United Nations.
Van Gerven, Dennis and George J. Armelagos (1983) Farewell to Paleodemography: A
    Reply. *Journal of Human Evolution* 12:352–66.
Walker, Philip (1985) Anemia among Prehistoric Indians of the American Southwest. In
    Health and Disease in the Prehistoric Southwest. Charles F. Merbs and Robert Miller,
    eds, pp. 139–64. Arizona State University Anthropological Research Papers 34.
    Tempe: Arizona State University.
—— (1986) Porotic Hyperostosis in a Marine Dependent California Indian Population.
    American Journal of Physical Anthropology 69:345–54.
Wood, Richard L. (1975) Erysipelothrix Infection. In *Diseases Transmitted from Animals to
    Man.* William T. Hubbert, William F. McCulloch, and Paul Schurrenberger, eds, pp.
    271–81. Springfield, IL: Thomas.

Chapter 17

Nelson

GENDER HIERARCHY AND THE QUEENS OF SILLA

Sarah M. Nelson

Recent scholarship has exposed some of the "self-evident" truths of the anthropology of the last century as being products of cultural blinkers which prevent a clear view of the evidence (Fee 1974; Tiffany 1979). Assumptions about the origins of gender hierarchy and the relationship of male dominance to the formation of states need to be re-examined in this light (Gailey 1985). While feminists have explicitly discussed these topics, sometimes using archaeological data in their discussions (Rohrlich 1980; Lerner 1986), mainstream archaeology has not often examined the gender assumptions implicit in their arguments (see the critique by Conkey and Spector 1984, as well as Zagarell 1986 for a recent exception). Theories of cultural evolution have been derived more from ethnographic than archaeological examples, since the major variables were thought to be difficult to retrieve archaeologically. Theoretical problems with universal explanations regarding the origin of the state include over-generalizing and a lack of attention to kinship structures (Rapp 1977). A combination of archaeological and ethnohistoric evidence can help to reveal our own cultural assumptions in formulations of cultural evolution.

The school of thought that perceives gender hierarchies in all societies (Rosaldo and Lamphere 1974:3) has largely been replaced by an awareness of variation in women's autonomy, power, and authority in prestate societies (Leacock 1978; Draper 1975; Ortner 1981:359; Sanday 1981:132). However, the more specific thesis that state-level societies are inevitably characterized by gender hierarchy, and indeed that other hierarchies are built on the model of inequality by sex and age (Flannery 1972; Service 1975; Sagan 1985; Rousseau 1985), has received less attention.

Rohrlich not only assumes that the formation of the state is based on inequality of women (1980:98), but asserts that the "critical factor in state formation is the emergence of patriarchy" (1980:76). Historical analyses of the antecedents of Western society also indict "patriarchy" and the "patriarchal family" as the source of gender stratification in archaic states (Lerner 1986:212). It is interesting to note that the equation of hierarchies with the state is not limited to Western writers. For example, in *Kuan-tzu*, a Chinese document written around the fourth century BC:

> In antiquity, before there was a distinction between prince and minister, superiors and inferiors, and before there was a union of husband and wife, consort and mate, people lived like beasts and lived in herds, and attacked each other by means of force . . . When superiors and inferiors had been established, the people formed an organization, and the state was founded.
>
> (Duyvendak 1928:103)

Archaeologists, on the other hand, tend to ignore gender stratification in their analyses of state formation, assuming that males are in "the competitive public arena vying for external power in contrast to the private arena of females" (Earle 1987:299), even in chiefdom-level societies.

Universality of female subordination at any stage is a proposition that should be scrutinized. Ruling women in chiefdoms and early states are not as uncommon as general theories about the origin of states would suggest. Women were eligible to rule in Celtic society (Muller 1987), in early Sumer (Rohrlich 1980), in early Japan (Wheatley and See 1978), and in the Silla state of Korea, to name a few. The actual rule by these women is more often acknowledged with reference to documents. Archaeologists tend to discount finds associated with women which, if male, would be considered evidence of very high status (Gilman 1981). Focusing on the high status of some women allows us to examine the supposed necessary connection between the origin of states and "patriarchy," between the formation of elites and the hierarchization of gender relationships (Service 1975; Sagan 1985), between militarism with territorial expansion and the lowered status of women (Harris 1977; Divale and Harris 1976), and to focus on the kinship group as a preservator of women's status (Sacks 1979).

An example of apparent gender equality in the Silla state on the Korean peninsula during the first to seventh centuries may shed some light on these questions. The discovery in 1973 that the largest and most elaborate of the Silla royal tombs in Korea contained a woman as its major occupant, complete with all the accoutrements of power of that early kingdom (Kim W. Y. 1981), has raised major questions about Silla history and society. Have the symbols been misinterpreted, and was not this queen the head of government? If she did rule, why is she missing from the king lists in both of the major Korean documents relating to this time although later ruling queens are included? How does this discovery fit into the social structure as it has been understood, with endogamous "bone ranks" each having its own appointed range of occupations, and sumptuary laws to keep individuals and families from rising above their own class? What was the position of women *vis-à-vis* the class hierarchy and the bureaucracy?

Clearly, wherever there are ruling queens, or even figurehead queens, the principle of royal descent overrides any gender hierarchy that might be present, demonstrating that there are hierarchies of hierarchy, that class may be more important than gender in many cases (Ortner 1981). Regarding the Silla example, we need to know whether there is any necessary relationship between gender hierarchy and the social, economic, and political systems, and whether gender equality applies to the lower classes as well as to the nobility.

Old Silla in documents and archaeology

The Old Silla kingdom was centered on the city of Kyongju, in southeastern Korea. The traditional dates for this kingdom are 57 BC to AD 668, although the earlier half of this period is generally not considered to be a state-level society. Old Silla ended when it conquered Paekche and Koguryo, the other competing states of the Korean Three Kingdoms period, forming United Silla. In this chapter "Silla" refers to Old Silla.

From 108 BC to AD 313 there was a significant Chinese presence on the Korean peninsula north of the developing Silla state, in the form of commanderies established by the Former Han dynasty expansion. With various border changes and revolts the Lolang colony, with its capital near present day Pyongyang, continued until it was extirpated finally by the Koguryo kingdom on its northern border in AD 313. Comments about the oddities of the unconquered regions of southern Korea are extant in Chinese documents, especially a section of the *Wei Shu* regarding the "Eastern Barbarians" from the third century AD. Neither the Silla nor the Paekche kingdom is named in that document; rather we read of the Three Hans, Ma-Han, Pyon-Han, and Chin-Han, of which the last is usually identified with Silla (Joe 1972:25). Chin-Han contained twelve "*guo*," a character that now is translated as "state," but is thought to refer to some less organized form, such as walled villages or towns protected by hill forts. One of these *guo* was Saro, a confederation of six villages, whose capital was at the present site of Kongju in southeastern Korea. Saro expanded by the conquest of neighboring states and ultimately became Silla.

The formation of the Silla kingdom was less influenced by China than the other two Korean kingdoms of the Three Kingdoms period. It is clearly an example of a secondary state, but the concept of "peer-polity interaction" (Renfrew 1982) is also relevant, for Silla's interactions with the other kingdoms of Korea and Japan were probably as critical as those with China in its early development. One of Silla's own traditions, recorded in the *Wei Shu*, is that some of its founders were Ch'in refugees from the harsh laws of the Chin dynasty of China, who came to the Korean peninsula "to escape the misery of forced labor" (Parker 1890:209). Their dialect was said to be like that of northwest China. Chinese sources additionally relate that in AD 37 a great many ("five thousand") refugees from the Lolang colonies fled to Silla and were apportioned among the villages (Kim C. S. 1965:160).

Archaeological discoveries suggest an intrusive population in the third to first centuries BC, with a new form of pit burial replacing the stone cist graves under dolmens of the Bronze Age. In the pit graves iron implements accompanied the dead, along with bronze weapons (Kim W. Y. 1982:26). Differentials of wealth are evident in these burials. The region around Kyongju, later Silla's capital, is one of two areas in South Korea with extensive early Iron Age sites. It is probably significant that both these areas are near outcrops of iron ores. In the Han river basin, semisubterranean dwellings and Mumun (Bronze Age) pottery are found associated with early iron artifacts, while in the southeast, iron has so far only been found in pit graves associated with Wajil and Kimhae (Iron Age) pottery. The techniques of iron working have been found to include both cast iron and steel, with technology equal to that of Han China. The technology may have been imported, but the metal was locally worked (Lee 1982).

Perhaps as early as the first century AD, a new variant appeared in that burial system. Stone cairns were raised over cobble-lined tombs, instead of simple earthen pits. The tradition of mounded tombs was long established in China, and was also practiced in the Lolang commandery in Korea. Thus, an inspiration for this new burial style is to be found close at hand.

Excavations in Choyadong, Kyongju, have been dated to the early centuries AD. One of the burials contained four mirrors in the style of the Former Han dynasty, helping to date the graves as well as demonstrating connections with China. Another set of graves, excavated in the vicinity of King Michu's tomb in Kyongju, is believed to date from the second and third centuries AD (Kim W. Y. 1974). Long-distance trade and human sacrifice were already evident. Round pits with horse skeletons were found outside human burials, along with multi-chambered tombs, which appeared to contain human sacrificial victims. Tomb 4 in Area C contained an elaborate glass bead of Roman type, with a round-eyed face in the bead. The excavators consider this to be evidence that long-distance trade was carried on at this early date (Kim and Yi 1975). At about this time in China, poems were being written celebrating foreign glass objects (Engle 1976:35), making it likely that China was the mediator of this trade.

Choi (1981) has seriated the Silla wooden chamber tombs under cobble and earth mounds, which date from about AD 350–720. These tombs show increasing amounts of high-status grave goods, although craft specialization can be inferred from the artifacts from much earlier times. Great artistry and technical sophistication in fabricating artifacts are hallmarks of this period. Glass vessels from the Western world are not uncommon in the high-status tombs, but only one Chinese artifact has been unearthed – a glazed brown ceramic bottle. This suggests the possibility of later trade not mediated by China, but how and by what route is not clear. Perhaps the paucity of Chinese goods merely indicates that they were not exotic enough for royal burials. Regardless of the source of trade goods, Sillan contact with China is attested to in various documentary sources.

Chinese manners and customs began to be adopted during the period of the mounded royal tombs. Chinese and Korean records concur that in the reign of King Chinji in the fourth century Korean rulers began to use the Chinese code of mourning and the custom of posthumous names for rulers. But not until the early sixth century did Silla begin to use the Chinese calendar instead of the native lunar reckoning, and to call the kings "wang" after the Chinese fashion, instead of using native Korean titles. By this time Buddhism was well established, literacy in Chinese was the rule in the court, and the Korean language was being written in Idu, using Chinese characters for their phonetic value to represent the sounds of Korean words. Alongside this sinicization, the Sillans maintained many of their ancient customs.

Silla society

The social system is the most thoroughly recorded subsystem of Silla. Class stratification was the basic building block of society. A system called *kolpum*, "bone ranks" (bone being the Korean metaphor for kinship), kept everyone in the same social position into which they were born. The highest group was the *songgol*, or Holy Bone, a quality required for the ruler until this group became extinct in the seventh century. Neither primogeniture nor patriliny was a necessary category in selection of the ruler, but *songgol* status was *sine qua non*. It appears that there was a rule of hypodescent in which both parents had to be *songgol* for the children to enjoy this status, but given *songgol* birth, "the holders of the highest status . . . were eligible for the throne regardless of sex" (Kim C. S. 1977). Only three families (Pak, Sok, and Kim) comprised the *songgol*, but not all branches of these families were among the Holy Bone. Endogamy within the *songgol* became ever more pronounced, with not only cousin marriages but marriages between niece and uncle occurring commonly in royal families, according to the lists of kings and queens.

Below the *songgol* were the *chin'gol*, the True Bone. Each rank in the government could be held only by a person of the appropriate social rank, and members of each wore robes of a distinctive color. The highest five ranks of the government could be filled only by *songgol* who wore purple, or *chin'gol* in red robes. The *ryuk-tupum*, "six head rank," were eligible to hold the four government ranks below those held by *chin'gol*; they were distinguished by blue robes. The next two state ranks could be filled by the "fifth head rank" wearing yellow robes, and the lowest four groups were *pyongmin*, commoners, not eligible for government service (Kim C. S. 1977). Under this system, "every individual in Silla was by birth assigned a specific status from which it was virtually impossible for him [sic] to escape" (Kim C. S. 1977:4).

Strict sumptuary laws also enforced the *kolpum* ranks. For example, male *chin'gol* were prohibited from wearing "embroidered trousers made of fur, brocade or raw silk," while among the prohibitions for female *chin'gol* were "hairpins engraved and inlaid with gems and jades" (Kim C. S. 1977:59). Wrinkled purple reindeer leather was not allowed as a material for boots for male *ryuktupum*, while male *odupum* were limited to cotton cloth for their underwear, and female *sadupum* could not use underskirts at all. *Chin'gol* were forbidden to hang carved wooden fish from the eaves of their houses, and the largest stable permitted commoners would accommodate only two horses.

Although there are champions for an interpretation of either matrilineality (Kim C. S. 1965) or patrilineality (Choi 1971:32) in early Silla, the relationships demonstrated by the king lists cannot be described by simple linearity. For instance, it was common for a ruler's daughter's husband to succeed to the kingship, and about equally common for the past ruler's brother or son to succeed, or both in no necessary order. Groups of endogamous families appear to have formed corporate descent groups without a unilineal principle at all, descent being reckoned bilaterally. Examining these patterns of succession, Grayson (1976:38) concludes that "women play important connective roles in [royal] succession. A new king will have as wife a close female relative of the former king." There is another possible way to view this pattern which I discuss in the conclusion.

While archaeology cannot confirm all the details of the social structure, excavated tombs from the Silla period show a great disparity in quality and quantity of burial goods, size of grave mound, and elaboration of tomb construction, even within the city of Kyongju itself. Some unexcavated mounds are connected with specific kings in popular lore, but not all the mounds have attributed occupants, nor do all rulers have an ascribed mound. Thus, the folklore of the tombs cannot be used to argue for or against tomb size alone as an indicator of prestige and the ability to mobilize labor.

The political system

Silla grew from a confederation of six villages which joined together because of "strong enemies nearby" (Ilyon 1972 [1281]), eventually to rule the entire peninsula. Not surprisingly, this change in scale was accompanied by changes in the structure of the government. Although the precise organization is unknown, glimpses of the original pattern are possible in the various historical texts. The foundation legend of Silla recounts the selection by the village elders of an exceptional individual as leader. This council of elders seems to have persisted throughout Silla's history, institutionalized as the *hwabaek*. In this body, all important matters had to be settled by unanimous consent. Although the council originally met at four sacred outdoor localities, in the mountains or by streams, eventually a hall was constructed next to the royal palace where the deliberations of this group took place.

According to the *Samguk Sagi*, the office of chief minister was established in AD 10, and the seventeen official ranks in AD 32. While these dates may be anachronistic, there is other evidence of centralized power, and hierarchies of power, even in the first three centuries. For example, there is the use of the word *guo*, "state," in the Chinese annals. The larger *guo* comprised more than 10,000 households, and even the smallest contained 600–700 families (Parker 1890:207). These units were composed of a capital, surrounding villages, and a special village with a religious function. In each capital there was a leader, a standing army, and an official house called *kwanga* (Kim C. S. 1965:48), whose function, according to the *San Guo Chih*, was to organize corvée labor to construct forts and other public works. While we have no specific data from Korea on the gender of the various officials, Japanese chronicles indicate female court officials in a system imported from the Korean Paekche Kingdom (Barnes 1987:87). Approaching the problem of what the Chinese meant by *guo* from the vantage point of early Japan, Wheatley and See (1978:20) conclude that "generally speaking, the chroniclers of Han times seem not to have used it in connection with societies totally without manifestations of hereditary inequalities and territorially defined institutions."

We do know that Silla (or its predecessor Saro) had organized armies which invaded other native *guo*, as well as the Chinese commanderies. It is recorded that in AD 104 the state of Silchikkok, which had previously been conquered by Saro, revolted. Not only was it crushed militarily, but the population was forcefully removed to another location, a feat which requires strong central power. Perhaps the date is wrong, but archaeology suggests endemic warfare even earlier than the first century. Details of the conquest of other small states by Silla abound in the *Samguk Sagi* and *Samguk Yusa*.

Corvée labor is also evidence of state power. An edict of AD 144 ordered the extension of irrigation works to increase the amount of land under cultivation and forbade the conscription of farm workers for public works during the agricultural season. In AD 231 the office of *Taejanggun*, chief military leader, was created and at about the same time a principal administrator was installed. The *Hou Han Shu* gives the titles of five ranks of village heads. Thus, the political system became increasingly centralized, with more and more differentiation of leadership positions, between the first and fifth centuries.

Symbols of power in the form of pure gold crowns hung with tinkling gold and jades, and gold belts with multiple pendants shaped as golden fish or made of curved jade jewels, have been unearthed in Silla tombs. Gilt-bronze crowns are sometimes found in lesser graves, but only the royal graves have sheet-gold crowns. The shapes used in the crowns are thought by scholars to be shamanic symbols, especially the uprights in the form of stylized trees and antlers. Inscriptions on objects in the Silla tombs are rare, and none found so far names the occupant of the tomb. The traditional ascription of certain mounds to particular rulers is the only clue to the identity of the interred, other than approximate dates inferred from imported objects which can be compared against the dates in the king lists.

Tomb 98 in Kyongju is an example of a royal burial. It is unusual in being a double mound, with one major burial in each half. One of the largest of all Silla tombs, it measures 23 m high, and the diameter of each mound is about 80 m, for a combined length of 120 m. This mound is so large that before excavation it was used as a natural hill, having houses built on its flanks with alleys between them.

The south mound, containing the burial of a male, is the earlier. Only a few teeth and a mandible remained at the time of excavation, from which the occupant's age was estimated at about 60 years. He was interred wearing a small gilt-bronze crown and "other personal ornaments were also of rather poor quality" (Kim W. Y. 1976:6). A separate pit beside the coffin contained over 2,500 artifacts, including a silver crown, two gilt-bronze crowns, weapons, pottery, and glass vessels identified as of Mediterranean manufacture. The iron weapons included 30 swords, 543 spears, 380 battle axes, and more than 1,000 arrowheads. Armor was included as well, even his silver leggings.

The person buried in the north mound was female, identified by an inscription on a silver ornament on one of her ceremonial belts. She was laid to rest wearing one of the most magnificent gold crowns yet found in Korea, as well as a gold belt with pendants of the type found only in royal graves. She wore five pairs of gold bracelets, gold earrings, and three necklaces. The total weight of her gold jewelry was nearly 4 kg. A Chinese brown-glaze pottery bottle buried with her is similar to examples unearthed from Chinese graves dated to the mid-fourth century. A Sassanian-style chased silver bowl was also found with the queen, possibly one of the silver wine cups noted by the *Samguk Sagi* as a gift to Silla from China (Kim W. Y. 1981).

Assignment of Tomb 98 to a specific ruler in the king list is a matter of controversy. The earliest time estimate is by Choi (1981), who places the south mound at around AD 400. This placement implies that the male occupant was King Naemul (reign 356–402); with a 46-year reign, he would have been elderly at death. Queen Poban, the consort, as the daughter of King Michu, was eligible to rule in her own right, by the rules as they have been inferred. Kim Won-Yong (1981) selects King Nulji (reign 417–58) as the likely occupant. Nulji died at age 56 and was likewise married to a king's daughter eligible to rule. Kim and Pearson (1977) suggest King Soji (reign 479–500), but this possibility seems unlikely, since his queen predeceased him. The problem of who are the occupants of Tomb 98 continues to be a matter of controversy.

The economy

The Silla state was largely agrarian, although its foundation was probably related to trade in iron and gold (Kim W. Y. 1982). The Chinese chronicles report that "the country produces iron, and the Wei, Wa, and Mahan all go to buy it; for purposes of barter the sole money exchange is iron" (Parker 1890: 210). The early

Chinese observed that "the land was fat and fair, and suited to the five cereals; they understand mulberry and sericulture, and the making of cloth fabric; they use oxen and horses in riding and carts" (Parker 1890:209). The arable land was considered to belong to the state itself and not to any individual, and thus a feudal system did not develop. Certain villages were expected to produce particular products, including various grades of cloth, metals, basketry, and paper (Choi 1971:66; Sohn, Kim, and Hong 1970:66). The farmers were taxed in both grain and labor, and the state kept grain warehouses from which grain was allocated in years of famine. Farmers' associations, called *ture*, are believed to date back to the Silla period (Shin 1985). Women's cooperative weaving may also have been organized into *ture* (Joe 1972). This suggestion is based on a tale about King Yuri (reign AD 24–57), who divided each *guo* into two teams, each headed by one of his daughters. A competition lasted for a month, after which the winning team was treated to a feast by the losers, followed by singing, dancing, and games (Shin 1985:6).

A thriving economy can be deduced from the sumptuary laws. Many kinds and qualities of cloth, blankets, saddles, shoes, and other manufactured products are prohibited for lower groups. However, reports of famines and floods appear in the chronicles frequently, indicating intermittent problems with the agricultural base.

The *Samguk Sagi* names "more than 90 occupational titles in the central government [among them] historians, mathematicians, doctors, astronomers, gardeners, tax collectors, metallurgists, leather and shoe specialists, butchers, sorcerers, guards, cotton and hemp specialists, wardens, druggists, warehouse keepers, sickle makers, temple officials, sewing and laundry girls, bookkeepers" (Kim C. S. 1974:36). Except in a few cases, gender is not specified, so we do not know how many of these occupations were gender-marked.

A census from the eighth century has survived, showing that the state kept careful records on all the villagers by sex and age groupings, as well as all the livestock and trees. Land was allocated with a constant amount for each adult, and was conceptualized as belonging to the state (Kim C. S. 1965). Division of labor by sex is alluded to in terms of women's weaving, but other documents make it possible to infer that both males and females were expected to work on the public labor projects.

Religion

Many important local deities were female, including the goddess of agriculture (Chee 1974:144). *Changsung*, representations of village guardian spirits, are still occasionally found in Korea (Kim T. G. 1983). They were always carved in male and female pairs, suggesting equality in the spirit world.

Ceremonies by and for the lower classes were conducted at the village level, and there are several reasons to suppose that women participated equally with men. In remote villages ceremonies to bless and purify the village are still conducted, presided over by a shaman, usually a woman called a *mudang* or, more politely, *manshin* (Kendall 1985). Not only could women become shamans, but women in Silla represented the majority of those who could deal with the supernatural (Kim Y. C. 1977:14), as they do at the present time. In fact female *mudangs* thrive in modern Korea. Several writers have seen in the *mudang* the reflection of a time in the past when women's roles had not been debased by Confucianism. Whether or not this is so, at the very least it can be said that women even at present are in no way excluded from ceremonial roles or contact with the supernatural on behalf of individuals or groups. Traditionally, *mudangs* even "presided in national ceremonies" (Kim Y. C. 1977:14). Even in Buddhism, women were relatively equal to men (p. 19).

Archaeological evidence of religion in Silla is limited by the fact that large ceremonial buildings did not become a part of the system until the advent of Buddhism in the sixth century. Sacred precincts called *sodo* were set aside, marked by a tall pole on which were hung a bell and a drum. Some of the same ideas may survive today in village sacred trees, and the bell and drum towers of Buddhist temples. Unfortunately, in terms of archaeology these places are invisible. Various bronze bells and bronze "ritual objects" of uncertain date have been discovered in caches, and they are often considered probable shaman's equipment (Kim W. Y. 1981). The archaeological record gives no hint as to the gender of their owner.

Gender stratification

The *Wei Chih* records disapprovingly that the people of Chinguk "drew no distinctions of age and sex" (Parker 1890:209). Confucian values, strongly male dominant, date from the fifth century BC (Joe 1972:97), and influenced Chinese foreign policy at least as early as the unification of all China by the Chin. The severe laws which helped the Chin dynasty conquer all of China in the third century BC are credited to a Lord Shang, who boasted about his accomplishments. Regarding the Chin conquest of their neighbors, he reported, "Formerly, the Jung and Ti barbarians of Ch'in, in their teaching knew no difference between father and son, and they lived together in the same room. Now I have altered and regulated their moral teaching and have made distinctions between men and women" (Duyvendak 1928:214). Some of these same Ch'in barbarians might have helped populate early Chin-Han as their own traditions suggest.

Another indication of the status of women in early Silla is found in the poorly understood society of the *wonhwa*, an association of girls, which later was transformed into the male institution of the *hwarang*. Even the *hwarang*, about which much is written, is not easy to understand. It had both a military and a moral training function, as well as esthetic activities and excursions to the mountains. Meaning "flower youth," it has been seen as having a homosexual base and as shamanistic (Rutt 1961), or as basically military. It is recorded that the *wonhwa* preceded the *hwarang*, but the girls quarreled, so its functions were turned over to boys. Each of the *wonhwa* were selected by the ruler for service to the state, and had "thousands" of followers.

Although the assumption of later scholarship and the language of the translators often seem to present the government bureaucrats as men only, the institution of *wonhwa* suggests that women were also involved in the government, for the *hwarang* was seen as a training ground for government leaders. Court functionaries from the more sinicized Paekche state included women (Barnes 1987:87) which may reflect a widespread pattern in southern Korea.

The extant portion of the eighth-century census previously discussed reveals a considerably greater number of females than males at each age level, especially adult. The total population in four villages was 884, of which 194 were adult males and 248 adult females (Kim C. S. 1965). This ratio could reflect a high military death rate for males, or might result from deception in reporting. The fact that there are more females than males in all age categories may indicate that the later Korean tendency toward preference for sons had not taken root at this late date, at least not to the extent of female infanticide.

The movement of women was not restricted. Prescriptions concerning certain kinds of saddles according to a woman's rank indicate that all women rode horses. In various tales, women are described as moving around the countryside independently. At least some women were educated, for we learn that the famous general Kim Yusin was "taught and instructed by his mother." Women were accorded respect in the family: the majority of examples of filial piety concern mothers, not fathers (Kim Y. C. 1977:44). The most compelling data concern the social system: "Women must have played an important role in the Silla social system, as it is through them that males could establish their claim to the throne. In addition, three women became ruling queens in their own right" (Grayson 1976).

Archaeological finds reinforce the interpretation of relative gender equality. Many burials are in male–female pairs in the regions surrounding Kyongju, with each person receiving roughly equal treatment in separate but overlapping mounds. In an extensive study of the artifacts from 155 excavated mounds, it was concluded that 52 per cent of the burials were male, based on the presence of weapons and armor (Ito 1971:25), further suggesting a lack of gender stratification. The excavated mounds may be skewed in favor of the nobility, but only a few are royal tombs.

The nature of Silla hierarchies

Although rigidly hierarchical in terms of social rankings, the structure of the Silla state is revealed as relatively simple. The social system was composed of strata to which each person was assigned at birth and from which there appears to have been no escape. Presumably the uppermost social level contained the fewest people, and the lowest level formed the bottom of a broad-based pyramid. The highest-ranking *songgol* must have been a small group to begin with, for they diminished in numbers over the centuries and died out in 654.

The political system was a reflection of the social system, and dependent upon it. One's place in the social system determined one's potential place in the political system, although there must have been fewer government offices than there were *songgol* and *chin'gol* to fill them.

The social/political system was so rigid and so well-established that it did not allow wealth to be used to usurp the place of status by birth. No incipient merchant class was permitted to develop. There were few means of becoming wealthy, because the economy was totally subservient to the state. Agricultural land was allotted by the state, and care was taken to extract the taxes and labor owed by each individual directly to the state. The mechanism for trade is unknown, but the exotic items from great distances found in high-status burials were probably limited to royalty and acquired in the form of gifts to the head of state. Sumptuary laws regulated everything from roofs to saddles, preventing persons from rising above their station in life, even if they could find the means to do it. The color-coded robes within the government must have helped to keep officials in their proper places as well. Until the extinction of the *songgol* the system seems to have maintained itself. *Chin'gol* factionalism then held sway (Kim C. S. 1969), but this was not class struggle. It was jockeying for power within the social group, not between classes. In the ninth century when the famous Chang Pogo, a commoner, created a trading empire extending to bases in China, his bid for political and social power in Korea was firmly crushed (Han 1970:115).

The shamanistic religious system had no separate hierarchy which could interfere with the power of the state. Each mountain and stream had its local deity, each village its guardian spirits. As long as there were *songgol*, the rulers may have performed rites on behalf of the state, since they were believed to be descended from gods. But there were no national deities. The local gods were worshipped by local people in local ceremonies, a decentralized system presenting no potential threat to the state. The power of Buddhism as an organized religion came later to Silla than to Koguryo and Paekche. It was not until the succeeding Koryo dynasty (936–1491) that Buddhist temples became large enough landholders to challenge the power of the state.

Sex and age as models of hierarchy

Let us return to the notion that "egalitarian societies" may have inequalities by sex and age, and the common assumption that the model for state-level inequality derives from the family, well articulated by Service: "All families, of course, have internal dominant-subordinate relationships, based primarily on age and sex differences" (Service 1975:71). The essential question is not how hierarchies came to be formed, but whether states necessarily entail gender inequality, using pre-existing gender hierarchy as a model for other kinds of inequalities. The Silla example suggest that gender inequality may arise well after the formation of a state.

A parallel question can be asked regarding age hierarchy. Trigger considers the extension of hierarchical patterns as deriving from the state. "Another unanswered question is whether the concept of relations based on inequality began with the state and only later was projected into family life and the activities of other small groups or whether such relations first developed within the nuclear or extended family and later were utilized in the construction of the state" (Trigger 1985:59). Examining patterns of physical punishment of children in early Egypt, Mesopotamia, and the Aztec state, he concludes that "the specific types of relationships found within the family in early civilizations were ones that were only possible within the broader context of inequality of the whole society and ultimately depended on the sanctions of the state."

Although Sacks (1979) finds the rise of the state destructive to women's positions in her African examples, she demonstrates that women could have equality in emerging complex societies. She sees corporate kinship groups as the protectors of "sisterly prerogatives," including partial control of group resources. Perhaps there is an analogy here with the Silla endogamous groups.

A basic problem with any analysis of the Silla case is the reification of the state in the literature on cultural evolution. A typical definition of the state includes a strong, centralized government, a ruling elite which controls the economy, and a monopoly on force, allowing the state to "draft soldiers, levy taxes, and exact tribute" (Flannery 1972:403). States also involve the shift from the principle of kinship to that of territory. How, then do we understand the Silla state? All the defining characteristics of a state were present, *except* that kinship, having become identical with the stratification system, was still an important organizational principle. (Perhaps we should think of this as an Asiatic Mode of Reproduction.)

Is Silla, then, not a state? The exercise of pigeonholing societies into typologies seems to be fruitful only in revealing anomalies, which may help to show variation in the processes of human social and political evolution. Theory suggests that ruling classes destroy kin groups. This destruction did not occur in Silla as long as the ruling classes were kin groups. If we accept Silla as a state, this example suggests that analyses which find the source of female inequality in surplus extraction (Gailey and Patterson 1987), in the elite control of production (Muller 1987), in militarism (Rohrlich 1980), or even in "generalized coercion" (Trigger 1985), are not sufficient. State-level political and economic power can coexist with relative gender equality, as long as kinship is the basic organizing principle of the elites.

Theories about state formation have been closely entwined with supposed male activities: warfare, the managerial system, and long-distance trade. Archaeology has compounded this bias by interpreting finds differentially according to gender and making unwarranted assumptions, as Shennan (1987:372) points out regarding the exchange of women. Trigger (1984:292) reminds us that "archaeological interpretations are subtly influenced by social and personal preconceptions of reality that preclude an awareness of alternative explanations which might encourage formal testing or of the actual limits within which a generalization holds true."

And what of the enigmatic burial in the north mound of Tomb 98? Based on the archaeological evidence alone, it would seem that this woman was the ruler, and the male in the south mound was merely a military leader. One could argue that they were co-rulers with complementary positions, or that the woman alone was the political/religious head of the state. Later Confucian (*Samguk Sagi*) and Buddhist (*Samguk Yusa*) scholarship, especially in the context of the Koryo dynasty, would both have preferred to suppress the fact of women rulers in earlier times. The three queens that *were* recorded in the king lists had no husband to whom the kingship could be ascribed. Genealogies of the relevant period – variously placed from the mid-fourth to the mid-fifth centuries – show that kings' daughters almost always became queens. For example, the wife of Nulji, the nineteenth king (reign 417–58), was the daughter, granddaughter, and great-granddaughter of ruling kings (and queens), and her daughter's son became the twenty-second king. Interpreting the queens as reigning themselves, or as co-rulers, is consistent with these data.

The specific puzzle of the queen in Tomb 98 may never be solved, but it is evident that Silla had found a way to create a stable state with a single hierarchical system. Women had always had a place in society equal to men, and there was no room in the structure for social climbing. Adding gender stratification might have upset the balance.

■   ■   ■

References

Barnes, Gina (1987) The Role of the *Be* in the Formation of the Yamato State. In *Specialization, Exchange, and Complex Societies*. E. M. Brumfiel and T. K. Earle, eds, pp. 86–101. Cambridge: Cambridge University Press.

Chee, Changboh (1974) Shamanism and Folk Beliefs of the Koreans. In *Traditional Korea, Theory and Practice*. A. C. Nahm, ed., pp. 141–57. Kalamazoo: Center for Korean Studies, Western Michigan University.

Choi, Byung-hyan (1981) The Evolution and Chronology of the Wooden Chamber Tomb of the Old Silla Period. *Hanguk Kogo Hakbo* 10–11:137–228. (In Korean.)

Choi, Hochin (1971) *The Economic History of Korea*. Seoul: The Freedom Press.

Conkey, Margaret and Janet Spector (1984) Archaeology and the Study of Gender. *Advances in Archaeological Method and Theory* 7:1–38.

Divale, William and Marvin Harris (1976) Population, Warfare and the Male Supremacist Complex. *American Anthropologist* 78:521–38.

Draper, Patricia (1975) !Kung Women: Contrasts in Sexual Egalitarianism in Foraging and Sedentary Contexts. In *Toward an Anthropology of Women*. Rayna Reiter, ed., pp. 77–109. New York: Monthly Review Press.

Duyvendak, J. J. L. (1928) *The Book of Lord Shang*. Chicago: University of Chicago Press.

Earle, Timothy (1987) Chiefdoms in Archaeological and Ethnohistorical Perspective. *Annual Review of Anthropology* 16:279–308.

Engle, Anita (1976) Glass Making in China. *Readings in Glass History* 6–7:1–38.

Fee, Elizabeth (1974) The Sexual Politics of Victorian Social Anthropology. In *Clio's Consciousness Raised*. M. Hartman and L. Banner, eds, pp. 86–102. New York: Harper Books.

Flannery, Kent V. (1972) The Cultural Evolution of Civilizations. *Annual Review of Ecology and Systematics* 3:339–426.

Gailey, Christine W. (1985) The State of the State in Anthropology. *Dialectical Anthropology* 9(1–4):65–90.

—— (1987) Culture Wars: Resistance to State Formation. In *Power Relations and State Formation*. Thomas C. Patterson and Christine W. Gailey, eds, pp. 35–56. Washington, DC: American Anthropological Association.

Gailey, Christine W. and Thomas C. Patterson (1987) Power Relations and State Formation. In *Power Relations and State Formation*. Thomas C. Patterson and Christine W. Gailey, eds, pp. 1–26. Washington, DC: American Anthropological Association.

Gilman, A. (1981) The Development of Social Stratification in Bronze Age Europe. *Current Anthropology* 22:1–8.

Grayson, James H. (1976) Some Structural Patterns of the Royal Families of Ancient Korea. *Korea Journal* 16(6):27–32.

Han, Woo-keun (1970) *The History of Korea*. Lee Kyng-shik, trans. Grafton K. Mintz, ed. Seoul: The Eul-Yoo Publishing Company.

Harris, Marvin (1977) *Cannibals and Kings: The Origins of Cultures*. New York: Random House.

Ilyon (1972) *Samguk Yusa: Legends and History of the Three Kingdoms* (1281). Tae-hung Ha and Grafton Mintz, trans. Seoul: Yonsei University Press.

Ito, Akio (1971) *Zur Chronologie der Frühsillazeitlichen Gräber in Südkorea*. Munich: Bayerische Akademie der Wissenschaften. New Series, Vol. 71.

Joe, Wanne (1972) *Traditional Korea: A Cultural History*. Seoul: Chungang University Press.

Kendall, Laurel (1985) *Shamans, Housewives, and Other Restless Spirits*. Honolulu: University of Hawaii Press.

Kim, Chae-kuei and Eunchang Yi (1975) *A Report on the Excavation of the Tombs at Hwangnam-dong, Kyongju*. Yongnam, Korea: Yongnam University Museum, Monograph 1.

Kim, Chong-Sun (1965) The Emergence of Multi-Centered Despotism in the Silla Kingdom: A Study of the Origin of Factional Struggles in Korea. PhD Dissertation, University of Washington.

—— (1969) Sources of Cohesion and Fragmentation in the Silla Kingdom. *Journal of Korean Studies* 1(1):41–72.

—— (1974) Slavery in Silla and Its Sociological and Economic Implications. In *Traditional Korea, Theory and Practice*. A. C. Nahm, ed., pp. 29–43. Kalamazoo: Center for Korean Studies, Western Michigan University.

—— (1977) The Kolp'um System: Basis for Sillan Social Stratification. *Journal of Korean Studies* 1(2):43–69.

Kim, T'ae-gon (1983) A Study on the Rite of *Changsung*, Korea's Totem Pole. *Korea Journal* 23(3):4–19.

Kim, Wong-Yong (1974) *Archaeology in Korea, An Annual Review of Korean Archaeology 1*. Seoul: Seoul National University, Department of Archaeology and Anthropology.

—— 1976 *Archaeology in Korea 3*. Seoul: Seoul National University, Department of Archaeology and Anthropology.

—— (1981) *Recent Archaeological Discoveries in the Republic of Korea*. Tokyo: UNESCO

—— (1982) Kyongju: The Homeland of Korean Culture. *Korea Journal* 22(9):25–32.

Kim, Won-Yong and Richard Pearson (1977) Three Royal Tombs: New Discoveries in Korean Archaeology. *Archaeology* 30(5):302–13.

Kim, Yung-Chung (1977) *Women of Korea: A History from Ancient Times to 1945*. Seoul: Ehwa University Press.

Leacock, Eleanor (1978) Women's Status in Egalitarian Society: Implications for Social Evolution. *Current Anthropology* 19(2):247–75.

Lee, Nam-kyu (1982) A Study of Early Iron Age Culture in South Korea. *Hanguk Kogo Hakbo* 13:39–59. (In Korean with English summary.)

Lerner, Gerda (1986) *The Creation of Patriarchy*. New York: Oxford University Press.

Muller, Viana (1987) Kin Reproduction and Elite Accumulation in the Archaic States of Northwest Europe. In *Power Relations and State Formation*. Thomas C. Patterson and Christine W. Gailey, eds, pp. 81–97. Washington, DC: American Anthropological Association.

Ortner, Sherry B. (1981) Gender and Sexuality in Hierarchical Societies: The Case of Polynesia and Some Comparative Implications. In *Sexual Meanings: The Cultural Construction of Gender and Sexuality*. Sherry B. Ortner and Harriet Whitehead, eds, pp. 359–409. New York: Cambridge University Press.

Parker, E. H. (1890) On Race Struggles in Korea. *Transactions of the Asiatic Society of Japan* 18(2):157–228.

Rapp, Rayna R. (1977) The Search for Origins: Unraveling the Threads of Gender Hierarchy. *Critique of Anthropology* 3(9–10):5–24.

Renfrew, Colin (1982) Socio-economic Change in Ranked Societies. In *Ranking Resource, and Exchange*. Colin Renfrew and Stephen Shennan, eds, pp. 1–8. New York: Cambridge University Press.

Rohrlich, Ruby (1980) State Formation in Sumer and the Subjugation of Women. *Feminist Studies* 6(1):76–102.

Rosaldo, Michelle Zimbalist and Louise Lamphere, eds (1974) *Women, Culture and Society*. Stanford, CA: Stanford University Press.

Rousseau, Jerome (1985) The Ideological Prerequisites of Inequality. In *Development and Decline, the Evolution of Sociopolitical Organization*. H. Claessen, P. van de Velde and M. S. Smith, eds, pp. 36–45. South Hadley, MA: Bergin and Garvey Publishers.

Rudolph, Susanne Hoeber (1987) Presidential Address: State Formation in Asia – Prolegomenon to a Comparative Study. *Journal of Asian Studies* 46(4):731–46.

Rutt, Richard (1961) The Flower Boys of Silla. *Transactions of the Korea Branch of the Royal Asiatic Society* 37:1–61.

Sacks, Karen (1979) *Sisters and Wives: The Past and Future of Sexual Equality*. Westport, CT: Greenwood Press.

Sagan, Eli (1985) *At the Dawn of Tyranny: The Origins of Individualism, Political Oppression and the State*. New York: Alfred A. Knopf.

Sanday, Peggy Reeves (1981) *Female Power and Male Dominance: On the Origins of Sexual Inequality*. New York: Cambridge University Press.

Service, Elman (1975) *Origins of the State and Civilization: The Process of Cultural Evolution*. New York: W. W. Norton.

Shennan, S. J. (1987) Trends in the Study of Later European Prehistory. *Annual Review of Anthropology* 16:365–82.

Shin, Yong-ha (1985) Social History of the Ture Community and Nongak Musik (I). *Korea Journal* 25(3):4–17.

Sohn, Powkee, Chol-choon Kim, and Yi-sup Hong (1970) *The History of Korea*. Seoul: UNESCO.

Tiffany, Sharon (1979) Woman, Power and the Anthropology of Politics: A Review. *International Journal of Women's Studies* 2:430–42.

Trigger, Bruce (1984) Archaeology at the Crossroads. *Annual Review of Anthropology* 13:275–300.

—— (1985) Generalized Coercion and Inequality: The Basis of State Power in Early Civilization. In *Development and Decline, the Evolution of Sociopolitical Organization*. H. Claessen, P. van de Velde, and M. S. Smith, eds, pp. 46–61. South Hadley, MA: Bergin and Garvey Publishers.

Wheatley, Paul and Thomas See (1978) *From Court to Capital: A Tentative Interpretation of the Origins of the Japanese Urban Tradition*. Chicago: University of Chicago Press.

Zagarell, Allen (1986) Trade, Women, Class and Society in Ancient Western Asia. *Current Anthropology* 27(5):415–30.

Chapter 18

WOMEN, KINSHIP, AND THE BASIS OF POWER IN THE NORWEGIAN VIKING AGE

Liv Helga Dommasnes

Viking society, as we think we know it, was a society of men: seafarers, robbers, warriors, traders, farmers, craftsmen, kings, and slaves. We know of course that there must have been women and children, but this fact rarely surfaces in our interpretations. Once we start thinking about this elemental flaw in our picture of Viking society, we shall also have to start reflecting on how our knowledge of the past is structured. It is evident that language plays a fundamental part in this structuring of knowledge. The concepts of modern languages are *our* tools for grasping past realities. But these concepts are products of our own time and reality.

This culture-dependency of conceptualisation is of course the main reason why women and children have largely disappeared from the past. As many have pointed out before me, archaeology was born at a time when women and children were not supposed to be visible, at least not in the public sphere (Mandt and Næss 1985; Stalsberg 1991). And the public sphere was exactly what interested Victorian men as well as those Scandinavian men then involved in forming archaeology as a tool in the process of nation-building.

When working with the Viking Age, we do have the support of some written sources as well as the archaeological material. As far as archaeologists are concerned, this seems to have been a hindrance more than a help. Perhaps archaeologists feel that this period is not exclusively their own and too close in time to be investigated through the evolutionary and other, general models they use on the distant past. Whatever the reason the fact remains that in Scandinavia archaeological sources relevant to the study of women's roles are more abundant from the Viking Age than from any other period, but relatively few archaeologists try to exploit

[handwritten top margin: No written accounts from Viking societies themselves – other cultures record]

their potential. The written sources, scarce as they are, seem to have gained precedence. And this, in spite of the fact that we know that the written sources are biased. With a few exceptions they all belong to a different culture; writing from Viking societies is scarce. Because they explicitly convey *literate* meaning, we can be reasonably certain that this meaning is that of early Christianity in the north, not Viking Age ideology (but see Lönnroth 1991). If we assume, as has been recently argued (Steinsland 1988), that the transformation from heathen to Christian religion was not gradual but represented a radical break, this should also influence our views on the transformation of traditions from the late Viking Age or shortly thereafter before they were finally written down in the twelfth or thirteenth centuries. One perspective that we can reasonably assume to have been heavily influenced by changing cultural values is that of women in particular and gender roles in general.

Property, rank, and gender

[handwritten left margin: Women connected to biological capacity]

Viking Age society, as presented in laws and sagas, is a markedly hierarchical society with thralls at the bottom – mostly outside the law – and earls at the top. Icelandic sagas, when they mention women as they quite often do, tend to stress their family connections on the one hand and their family loyalty on the other. The popular image of Viking Age woman seems to be that of the ardent protector and, if need arise, avenger of family honour, like Gunhild in one of the Edda poems. This may or may not have been one aspect of women's role in Viking society. The general picture we get from a critical review of the written sources is that women of good family were respected, but they were not equal to men by any standard. Their work, which must have been very important to the economy of the farm, was mainly indoors, in the house or barn, while the public functions seem to have been the prerogative of men. Still, these positions were not definitely closed to women.

[handwritten left margin: ① women given some freedoms – but were these just false freedoms – given by men just to satisfy women (keep them in line)]

Under certain conditions a woman had the right to own family property (*oðall*). In that capacity she also had the right to vote at the legislative assembly, even though participation was voluntary for women (and disabled farmers). In Iceland women are even known to have been *goðar*, chieftains, fulfilling a religious and political function, if the sagas are to be believed, although they did not then have the political and legal authority of a male *goði*. In marriage a woman had some economic freedom, in that she ruled over some of the common property, generally a third; the dowry would be hers alone. Daughters had the right to inherit although their share was smaller than that of sons and primarily restricted to movables. *[handwritten: Given just enough, but not enough to have any power]*

The picture presented above is based exclusively on written sources and can thus be assumed to represent the ideal, or ideological, as filtered through the mesh of Christian authorship. Despite their flaws these sources provide a frame of reference in which to work when discussing social structures. They also allow us to raise the question of the relationship between ideology and practical life.

What do material remains tell us about hierarchical structures or about the position of women? This last question in particular interested me when I first started working on the western Norwegian Viking Age in the early 1970s. Because of the abundant sources, the Viking Age seemed a good place for an archaeologist to start her or his attack on established "truths" about the past. In recent years a number of studies relevant to this problem have been published, but unfortunately not all in English. I am very grateful to the authors and shall draw heavily on their results in my presentation. But first I shall give a brief review of my own results, based on an examination of early Iron Age archaeological remains, mainly from western Norway (Dommasnes 1976; 1982; 1987). Since the archaeological sources from the Viking period are mostly graves, these had to form the basis of my investigation. Lewis Binford's (1971) assumptions about the relationship of social complexity and status differentiation in death were taken as the point of departure.

One of the main conclusions of my investigation of Viking Age gender-structure in western Norway was that high status for women, as measured by grave-furnishings and the size of the covering mounds, was associated both with conditions favourable to agriculture and with older settlements. In this area at least, the most and the richest women's graves were found on the long-established farms, going back to the early Iron Age or even earlier. There also was a definite correspondence between areas with a high percentage of female graves and imported goods, which came mostly from the British Isles. This was evident from the tenth century onwards, which was not only the start of the Viking expansion towards the west, but also a period of internal unrest with rival, local kings, and the beginning of the unification of the country. The local kings or chieftains had the right to demand certain military assistance from the farmers within their area. We can assume that this right was occasionally called upon (Lindkvist 1991). Internal and external demands thus combined to take men away from the farm. Perhaps the men's absence paved the way for women's economic power, for they had to take over full responsibility for what went on at home, which may be reflected in the growing percentage of female graves during the Viking period, after a long decline (see below). These interpretations are strengthened by the fact that these rich burials are found mostly in coastal areas. Even though I claimed this economic potential must have been embedded in an ideology allowing women this kind of authority, such an explanation is not satisfactory, mainly because it is one-dimensional.

Norwegian archaeologist Mari Høgestøl (1983) has recently made an analysis of graves from the district of western Agder in southern Norway. Her analysis includes graves from the Roman, Migration, Merovingian, and Viking periods, thus obtaining a greater depth of time than my study. When possible she also had the skeletal remains from the graves analysed osteologically to determine age and sex. Høgestøl's (1983, 193) conclusions are interesting: in the Roman period the ratio of male to female burials is 1:7, in the Migration period 1:3, and in the late Iron Age 3:2.

Even if one takes account of her cautionary remarks that the female graves probably are over-represented in the Roman sample, the pattern is clear: a steady, relative increase of male graves during the Iron Age. Comparisons with other districts where determinations of sex were made on an osteological basis show a repetition of this pattern, as do analyses of Swedish grave-fields from the Roman period (*ibid.*, 194–7).

Høgestøl also investigated the degree of sex – or gender – differentiation in the graves, concluding that there was no definite indication of such a differentiation in the Roman period, some in the Migration period, which later became more marked in the late Iron Age. Likewise, women's graves showed the most variation in grave-furnishings and building in the earlier Iron Age, men's in the later Iron Age. This last observation corresponds with my own analysis of Viking Age burials from the district of Sogn. We both then chose to interpret the variation as an expression of different social roles.

Høgestøl's data did not allow a successful analysis of the relationship between sex, age, and grave-furnishings. Such an analysis has been made on Danish Iron Age burials, however. This analysis disclosed that while, among men, young adults were given the richest grave-furnishings, women were given more equipment the older they were (Sellevold *et al.* 1984, 68). If read in terms of status, high status was for young men and old women.

What is gender? The discussion till now has been mostly related to differentiation of sex with little attention paid to the concept of gender, although the question of gender roles has been implicit in the interpretations given. In modern feminist discussion the term sex is used for biological sex only. Gender is used for "social sex", or rather, social roles considered feminine or masculine respectively. While there must necessarily be a certain correspondence between biological and social sex in order to render the term "gender" meaningful, this correspondence is not absolute. Women may have roles considered essentially masculine, and vice versa. More importantly, the content of gender roles is by definition understood as culturally defined. Consequently we should not only expect gender roles to be different in different cultures, but also to change over time in one and the same culture. Gender roles can be seen as conditioned by culture but also as one important element in defining culture. This aspect of gender-structures is important to modern feminism and has led to the investigation of, among other things, the relationship between gender and power-relations, since gender-relations as we know them are also power-relations. Related to power are the two concepts of authority and influence. In this perspective gender-relations must also play an important part in any discussion of kinship and power, two of the themes explored in this volume.

So now let us examine the concepts of kinship and power, especially authority and influence, in terms of the archaeological evidence presented above and further historical and religious data, and present our interpretations from a gender perspective.

Kinship and power

Power was inherited

In old Norse society kinship and power seem to have been related in the sense that power resided in the family (*ætt*) rather than in individuals. It is also generally assumed that this was a male-dominated society, women being relegated to their role of exerting influence behind the scenes. Even if this was the case, it seems probable that nuances can be found if these questions are considered anew in light of the archaeological evidence presented above, and if perspectives are adopted to understand the influence of ideology (tradition) and gender-relations.

The *ætt*, or family, was the basic unit in Viking society, fundamental to alliances and loyalties. The head of the family was normally a man; inheritance went through the male line. A daughter was married away and due consideration taken to the importance of forming appropriate alliances through the marriage. But within this system women had some rights: a daughter would inherit, although less than her brothers; once married (and after some time), she obtained disposal over part of their property; the dowry would always belong to the woman, even after a divorce; and a widow had full disposal of her property.

Women obtained power thru family - men

Family ties can be assumed to be reflected in burials. Analyses of Swedish grave-fields have disclosed groupings that can be interpreted as family plots (Johnsen-Welinder and Welinder 1973, 61 and 72ff). In western Norway no such grave-fields have been completely excavated, but here there are rather big grave-mounds containing many burials. An analysis of such mounds from the late Iron Age in the district of Sogn showed that a greater percentage of women's graves than men's came from big mounds (more than 15 metres in diameter). However, the women's graves in those big mounds are with one single exception secondary burials. Secondary burials are generally twice as common among women as among men (Dommasnes 1976, 75). A tentative explanation of this phenomenon would be to interpret the grave mounds, which seem to have been built rather close to the farmhouses, as family graves originally built perhaps over the founding father. The fact that women's graves are almost never primary seems to confirm the notion of a gender-based, hierarchical society.   *Women were buried in a group*

Not given individual grave

At the same time, the 3:1, male:female ratio in the graves, along with the observation that relatively more female than male graves were placed in big mounds, suggests that a more select group of women than men received the kind of considerate burial that archaeologists are able to identify. Analyses of objects found in the graves, both in western Norway and in Agder, point in the same direction. Assuming that a family would have roughly the same number of men and women, we must conclude that just being a member of the family did not justify an elaborate funeral, at least not for women. Based on an analysis of grave-goods, I have suggested that one of the extra qualifications needed would be economic in character: a woman who took good care of the family property while the men were away would be recognised for her skill and honoured in this way. Of course one can also speculate that among the graves we find are those of the few women in charge of family property, widows in full posession of their own property, or women who held religious positions of importance. I shall return to this last point after a short dicussion of the ways and means to power open to Viking Age women.

Power can be power over people, over property, or even over forces outside the immediate environment. One can distinguish between power *over* (people) and power *to* (do things). Power implies *influence* as well as *authority*. This last concept is here understood as "the right to make a special decision and demand obedience" (Sanday 1974, 190). Authority thus becomes acknowledged power.

Ideology behind power

Public positions of power and authority, whether they were based on economic, legal, or military supremacy, seem to have been reserved for men, even though women could gain access to them under certain circumstances. As mentioned above, a widow had the right, but not the duty, to be present at the legislative assembly. When Icelandic sagas mention female *goðar,* it seems that they must have had full religious authority, although they did not have legal power equal to men in the same position (Steinsland 1985, 35).

Influence, on the other hand, women had. The sagas in particular paint a picture of Viking Age women as ardent defenders of family honour, urging their men to revenge. In the relationship between husband and wife their family connections would play an important part.

While women may not have had power over people like men, we must be allowed to assume that in the domestic sphere women had power to make decisions of far-reaching consequences to the entire household. As managers of all kinds of farm products, such as food, textiles, and hides, it was in the hands of the wife to see to it that the often quite big household of many generations, servants, and animals came safely through the winter. In this capacity she must have had decisive influence in the disposition of these goods and thereby over family economy.

The only kinds of tools, according to the grave-goods, that were reserved for women only were textile implements. These are also found on house-sites, where strikingly there seems to be an abundance especially of spindle-whorls. From the deserted Viking Age farm in Ytre Moa, Sogn, we know eleven (Bakka n.d.), while an incomplete excavation of a house-site at Dale, Høyanger, further west has yielded eight (Randers 1987). Could it be that Viking women specialised in cloth production for sale, and thereby created their own, "independent" economic basis? In a dissertation analysing textile fragments from northern Europe, Danish archaeologist Lise Bender Jørgensen (1986, 175) suggests that the fine woollen cloth so much appreciated in the Viking Age may have been produced just here, in western Norway. If so, women in Sogn had a product very much sought after in international trade, and the concentration of female graves in areas where imported goods are common, noted earlier, becomes immediately comprehensible.

There can be no doubt that material and economic conditions are important in an analysis of power. One should not forget, however, the importance of custom, or tradition, in the religious sphere. In pre- and protohistoric societies I do not find it useful to distinguish between ideology and religion. Instead I would like to adopt the definition of religion suggested by Ragnhild Bjerre Finnestad (1986, 23):

> I employ a concept of *culture* which includes the system of comprehensive religious outlooks on life – imbedded in all cultural manifestations, pertaining directly or indirectly to all activities of society.
>
> . . . On the other hand, the pragmatic, utilitarian aspect of culture is included in the definition of religion which I employ: I do not define *religion* as something which is not pragmatic-and-useful in the struggle for existence.

This implies that even if we can see an immediate, economic or functional explanation of a phenomenon, the rationalisation for ordering things or acting in just this way may be religious. In this wider sense religion is a way of creating order in the world, transcendental or material. At the same time religion is no more static than other aspects of culture. Interpretations and emphases on different aspects of the religious system may change as a response to changes in society and environment. Such a shift in emphasis seems to have taken place in Norse societies during the Iron Age. Gro Steinsland (1979; 1985), another historian of religion, has pointed out that in the pre-Viking Iron Age, up to about AD 600, the emphasis seems to have been upon a fertility cult, in which woman played an important role, while a warrior cult took precedence, at least in parts of Scandinavia, during the Viking period. But she also points out that there were remnants of a fertility cult even in the late Viking Age. This cult was private in the sense that it took place on individual farmsteads. It was performed by women (Steinsland and Vogt 1981), perhaps most often by old women (Steinsland 1985, 36), which would help explain why old women seemed to obtain high status as measured by grave-goods, if conditions in Denmark and Norway offer valid parallels. Steinsland also points to the fact that the areas of Sogn where the concentration of rich Viking Age women's graves are found are also areas where place-names testify to a strong fertility cult, and she suggests that those buried here may have been women who had important functions in this connection.

In any case, such a change of emphasis in the religious sphere offers an alternative frame of reference for understanding the change in women's social positions as reflected in burial customs. In my opinion this is merely moving a step further in trying to discuss the ideological basis for gender differentiation.

Such an interpretation also seems to offer a better explanation than does a purely economic model for Mari Høgestøl's data, showing a steady decline in women's position during the Iron Age (although I do not think one should make generalisations from this). If we accept that women as a rule play important parts in fertility religions and their cults (Eliade 1978, 40ff), as they seem to have done in old Norse religion, it becomes reasonable to assume that as the fertility cult lost its dominant position, the foundation for some of women's sources of power and authority disappeared. Not only were women no longer essential as cult performers but the very justification for some of their influential social roles disappeared. Should we assume that as the fertility cult was relegated from the public to the private (farm) sphere of life, so too was the basis for women's power and influence? To support such a hypothesis more investigations are needed, especially regarding religious manifestations and gender roles in the age preceding that of the Vikings.

Until now archaeological gender studies in Norway have concentrated on Viking Age material simply because the burial customs in this period were such that it seems possible to distinguish between men's and women's graves. Fortunately the centuries before the Vikings are now finally coming into focus. Two important projects dealing with problems relevant to the one in question are now in progress: one is a combined osteological and archaeological analysis of Iron Age grave-finds from the entire country (Næss and Sellevold forthcoming); the other is an investigation of pre-Viking, Iron Age graves from the district of Sunnmøre, western Norway, with special attention paid to the roles of women (Hjørungdal forthcoming). If analysed within a proper theoretical framework, these investigations should be able to generate data of great relevance to many of the questions raised in this volume.

■ ■ ■

References

Bakka, Egil n.d. *Excavation report from Ytre Moa, Årdal, Sogn.* Topographical archives, Historical museum, Bergen.

Bender Jørgensen, Lise (1986). *Forhistoriske textiler i Skandinavien. Prehistoric Scandinavian Textiles*, (Nordiske Fortidsminder, series B, 9), København.

Binford, Lewis (1971). "Mortuary practices: their study and their potential" *American Antiquity* 36, 6–29.

Bjerre Finnestad, Ragnhild (1986). "The part and the whole: reflections on theory and methods applied to the interpretation of Scandinavian rock carvings" in Gro Steinsland (ed.) *Words and Objects: towards a dialogue between archaeology and history of religion,* 21–31. Oslo Univ. Press, Oslo.

Dommasnes, Liv Helga (1976). "Yngre jernalder i Sogn – forsøk på sosial rekonstruksjon". (Unpublished masters degree, University of Bergen).

—— (1982). "Late Iron Age in western Norway: Female roles and ranks as deduced from an analysis of burial customs" *Norwegian Archaeological Review* 15, 70–84.

—— (1987). "Male/female roles and ranks in late Iron Age Norway" in Reidar Bertelsen, Arnvid Lillehammer and Jenny-Rita Næss (eds.) *Were They All Men?*, 65–78. (AmS Varia 17), Stavanger.

Eliade, Mircea (1978). *A History of Religious Ideas. 1. From the Stone Age to the Eleusinian Mysteries.* Univ. of Chicago Press, Chicago.

Hjørungdal, Tove forth. (1991). *Det skjulte kjønn. Patriarkal tradisjon og feministisk visjon i arkeologin belyst med fokus på en jernalderkontekst.* Acta Archaeologica Lundersia. Series in 8°. Nr. 19. Lund.

Høgestøl, Mari (1983). "Gravskikk og kjønnsrelasjoner" (Unpublished masters degree, University of Oslo).

Johnsen-Welinder Barbro and Stig Welinder (1973). *Järnåldersgravfäl i Mälardalen.* (Acta Archaeologica Lundensia. Series in 8° Minore 2), Lund.

Lindkvist, Thomas (1991). "Social and Political Power in Sweden 1000–1300: Predatory Incursions, Royal Taxation, and the Formation of a Feudal State," in R. Samson (ed.) *Social Approaches to Viking Studies,* Glasgow, Cruithne Press, pp. 137–146.

Lönnroth, Lars (1991). "Sponsors, Writers and Readers of Early Norse Literature," in R. Samson (ed.) *Social Approaches to Viking Studies,* Glasgow, Cruithne Press, pp. 3–10.

Mandt, Gro and Jenny-Rita Naess (1986). "Hvem skapte og gjenskaper vår fjerne fortid?" *Kvinner i arkeologi i Norge* 3, 3–28.

Naess, Jenny-Rita and Berit Sellevold forth. "Iron Age man in Norway".

Randers, Kjersti (1987). *Bosetningsrester fra middelalder.* (Topographical archives, Historical museum), Bergen.

Sanday, Peggy R. (1974). "Female status in the public domain" in Michelle Zimbalist Rosaldo and Louise Lamphere (eds) *Woman, Culture and Society,* 189–206. Stanford Univ. Press, Stanford.

Sellevold, Berit, Ulla Lund Hansen and J. Balslev Jørgensen (1984). *Iron Age Man in Denmark.* (Nordiske fortidsminder), København.

Stalsberg, Ann (1991) "Women as Actors in North European Viking Age Trade," in R. Samson (ed.) *Social Approaches to Viking Studies,* Glasgow: Cruithne Press, pp. 76–84.

Steinsland, Gro. (1979). "Den gamle tro" in Ingrid Semmingsen, Nina Karin Monsen, Stephan Tschudi-Madsen and Yngvar Ustvedt (eds) *Norges Kulturhistorie* 1, 129–63. H. Aschehoug and Co., Oslo.

Steinsland, Gro (1985). "Kvinner og kult i vikingtid" in Andersen, Randi, Liv Helga Dommasnes, Magnús Stefánsson and Ingvild Øye (eds) *Kvinnearbeid i Norden fra vikingtiden til reformasjonen,* 31–42. Bergen.

Steinsland, Gro (1991). "Religionsskiftet i Norden og Veluspá 65," in Ero Steinsland, Ulj Drobin, Juha Pentiköinen and Preben Meulengracht Sørenen (eds) *Nordisk hedendom. Et Symposium.* Odense.

Steinsland, Gro and Kari Vogt (1981). "Aukinn ertu Uolse ok vpp vm tekinn. En religionshistorisk analyse av Volsapáttr i Flateyjarbók" *Arkiv för Nordisk filologi* 96, 87–107.

PART VII

New narratives, new visions

INTRODUCTION

The studies presented above take gender as an interesting and important dimension of social difference. They show how archaeologists can study gender differences, and present a variety of conclusions about the human past that challenge our Euro-centric assumptions. Among these conclusions are:

1. that gender does not always correlate with biological sex;
2. men and women may have separate prestige and power systems;
3. the basis of men's and women's power may change from time to time and place to place; and
4. material tasks, tools, and symbols help to define and change gender roles and prestige hierarchies.

Recently, some authors have begun to ask whether the very practice of archaeology can change by considering gender differences, and gender diversity. New ways of thinking, and new ways of writing are emerging.

One thread in this increasingly complicated task asks whether women may tend to do archaeology differently from men (Gero 1996; see also studies of women in science such as Keller 1985, Harding 1986), in many cases taking a more personal or empathetic approach to understanding past lifeways, in contrast to masculine emphases on objectivity, proof, and professional competition. Although the women's movement of the 1960s had little direct effect on archaeological theory and practice, individuals were affected, and there have always been individual women who broke barriers and subverted conventions.

One woman archaeologist who has yet to attract the attention of feminist biographers is Emma Lou Davis. Sculptor, wild woman, and archaeologist, Davis spent many years researching the prehistory of the China Lake area of Southern California in the 1960s and 1970s, long before the emergence of gender archaeology. She proved her ability to write with scientific detail demanded by her colleagues of her research as it unfolded, but refused to leave out the story of discovery, and the story of Paleoindian men, women, and children, as she saw it. She realized that the difference between the orientation to her work and that of other archaeologists had much to do with gender. In the preface to her book, *The Ancient Californians: Rancholabrean Hunters of the Mojave Lakes Country*, excerpted in chapter 19, her colleague Richard Shutler wrote,

> Dr Davis is indefatigable, which is not surprising when you consider that she walked across Siberia and China in 1936 and 1937. Further evidence of her tenacity came to light when she had to reconstruct her MA thesis after the original copy and material were burned in a house fire in 1961. She received her PhD from UCLA in 1964, somewhat later in life than most of us, and since that time she has been involved constantly with interdisciplinary field research and reporting.

Janet Spector's monograph *What this Awl Means: Feminist Archaeology at a Historic Wahpeton Village* (chapter 20), takes an explicitly feminist viewpoint. But it has much in common with Davis's earlier efforts because both are built around narratives – the story of the author's interests and motivations, the story of daily life in the field doing research, and admittedly imaginative accounts of what life was like in the past, thoroughly grounded in the detailed recording demanded by traditional archaeological methods. We present below the beginning and concluding sections of Spector's first chapter, "Archaeology and Empathy," in which she details her personal and professional interest in archaeology, and the story of how she came to work with descendants of Native Americans who lived at the historic village she and her field school students excavated. The first few paragraphs of her narrative about life at the Little Rapids Site provide a taste of her innovative approach.

We conclude with A. Bernard Knapp (chapter 21), who reminds us that males are 49 per cent of humankind, and thus 49 per cent or so of our human past. While a gendered archaeology can be a feminist archaeology, it can also be a masculinist archaeology. But this is not an archaeology based on the traditional implicit assumptions of male dominance and female passivity or invisibility. It is, instead, one that recognizes that identifying and critically analyzing both masculine and feminine roles and interrelationships is the key to removing Euro-centric biases in our reconstructions of the past.

■ ■ ■

Further reading

Claassen, Cheryl (ed.) (1994)
Conkey, Margaret W. and Ruth E. Tringham (1996)
Harding, Sandra (1986)
Keller, Evelyn Fox (1975)
Meskell, Lynn (1996)
Moore, Henrietta (1988)
Tringham, Ruth E. (1991)
Yates, Tim (1993)

■ ■ ■

References

Claassen, Cheryl (ed.) (1994) *Women in Archaeology*. Philadelphia: University of Pennsylvania.
Conkey, Margaret W. and Ruth E. Tringham (1996) "Cultivating Thinking/Challenging Authority: Some Experiments in Feminist Pedagogy in Archaeology," in R. P. Wright (ed.) *Gender and Archaeology*, Philadelphia: University of Pennsylvania Press, pp. 224–250.

Gero, Joan M. (1996) "Archaeological Practice and Gendered Encounters with Field Data," in R. P. Wright (ed.) *Gender and Archaeology*, Philadelphia: University of Pennsylvania Press, pp. 251–277.

Harding, Sandra (1986) *The Science Question in Feminism*. Ithaca, New York: Cornell University Press.

Keller, Evelyn Fox (1985) *Reflections on Gender and Science*. New Haven: Yale University Press.

Meskell, Lynn (1996) "The Somatization of Archaeology: Institutions, Discourse, Corporeality," *Norwegian Archaeological Review* 29(1):1–16.

Moore, Henrietta (1988) *Feminism and Anthropology*. Minneapolis, Minnesota: University of Minnesota Press.

Tringham, Ruth E. (1991) "Households with Faces: The Challenge of Gender in Prehistoric Architectural Remains," in J. M. Gero and M. W. Conkey (eds) *Engendering Archaeology: Women and Prehistory*, Oxford: Basil Blackwell, pp. 93–131.

Yates, Tim (1993) "Frameworks for an Archaeology of the Body," in C. Tilley (ed.) *Interpretative Archaeology*, Providence, Rhode Island and Oxford: Berg, pp. 31–72.

Chapter 19

THE ANCIENT CALIFORNIANS:
Rancholabrean Hunters of the
Mojave Lakes Country

Emma Lou Davis

Preface

In looking back over this book, I can now see how experimental
it is. The significance of many kinds of information became clearer
as different arrangements of them were tried, changed or discarded.
Many isolated and widely spaced facts have been stretched to the
limit to connect them and thereby bring into focus some measure
of reconstruction of ancient and insecure lifeways over a vast passage
of time.

The last of the saber tooth cats and the first of the humans
drifted in and out of this valley as transients during uneasy times
when there were extreme and rapid changes in the lake and general
climate. A challenging existence was everybody's lot. Passing
millennia saw Lake China transformed from a wind-ruffled inland
sea, to expanses of pond and marsh, to desert floor; and sequentially change back.

Doing this work and organizing it together in a coherent record
has been a growth experience. Slowly, but clearly, I saw how little
I knew as the synthesis progressed.

This is a very female book. Hopefully, it contributes a different
voice, different attitudes and values from male traditions of archaeological writing in which, somehow, the actors become lost in the
gimmicks and stage props. The carefulness is the same. There may
be more devotion to detail (women always have been good at
remembering where things should be put on shelves!). But the focus
has been on the people, their diversity, their energy and inventive-
ness. At first unknown, they gradually materialized and became
friends – the woman who made those two nearly identical skinning

knives; the man who threw away a base of a broken lanceolate knife on Stake 25, and dropped its companion piece in a camp at 25 NW.

This is not a book about full-time Elephant Hunters (a male myth, not substantiated by our information). It is about peoples of the marsh: setting snares for musk-rats and nets for ducks; gathering eggs on a spring morning when brant were feeding; when there was enough dried horse meat in camp to tide the family over until the next camel. These were people who spent spring and fall near flyway marshes, summers in higher pastures and forests and autumn collecting winter stores — nuts for caches, berries for pemmican — in a round of life.

E. L. D.
July 1975

Introduction
The Mojave Desert

The Mojave Desert is among all things contradictory — inner visions and drab flats; rock needles and swamp muck; black basalt against a neon sky, above a translucent, perfect flower growing without visible stem on the gravel floor. Storms explode in a riot of wild yells and downpour. Evening is tranquility, a song singing to itself. And there are few other places where you get such tired, frozen feet.

This beautiful place is a country of color and shadow — tiny plants, nocturnal animals, salt flats and gravel windrows inside a rim of volcanic mountains. When day breaks, every mountain stands out clean, every little cloud shines. During the wheeling hours of day, the light changes to a flat blank and sweat runs down from hidden springs in our hair until shadows lengthen, each granule and artifact casting its own, and we reach for jackets. As shadows lengthen, the desert world begins its color transformations: rusts, ochres, purple-brown, black and electric blue. And at night, moonshine turns it to sea.

This is the last of the quiet places, so silent that flight feathers of ravens overhead cut the air like tearing silk.

During five years we worked here very slowly, only on occasional weekends as the Naval testing schedule permitted — a slowness that proved to be a great asset. It forced us to rethink our work, improve our techniques, and soak ourselves with the environments and materials of a long study in prehistory. We set ourselves well-measured deadlines and met them: this interim report is one of those nodal points, a good stopping place at which to pause and review what has been done — to pull it all together — before proceeding into the next stages of the work. For me, this was a continuous period of growth and insight, a period when strong bonds formed with my co-workers. I also learned to love the desert. And finally, during four months of daily work with the artifacts, a strange bridge gradually formed between myself and the stone, like an intense involvement. It was a two-way communication in which I talked and sang to them like an Eskimo sculptor with a fresh block of ivory – singing "who are you who lives in there?" – and they replied in kind. It was during this period that the knowledge and perceptiveness of my friends, particularly Gena Van Camp, guided some of the way across under-water stepping stones to the past. The stepping stones were the tools.

Scope of the report

This report is a preliminary one, a first scan of what has been accomplished so far during the first five years of the China Lake Program. The report reviews this work, resorting and arraying masses of raw data, which comprise the following:

1   More than 5,347 artifacts;
2   more than 15,700 flakes;
3   plane table mapping of more than 3km^2 of PaleoIndian site surfaces;
4   initial studies of the late Pleistocene geology of Lake China;
5   identification and cataloging of more than 900 bone fragments of a Rancholabrean fauna;
6   correlations of certain faunal elements with PaleoIndian hunting and butchering activities;
7   initiation of palynological and paleoecological studies;
8   preliminary classification of all artifacts by the following three criteria: function; degree of weathering; morphology. This sorting has produced some new and unexpected tools, such as Time-marker Groups (The Core Tool Tradition); Phase Groups (like Classic Clovis vs. Proto-Clovis); and such use categories as crescentics and crescents, cutters and "steak knives";
9   recording on edge-punched cards of 412 key artifacts used in defining the various classes;
10 backhoe trenches and test excavations to discover stratigraphies and correlations with artifacts.

The work of arraying and synthesizing also has generated an extensive structure of hypotheses for interpretations of both parts and the whole of a vast, disparate corpus of information:

1   a time scale for culture-historical changes;
2   tentative seriation of the stone tools into long (but interrelated) technological sequences with a possible time-depth of 45,000 years;
3   recognition of the value for PaleoIndian studies of these broad and open categories, as opposed to rigid sterility of a narrow typological approach.

Eventually, the organized body of data and web of testable hypotheses will prove ideal for sophisticated, multivariate analysis. However, in this first presentation, only the simplest scaling will be attempted. First, we must become very clear about what questions need to be asked, and how best to answer them, using every means at our disposal. If digital mathematics does it — we will use statistics; if analog simulations are most heuristic, they will be used; and we know that intuition is an ultimate form of wisdom. This preliminary array of digested information is a firm base for many future, investigative enterprises.

Beginning and development of the Lake China project

Early in September 1969, two college students named Dick and Bill Fagnant came down from the China Lake Naval Weapons Center with a large grocery box full of artifacts, which they wanted appraised. The contents were startling: fluted knife/points; end scrapers; beaks; choppers that almost were obliterated by weathering; and long ovate knife/points as deeply eroded as the choppers. There was no doubt that the Fagnants had found their way onto PaleoIndian sites of major importance. I immediately made arrangements with the China Lake Command to visit the area, which was well protected because it happened to be in the middle of the bombing ranges.

Two weeks later on a blistering afternoon, a small group of us climbed out of our vehicles on G-1 Road, a lateral across the Naval Weapons Center testing areas in the basin of Pleistocene Lake China. We were an assorted crew of civilian professionals from the Base, college students, members of the Mojave-Sierra Archaeological Society and my assistant and I from the San Diego Museum of Man. We fanned out and started crunching over gravelly slopes led by the young Fagnants, who knew the district well and had marked various site localities on a topographic quadrangle sheet. The "sites" didn't look like much — a lot of gravel, some sand, a few playas, an occasional pile of tufa and a weatherbeaten flake or artifact at rare intervals with only an occasional concentration. However, judging by the Fagnant collection, this impoverished-looking landscape contained "sign" of a poorly defined culture called Lake Mojave, and an equally elusive one called Clovis (known on the High Plains from an association of large, fluted implements and dead mammoths). In California, no one, particularly ourselves, had any clear idea of the characteristics, dates or interrelationships of these cultural will-o-the-wisps. On the basis of five years of painstaking work since that time, however, we are now able to point out certain kinds of reasonable relationships and sequences, and have outlined a model (seriated on the basis of weathering of the artifacts coupled with their morphology and technology) of the suggested cultural history of this region over the past 45,000 years, which may prove useful while it lasts.

In the beginning, it would be difficult to imagine a major search in prehistory starting with a scantier foundation in theory, despite the extensive structure of ideas that has since grown out of our work like a seedling. As time passed and we became more discerning, we were able to make advances in both procedures and interpretations.

1   A sampling program was devised, which was adequate for a huge area.

2   A system of survey squares, each 305 meters on a side was established, together with simple but efficient methods of mapping, artifact harvesting and recording (see also Davis 1975).

3   We developed initial hypotheses, tested and scored them and changed them as needed.

4   By departing from opinions in the literature, we discovered new, functional classes of tools – little scalpels, women's work implements and butchering equipment.

5   Also, new theories about the origins and culture/historical position of the assemblage called Lake Mojave and its relation to Clovis were postulated.

6   In the final stages of artifact analysis and review, the tools began to array themselves into novel sequences, suggesting new progressions of cultural developments in our sampling area as well as time depths of human activities in the Great Basin Lakes Country (Russell 1889), which might be far greater than expected.

But in 1969 we had little concept of how widely PaleoIndian tools were scattered in the basin of Lake China. There was as yet no way of knowing what we were seeking – anything and everything, really. We walked for miles, looking and taking notes. There was so much, yet so little knowledge about it.

Concluding Remarks
Excerpt from summary

During five years of weekend field work in China Lake Basin, we approached the Mojave Desert with work philosophies and practical strategies different from those that customarily have been used. We viewed the desert as a whole environment and the scraps of PaleoIndian "signs" as part of a total life-style within this ecosystem. Also, we were forced to devise simple, intensive tactics of mapping, spotting, recording and collecting stone and bone (see Davis 1975). By treating the Mojave as delicately as though it were a French cavern, we were able to squeeze a small amount of cavern information out of it – for it is an open "cavern" with refined layering. This was our major discovery. Therefore, we harvested unaccustomed information and generated deviant hypotheses to explain it.

This report is a first scan of a large corpus of unreported data. It is highly experimental. Postulates and their corollaries have evolved along growth lines of speculation, leading to unexpected and unifying possibilities.

■ ■ ■

References

Davis, Emma Lou (1975) "The 'Exposed' Archaeology of China Lake, California," *American Antiquity* 40: 154–177.

Russell, I. C. (1889) "Quaternary History of Mono Valley, California," Department of the Interior Geological Survey, Eighth Annual Report to the Director 3: 261–394.

Chapter 20

Spector

WHAT THIS AWL MEANS:
Feminist Archaeology at a Wahpeton
Dakota Village

Janet D. Spector

When I excavate sites and touch things that have lain untouched
for centuries, I know why I am an archaeologist. But until now,
when I wrote about those sites and objects, I felt no connection
with the past, my own or that of the people whose cultural land-
scapes I had unearthed. Writing "What This Awl Means," a story
about a Dakota girl who lost a carved awl handle a century and a
half ago, brought back thoughts and feelings I had experienced as
a young girl drawn to archaeology. As I learned about the discipline – and, especially, how to write about archaeology for academic readers – I found myself increasingly distanced from the question that had fascinated me since childhood: what was life like for
people in the past? While composing the awl story in place of the
standard archaeological report or scholarly article, I was reminded
of my original reasons for wanting to be an archaeologist. These
motives are empathetic – a longing to discover essences, images,
and feelings of the past – not detached, distanced, objective.

It took me a long time to reconnect with the past. My interests in archaeology and Indians began in the late 1940s in Madison,
Wisconsin, when my grandfather walked with me and my friends
to the zoo in Henry Vilas Park. Our route took us through
unmarked Indian burial mounds on a ridge above the park. I do
not recall his ever telling us anything about the mounds or the
people who built them. I doubt that my grandfather, who had fled
Russia around 1890 to escape pogroms against Jewish people, knew
anything about Indians, though his experiences with persecution
were not so different from theirs. I knew virtually nothing about
the Indian mounds except that they were an important, memo-
rable part of my early sense of place.

When I was five, we moved to a Madison neighborhood called Nakoma. We lived on the corner of Cherokee Drive and Shawnee Pass. Almost every street had a real or made-up Indian name: Manitou Way, Waban Hill, Hiawatha Drive, Seminole Highway, Iroquois Drive, Huron Hill. No teachers at Nakoma Elementary School or Cherokee Junior High School thought to tell us how these place-names were selected, let alone anything about the peoples we knew of in this peculiar way.

I remember walking down Cherokee Drive on trash pick-up day and looking in cans to see what broken appliances, gadgets, and other interesting junk neighbors had thrown away. I also liked to scavenge for objects lost in the dry creek near Cherokee Drive. Kids often went to the creek for smoking or other forbidden acts, and sometimes I found clues to children's secrets: a jackknife or a cigarette lighter.

I trace the roots of my interest in archaeology to these childhood wanderings among Indian mounds and along streets bearing Indian names in search of things that people abandoned or lost. Of course the peoples named Huron, Seminole, Iroquois, Cherokee, or Shawnee – groups separated by culture, language, and hundreds of miles when they first encountered Euro-Americans – never lived in my neighborhood or even in Wisconsin. No one ever told me about them or their histories, but I wondered what life was like when other Indian peoples lived in my neighborhood.

I began studying archaeology in 1962 as a freshman at the University of Wisconsin at Madison, but I found the subject much less interesting than I had expected. This disappointed me, since I had decided in the ninth grade to become an archaeologist, despite having been told that girls could not be archaeologists and not knowing what it took to become one. With a few exceptions the readings in undergraduate courses bored me. I despised being required to memorize the esoteric names and obscure traits that defined types of stone tools and pottery. These types constituted the "archaeological cultures" that students dutifully charted through time and space on their final exams. I learned from these courses that archaeologists apparently considered artifact classification more important than the people who had made the tools, about whom very little was said. The archaeology I was taught was objective, object oriented, and objectifying.

Fortunately, in the summer after my sophomore year and throughout my undergraduate years, I had the opportunity to do fieldwork under the supervision of Joan Freeman, an archaeologist for the Wisconsin Historical Society. At the time, women field directors were as unusual as opportunities for women students. I went on my first "dig" in 1964. After a few weeks of practice, we began excavating a site in southern Wisconsin, inappropriately named "Aztalan" by early nineteenth-century observers. They believed that the site's sophisticated remains could not have been left by local Indian people, and they concluded erroneously that Aztecs or colonists from Mexico at one time occupied Wisconsin (Freeman 1986, 355).

Aztalan refueled my interest in archaeology. I remember sitting at the top of a huge, reconstructed earthen temple mound, one of several sacred places at the site, watching a thunderstorm approach. Filled with awe, I ached to know about the Indian people who had built this impressive place several centuries earlier and had left it long before Euro-Americans arrived in the area. I had no idea how or why the Indians built the pyramid, what they did there, or how they explained thunderstorms. Questions like these drifted through my mind as I worked.

For almost a decade of summers I excavated at Indian sites in Wisconsin. At each I imagined being transported into the past and through the empathetic barrier that separated me from the people who once used the broken tools, ornaments, containers, and plant and animal remains we carefully exposed with our trowels. I knew that their world was very different, but I had no framework for understanding it, just the intense wish to know about their perspectives and perceptions.

Neither professors of archaeology nor authors of archaeology texts suggested that we might get closer to these people by studying contemporary Indian languages, religions, or philosophies. They implied that too much time had elapsed, too much change had occurred, too much history separated people from their pasts. People occupied these "prehistoric" sites long before traditional Indian culture had "disintegrated" through contact with Europeans. Contemporary Indians were disconnected from their ancestors. But no one I knew ever bothered to ask Indian people about these notions. . . .

I began writing this book about Little Rapids with several goals in mind. First, I wanted to communicate in an easily accessible way what we had learned about the Wahpeton community during a turbulent period of its history. Second, I wanted to highlight women's activities and the relations between men and women, topics typically ignored in archaeological writings. Third, I wanted to incorporate Dakota voices, visions, and perspectives into the story.

Initially, I returned to my earlier analysis of Dakota men's and women's activities, hoping to expand that study. I started with two sets of data: information and artifacts from the Little Rapids site, now mapped, sorted, identified, and counted; and documentary evidence from nineteenth-century written accounts, organized into tables with titles such as "Gender-Specific Task Inventory: Women/Men," "Task Seasonality," "Task Materials: Women/Men," and "Men's and Women's Material Inventory." Although Euro-American men wrote most of the nineteenth-century descriptions of Dakota life, several women also left eyewitness accounts. In addition, Charles A. Eastman (Ohiyesa), a Wahpeton man, recorded experiences from his childhood in the mid-1800s (C. Eastman [1902] 1971). These remarkably consistent sources often included detailed descriptions of men's and women's work and activities. During the digging we had recovered evidence of numerous resource-procurement, processing, and storage activities; signs of clothing, tool, ornament, and ammunition manufacturing; and traces of housing. Through close analysis of the tasks as described in the literature, I hoped we could link elements of the Little Rapids archaeological assemblage to the men, women, and children who lived in the community.

Yet as I pursued this approach and, at the same time, reflected on my recent experiences with Dakota people at the site, I became dissatisfied. I found the task-differentiation approach too constraining as a way of writing about what life was like for the nineteenth-century people. Like other taxonomic schemes, it generated distanced and lifeless representations of the past. This was not how I wanted to portray the Wahpeton people who had lived at the site when Euro-Americans began moving into the territory. So, finally, I put aside my tables enumerating activities, schedules, spaces, and tools and began to experiment with a new way of presenting the past.

I turned my attention to an artifact that we had discovered in 1980 in a garbage dump. It was a small antler awl handle, about three inches long and delicately inscribed with a series of dots and lines. The handle would have held a short, pointed iron tip of about the same length, making a tool for perforating leather and other materials. I felt certain that a Wahpeton woman had once used the tool at Little Rapids and that its inscriptions conveyed a great deal about her accomplishments to those who understood their meaning. The awl handle became an important symbol to me.

In response to this evocative find, I wrote the story of how the awl might have been used and lost. In many ways, that work represents the culmination of what I have learned between the time of my visits to the mounds in Madison with my grandfather and my visits to the mounds at Little Rapids with members of Mazomani's family. Through this account I hope to give readers a sense of Dakota culture in those times and to stimulate curiosity about the site and the people who left no written records of themselves.

The chapters that follow the story unravel it. They incorporate voices and viewpoints other than my own – those of the Dakota people, as well as the fur traders, officials, explorers, and missionaries that the Indians encountered, sometimes in harmony but more often in conflict. Throughout I have tried to convey the turmoil of the times and to avoid the rhetoric of archaeology that frequently obscures the people being studied.

Shaping my work are the ongoing tensions between archaeologists and Indian people. These conflicts exemplify the archaeological premise that the past shapes the present. A viewpoint archaeologists less often acknowledge is that the present shapes our rendering of the past.

What this awl means

The women and children of Inyan Ceyaka Atonwan (Little Rapids) had been working at the maple sugar camps since Istawicayazan wi (the Moon of Sore Eyes, or March). At the same time, most of the men had been far from the village trapping muskrats. When Wozupi wi (the Moon for Planting, or May) came, fifteen households eagerly reunited in their bark lodges near the river. Hard work lay ahead; they needed to replenish their stores of food and other supplies consumed over the long winter.

In the first days after their return, the women repaired the houses they would be living in for the next few months. They reinforced or replaced the basswood-bark lashing holding the wood pole framework together. Then they reset the wall posts, roof rafters, and sections of the elm bark walls and roof that harsh winter winds, ice, and snow had dislodged. Several of the older lodges had been damaged beyond repair, so the women cleared and leveled the ground with their hoes to prepare for new dwellings. Soon everyone in the community moved from their portable, skin-covered tipis, which they used during the winter months and while traveling, into the cooler summer lodges.

Most of the men and boys spread out from the village daily to fish or hunt ducks, turtles, and small game. Meanwhile, groups of women and girls collected firewood and building supplies and gathered the late spring vegetables and fruits beginning to appear in the surround. After the kernels sprouted, they planted it in the rich soil near the slough where wild artichokes grew. . . .

Mazomani and Hazawin (Blueberry Woman) were proud of their daughter, Mazaokiyewin (Woman Who Talks to Iron). The day after visiting Faribault [the trader], they had given her some glass beads and a new iron awl tip. The tip was the right size to fit into the small antler handle that Hazawin had given Mazaokiyewin when she went to dwell alone at the time of her first menses. Mazaokiyewin used the sharp-pointed awl for punching holes in pieces of leather before stitching them together with deer sinew. Though young, she had already established a reputation among the people at Inyan Ceyaka Atonwan for creativity and excellence in quillwork and beadwork.

Mazaokiyewin's mother and grandmothers had taught her to keep a careful record of her accomplishments, so whenever she finished quilling or beading moccasins, she remembered to impress a small dot on the fine awl handle that Hazawin had made for her. When Mazaokiyewin completed more complicated work, such as sewing and decorating a buckskin dress or pipe bag, she formed diamond-shaped clusters of four small dots which symbolized the powers of the four directions that influenced her life in many ways. She liked to expose the handle of this small tool as she carried it in its beaded case so that others could see she was doing her best to ensure the well-being of their community.

When she engraved the dots into her awl handle, she carefully marked each one with red pigment, made by boiling sumac berries with a small root found in the ground near the village. Dakota people associated the color red with women and their life forces. Red also represented the east, where the sun rose to give knowledge, wisdom, and understanding. Red symbolized Mazaokiyewin's aspirations to these qualities . . . .

■ ■ ■

References

Eastman, Charles A. [1902] (1971) *Indian Boyhood*, New York: Dover Publications, Inc.

Freeman, Joan E. (1986) "Aztalan: A Middle Mississippian Village," in W. Green, J. B. Stoltman and A. Kehoe (eds), Special Issue, *The Wisconsin Archaeologist* 67(3–4):339–64.

Chapter 21

BOYS WILL BE BOYS
Masculinist Approaches to a Gendered Archaeology

A. Bernard Knapp

The study of gender in archaeology has made significant strides since the ground-breaking article of Conkey and Spector in 1984 (Zarmati 1994). Male archaeologists, however, continue to show reluctance in adopting gender as a key concept in archaeological theory. This seems all the more curious since "masculinist" writers have been treating gender-related concepts in an intelligent and informed manner for at least the past decade (e.g., Connell 1987, 1995; Seidler 1989; Stoltenberg 1989). Since many feminists equate "masculinist" with male dominance, my use of the term "masculinist" may be disquieting. I would like to suggest here an alternative meaning for those who associate the term "masculinist" exclusively with a reactionary, gender-biased, androcentric position. In this paper, "masculinist" is used exclusively as a gender-based concept widely adopted by psychologists, social scientists, historians and literary critics to define or categorise both a contemporary social movement and an academic position, each of which attempts to formulate the masculine subject. Furthermore, I argue that masculinity, or better, masculinities, must become a focus of gender-based social or cultural enquiry, not least because the social sciences have for so long presented men as gender-neutral and thus as universal, but also because – in my opinion – there is no point in replacing an androcentric account of the world with a gynecentric one. An exclusionary, feminist worldview is no less likely than any other to obliterate the significance of gender, or to portray gender asymmetry as a consequence of other, somehow more "essential" forces.

Archaeologists of whatever gender need to rethink their traditional research priorities and writing styles, as well as the objects and subjects of their study. Feminist theory has proved to be a fulcrum for the study of gender in archaeology because it has paid closer attention to gender as an analytical category than any other body of theory. I proceed in this paper by looking briefly at the background of feminist scholarship, after which masculinist reactions to feminism are defined: in many ways, masculinist approaches may be regarded as heavily reliant on feminist scholarship. One important contribution of masculinist research has been to insist upon the existence of divergent, multiple masculinities rather than the binary oppositions that once characterised most gender-based research. In drawing upon a cross-section of new studies on masculinities, I want to emphasise that an engendered archaeology must involve both women and men. The study of sexual, social and gender issues should not become the exclusive domain of either women or men; the goal is an archaeology informed by feminism, one that looks critically at theories of human action and uses archaeological data to challenge existing structures of knowledge.

Feminist and masculinist

The women's liberation movement emerged forcefully during the 1960s when it began to make noticeable inroads into a complacent, strongly male-dominated American society. Before long, the corporate world and Madison Avenue had co-opted the movement for purely economic ends: "You've come a long way, baby" (advertisement for Virginia Slims cigarettes) was a typical example. The co-optation, however, was purely economic, since the women's liberation movement was far too controversial socially and politically. Alongside the student and civil rights movements in the USA, and the New Left movement in Britain, a new kind of women's scholarship emerged (e.g., Strathern 1972; Weiner 1976), while a flood of political commentary and soul-searching associated with the movement led to a very different way of looking at the world (e.g., Rosaldo and Lamphere 1974).

The male reaction to feminism that emerged over the succeeding two decades took two main directions, while gay scholarship evolved in other directions:

1   *reactionary masculinities*: the "weekend warriors", "wild men" who engaged with their "Zeus energy" and communed with nature, legend, myth and other "real men";

2   *motivated masculinities*: "feminist" writers who took on board the radical implications and ideology associated with feminism in their writing on masculinity.

The authors engaged in reactionary masculinities tend to be psychologists or else to write with a psychological orientation; those engaged in motivated masculinities tend to be sociologists, and to write with a strong political commitment. Robert Bly's *Iron John* (1990) is the most notorious of the biosocial, almost mythological, writings where biological sex is seen as the fundamental difference between genders. The most compelling of the motivated masculinity studies is perhaps John

Stoltenberg's *Refusing to be a Man* (1989), where the political becomes intensely personal, and where all gender-based research stems from radical feminism.

But how has "masculinist" theory contributed to the study of gender, and how might it contribute to a gendered archaeology? Can men study gender and masculinity using feminist insights but avoiding an androcentric perspective? Masculinist approaches are usually regarded with extreme scepticism, not least because feminists are concerned that masculinist writers will simply co-opt all of the advances made since the 1970s (Canaan and Giffen 1990; Hammer 1990). Of course, such concerns are entirely justified in response to reactionary writers, but otherwise they may prove to be counter-productive to a holistic study of gender that incorporates females, males and any of several other possible realities (Cornwall and Lindisfarne 1994: 29–34).

A feminist political position logically regards "men" or "male" as an oppositional category (Threadgold and Cranny-Francis 1990). Yet some of the critiques of "radical" or "cultural" feminism which appeared in the American literature of the 1980s (e.g., Jaggar 1983; Ringelheim 1985) articulated well the general objections to a "remedial" feminism that simply inverted the gender categories it meant to challenge (Alison Wylie, personal communication). Along with the classical self-critique by Rosaldo (1980), these writings represent a burgeoning feminist literature and practice which questioned an essentialist myopia and certain, narrowly focused, approaches in feminist political theory and enquiry.

Assertions about gender differences are bound closely to specific political positions, but gender does not conform to any fixed identity nor does it preordain any inevitable type of human action (Lorber 1994: 80–96). On the contrary, gender identity is tenuously constituted in time and through space, and gender differences are built and maintained through discourses pertaining to agency, identity and causation (Strathern 1988: 5; Butler 1990: 140). For some, gender is regarded as nothing more than a performance, one way that human agents negotiate their social reality (Morris 1995). Some feminists, moreover, believe that gender should be eliminated as an organising principle in post-industrial and post-colonial society (Lorber 1986: 568; Coltrane 1994: 43). Still others argue that there is no distinction between sex and gender, and that it is no longer acceptable to advocate biological sex as the basis from which the cultural construction of gender proceeds (e.g., Laqueur 1990; Butler 1993: 1; detailed arguments in Knapp and Meskell 1997).

The ideologies that privilege both men and women have been termed "hegemonic masculinities" (Carrigan *et al.* 1985), which themselves necessitate an "essentialist", male/female binary system. Binary approaches have always formed an integral part of Western metaphysics, and contain an inbred, judgmental bias which privileges one over the other (Bruner 1994: 98; Conway-Long 1994: 77). Postmodernist theory largely ignores such biological, dualistic typologies and views gender as a spectrum, rather than a dichotomy. Postmodernist studies, however, have yet to reconcile satisfactorily the binary typology of human beings with the culturally-fashioned spectrum of gender (di Leonardo 1991; Wylie 1991). No matter how central this biological dualism may be to human culture, gender does not simply follow on directly from sex.

The movement of human beings between the diverse social aspects of their lives, and the pluralistic elements on which these movements depend, help to conceptualise gender (Strathern 1988). This somewhat radical notion of "personhood" makes it possible to think about difference beyond binary opposites. The category of "woman," or "feminist," is no more monolithic than that of "man," or "masculinist." Masculinity, then, like femininity, is a relational construct: understanding gender in relational terms is important because hegemonic masculinities function best when they assert their power over some "other" group or individual. Power relations between different men also involve struggles to define hegemony, and so serve to construct different masculinities. It should be apparent that no single factor constitutes masculinity: it is not only divergent and often competing, but above all continuously changing.

Analysing the nature of difference has always been central to anthropology: one way to validate both difference and similarity, and at the same time to highlight both human agency and structural pattern, is to delineate the motivations, conditions and settings through which gender becomes salient in everyday life (Coltrane 1994: 57; Lorber 1994: 172–193). There is a constant, active process in which gender is created and re-created, in response to specific tasks, roles and changing power relations. Gender is never static, but instead interacts with the structures that surround it and the agents that act it out (Kaufmann 1994: 147). The systematic study of these "gender strategies" (Hochschild 1989) helps in understanding their origin and the way that they are constructed and used within various cultural, economic, institutional and spatial contexts.

Gendering archaeology

In what follows, my aim is simply to outline briefly what I regard as the most problematic as well as the most promising aspects of a gendered archaeology. The feminist critique of academic research traditions has proceeded in stages, from exposing androcentrism, to "remedial" research, and finally to reconceptualisation. Archaeologists, in turn, have engaged with gender in at least two distinctive ways (Conkey and Tringham 1995):

1   the "add women and stir" approach (cf. Conkey and Spector 1984), where gender issues are tacked on to existing, usually androcentric, paradigms.
2   the "gender attribution" approach, which is essentially static and fails to engage any of the rich theoretical resources on gender (Conkey and Tringham 1995; Dobres 1995).

The fundamental critiques of essentialism that have appeared during the last decade (e.g., Spelman 1988; Fuss 1989) have been pivotal in the shift from an "add women and stir" approach to programmes of feminist research that accept the challenge in taking gender seriously as a category of analysis (Alison Wylie, personal communication). Within anthropology, recent feminist thought has focused on analysing gender differences in relation to class, age, culture, ethnicity and identity (e.g., Moore 1988, 1995; di Leonardo 1991; Conkey and Tringham 1995). More recent work on the anthropology of sex and gender revolves in large part around the concept of the body as an essential site for theorising about society and the self (e.g., Shilling 1993; Grosz 1994; Morris 1995). Within archaeology, gender increasingly is accepted as a key organising principle of all human beings through time and space (Conkey and Spector 1984); accordingly it should be recognisable in the material remnants of past human groups and individuals (Roberts 1993: 18; Beck and Balme 1994: 39–40).

Roberts (1993: 18–19) distinguishes what she terms a "gendered archaeology", which rejects the binary oppositions and biological determinism implicit in earlier gender-based research and in structuralist or post-structuralist approaches in archaeology (Conkey and Gero 1991: 8; Gilchrist 1991: 488). Despite these ideals and desiderata, there remain certain problems in making gender a central concern of archaeology. Although Conkey and Gero (1991: 11) have emphasised that a gendered archaeology is not dependent on the actual visibility of various gender categories in the archaeological record, certain questions seem inescapable: for example, if we regard material data as a record, how does the evidence indicate different kinds of gender-based activity? Alternatively, if we regard the material record as text, and agree that certain codes may signify gender in particular socio-cultural contexts, how are such texts to be read (Barrett 1988: 12)? Even where the use of cross-cultural data derived from an ethnoarchaeological or ethnohistoric approach allow us to link certain materials, tools or trinkets to gender-specific activities, is it justifiable to retrodict present or recent cultural expressions of gender into the remote past?

Archaeologists should not attempt to understand gender simply in terms of female or male activities, or their residues. At a minimum, this paper suggests that the categories female and male, or feminine and masculine, have been destabilised substantially, and that multiple genders must be acknowledged. Gender, moreover, is based not just in material or economic conditions, but also in the structuring of ideology (Dommasnes 1990: 29). If gender serves to constitute social relations, then it may be constructed as a relationship, while gender categories may be reproduced as a relationship in which women, men or others control specific cultural-resource sets (Rosaldo 1980). A gendered archaeology therefore accepts that gender is based on culturally perceived and inscribed similarities and differences between and among diverse human individuals (Gilchrist 1991: 497).

Feminist and masculinist theory alike are critical for studying gender in archaeology, not least because they promulgate a pluralistic approach or multiple interpretations while rejecting "runaway relativisms" (Conkey and Tringham 1995). Ambiguity is inherent in the archaeological record, and alternative interpretations are inevitable. Moreover, the recognition of difference and ambiguity encourages dialogues between data and theory, past and present, writer and reader, text and context. Feminist theory not only offers insight into the way gender affects and is affected by social being and social practice, it also challenges contemporary "scientistic" reconstructions of the past that proclaim "truth" or exclusive knowledge (Conkey and Tringham 1995).

Conclusion

"Malestream" archaeologists still regard gender as an intractable field of discourse. Indeed, the study of gender and the issues raised by feminist theory present real challenges to archaeology, which must be confronted if ever we wish to incorporate gender as a dynamic, historical process, or to produce better understandings of the past. Feminist theory can help archaeologists to balance objectivism against extreme relativism, and to realise a more encompassing archaeology that acknowledges contexts, contingencies and ambiguities. Based as it is in categories and typologies, archaeology can only benefit from placing gender at the analytical centre of the categories and typologies we construct. Engaging gender in this manner should also help archaeologists to comprehend the social construction of particular human roles and relationships, and to foreground the individual as an active social agent.

If it is true that the study of the human past thus far has involved largely an appraisal of patriarchy (Kokkinidou and Nikolaidou 1993: 163), the significance of feminist theory and gender in archaeology will only be realised when androcentric attitudes are demolished and bridges built to integrate gender fully within the wider discipline (Gilchrist 1991: 500).

Fotiadis (1994: 546) points out that authors must pass an "epistemological tribunal" even to discuss an "engendered" archaeology or to critique "malestream" practices, and of course to ensure that the work represents "legitimate disciplinary pursuits". If, as seems evident (e.g., Hodder 1991: 10), a backlash against theoretical archaeology asserts itself in the wake of the processual/postprocessual debate, an archaeology informed by feminist theory may discover that the archaeological establishment has become even less receptive to their ideas.

Finally, it is necessary to consider the wisdom of arguing that a total commitment to feminist archaeology must result in a new archaeology, where both the praxis and theory of the discipline must be radically transformed (Dommasnes 1990: 28; Conkey and Tringham 1995). In terms of social change, this presents a real dilemma: while such a transformation must remain a feminist goal, and although gender cannot be separated from other archaeological concerns and marginalised as a "speciality" within the discipline (Conkey and Gero 1991: 17), I reiterate that it will do no good simply to replace an androcentric archaeology with a gynecentric one.

I have argued in this study that gender forms an important theoretical aspect of work by "masculinist" writers, and that careful attention to this work can help archaeologists to engage the study of multiple, engendered pasts. The critical point is that a gendered archaeology must involve both women and men in order to make gender a more dynamic, multifaceted concept within archaeological interpretation. Any serious debate on gender within a social archaeology must engage both feminist and masculinist perspectives, reconceptualise the categories within which we construct the past, and define new and alternative modes of archaeological discourse and interpretation.

■ ■ ■

References

Bacus, E., Barker, A.W., Bonevich, J.D., Dunavan, S.L., Fitzhugh, J.B., Gold, D.L., Goldman-Finn, N.S., Griffin, W. and Mudar, K.M. (1993) *A Gendered Past: A Critical Bibliography of Gender in Archaeology*. Ann Arbor: University of Michigan. University Museum of Anthropology, Technical Report 25.

Barrett, J.C. (1988) "Fields of discourse: reconstituting a social archaeology". *Critique of Anthropology*, 7(3):5–16.

Beck, W. and Balme, J. (1994) "Gender in aboriginal archaeology: recent research". *Australian Archaeology*, 39:39–46.

Bly, R. (1990). *Iron John: A Book About Men*. Rockport, Mass.: Addison-Wesley Publishing.

Bruner, E.M. (1994). "Abraham Lincoln as authentic reproduction: a critique of postmodernism". *American Anthropologist*, 96:97–415.

Butler, J. (1990) *Gender Trouble: Feminism and the Subversion of Identity*. London and New York: Routledge.

—— (1993) *Bodies that Matter: On the Discursive Limits of Sex*. London and New York: Routledge.

Canaan, J.E. and Giffen, C. (1990) "The new men's studies: part of the problem or part of the solution?" In J. Hearn and D.H.J. Morgan (eds) *Men, Masculinities and Social Theory*, London: Unwin Hyman, pp. 206–214.

Carrigan, T., Connell, R.W. and Lee, J. (1985) "Towards a new sociology of masculinity". *Theory and Society* 14:551–603.

Coltrane, S. (1994) "Theorizing masculinities in contemporary social science". In H. Brod and M. Kaufmann (eds) *Theorizing Masculinities*, London: Sage, pp. 39–60. Research on Men and Masculinities 5.

Conkey, M.W. and Spector, J.D. 1984 "Archaeology and the study of gender". In M.B. Schiffer (ed.) *Advances in Archaeological Method and Theory* 7:1–38. New York: Academic Press.

Conkey, M.W. and Gero, J.W. 1991 "Tensions, pluralities, and engendering archaeology: an introduction to women in prehistory". In J.W. Gero and M.W. Conkey (eds) *Engendering Archaeology: Women and Prehistory*, Oxford: Basil Blackwell, pp. 3–30.

Conkey, M.W. and Tringham, R.E. 1995 "Archaeology and the goddess: exploring the contours of feminist archaeology". In A. Steward and D. Stanton (eds) *Feminisms in the Academy: Rethinking the Disciplines*. Ann Arbor: University of Michigan Press. pp. 199–247.

Connell, R.W. 1987 *Gender and Power: Society, the Person, and Sexual Politics*. Oxford: Polity Press.

—— 1995 *Masculinities*. London: Polity Press.

Conway-Long, D. 1994 Ethnographies and masculinities. In H. Brod and M. Kaufmann (eds) *Theorizing Masculinities*, London: Sage, pp. 61–81. Research on Men and Masculinities 5.

Cornwall, A. and Lindisfarne, N. 1994 "Dislocating masculinity: gender, power and anthropology". In A. Cornwall and N. Lindisfarne (eds) *Dislocating Masculinities: Comparative Ethnographies*, London and New York: Routledge, pp. 1–10.

Di Leonardo, M. (ed.) 1991 *Gender at the Crossroads of Knowledge: Feminist Anthropology in the Postmodern Era*. Berkeley: University of California Press.

Dobres, M.-A. 1995 "Beyond gender attribution: some methodological issue for engendering the past". In J. Balme and W. Beck (eds) *Gendered Archaeology: Proceedings of the Second Australian Women in Archaeology Conference*, Canberra: ANH, Research School of Pacific and Asian Studies, Australian National University. Research Papers in Archaeology and Natural History 26, pp. 51–66.

Dommasnes, L.H. (1990) "Feminist archaeology: critique or theory building?" In F. Baker and J. Thomas (eds) *Writing the Past in the Present*, Lampeter: Saint David's University College, pp. 24–31.

Fotiadis, M. (1994) "What is archaeology's 'mitigated objectivism' mitigated by? Comments on Wylie". *American Antiquity* 59:45–555.

Fuss, D. (1989) *Essentially Speaking: Feminism, Nature and Difference*. New York and London: Routledge.

Gero, J.M., and Conkey, M.W. (eds) 1991 *Engendering Archaeology: Women and Prehistory*. Oxford: Basil Blackwell.

Gilchrist, R. (1991) "Women's archaeology? Political feminism, gender theory, and historical revision". *Antiquity* 65/248:495–501.

Grosz, E. (1994) *Volatile Bodies*. St Leonards (Sydney): Allen and Unwin.

Hammer, J. (1990) "Men, power and the exploitation of women". In J. Hearn and D.H.J. Morgan (eds) *Men, Masculinities and Social Theory*, London: Unwin Hyman, pp. 21–42.

Hochschild, A. (1989) *The Second Shift*. Berkeley: University of California Press.

Hodder, I.A. (1991) "Interpretive archaeology and its role". *American Antiquity* 56:7–18.

Jaggar, A.M. (1983) *Feminist Politics and Human Nature*. Totowa, NJ: Rowman and Allanheld.

Kaufmann, M. (1994) "Men, feminism, and men's contradictory experiences of power". In H. Brod and M. Kaufmann (eds) *Theorizing Masculinities*, London: Sage, pp. 142–163. Research on Men and Masculinities 5.

Knapp, A.B. (1996) "Archaeology without gravity: postmodernism and the past". *Journal of Archaeological Method and Theory* 3: 127–158.

Knapp, A.B. and Meskell, L.M. (1997) "Bodies of evidence on prehistoric Cyprus". *Cambridge Archaeological Journal* 7: 183–204.

Kokkinidou, D. and Nikolaidou, M. (1993) *I Arheoloyia ke i Kinoniki Taftotita tu Filu: Prosengisis stin Eyeaki Proistoria*. Thessaloniki: Vanias Editions. (in Greek, English summary)

Laqueur, T. (1990) *Making Sex: Body and Gender from the Greeks to Freud*. Cambridge, Mass.: Harvard University Press:

Lorber, J. (1986) "Dismantling Noah's ark". *Sex Roles* 14:567–580.

Lorber, J. (1994) *Paradoxes of Gender*. New Haven and London: Yale University Press.

Moore, H.L. (1988) *Feminism and Anthropology*. Cambridge: Polity Press.

Moore, H.L. (1995) (ed.) *The Future of Anthropological Thought*. London and New York: Routledge.

Morris, R.C. (1995) "ALL MADE UP: Performance Theory and the New Anthropology of Sex and Gender". *Annual Review of Anthropology* 24:567–592.

Ringelheim, J. (1985) "Women and the holocaust: a reconsideration of research". *Signs* 10:741–761.

Roberts, C. (1993) "A critical approach to gender as a category of analysis in archaeology". In H. du Cros and L. Smith (eds) *Women in Archaeology: A Feminist Critique*, Canberra: Dept of Prehistory, Research School of Pacific Studies, Australian National University. pp. 16–21. Occasional Papers in Prehistory 23.

Rosaldo, M.Z. (1980) "The use and abuse of anthropology: reflections on feminism and cross-cultural understanding". *Signs* 5:389–417.

Rosaldo, M.Z. and Lamphere, L. (eds) (1974) *Women, Culture and Society*. Stanford: Stanford University Press.

Seidler, V.J. (1989) *Rediscovering Masculinity*. London and New York: Routledge.

Shilling, C. (1993) *The Body and Social Theory*. London: Sage.

Spelman, E.V. (1988) *Inessential Woman: Problems of Exclusion in Feminist Thought*. Boston: Beacon Press.

Stoltenberg, J. (1989) *Refusing To Be a Man: Essays on Sex and Justice*. Boulder, Oxford: Westview Press.

Strathern, M. (1972) *Women in Between: Female Roles in a Male World. Mount Hagen, New Guinea*. London: Seminar Press.

Strathern, M. (1988) *The Gender of the Gift: Problems with Women and Problems with Society in Melanesia*. Berkeley: University of California Press.

Threadgold, T. and Cranny-Francis, A. (eds) (1990) *Feminine, Masculine and Representation*. London: Allen and Unwin.

Weiner, A. (1976) *Women of Value, Men of Renown*. Austin: University of Texas Press.

Wylie, A. (1991) "Feminist critiques and archaeological challenges". In D. Walde and N.D. Willows (eds) *The Archaeology of Gender*, Calgary: Archaeological Association of the University of Calgary, pp. 17–23.

Zarmati, L. (1994) Review of Bacus *et al.* 1993, in *American Journal of Archaeology* 98:773–774.

INDEX